PRINCIPLES
OF REASONING

PRINCIPLES OF REASONING

Lilly-Marlene Russow
PURDUE UNIVERSITY

Martin Curd
PURDUE UNIVERSITY

St. Martin's Press
New York

Editor: Don Reisman
Project Management: Editing, Design & Production, Inc.
Cover Design: Darby Downey

Library of Congress Catalog Card Number: 88–60527

Manufactured in the United States of America.

32109

fedcba

For information, write:
St. Martin's Press, Inc.
175 Fifth Avenue
New York, NY 10010

ISBN: 0–312–17506–X

Acknowledgments

Albert Shanker, "Unfair Hurdles for Teachers," © 1984 American Federation of Teachers.
Saul Hormats, "Yellow Rain," *Washington Post,* 26 February, 1984, reprinted by permission of the
author.
April 6, 1983 editorial, "Keeping Lawyers Out of the Hospital," reprinted by courtesy of the *Purdue
Exponent.*
Kathleen Okruhlik, "Pornography and Censorship," reprinted by permission from the *Westminster
Institute Review,* Vol. 2, No. 4, © 1983, published by the Westminster Institute for Ethics and
Human Values, 361 Windermere Road, London, Ontario N6G 2K3. All rights reserved.
Stephen Stich, "Forbidden Knowledge," reprinted by permission of the author; *Science and the Public
Interest: Recombinant DNA Research,* pp. 206–215, 1978, Indiana University Foundation.
"Handgun Bans—Facts to Fight With," p. 4, reprinted from *Guns & Ammo Annual,* 1984.

Preface

All textbooks on "critical thinking," "informal logic," and "reasoning" aim at teaching students to distinguish between good and bad arguments, but there is little agreement about how this goal is best accomplished. Our approach is characterized by two basic commitments. First, we are convinced that it is essential to present a structured framework within which to analyze and evaluate arguments, one that is based on an appreciation of the principles that underlie good reasoning. Second, we believe that the ability to construct good arguments should be developed along with the ability to analyze and evaluate them.

The first of these commitments shapes both the organization and the content of this textbook. Chapter 1 deals with the basic aspects of arguments: their structure, how they differ from other forms of discourse, and their role in justifying beliefs and extending knowledge. This discussion allows the student to understand why the traditional concepts of validity and soundness are appropriate categories for evaluating arguments, which, in turn, provides a basis for justifying the specific methods of evaluating arguments presented in subsequent chapters.

Chapters 2, 3, and 4 study the different kinds of argument produced by categorical, propositional, and inductive reasoning. In each case, the approach is grounded in an explanation of the standards and methods of evaluation. Venn diagrams, truth tables, and simple random sampling are important topics here.

Chapter 5 draws on the material from previous chapters to provide a structured framework for reconstructing and evaluating extended arguments. Chapters 6, 7, and 8 focus on the interpretation and evaluation of the kinds of statements that often appear as premises of arguments. Chapters 9 and 10 apply the principles previously articulated to the special cases of practical, legal, and causal reasoning. The emphasis throughout is on understanding how arguments work and the principles that should guide their evaluation.

If students understand the principles that underlie good reasoning, they are better able to construct good arguments of their own. Emphasizing the constructive side of reasoning is the second major goal of this book. Thus, discussions of each major topic include suggestions about how the principles of reasoning can guide the development of good arguments. Similarly, some of the practice exercises ask students to develop arguments, not just to criticize them. The Extended Arguments in Appendix I also provide a starting point from which students may develop their own arguments in homework exercises, small-group discussions, and papers. Answers to questions marked with an asterisk can be found in Appendix II.

Principles of Reasoning contains more material than most instructors will cover in a single semester. Consequently, it is possible to choose one of several different approaches, and to tailor a class to special interests. Here are a few possibilities:

Scientific Reasoning: Chapters 1, 2, 3, 4, 8, 10.

Prelaw: Chapters 1, 2, 3, 5, 7, 9.

Reasoning and Persuasive Writing: 1, 2, 3, 4, 5, 6.

Acknowledgments: We would like to thank the following reviewers for St. Martin's Press, who offered valuable suggestions for developing our final draft of the manuscript: Robin A. Assali, San Francisco State University; Tom Bridges, Montclair State College; William A. Drumin, King's College; Colonel Anthony E. Hartle, United States Military Academy; Lenore Langsdorf, The University of Texas at Arlington; Harvey Siegel, University of Miami; and Elliot Sober, University of Wisconsin—Madison.

We would like to thank Maricia Moudy for her help in preparing the manuscript, and William Rowe for his unwavering support. We are also grateful to our students, who, for the past five years, have helped us refine our approach, clarify explanations, and to develop useful exercises. Most of all, we thank Patricia Kenig Curd and James Whyte Stephens for their encouragement, patience, and understanding.

Lilly-Marlene Russow
Martin Curd

A more complete explanation of the organization of the exercises and the corresponding answers in Appendix II is contained in the Instructor's Manual (present at the back of this volume—if marked "Instructor's Edition"—or available upon request from the publisher).

Contents

CHAPTER
1

An Introduction
to Arguments

Every day we confront the problem of deciding what to believe and how to act. Critical thinking helps us make these decisions rationally and reliably.

In rationally deciding what to believe, we must seek reasons or evidence that would justify our acceptance of statements as true. Similarly, in rationally deciding how to act, we must decide whether to accept as true a statement describing our best course of action, given the circumstances and what we wish to achieve. Thus, in both cases, our primary concern as rational decision makers is to decide which statements we should accept as true. The best method for deciding about the truth of statements is reasoning. Thus, reasoning is the key to rational decision making.

Reasoning has two sides, the **constructive** and the **analytical**. On the constructive side, we gather information and then decide where it points, what conclusion to draw. On the analytical side, we evaluate other people's reasoning by asking whether they have considered the relevant facts and arrived at their conclusions in a reliable way. The two sides are closely related. When we construct a chain of reasoning, we also act as our own critic, rejecting bad reasoning and preferring good. When we analyze another person's argument, we ourselves engage in constructive reasoning. Both construction and analysis use the same rules for good reasoning.

Reasoning and Arguments

When we say that two or more people are "having an argument" we mean merely that there is heated debate going on, or an expression of disagreement, whether or not it involves any reasoning. This is *not* the sense of "argument" that interests us. Throughout this book the term *"argument"* refers to something produced through reasoning. More precisely, an **argument** is a set of statements—one the **conclusion** and the rest **premises**—with the premises intended to support the conclusion or give reasons for thinking that the conclusion is true.[1]

Reasoning can be more complex than just giving a single argument. It might consist of several arguments, some for and some against a particular idea; or it may be a chain of arguments, with some leading to ideas that serve as parts of another argument. For example, a statement might be the conclusion of one argument and then be used as a premise in another.

The conclusion of an argument and each of its premises must be a **statement** or a group of statements. Statements are either true or false; they assert, either truly or falsely, that something is the case. Statements are expressed either by uttering a string of words or by writing them down in **sentences.** For example, the sentence "Harare is the capital of Zimbabwe" expresses a statement because it makes a claim that is either true or false.

Not all sentences express statements. For example, genuine questions are not statements, nor are commands such as "Do not feed the animals!" Genuine questions must, however, be distinguished from **rhetorical questions,** which are not questions at all, but statements. For example, "Who can deny that apartheid is morally repugnant?" is not a request for information but a forceful way of asserting that apartheid is morally repugnant. Similarly, in certain cases, commands and exhortations should be interpreted as statements when they appear as the conclusions of arguments. For example, "Vote for Brown because she is the best candidate for mayor," is really an argument in which the conclusion is the statement "You should vote for Brown."

The same statement can be made with different sentences in different languages (e.g., "It is raining," "Il pleut," "Es regnet") and with different sentences in the same language (e.g., "John is taller than Peter," "Peter is shorter than John"). Some sentences express several statements (e.g., "Albany is the capital of the state of New York but is smaller than New York City.").

Of particular importance in arguments are sentences that use "either . . . or . . ." and "if . . . then . . ." The sentence "Either Jones is at home or he is at work," expresses a single statement. It does not assert that Jones is at home, nor does it assert that he is at work; it states only that one or the other of these alternatives is the case. Similarly, "If Brown receives the backing of the labor unions, she will win the election," asserts only a single conditional statement about what will happen if Brown is supported by the labor unions. Finally, an argument can be expressed by a single sentence if the sentence contains at least two appropriately linked statements, for example, "This law must be struck down since it discriminates against the handicapped."

Arguments are meant to support their conclusions, and thus *rationally* motivate us to accept their conclusions *as true*—to believe them. They purport to represent good reasoning that is a reliable decision-making process. Giving an argument is thus distinct from following hunches or intuition, trying to persuade through emotional appeals or trickery, simply stating one's opinion, however forcefully or eloquently, and merely describing the position one wishes others to adopt without providing any supporting reasons.

A hunch or intuition stands alone. To call something a hunch implies that one has no evidence for it and it is not the result of reasoning. Trickery or emotional appeals may lead someone to accept a statement, but they work by short-circuiting the reasoning process. Mere descriptions or statements of opinion simply put forward a point of view without any reasons or evidence. Since these procedures are irrelevant to the truth of statements, they are unreliable. By contrast, arguments aim to give reasons in the premises that *are* relevant to the truth of their conclusions. Thus, if an argument is good, it can rationally motivate us to accept its conclusion on the basis of its premises.

Deciding whether a piece of writing constitutes an argument, or contains one, is sometimes quite difficult. Although we cannot list all the ways that something can fail to be an argument, some cases occur sufficiently often to warrant our attention.

Causal claims are not arguments; rather, they are statements, which are either true or false, about the cause of an event or a state of affairs. Typically we already know something is the case, or a certain event has occurred, and want to know its cause. Thus, we do not have a conclusion whose truth may be in doubt, which needs to be supported by citing premises.

Causal claims are easily confused with arguments because they often use the same clue words such as "because," and "as a consequence of." Contrast the causal claims in 1:1 with the arguments in 1:2:

1:1.   The pipe broke because the water inside it froze.

Catherine believes in strict discipline because she was bullied at school.

The reason Jane was ignored was that she was poorly dressed and shy.

1:2.   Because all even numbers greater than 2 are divisible by 2, all primes greater than 2 are odd.

Because water expands when it freezes, it can exert huge pressures inside a closed container.
Sodium is monovalent. As a consequence, it combines vigorously with chlorine.

In examples 1:2 we are not claiming that one event or state of affairs is the cause of another, but rather that one statement (the conclusion) is true because some other statement is true. It is important to bear in mind, here, the different meanings of "giving an explanation." In one of its senses, to give an explanation is just to assert a true causal claim. Thus, we explain the bridge's collapse by asserting the event was caused by metal fatigue in the girders. In another of its senses, giving an explanation involves justifying that the causal claim is true. This is done with an argument showing that the bridge's collapse could have been predicted from a knowledge of the metal fatigue, other initial conditions, and the relevant scientific laws.

Explanations of a person's beliefs or behavior that involve attributing to her the awareness of an argument or of a chain of reasoning are not, themselves, arguments. Sometimes such explanations describe the reasons someone changed her mind.

1:3. Sally thought it must be sunset because the sun lay on the Pacific horizon; but then she remembered that she was in Japan and realized it was dawn.

In this example, it is either true or false that Sally changed her mind for the reasons given. Hence, 1:3 is a statement, not an argument. In cases like this, an argument has been **mentioned** or referred to, but not **used** by the author to reach a conclusion. Rather, the author is claiming, either truly or falsely, that someone else used the argument mentioned to reach a conclusion.

Attributions of arguments are not themselves arguments.

1:4. Aquinas argued that, since the existence of any object is an empirical question, there can be no *a priori* proof of God's existence.

Even when the argument in question is quoted verbatim and set off in quotation marks, the assertion that so-and-so made such an argument is a true or false statement, not an argument. Indeed, the argument under discussion may be cited in order to criticize it, not to endorse it. Aquinas's argument has been *mentioned* in 1:4 but not *used*.

Statements that merely assert someone used an argument to reach a conclusion must be carefully distinguished from *arguments* in which the author *endorses* someone else's reasoning for a conclusion. In these cases the author is asking us to accept a conclusion as true on the grounds that so-and-so, a presumed expert, gave a good argument for it. Consider the following example:

1:5. The current tax codes must be reformed. In the most recent issue of *The Spectator,* the British Prime Minister, Margaret Thatcher, argues convincingly that passage of the tax code reform bill is absolutely vital if we are to encourage capital investment in Britain's industries.

Here, the author's argument rests on Thatcher's authority as a reliable judge of such matters; Thatcher's own argument rests on the soundness of her reasoning from whatever premises she offers.[2]

Finally, it should be remembered that even bad arguments are still arguments. However fallacious, weak, or question-begging someone's reasoning may appear to be, if it involves reasoning from premises to a conclusion, then it is an argument.

EXERCISES

For each of the following examples, decide whether or not it is an argument. Briefly explain your judgment.

1. Harold believes that environmental concerns are important because that is the way he was brought up.

2. According to evidence given in a recent Miami case, 25 percent of traffic radar speeding tickets are in error. That's why you need a Fuzzbuster II Radar Detector.

*3. There are no proofs that God exists. But there are also no proofs that God does not exist.

4. Should the legal age for a driver's license be raised to 18 in all states?

5. Because a variety of conditions exist among the states, it is essential that each state adopt its own drivers' regulations. Idaho, for example, is 12th in geographical size, with a population of less than 1 million. Many highways are in rural areas with little traffic, and young teens need an operator's permit to drive to school or to transport family farm supplies.

*6. It is an illusion to think a utopian society could exist without any form of legal regulation. Bertrand Russell argued that even in an anarchist society, there would have to be laws to prevent theft and other such violent actions. He believed that even if destitution were eliminated in such a society, some men would want more than others and would, individually or in groups, take it.

7. As the oldest of 11 children (all married) I'd like to point out that our combined family numbers more than 100 who vote only for pro-life candidates. Pro-lifers have children; pro-choicers do not. (Letter to the editor, *Time,* 7/30/79.)

8. Aside from a few countries in very modern times, poverty is the common condition of mankind. But revolution is neither ubiquitous nor permanent. We need, therefore, something beyond poverty and misery to explain why there is revolt in some places and not others. (From Charles Krauthammer, "Terror and Peace: The 'Root Cause' Fallacy," *Time,* 9/22/86.)

9. A recent New York Times–CBS News national poll purports to show

*Answers to questions marked with an asterisk can be found in Appendix II.

that 72 percent of the American people are willing to undergo urine testing for drugs in the work place.

*10. The other reason I oppose the ERA is because of Section 2, which says: "The Congress shall have the power to enforce by appropriate legislation the provisions of this Article." This section shifts vast power from the states to the federal government, and I do not think that the federal government should be given another whole area of power it never had before.

Getting to the Point: The Conclusion

The purpose of an argument is to give reasons for thinking its conclusion is true. Thus, to evaluate how good an argument is, we must begin by identifying its conclusion, that is, what is being argued for. The more lengthy or unclear the argument, the harder this first step becomes. This is especially true when one is dealing with a **complex argument** or **argument chain** consisting of several **intermediate steps.** Each of these steps might be an argument with a conclusion of its own. These **intermediate conclusions** then combine to support the **final conclusion.**

There are three general rules to follow in looking for the *final conclusion:*

1. Ask yourself what the main idea is. What is the author trying to establish or work toward?

2. In a complex argument or argument chain, determine what the intermediate steps point to. Do the intermediate conclusions contribute to the support of one overall idea? More generally, which statements lead to or support other ideas?

3. Look for **clue words** that indicate the author's organizational scheme.

When presenting an argument of your own, you can use **clue words** to direct attention to your conclusion. The following words are often used to signal that a conclusion follows:

consequently	it follows that
therefore	suggests that
this proves that	points to the fact that
so	entails
since this is so	implies
hence	thus

In arguments which use no clue words, we must rely on the first two rules. In complex arguments or argument chains that do contain clue words, the clue words might signal the conclusion of an intermediate step, thus directing our attention away from the final or main conclusion. For this reason, even when clue words are present, it is advisable to test the use of the third rule with the other two rules. To illustrate this point, consider argument 1:6:

1:6.   Age discrimination is often fostered by economic motives, since younger workers generally have less experience, and hence can be hired more cheaply.

The clue word "hence" directs our attention to the claim "[Younger workers] can be hired more cheaply," but this is not the final conclusion. If we look for the main idea, we see that it is the first statement, "Age discrimination is often fostered by economic motives." The claim "[Younger workers] can be hired more cheaply," is the conclusion of an intermediate step in the chain of reasoning.

To see how the three rules operate in a more complex argument, consider example 1:7, in which each sentence has been numbered for ease of reference:

1:7.   (1) Should we repeal the present 55 mph speed limit? (2) This question cannot be decided on economic grounds alone. (3) Raising the speed limit to, say, 70 mph will save time in transporting goods and hence tend to reduce costs. (4) But it is unlikely that this will result in a significant economic benefit, since driving at higher speeds consumes more fuel. (5) Even critics of the present speed limit concede that it has helped to reduce the number of deaths and injuries in automobile accidents. (6) The vast amount of money we spend on health care shows that saving lives is more important to us than saving dollars. (7) The 55 mph speed limit saves lives, and the economic advantages of changing it are uncertain. (8) So it should be retained.

The first rule directs us to look for the main idea. At first we might think that the main idea is expressed in the second sentence, but, reading further, we see that the overall point the author is trying to establish comes right at the end in sentence 8.

The second rule serves as a check on the first. Having picked out "It [the 55 mph speed limit] should be retained" as the final conclusion, we now go back to see which of the other statements point toward that idea and support it. The statements that support the final conclusion most directly are "Saving lives is more important to us than saving dollars" (from sentence 6), "The 55 mph speed limit saves lives" (from sentence 7), and "The economic advantages of changing it are uncertain" (from sentence 7). The first two of these are intermediate conclusions that work together to support the final conclusion. Each of these, in turn, is supported by further statements in sentences 5 and 6. The main support for regarding the economic advantages of a change as uncertain comes in sentence 4.

The third rule is the simplest, but needs to be applied thoughtfully. Argument 1:7 contains three different clue words or phrases which signal that a conclusion follows: "hence" (in sentence 3), "shows that" (in sentence 6), and "so" (in sentence 8). Only the last of these indicates the final conclusion, and might conceivably have been omitted. "Shows that" signals an intermediate conclusion in the overall argument. "Hence" points to the conclusion of an entirely separate argument.

Sometimes a conclusion is signaled not by using clue words, but by **juxtaposition.** It is a common practice to make a claim (the conclusion), and then follow it with a statement of the evidence that is supposed to support it (the premises).

Finally, some arguments have final conclusions that are not explicitly stated at all. These arguments have **implicit conclusions,** since it is often rhetorically effective to let readers "draw their own conclusion." In these cases the premises are usually presented in such a way that there is only one "obvious" conclusion to draw from them. Thus, the reader is not really drawing his own conclusion but merely making explicit the implicit conclusion the author intended.

EXERCISES

For each of the following arguments state the final conclusion in your own words. Is the conclusion explicit or implicit? Put brackets around any clue words that indicate conclusions and identify the ones that indicate the final conclusion. Where possible, underline the portion of the passage that comes closest to stating the final conclusion.

1. If you want effective relief, buy Bayer; it contains the ingredient doctors recommend most.

2. This must be a diamond, since it will scratch glass.

3. This is a diamond; therefore it will scratch glass.

*4. By voting themselves a hefty pay raise, congressmen proved that they are not interested in fighting the budget deficit.

5. Pit bulls are dangerous dogs. According to the Humane Society of the United States, in the 4 years since July 1983 pit bulls have been responsible for 20 of the 28 deaths after dog bites in the nation, including all 5 in 1987. The breed accounts for no more than 1 percent of all dogs in the nation.

6. Either the mind is material or it is immaterial; that is demanded by logic. If the mind were immaterial, we would have to deny that it is in the person's body, because immaterial things are not physically located anywhere. Since the mind is in the body, the mind must be material.

7. Linus Pauling told his audience that vitamin C must be taken in doses much higher than those recommended by the FDA. This contrasts with the way therapeutic drugs act. He said: "Too large a dose, no matter how useful the drug, can be deadly. Vitamins, however, are natural

substances, and mankind has become accustomed to them through the ages, so one can't take too much vitamin C."

8. Chimpanzees learn language much more slowly than people, and require special tutoring. So with chimps we can get a better perspective on both the factors that facilitate the learning and the factors that interfere with the learning. For example, we can completely control their training. We can make the chimps proficient in some areas of language, but not in others; we can systematically emphasize certain aspects of their language learning.

*9. In the fury that surrounds the debate about school prayer, it is sometimes forgotten that prayer is an essential part of religion. To permit school prayer is, therefore, virtually the same as endorsing religion. What can be said, then, for religion? Not much, I'm afraid. Indeed, religion is dangerous. It has spawned numerous wars throughout history. Today, it continues to sow the seeds of discontent and destruction in Northern Ireland and the Middle East. It divides people by emphasizing their differences rather than their similarities. It breeds intolerance of people of opposed views. Is there any doubt, therefore, that the responsible citizen should oppose school prayer?

*10. If sexual orientation is something over which an individual—for whatever reason—has virtually no control, then discrimination against gays is deplorable, as it is against racial and gender classes, because it holds a person accountable without regard for anything he himself has done. And to hold a person accountable for that over which he has no control is one of the central forms of prejudice. Looking at the actual lived experience of gays in our society, it becomes clear that sexual orientation is not likely a matter of choice. For coming to have a homosexual identity in our culture does not have the structure of decision-making. (From Richard D. Mohr, "Gays and the Civil Rights Act," *QQ: Report from the Center for Philosophy and Public Policy,* Spring 1984; *QQ*, an abbreviation for "questions," is a quarterly newsletter published by the University of Maryland.)

Giving Reasons: The Premises

The premises of an argument are those statements that lend support to the conclusion. From our earlier discussion of arguments, it is clear that the support we are looking for is of a special kind. We want reasons that point to the truth of the conclusion. Thus, reasons or premises must be distinguished from the following sorts of statements that often occur in the course of a discussion:

1. Introductory remarks that merely mark out the topic, set the context, or explain why someone might be interested in the issue.

2. Comments that merely restate or elucidate a position without giving reasons that support it.

3. Mere persuasion, such as use of emotional language or seductive appeals that are not evidence for the truth of the conclusion.

4. Disclaimers, that is, remarks that discount a statement or possible criticism without actually providing an argument, such as "One might think that taxes should be increased, but I oppose any such measure."

Consider the following pair of examples:

1:8. Many of the biologists in the environmental movement support left-wing causes.

1:9. Since none of those who declare that nuclear power plants are safe is willing to live within a mile of one, we should be skeptical of such claims.

Unlike 1:8, 1:9 is clearly an argument. In 1:9 there is a conclusion and a statement, which is a reason, however weak, for thinking that the conclusion is true. On the face of it 1:8 is just a single statement, and hence not an argument. But if we encountered 1:8 in the context of a debate over which scientists we should trust on environmental issues, we might be justified in regarding it as an argument with the implicit conclusion that we should ignore the views of many biologists in the environmental movement. But the only reason given for this implicit conclusion is that these biologists are supporters of left-wing causes, which is irrelevant to its truth. Thus, if 1:8 is an argument it is a very bad one.

Examples like 1:8 raise difficult issues about when something should be considered an argument. If it is clear from the context that someone has reasoned, however poorly, from one statement or statements to another, then we should treat those assertions as an argument, adding the implicit conclusion, if necessary.

Just as there are words that signal a conclusion, there are also terms that are often used to identify premises. The clue words on the following list may be introducing a premise. If you are presenting an argument, you can use these signals to help your audience identify your premises more readily:

since	for the reasons that
because	may be deduced from
as shown by	follows from
seeing that	may be inferred from
is proved by	is suggested by

As with clue words for conclusions, you should not rely blindly on these signals. Check to make sure that what you have identified is actually a premise. For example, the word "since" does not always indicate a premise, since it can be used in a temporal sense (e.g., "Personal computers have become much more powerful since they were first introduced in the 1970s"). "Because" is sometimes used in stating a claim about the cause of something rather than stating a reason for thinking a statement is true (e.g., "The car stopped because it ran out of gas").

To sum up. The first step is to ask whether we have an argument at all. If there is no conclusion, either implicit or explicit, there is no argument. If there is a conclusion, we must locate the premises. The premises are those statements that provide evidence that the conclusion is true; other statements might "color," explain and clarify, or set the stage for the conclusion without giving reasons, but these are not premises. These remarks apply to both the constructive and analytical enterprises.

When trying to create or evaluate an argument, we must direct our attention to the premises or reasons, and refuse to be distracted by the other sorts of statements. Clue words often help us to identify the premises.

EXERCISES

I. In each of the following examples, decide whether reasons (premises) are being given to support the truth of a conclusion. Identify the premises (if any), being careful to distinguish them from introductory remarks, restatements or elucidations of a position, mere persuasion, and disclaimers. Briefly justify your answer.

1. Pornography will be an important topic in the upcoming elections, since some local groups will only support candidates who are perceived as being "tough" on pornography.

2. Pigs are quickly replacing dogs as laboratory animals because their use provokes less of an outcry from the public.

3. Since fundamentalist forms of Christianity have become more popular, the government has been under increasing pressure to clarify the doctrine of "the separation of church and state."

*4. Ted Kennedy has long been affiliated with antigun groups; therefore, his arguments in favor of gun control cannot be taken seriously.

5. Since people who can handle poison ivy with no ill effects can lose their immunity at any time, they should avoid unnecessary contact with the plant.

6. If we are to regain our position as a scientifically advanced nation, we must increase aid to elementary schools, for lack of basic education at the earliest stages can never be overcome.

7. Quite simply: The showpiece of our collection! Owning our Eiderdown Comforter is a remarkable opportunity, like owning a rare antique. Because eiderdown is so rare and of such superior quality, it is coveted by connoisseurs around the world.

*8. Stealth's invisible. Enemy radar can't see it. And, it's the newest electronic marvel to come off the drawing board. Now, you may be thinking that there's not much in common between a Stealth Bomber and an automated cassette deck. After all, a Stealth Bomber can't fly backward. But wait, before you decide. This automated auto-reverse deck has a "radar avoidance system" called dbx. No, it's not an MX missile. But if the Stealth Bomber is invisible to radar, wait till you hear how "invisible" tape hiss will become to your ears with this dbx deck. [From Dak Industries Inc. Winter 1986 catalog.]

9. Much of the power drawn from your amplifier is used to drive your woofers. When you drive the amplifier too hard, it clips and you end up with distortion. A subsonic filter removes a lot of nonmusical material *you can't hear* that exists below 20 hz. So, it relieves your amplifier of a lot of work. It doesn't actually create more watts (please, no letters from my "technical" friends) for your amplifier. But, it's like turning off the air conditioning in your car. It saves you using about 7 hp of what you have. And therefore, you'll have more watts for clean powerful-sounding music. [From Dak Industries Inc. Winter 1986 catalog.]

10. People cooking live lobsters believe that dunking arthropods in boiling water does not cause them pain. This common view of pain in invertebrates has now been challenged, at least with regard to spiders. Honeybee venom and wasp venom injected into the leg of some types of spider cause the spider to detach the affected leg. Because the response is so swift, the venom has little chance to reach the spider's body. Spiders that do not discard their legs when stung in the leg usually die. Thus, discarding the leg has definite survival value. Although this behavior in itself does not prove that some spiders feel pain, the components of the venom associated with leg detachment suggest that these spiders do feel pain. Melittin, histamine, phospholipase A_2, and serotonin, found in the venoms, are known to cause human pain. [Adapted from *The Science Almanac: 1985–1986 Edition,* ed. by Bryan Bunch (Garden City, NY: Anchor Books, 1984), p. 169.]

II. Apply the instructions for Part I to the indicated passages in Appendix I. The first number refers to the argument, and the second number to the numbered paragraph within the argument. Thus, 3–2 refers to Extended Argument 3, paragraph 2.

1. 1–1.		6. 5–2.	
2. 1–8.		7. 5–11.	
3. 2–2.		*8. 6–1.	
4. 2–6.		9. 6–5.	
5. 3–2.		10. 8–17.	

III. In each of the following exercises a statement labeled "C" is followed by a list of numbered statements. For each exercise, decide which of the numbered statements can be used as a reason in support of statement "C."

1. (C). The attempt to unionize university professors has been a failure.
(1) The majority of university professors have chosen not to join the unions that are available.
(2) The unionization of professionals is a bad idea.
(3) Only "losers" join such unions.
(4) Where unions have formed, they have had little impact on policy making.
(5) Unionization simply will not succeed in an academic environment.

2. (C). Science students should take more liberal arts courses.
(1) People who take nothing but science courses are usually nerds.
(2) Liberal arts courses are an important part of the curriculum.
(3) People who take liberal arts courses are better able to cope with a changing world.
(4) It is easier to get an "A" in liberal arts courses than in science courses.
(5) Liberal arts professors are more sophisticated than science professors.

Outlining the Structure of Arguments[3]

If all arguments consisted of just a few premises all leading directly to a single conclusion, our task would be easy. Unfortunately, things are rarely that simple. As noted earlier, we can sometimes have **argument chains;** moreover, premises can work together or independently to support a conclusion, or one premise might be used to support two different conclusions.

To analyze more complex arguments, it is helpful to have a technique for outlining their structure. This outlining technique can also be used in planning an argument, but first we will concentrate on its application to arguments we wish to analyze. The procedure has three steps:

1. Find the final conclusion, underline it, and put brackets around it. If the final conclusion is implicit or if it has not been appropriately stated, write out the conclusion in your own words and label it "C." You may find it helpful at this stage to circle any clue words.

2. Enclose each separate premise in brackets, and assign each a number. If you are not sure whether or not something is a premise, go ahead and give it a number, but be prepared to leave it out later, if it turns out not to be a premise. Take care to separate each distinct thought, but do not break up a single idea. If the conclusion has also been bracketed, give it a number.

3. Draw an outline of the argument by writing down the number assigned to the conclusion (or, where appropriate, the letter "C") and arrows point-

ing from the numbers of statements that directly support the conclusion. Continue adding arrows and plus signs, where appropriate, as explained in the following.

Argument 1:10 is an example of a very simple argument and its outline:

1:10. [¹Animals feel pain just as people do]; {therefore,} [²*it is wrong to torture them*].

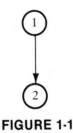

FIGURE 1-1

The conclusion is: "It is wrong to torture (animals)"; the clue word "therefore" introduces it. The only other statement is a premise that points to the conclusion, and this is indicated by the arrow in the outline, which points from 1 to 2. Before considering more complicated arguments and their outlines, a few potential difficulties should be noted.

First, the conclusion is not always stated, or it may be stated in the form of a rhetorical question or in some other oblique way. In these cases, formulate a statement of the conclusion in your own words; make a note of it, and refer to it in your outline as "C." You can indicate that "C" is a restatement of a certain oblique statement, by noting on your outline "C = X," where X is the number of the appropriate statement. Thus, if (1:10) had as its second sentence, "Why, then should we feel we can torture animals without justification?" instead of the original version, we should rewrite the conclusion (C) as "We should not feel that we can torture animals without justification," and our outline would look like this:

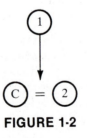

FIGURE 1-2

Second, we sometimes encounter two or more statements in an argument that say the same thing or convey the same idea, perhaps with slightly different emphasis, but with no change in content. If you notice this as you are assigning numbers, you can give equivalent sentences the same number. If you discover the similarity later, you can use an equals sign to connect them in the same way that the conclusion, C, is connected to the sentence it is equivalent to. Thus, 1:11 might be outlined as indicated:

1:11   [¹Gun control legislation should be one of our top priorities], {since} [²that is the only way to cut down on the number of irresponsible people with easy access to handguns.] [¹*We must,* {therefore,} *work hard toward the implementation of such legislation.*]

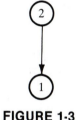

FIGURE 1-3

If we had failed to notice that the third sentence expressed the same thought as the first, we might have assigned it the number "3," in which case the outline would look like this:

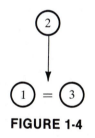

FIGURE 1-4

The final potential difficulty actually includes two things, both connected with the problem of bracketing individual statements correctly. Statements do not always coincide with sentences, so if a sentence contains two distinct statements connected by "but," "and," or a similar conjunction, we should distinguish the statements, and give each its own number. Thus, the sentence "All citizens of a country have an obligation to obey the laws of that country, but this obligation does not override the greater duty to do no wrong" should be broken up into two distinct statements, separated by the word "but."

The second consideration when bracketing statements is that we must be careful not to break up unified statements. This temptation is especially strong when we are dealing with a complex sentence with the form "if . . . , then . . .", or "either . . . or . . . ," or some form equivalent to either of these.

The sentence "If animals feel pain the same way humans do, then it is wrong to torture them" does not contain two separate statements, one to the effect that animals feel pain, and the other claiming that it is wrong to torture them; the sentence remains neutral about whether they do feel pain and whether it is wrong to torture them. Rather, it expresses a *relation* between these two factors; it presents the idea that feeling pain and the wrongness of torture are linked. So it would be wrong to break these two factors apart. We must enclose the whole statement in a single pair of brackets, and give it one number. The same holds true of the examples in 1:12:

1:12. Either you pay me now or you pay me later.

When it snows, my car won't start.

He who hesitates is lost.

If Yossarion is sane and he recognizes that flying missions endangers his life, then he would not fly his missions.

A person can be elected president only if he or she receives a majority of votes in the Electoral College.

The general principle is to watch for statements that express a relation between two or more factors, and avoid breaking them up. These relations are most commonly found in "if . . . then . . ." statements, "either . . . or . . ." statements, or variations of these forms.

More complex arguments require more complex outlines. We might, for example, have an *argument chain,* in which case one of our statements may be the conclusion of a preliminary argument, and serve as a reason for the final conclusion. This can be seen in the outline of the passage discussed in the section Getting to the Point: The Conclusion.

1:13. [¹*Age discrimination is often fostered by economic motives,*] {since} [² younger workers generally have less experience,] and {hence} [³can be hired more cheaply.]

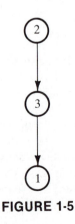

FIGURE 1-5

Many arguments give more than one premise for a conclusion. Frequently, the conclusion depends on both premises taken together. Sometimes, but not always, this connection is signaled by a conjunction such as "and." The fact that two premises are dependent on each other is indicated in the outline by a plus sign between the numbers of the two statements, as shown in the outline of example 1:14:

1:14. [¹*A university education should not emphasize career-training courses at the expense of the liberal arts*]. After all, [²one's college years are meant to be a time for intellectual growth and maturation,] but [³career-training courses usually emphasize unquestioning assimilation of the right answers.]

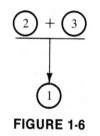

FIGURE 1-6

The point to note is that neither (2) nor (3), alone, gives any reason for the conclusion. They must be combined before they become relevant to (1).

It makes sense to have an arrow *leading from* a plus sign to a number, because that indicates that combining two statements produces something that supports the conclusion. We never have an arrow *pointing to* a plus sign; it must always point *to* a conclusion, either an intermediate conclusion or the final one.

Alternatively, we may have arguments in which two premises work *independently* to support the conclusion. Each one, taken in isolation, lends at least some support to the conclusion. Example 1:15 and its outline show how this is handled:

1:15. [¹The 55 mile an hour speed limit reduces the number of traffic accidents], and [²it cuts down on fuel consumption,] {so} [³*it ought to be retained*.]

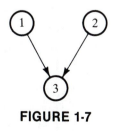

FIGURE 1-7

In complex arguments, several of these things may be going on at once, but the outlining method remains basically the same. In an argument with more than two or three statements, it may be easier to start with a small chunk here and there, before trying to combine all the various pieces into one outline. This step-by-step process is illustrated for example 1:16:

1:16. The widespread alarm about use and abuse of drugs in sports probably arises from some genuine, and perhaps rational, concern; but [¹*It is difficult to discern the basis for that concern in present policies and discussions.*] [²If it is based on unfairness, it is irrational.] {For} [³there are far greater sources of unfairness.] And [⁴whatever is due to drugs can be neutralized by a system that allows all athletes equal access to drugs.] [⁵If it is based on paternalism, it is disingenuous and misplaced.] {For} [⁶the risks of sport itself far exceed the demonstrated risks of those drugs that arouse the greatest concern.] [⁷If it is based on some notion of naturalness, we need more conceptual work to tell us why synthetic vitamins are considered natural, and naturally occurring hormones are considered unnatural.] [⁸We are not even clear on the moral difference, if any, between a food and drug,] [⁹nor is there a clear understanding of those terms.] (From Norman Fost, "Banning Drugs in Sports: A Skeptical View," *Hastings Center Report,* August 1986.)

After picking out and underlining the conclusion, and bracketing and numbering the various statements, you might notice a few of the closer connections.[4] Thus, Stage 1 of the outline might be rather fragmented, representing those connections that are easier to spot, such as the following:

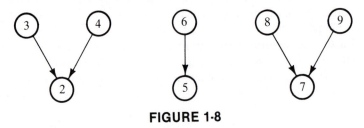

FIGURE 1·8

Once we have done this, it becomes easier to see how these various pieces can be combined to make up the full outline:

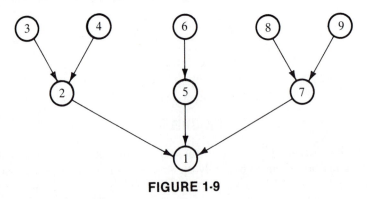

FIGURE 1·9

Here is another example that illustrates a common pattern in reconstructing arguments.

1:17. [¹Darwin's theory of evolution denies that we are all descended from Adam and Eve.] {It does so because} [²it claims that we are descended from monkeys,] {because} [³the Bible says that we are descended from Adam and Eve.] {This shows that} [⁴Darwin's theory is inconsistent with the Bible.] [⁵Only things that are consistent with the Bible can possibly be true.] {This follows from the fact that} [⁶anything inconsistent with the truth cannot be true.] {So} [⁷*Darwin's theory should not be taught in our schools.*]

Step 1 yields the following:

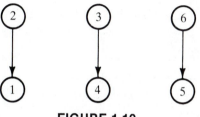

FIGURE 1-10

Each of these inferences is indicated by clue words and phrases. Since none of these intermediate arguments have any statements in common, we need to combine them in a reasonable way to produce a diagram with number (7) as the final conclusion.

Step 2, gives the following:

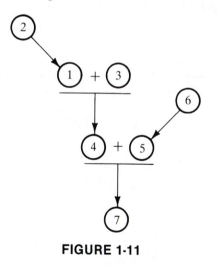

FIGURE 1-11

The reason for taking (1) and (3) *together* to yield (4) is primarily logical. It is also suggested by the order in which the material is presented. The inconsistency of Darwin's theory with the Bible logically requires not only a statement (3) about what the Bible claims, but also an assertion (1) that Darwin's theory denies this claim. The author first establishes (1) by an inference from (2); the author then asserts premise (3) and concludes with (4).

The inference from (4) and (5) to (7) involves an implicit premise to the effect that only things that can possibly be true should be taught in our schools. Statements (4) and (5), *together,* logically imply that Darwin's theory cannot possibly be true. Though it is not explicitly stated, the author intends this implicit intermediate conclusion to be combined with the implicit premise to yield the final conclusion. Since this implicit step is obvious, we have not represented it on our diagram. Such implicit steps, involving intermediate implicit premises and conclusions, are a common feature of arguments.

Strictly speaking, each premise of an argument should be expressed by a complete sentence, not a sentence fragment. Although we have been using sentence fragments to stand for entire premises when the meaning is clear, you will occasionally find it necessary to write out some of the premises as complete sentences. Example 1:18 illustrates this:

1:18. {Since} [¹diamond scratches glass] and [²transmits light,] while [³graphite does not,] clearly [⁴*there is a structural difference between these two forms of carbon.*]

To fully understand the structure of this argument, we must expand on statement (3) by spelling out the implicit contrast with statements (1) and (2); we do this by writing out two full sentences and labeling them "3a" and "3b":

3a: Graphite does not scratch glass.

3b: Graphite does not transmit light.

Using these new statements, we can outline the argument this way:

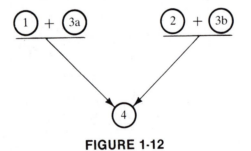

FIGURE 1-12

EXERCISES

For each of the following, give a complete outline of the argument.

 1. If we raise taxes, businesses will pass their increased costs on to consumers. So a tax increase will fuel inflation.

2. The protein in grain is good but not what nutritionists term "complete." Unlike, say, the protein in meat or fish, cereal protein is deficient in certain amino acids, which are protein's building blocks. (From *Consumer Reports,* October 1986, p. 630.)

3. Having an all-volunteer army produces a higher percentage of recruits who have graduated from high school, and it improves morale. So the draft should not be reinstated, except in a national emergency.

4. Computers never produce anything original because they merely follow their programs, and following a program is not a creative activity.

5. If we want to decrease unemployment, we must develop more adult education courses, for many chronically unemployed people are illiterate and thus have a harder time finding a job.

6. Electronic devices using solid-state components would be useless in a nuclear war because these components are easily damaged by ionizing radiation and thus the devices would cease to function properly. Hence, all vital equipment should use vacuum tubes and fiber optics wherever possible.

7. Physicians should make every effort to identify the organism that is causing an infectious illness, for then they can use specific drugs against that organism instead of wide-spectrum antibiotics. This is desirable because specific drugs have fewer unwanted side effects and their use is less likely to produce multiple drug resistance.

*8. The "total energy" of a physical system, a meaningful concept for flat space, is a meaningless concept if we allow for arbitrary space curvature. Since the space of the entire universe can curve, the total energy of the universe is thus simply not a meaningful concept. This conclusion, that the concepts of total energy and total energy conservation do not apply to the whole universe, is quite startling—but true. It implies that if we are to define nothing—the vacuum state—as it might apply to the whole universe, then we ought to look for features of the vacuum that do not use the concept of "total energy." [From H. R. Pagels, *Perfect Symmetry* (New York: Simon & Schuster, 1985), p. 329.]

9. God could not have created the world three days before he created the sun. Either the concept of a day is not defined by reference to the sun, or there could not have been a world three days before there was a sun, since if a day is defined this way, there would be no way of measuring days before there was a sun. The concept of a day is defined as a period between one sunrise and the next; therefore, it is defined by reference to the sun. Thus, it follows that some of the things in the Bible are false.

10. Is there an unworthy cause in the land that will not try a free speech defense? In fact, we tamper with free speech all the time, especially in mass media. The censorship codes for television are elaborate and strict:

no four-letter words, no nudity, no Marlboro man. Speech is massively controlled on mass media for good reason: it has mass effects, some of them bad. There are certain things we agree we don't want television promoting, and we are willing to make TV speech a bit less free as a consequence.

When it comes to censorship of television, the question is not whether, but for what. The what cannot be trivial. It must be important, as important as deglamorizing smoking. It is hard to see why deglamorizing alcohol fails to meet that standard. (From *The Washington Post News Weekly Edition,* June 10, 1985.)

11. The Post-ABC News survey focused mainly on voters who knew the polls showed Reagan ahead, for logic suggests that only among them could the polls have had an effect.

By rights, if opinion polls draw people to the frontrunner, then Reagan voters more than Mondale voters would know what the polls were showing. But that was not the case.

Among Reagan voters, 74 percent stated correctly that the president was ahead in the polls before the election. Among Mondale voters, 84 percent knew it. (From *The Washington Post News Weekly Edition,* June 10, 1985.)

12. Perhaps the most common argument offered by creationism against evolution is an attempt to discredit the fossil evidence for evolution by pointing to the relative scarcity of transitional forms. However, this is a poor argument, for at least three reasons. First, in order to embarrass evolution, it would be required that evolution *predicts* that there should be numerous transitional fossils. In fact, however there is reason to believe that major evolutionary change occurs when a *small* population becomes reproductively isolated, and that such a major change occurs over a relatively *short* period of geological time. Thus, on this view, there should be a relative scarcity of transitional fossils. The second point is that, nonetheless, there are transitional fossils. The therapsids provide numerous links between reptiles and mammals, and *Archaeopteryx* is a clear intermediary between dinosaurs and birds. Finally, whatever the problems associated with the fossil record, what we find does not look at all as it would be expected to if God created all varieties of life at the same time. In the very oldest layers, we find only the remains of microorganisms. Only later do we find soft-bodied animals and hardbodied creatures appear in still more recent layers. If creationism were true, we would expect the fossil record to have the structure of a wellstirred stew, with trilobites and tigers, dinosaurs and donkeys all side by side. This is anything but what we do find. (From A. Stairs, "The Case Against Creationism," *QQ* Spring 1982.)

*13. Animal liberationists insist that we have a moral obligation to efficiently relieve animal suffering. The misery of wild animals is enormous. In the natural environment nature ruthlessly limits animal populations by doing violence to virtually every individual before it reaches maturity. The path from birth to slaughter, however, is nearly always longer and less painful in the barnyard than in the woods. Thus, the most efficient way to relieve the suffering of wild animals would be to convert our national parks and wilderness areas into humanely managed farms. It follows, therefore, that animal liberationists cannot be environmentalists since they must be willing to sacrifice the authenticity, integrity, and complexity of ecosystems for the welfare of animals. (Adapted from an article by M. Sagoff in *QQ* Spring 1984.)

14. The greatness of our political system is that it not only guarantees us freedom of conscience, but also permits us to vote our conscience. When "pro-choice" groups urge congressmen to support federal funding for abortions, they are exercising their democratic rights. So too are theologians who urge a nuclear freeze. How can it be, then, that when others, like myself, support candidates who advocate the protection of unborn children or voluntary prayer in our schools, we are ostracized as un-American or worse? When those calling themselves liberals register new voters, they are said to enlarge the democratic process. Yet when I and my compatriots urge fellow believers to vote, we are condemned for mixing church and state. (Adapted from a passage by the Reverend Jerry Falwell in *Newsweek* 9/17/84.)

15. Our silence about the explicit contents of cultural literacy leads to the following result, observable in the sociology of the verbal SAT. This exam is chiefly a vocabulary test, which, except for its omission of proper names and other concrete information, constitutes a test of cultural literacy. Hence, when young people from deprived backgrounds ask how they can acquire the abilities tested on the verbal SAT, they are told, quite correctly, that the only way to acquire that knowledge is through wide reading in many domains over many years. That is advice that deprived students already in high school are not in a position to take. Thus there remains a strong correlation between the verbal SAT score and socioeconomic status. Students from middle-class and upper-middle-class backgrounds get their knowledge for the verbal SAT not just from reading, but through the pores, from talk at home and social chitchat. (From E. D. Hirsch, Jr., "Cultural Literacy and the Schools," *American Educator,* Summer 1985.)

16. Passions have always run high in the debate over animal experimentation; scientists charge groups like the Animal Liberation Foundation with a warped ethic that places animals before people, and pro-animal activists tell stories of terror and torture in the labs. But thanks to burgeoning numbers and increased sophistication, the animal defenders appear to be gaining an edge. An estimated 400 groups with 2 million dues-paying members are crusading to stop the use of animals in experiments, and they are scoring victories that could radically change the ways of science. Within the last year three states have banned the use of pound animals for research, universities have set up centers to seek alternative approaches, and regulatory agencies are beginning to curb decades-old testing techniques.

*17. *Forbidden Planet,* a 1956 MGM film, takes place on the distant planet Altair 4, in the year 2200. A rescue expedition from Earth finds only two survivors of an earlier landing party, Dr. Morbius and his daughter, along with the remnants of a long-extinct, highly advanced civilization, the Krell. An 8,000-cubic-mile power plant has continued to maintain itself for the 200,000 years since the Krell race vanished. It is powered by 9,200 nuclear reactors buried deep inside the planet. At the end of the film, the rescue party escapes in the nick of time as the planet is destroyed by an explosive chain reaction in the thermonuclear furnaces. This explosion of the entire planet is implausible. Since Altair 4's surface gravity nearly equals that of the Earth, we may infer that the size of the planet is also similar. Even exploded simultaneously, 9,200 of our most powerful hydrogen bombs would not destroy a planet of Earth's size. One can only conclude that the Krell nuclear power plants are each immensely greater, if they are to explode, than any hydrogen bomb built by man. Besides, why would the Krell build in a simple mechanism to destroy their entire planet? (Adapted from L. W. Dubeck and S. F. Moshier, "Teaching Fact with Fiction," *American Educator* Winter 1985.)

Constructing Arguments

The outlining technique discussed in the section Outlining the Structure of Arguments is useful in another way. It can help you plan and organize your own arguments, by making you think about the connections between ideas before you try to construct a full argument. The outlining technique is the same: arrows run from reasons to the ideas they support, reasons can work independently or dependently, and we might have argument chains. The only difference is that you will be supplying the claims that are organized by the outline.

Often we argue for a conclusion simply by giving a reason. For example, if a person is asked whether she thinks a university ought to offer all of its courses solely on a pass/no-pass (P/N) system, she might say "Yes, because that would encourage people to take new courses that they would be afraid to take otherwise." If we number the two ideas, we get:

1: A university ought to grade solely on the P/N system.[5]

2: P/N systems encourage people to take new courses.

Since there are only two statements here, there is not much to organize.

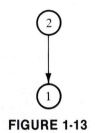

FIGURE 1-13

Someone who disagrees with this conclusion (1) might list his reasons as follows:

3: Grades are the best measure of performance in a class.

4: Without some measure of performance, it is impossible to tell how well a student has mastered the course material.

Once these reasons have been articulated, we can step back and ask how they are best related to the conclusion and to each other. Together they seem to work to support the conclusion that we ought to retain grades, but each by itself does not get us very far. So our outline would look like this:

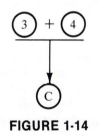

FIGURE 1-14

Note that in this case, the conclusion (C) has not yet been explicitly formulated. There are several choices for (C) that would be inconsistent with conclusion (1) of the first argument. At this stage, (C) may be as broad as "A pure P/N system is undesirable." If further reasons are thought of and incorporated into the argument, we may want to go back and refine the conclusion.

This procedure for creating an argument can be summarized as follows:

1. Try to develop a preliminary statement of the conclusion, of what you are arguing for. As you think about the subject more, do not hesitate to go back and change this statement to make it clearer, more precise, or a more accurate representation of the position you want to defend.

2. Make a list of the ideas you think are relevant to that conclusion and assign each a number. At this stage, do not worry about connections or development; that will come later.

3. Try to find an outline that reflects the natural or intuitive connections

between these ideas; in doing so, you may find yourself adding ideas to the list to fill out the outline.

This procedure is not really needed if you have come up with only one or two ideas. (Even here, though, it gives you time to stop and think whether your numbered statements really point to or support your conclusion, and whether they work together or independently.) When you come up with a longer list, the outlining technique allows you to break down the task of organizing your thoughts into more manageable parts. Consider the following list of reasons for advocating a complete P/N grading system:

1: Students will experiment with new courses.

2: It decreases the chances that students will become discouraged and think they are "no good."

3: By deemphasizing grades, we redirect attention to gaining knowledge.

4: Students would be less inclined to cheat and to plagiarize.

5: It would reduce harmful competitiveness between students.

6: It is more in keeping with academic, liberal arts ideals.

7: Grades produce too much stress.

8: Grades are often arbitrary.

This list moves from one strand of thinking to another, and we would like to organize these ideas into an argument that is more focused and easier to follow. To do this, we need to organize some of the subsections, and then tie the subsections together. Noting that some of the statements relate to reducing the negative effects of grades while others emphasize the positive value of the P/N system, we might begin with one of those areas.

If we look for the positive side, we note that **1, 3,** and **6** emphasize the beneficial value of the P/N system, rather than the defects in the conventional grading system. (Since the statements are just meant as starting points, there are many other equally good ways of grouping them. Remember that you are trying to develop an organizational pattern, not discover one that is already determined.) Statement **1** suggests that students are more likely to get a broader education, and **3** speaks of renewed attention to gaining knowledge rather than simply getting good grades. Both of these are aspects of the liberal arts ideal. Thus, we can begin our outline this way:

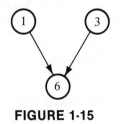

FIGURE 1-15

Alternatively, if we think that students will feel freer to experiment because they are more interested in knowledge than grades, our outline would look like this:

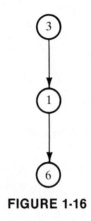

FIGURE 1-16

Going back to our list, we now note that several of the statements **2, 4, 5, 7** have to do with the bad effects of a conventional grading system, but no general statement conveys the broader objection.[6] So we add to our list the following:

9: Conventional grading systems have undesirable effects on the students.

10: Universities and colleges should abandon conventional grading systems.

The bad effects mentioned in **9** are regarded as a reason for thinking that conclusion **10** is true.

In planning this part of the outline, we note that "harmful competitiveness" could be a reason for thinking that grades provide a motive for plagiarism, but that it is also an undesirable consequence in itself. We can indicate its dual role on our diagram:

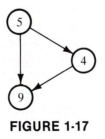

FIGURE 1-17

The complaint about stress **7** also occupies a multiple role, so our final outline of this section will look like this:

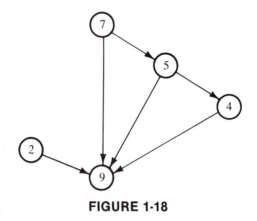

FIGURE 1-18

The only statement we have not yet used is **8,** which states that grades are often arbitrary. Statement **8** suggests that there might be something wrong with the whole idea of giving grades. Depending on our goal and audience, we may decide to pursue this topic by adding further ideas to our list, and formulating a new section of the outline, or we may decide to abandon **8** as unhelpful. If we do, we can try for a final formulation of our position, and bring together all the sections of the argument. In doing so we may notice other connections between ideas, for instance, the thought that stress, and fear of failure, is what often discourages students from taking a wide variety of new courses. These connections can also be indicated on the outline.

If we now wanted to present our argument in words, we could simply begin at the top of one branch of the outline and follow it down step-by-step, reformulating our numbered statements to make their place in the development clearer. When we had completed one branch, we would move to another, until the entire argument has been followed through to its final conclusion.

In subsequent chapters we will see how the arguments implicit in this outline can be constructed in the strongest possible way. We will learn to recognize what sorts of evidence might be relevant, how the premises must be formulated, and so on; but even before we learn to do all of this, the technique of using an outline to plan an argument is helpful. It helps us group related ideas together, and gives us time to think about the relations between these ideas—which ones lead to what, and how they fit together. It helps us locate gaps, and gives us an opportunity to supply missing pieces. By working out the pattern of the argument before we state it in final form, we can offer our ideas (which started off as numbered statements formulated in no particular order) in a way that shows our audience how they fit together. This ability to develop a clear and well-organized argument provides a firm foundation for learning how to reason correctly.

EXERCISES

I. For each of the following lists of ideas, develop an outline that organizes them in a natural way.

List 1:

(C) The Federal government should reinstitute the draft.

(1) It is important to have a trained army for purposes of defense.
(2) The volunteer army has proven to be an unfair system, putting the heaviest burden on minorities.
(3) It would reduce unemployment.
(4) It would provide many young people with skills and experience that will help them find jobs in civilian life.

List 2:*

(C) Public schools should give equal time to creationism when evolutionary theory is taught.

(1) Some people believe that evolutionary theory is contrary to their religious beliefs.
(2) Science is not cut-and-dried; there is room for disagreement.
(3) Students should be taught alternative explanations that illustrate the problem of choosing between conflicting theories.
(4) The Constitution guarantees freedom of religion.

List 3:

(C) Creationism should not be taught as an alternative to evolutionary theory.

(1) Most scientists do not accept creationism as a good theory.
(2) Evolutionary theory represents the best available explanation.
(3) If we teach creationism, we should also teach all the other versions of creation that are discussed in religion and myth.
(4) The only reason for introducing creationism is to illustrate accounts that rely on something other than scientific reasoning.
(5) Portraying the adoption of a scientific theory as merely a matter of individual choice unnecessarily confuses a school-age child.
(6) Positive arguments in favor of creationism ultimately rest on reference to the Book of Genesis rather than on empirical evidence.

II. Develop your own list of ideas for or against the following positions. Make up an outline to go along with your list.

1. The federal government should reinstitute the draft.

2. Public schools should give equal time to creationism when evolutionary theory is taught.

3. Colleges should abandon the present grading system and adopt a Pass/No Pass system.

4. Colleges and universities should consider moral issues when they make investments in stocks; for example, a college should not invest money in a firm that does business with the government of South Africa.

5. All states should enact "deposit laws" imposing a mandatory deposit on beverage containers.

III. Imagine that you are writing a letter to the Editor of your local or campus newspaper. Write such a letter using one of the outlines you developed in Section II.

Validity and Soundness

The main goal of critical thinking is to evaluate arguments. The first steps toward this goal are to locate the conclusion, find the premises, and outline the structure of the argument. We now discuss the question of evaluation.

Two main factors make an argument good or bad: (1) the relationship between the premises and the conclusion and (2) the status of the premises. We first concentrate on the relationship between the premises and the conclusion.

At this point, we introduce two concepts for evaluating arguments. The first, **validity,** has to do solely with the relationship between the premises and the conclusion; the second, **soundness,** concerns both the relationship between the premises and the conclusion, and the status of the premises.

To understand the concept of validity, we should remember that the purpose of an argument is to present a reliable form of reasoning, and reliability involves truth. Ideally, we want arguments that have the following feature: if we start with true premises, they must lead us to a true conclusion. In other words, we want our arguments to be **truth-preserving.** An argument that is truth-preserving in this way is called a **valid,** or **deductively valid,** argument.[7] With this in mind, we can define a valid argument in any one of three equivalent ways:

1. An argument is valid if and only if it is not logically possible for its conclusion to be false when all its premises are true.

2. An argument is valid if and only if its conclusion follows logically from (or is logically implied by) its premises.

3. A valid argument is one in which its premises are related to its conclusion in such a way that if all its premises were to be true, then its conclusion would also have to be true.

Though these definitions are all equivalent, the first is sometimes more useful, especially when it is not clear to us whether or not the premises of an argument logically imply its conclusion.

It follows from our definitions of validity that any argument that is not valid is **invalid** and vice versa: both of these terms are "all or nothing." If an argument cannot guarantee the truth of its conclusion on the basis of the truth of its premises, it is simply invalid. There is no such thing as an argument that is somewhat valid, or mostly invalid. Remember, the terms "valid" and "invalid" describe arguments, not isolated statements. Similarly, the terms "true" and "false" should be used only to describe statements, not arguments.

How do we tell when an argument is valid? An argument is valid when it exemplifies a **valid form of argument.** By a valid form of argument we mean a pattern such that any argument with that form or following that pattern *exactly* will automatically be valid.[8]

To examine the form of arguments more easily, with fewer distractions, we will frequently substitute symbols or letters for actual words, phrases, or statements. This allows us to look at the form completely apart from the specific claims made by the premises. We can show, for example, that any argument of the form "All A's are B's, All B's are C's; thus, All A's are C's" is valid, which tells us that whenever we substitute things for A, B, and C that make the premises true, the conclusion will be true too. Of course, if our substitutions make one or both of the premises false, then anything can happen—the conclusion might be true, or it might be false, even though the argument is still valid.

Each of the following examples is a valid argument; all of them follow exactly the same valid pattern.

1:19. All whales are fish, and all fish are cold-blooded; therefore, all whales are cold-blooded.

1:20. All whales are fish, and all fish live in water; so all whales live in water.

1:21. All whales are fish. All fish suckle their young. Therefore, all whales suckle their young.

1:22. All whales are mammals. All mammals suckle their young. So all whales suckle their young.

Each of these arguments is valid, even though three of them have at least one false premise, and one has a false conclusion. Each argument is valid because *if* all its premises *were* true, its conclusion would also have to be true; all four arguments exemplify the same valid form of argument. Argument 1:22 illustrates the fact that if a valid argument does have all true premises, the conclusion must also be true. On the other hand, if one or more of the premises of a valid argument is false, the conclusion might be true or it might be false; there is no guarantee either way.

How do we show that an argument is invalid? This can be difficult, since many invalid arguments have true conclusions. The crucial point is to prove that even if all the premises were true, the conclusion could still be false. For that reason, paying attention to the *form* of the argument can help us. So we begin by learning how to identify an invalid form of argument.

Since an **invalid form of argument** leaves open the possibility that true premises can lead to a false conclusion, we can show that a form is invalid by constructing an example of an argument following that form in which all the premises are true and the conclusion is false. Consider example 1:23:

1:23. If the president resigned yesterday, then the vice-president has become president. The president did not resign yesterday, and so the vice-president has not become president.

Although 1:23 may appear to be valid, it is actually invalid, and this can be discovered by examining its form. The form of argument 1:23 is: "If p then q; not p; therefore, not q." We can show that this form is invalid by substituting statements for p and q that make all the premises true and the conclusion false, as in example 1:24:

1:24. If Margaret is a Purdue graduate, then Margaret is a human being. Margaret is not a Purdue graduate, and so she is not a human being.

Given that Margaret is a human being, but not a Purdue graduate, 1:24 conclusively shows that in all arguments of this form, the truth of the premises does not guarantee the truth of the conclusion; therefore, this is an invalid form of argument.

We saw earlier that any argument that exemplifies a valid form of argument is a valid argument. Unfortunately, things are not as simple with invalid forms of argument, since one argument may exemplify many different forms. If we used "r" to stand for the entire first premise, "s" to stand for the second premise, and "t" to stand for the conclusion, we could also describe the form of argument 1:22 as "r and s; therefore, t." In fact, *any* argument with two premises will exemplify this invalid form. For this reason, the mere fact that an argument exemplifies an invalid form does not imply that the argument is invalid. An argument is invalid only if *all* the forms it exemplifies are invalid. In practice, the number of forms that might be valid for any given argument is extremely limited, so we can readily see which forms are worth testing.

It follows that in most cases we cannot tell if an argument is valid just by noting whether its premises and its conclusion are actually true. A valid argument can have any combination except all true premises and a false conclusion. An invalid argument can have any combination whatsoever: all true premises and a true conclusion, all true premises and a false conclusion, some false premises and a false conclusion, or some false premises and a true conclusion. Thus, a false conclusion can be the result of either a valid argument or an invalid one. The key to discovering if it is valid is to ask whether it is ever *possible* for all the premises to be true and the conclusion false. If it is possible, then the argument is invalid. Only when that possibility is ruled out is the argument valid.

The second concent, **soundness**, builds on the idea of validity. A sound argument must satisfy two criteria: it must be a valid argument, *and all* its premises must be true. If either of these criteria is not met, the argument is unsound. This definition tells us two things. Like validity, soundness does not admit of degrees—an argument is either sound or it is unsound. Second, a sound argument always has a true conclusion. To determine whether an argument is sound (in contrast to determining its validity) we must evaluate both its form and the truth of its premises. Evaluating the truth of statements on the basis of their content is discussed in later chapters. For the moment we will concentrate on validity.

EXERCISES

I. For each of the following questions construct an argument with just two premises by choosing three different statements from the following list. Use only statements from the list, and make sure that your arguments satisfy all the conditions.

List:

a. All dogs are cats.
b. All dogs are fish.
c. All dogs have eyes.
d. All cats have eyes
i. All fish can breathe in water.
j. All things with gills can breathe in water.

e. All cats have gills.
f. All fish are cats.
g. All fish have gills.
h. All fish are dogs.

*1. A valid argument with a true conclusion, one true premise and one false premise.

2. A valid argument with a false conclusion and two false premises.

3. A valid argument with a true conclusion and two false premises.

4. An invalid argument with two true premises and a true conclusion.

5. A sound argument with two premises.

II. Answer the following questions, and explain your answers.

*1. Can a valid argument lead to a false conclusion? If so, what do we know about its premises?

2. If we have an argument in which all the premises and the conclusion are true statements, can we tell anything about its validity?

3. If you know that an argument is valid, and has a true conclusion, does this imply that all of its premises are true?

4. If all the premises of an argument are false and its conclusion is true, can we tell if the argument is invalid?

5. Can a sound argument ever have a false conclusion?

6. Can a valid argument be unsound? Can a sound argument be invalid?

*7. If an argument has a conclusion that says exactly the same thing as one of its premises, is the argument valid or invalid?

8. Consider the following argument: "Some terriers are obedient, and all

my dogs are terriers; therefore, some of my dogs are obedient." Is it possible for the premises of this argument to be true and its conclusion false? What does this tell you about the argument's validity? What can you say about the argument's soundness?

9. A contradiction is defined as a statement that cannot possibly be true (e.g., Paris is in France and Paris is not in France); if one of the premises in an argument is a contradiction, is the argument valid? Is it sound?

10. If the conclusion of an argument repeats exactly one of its premises, can the argument be sound?

Truth, Relativism, and Skepticism

Up to this point we have assumed that the notion of truth is straightforward and unproblematic. Thus, in defining a sound argument as one that is valid and has all true premises, we have said nothing about how we *know* whether the premises are true. In our illustrations we have simply taken for granted that we all *believe,* for example, that whales are not fish but mammals, and that these beliefs are true. But when we turn to real-life arguments about matters of importance, in which people often hold conflicting beliefs, it becomes much harder to decide who, if anyone, is right. In fact you might think that there is something fundamentally wrong with even trying to judge who is correct about controversial issues of morality and values. This section addresses some of these general questions about truth and knowledge.[9]

First there is the question of truth. Throughout this book we assume that for any proposition or statement, either it is true or it is false. Thus, even when there is doubt and uncertainty about the truth of a given proposition, we still insist that it has a truth value, that either it is true or it is false, even if we do not *know* which it is. This is known as the **objective concept of truth.**

The objective concept of truth stands in contrast with the view that some propositions are true (or false) but only *relative to the person who believes them.* On this **relativist conception of truth** a proposition such as "Capital punishment is wrong" might be true for Smith but false for Jones, or true for the British but false for Americans. Often this relativism about truth stems from a desire to be tolerant of the "private" beliefs of others (on questions such as morality, diet, and religion) and from an awareness of cultural diversity. (Different cultures have held, and continue to hold, widely different beliefs about sex, punishment, justice, and so on.) But when one examines this proposal in detail, many problems become evident.

The most fundamental objection to relativism is that it confuses truth with belief. Consider the following statement:

1:25. The earth is at the center of the universe.

Many ancient Greeks believed 1:25 to be true and did so for excellent reasons, given the evidence available to them. But their belief, though rational, was false. The truth or falsity of statements like 1:25 depends on matters of fact, on the way the world is, regardless of what people believe. Nothing would seem to be gained by saying that the proposition that the earth is the center of the universe was "true for the ancient Greeks" but "false for us." All this boils down to is the simple observation that the ancient Greeks believed differently from us and that we now have good reasons for thinking they were mistaken.

The same distinction between (objective) truth and belief holds with respect to statements expressing moral judgments. Consider example 1:26:

1:26.   Abortion is morally wrong.

Admittedly, the truth or falsity of 1:26 does not seem to depend on facts about the physical world in the same way that 1:25 does. But it is hard to see what "1:26 is true for Smith but false for Jones" really means, except that Smith believes abortion is wrong (i.e., that Smith believes 1:26 is true), and Jones believes otherwise. Indeed, if Smith and Jones were to engage in a debate about the morality of abortion, their very discussion would presuppose that there is a correct (i.e., true) answer to the question "Is abortion morally wrong?" If there were nothing more to truth than what people happen to believe, discussion and debate would be pointless.

Insisting on the objective concept of truth, and thus holding that all propositions, including those about morality and values, have a truth value independent of what people believe does not lead to intolerance or dogmatism. Even though we think our beliefs are (objectively) true, and that people who disagree with us are wrong, there is always the possibility that we are mistaken. We should be prepared to evaluate our own arguments in support of our beliefs, as well as the arguments for conclusions we disagree with. The following chapters show how we can often reach a detailed and objective judgment about the merits of arguments and the likelihood that their conclusions are true.

Even after evaluating an argument as carefully as we can, we might still be unable to determine whether its conclusion is true. In such cases the correct judgment to make is simply that we do not know where the truth lies. Even though there is a truth of the matter, we have not been able to discover it. There is no guarantee that critical thinking will always yield certainty.

Honestly admitting that we lack certainty in some areas is not the same as, nor does it imply, abandoning all standards of rationality. In discussions of controversial issues one sometimes hears statements to the effect that "Everyone is entitled to his own opinion" or that "My beliefs are just as good as anyone else's." This may sound like tolerance, but it more often disguises an unwillingness to develop and evaluate arguments in a rational and objective way. The person who refuses to offer reasons for his beliefs or who has no interest in evaluating the arguments for positions he disagrees with has a closed mind, not a tolerant one.

Our second question, "How do we *know* that any statement is true?" is difficult to answer. Someone who doubts that we know anything (or who denies that we have knowledge in some particular area such as religion or morality) is a **skeptic**. The best reply to skepticism is to explain how knowledge is possible.

A good starting point is to ask ourselves what things we are sure we know, beyond reasonable doubt. There are some things we are more sure about than others, and there are many propositions whose truth is not seriously in doubt at all. Usually the beliefs of which we are most sure are reports of our personal experiences and claims about observable matters of fact that everyone agrees on. Examples are claims such as Kansas City is in Missouri, no one enjoys being in pain, Jones told me yesterday that he has a new car.

It is important to stress here that immunity to doubt and unanimity of opinion do not guarantee truth. After all, it is logically possible that one's memory is defective or that we are all victims of a mass hallucination. The point is that *unless we have a positive reason for doubting the claims we are surest about, then we are justified in accepting them as true.* The quest for knowledge has to start somewhere, and it seems only reasonable to begin with those statements for which we have the best justification.

We extend our knowledge by reasoning, by constructing arguments that lead us from premises that are most secure for us, to conclusions about matters that might initially be in some doubt. Of course, this account of how we come to know things is to some extent an idealization. Only rarely will our starting premises have that maximal degree of certainty that is our ultimate goal.

Consider example 1:27:

1:27. Do I know that Jones has a new car?

I might reason as follows: Jones told me yesterday that he has a new car. Therefore, he has a new car. Now, I am certain that the premise is true since it was only yesterday that Jones spoke to me and my memory about recent events is reliable. But the conclusion does not follow logically from the premise. It is logically possible that the conclusion is false even though the premise is true. For the argument to be valid, an additional premise is required about Jones's veracity. So we get:

1. Jones told me yesterday that he has a new car.

2. <u>Jones was telling the truth.</u>

3. Jones has a new car.

Unlike the first version of the argument, this one is valid. I have no doubt about the first premise but what about the second? Do I know for sure that Jones was not lying? I must now focus on my reasons for thinking that Jones was being truthful. I might consider arguing for premises 2, constructing the best argument I can for it.

Let us suppose that I have good reason to believe Jones usually tells the truth unless he has a reason for lying, and conjoin that with another premise that Jones had no reason for lying to me about his new car. Does this, finally, establish that I *know* Jones has a new car? The answer is that *I have shown that my belief is justified* and, depending on the context, this may suffice to warrant my claim to know.

In general, knowledge requires both that my beliefs are justified and that they are (objectively) true. In showing why I think I am justified in holding them I am, at the same time, showing why I think they are true. The real issue in explaining how we know things is **justification:** *Is our justification good enough to warrant our claim that we not only believe certain things, but actually know them?*

Since justification comes in degrees of strength from very strong to very weak, how good my justification has to be will vary with the context. What is good enough in everyday contexts ("I saw Jones's new car parked across the street") may not be good enough in a court of law ("How did you know it was Jones's car and not someone else's that is the same model and color?")

Though what counts as sufficient justification to license a knowledge claim is relative to the context, this does not mean that we have given up the objective concept of truth. We are *not* saying that whether "Smith knows that p" is true depends on the context. Rather we are maintaining that whether Smith is warranted or *justified in claiming to know p* will depend on the context. In *all* settings it continues to be the case that if p should be false, then regardless of what Smith and others believed, none of them knew p. Examining our justification is our best and only way of finding out which of our beliefs are true and which of them qualify as knowledge, but it is not infallible.

Notes

[1]The reason for saying "intended to" here is that some arguments are bad. Though the person giving the argument intends that the premises rationally support the conclusion, they might not do so. Also, we say "support" rather than "prove" or "establish" because some good arguments (e.g., inductive ones) are less than conclusive.

[2]For more on the evaluation of such appeals to authority, see the discussion in Chapter 7.

[3]The technique for outlining arguments used in this section is adapted from Monroe C. Beardsley, *Practical Logic* (Englewood Cliffs, NJ: Prentice-Hall Inc., 1950), and Stephen N. Thomas, *Practical Reasoning in Natural Language* (Englewood Cliffs, NJ: Prentice-Hall, Inc., 1977).

[4]You may wonder why the last sentence has been divided into the two statements 8 and 9. Does this not violate our rule that we should never break up an "either . . . or . . ." statement? The answer is "No." In this example, "nor" means "and it is not the case that. . . . " In general, "neither A nor B" means "A is not the case, and B is not the case."

[5]Feel free to state your ideas briefly, as long as you capture the substance of your reasons and conclusion.

[6]When we do this, we revise the emphasis of some of our original statements. Thus, we

are now thinking of (4) as the claim that grades push some people to plagiarism. The basic idea is the same; we can worry about precise formulations once we have decided how the argument should be organized.

[7]The terms "valid" and "deductively valid" are equivalent, and can be used interchangeably. The only reason for adding the term "deductively" is to emphasize the difference between *deductively valid* arguments and *inductively strong* arguments. The concept of the inductive strength of arguments is analyzed in Chapter 4. Here it is sufficient to note that deductive validity is the only sort of validity there is.

[8]It may be noted that there are many valid arguments, according to the fundamental (semantic) definition of validity (definition 1), that do not possess a valid argument form in either categorical or propositional logic. For example, "John runs quickly" validly entails "John runs." Definition 1 guides us in what we recognize as a valid form of argument. Unfortunately, the construction of such systems of logic is still incomplete. So there remain valid arguments that, as yet, are not recognized as instantiating a valid (syntactical) form of argument.

[9]For a more detailed account of these matters, see N. L. Gifford, *When in Rome: An Introduction to Relativism and Knowledge* (Albany: State University of New York Press, 1983).

CHAPTER

2

Categorical Reasoning

In Chapter 1, we introduced the concept of a **deductively valid argument**. In this and following chapters, we will learn to analyze and evaluate several different forms of argument. Our purpose is to understand what makes these forms of argument valid or invalid. We want to see how premises can be related to a conclusion in such a way that their truth guarantees the truth of the conclusion. Remember, in a valid argument, if all the premises are true, then the conclusion must also be true. By understanding validity, we will be able to recognize and construct truth-preserving arguments.

One common form of reasoning involves statements that put things into **categories** or **classes**. Examples of such statements are "Dogs are mammals," "All the people in this room are over four feet tall," "None of the numbers between 8 and 10 is prime," and "Some of the numbers between 3 and 8 are prime." From some statements about classes, we can deduce further statements. For example, from "All the people in this room are over four feet tall," and "Anyone who is over four feet tall is taller than Marvin," we can validly infer "Everyone in this room is taller than Marvin." All the arguments we will study in this chapter resemble this inference, since they are composed entirely of statements that put things into classes or categories. Such arguments are known as **categorical arguments**; individual statements about classes are called **categorical statements**.

Categorical Statements

In English we have many ways of conveying the same idea: for example, all college students are literate, every college student is literate, only literate people are college students, college students are all literate. Although these variations are important stylistic devices, for the purposes of studying the structure of arguments it is useful to settle on a single way of describing the same relation between classes. For that reason, logicians have developed a **standard form for categorical statements**.

First, we standardize the way of referring to classes or categories. The convention is to use only nouns or noun phrases such as "mammals," "literate people," and "things that weigh more than 30 pounds." If a statement uses something other than noun phrases, we must rewrite it. Preserving consistency will later allow us to exhibit the forms of categorical arguments. Here are some examples:

2:1. All college students are literate = All college students are literate people.

All clowns make children laugh = All clowns are people that make children laugh.

All ducks swim = All ducks are things that swim = All ducks are swimmers.

I find bad arguments wherever I go = All places to which I go are places where I find bad arguments.

Whenever Sheila eats garlic, she gets heartburn = All times when Sheila eats garlic are times when she gets heartburn.

These examples show the most common ways of putting sentences into the form of categorical statements that contain noun phrases linked only by "are," or, less commonly, "is." "All clowns are sad," can be thought of as relating the class of clowns to the class of sad people, or to the class of sad things. The general rule is to transform adjectives and verbs into noun phrases by attaching them to a word like "things." "All ducks swim," for example, relates the class of ducks to the class of swimming things. Thus, we can insert the verb "swim" into the phrase "things that ———," yielding "All ducks are things that swim."

Sentences that begin "when," "whenever," "never," "where," "nowhere," or "wherever" are usually about times or places. Thus, "when" may become "times at which" or "times when;" "where" becomes "places where." In this way, even sentences that do not seem to be about classes can be put into categorical form.

Many sentences do not follow any of the patterns discussed so far. In these cases, try to describe the group or class of things that the sentence is about. Consider, for example, "He who lives by the sword, dies by the sword." This sentence is about people who live by the sword. Thus, it can be rewritten as "All people who live by the sword, die by the sword." Following the noun–verb pattern discussed previously, we can now transform it into "All people who live by the sword are people who die by the sword." This technique of deciding what the sentence is about, what the subject class is, and how it can be described, enables us to put a wide variety of sentences into categorical form.

There are only four **standard forms of categorical statement**. Each kind of statement is associated with a particular letter: either A, E, I, or O. In the following table, the letter "S" is used as a placeholder for the **subject term**, and "P" is a placeholder for the **predicate term** of the statement. Here are the four forms:

TABLE 2-1

NAME	FORM	EXAMPLE
A	All S's are P	All authors are egotists
E	No S's are P	No sharks are mammals
I	Some S's are P	Some students are seniors
O	Some S's are not P	Some dogs are not hounds

The subject terms and predicate terms of the examples are written as *noun phrases*, even when it sounds awkward. When we consider whole arguments, this allows us to use exactly the same phrase in a number of places, without changing the category we are talking about. Such changes can occur if we refer to a group first with an adjective, then with a noun, and then with a verb. Using only noun phrases safeguards against grammatical variations that can produce unwanted shifts in meaning.

The meaning of each of the four kinds of statements deserves careful attention, since we tend to assume too much in some cases. For example, the (A) proposition, "All S's are P," tells us that anything that is an S must also be a P, but it leaves open the possibility that there are no S's. It is perfectly acceptable to say that all unicorns have horns, or, to put it into standard form, "All unicorns are things with horns," even though there are no unicorns. An (A) proposition tells us that the S-class is completely contained in the P-class, but it does not tell us whether or not the S-class has any members. (E) propositions are similar in this respect to (A) propositions. Thus, an (E) proposition can be read as "Nothing that is an S can also be a P." This leaves open the possibility that there may be no S's.

We must also be careful in dealing with (I) propositions. When hearing that some of the people in this room are college students, people often assume that some are, and some are not. But this goes beyond what the sentence actually says, and may be an unwarranted assumption.[1] What the statement actually means is just that at least one person in this room is a college student. In general, an (I) proposition means that there is at least one thing that belongs both to the S-class and the P-class. Thus, if I see a college student walk into a room full of people,

I am justified in claiming "Some of the people in the room are college students." It may be that everyone else in the room is a college student too; but the sentence I have uttered is neutral with respect to this possibility.

Like (I) propositions, (O) propositions make a claim about something that exists. An (O) proposition says that there is at least one thing actually existing in the world that belongs to the S-class but does not also belong to the P-class. This is consistent with all S's being outside the P-class, or with some of them being inside and some outside. Like the (I) proposition, the (O) proposition does not permit any further inferences about other things in the S-class.

Many English expressions can be easily translated into one of the four standard forms. All we need to do is decide whether the statement is about every member of the S-class, or just some of them, and whether it tells us that the S's are included in or excluded from the P-class. "Every" and "any" introduce sentences that are about all S's and are translated as (A) propositions. Sentences beginning "a few" or "at least one" tell us about some of the S-class, and are usually translated as (I) or (O) propositions.

Expressions containing "only" can be confusing. "Only S's are P," means "All P's are S" (reversing the subject and predicate terms). "Not all S's are P" or, less commonly, "All S's are not P" becomes "Some S's are not P." We must also be careful to distinguish "only" from "the only." "The only S's are P," translates as "All S's are P." Here are some examples of sentences using these forms:

2:2. Only seniors can graduate = All people who can graduate are seniors.

Mysteries are the only books I enjoy reading = All the books I enjoy reading are mysteries.

Not all politicians are crooks = Some politicians are not crooks.

All that glistens is not gold = Some things that glisten are not gold.

The only people at the meeting were Armenian = All the people at the meeting were Armenian.

These examples illustrate the importance of restricting one's translations to one of the four standard forms of categorical statements. Because of its ambiguity, "All S's are not P" is not an acceptable form. Most of the time, as in the examples in 2:2, it means "Some S's are not P," but sometimes it means "All S's are non-P's," as in "[All] juniors are not seniors."

The statement "No one can become president unless she is at least 35 years old," asserts that being at least 35 years old is one of the **necessary conditions** for becoming president. Failing to meet that condition guarantees that one cannot become president. Obviously, it is *not* also being claimed that being at least 35 years old is **sufficient** for becoming president. There are many other conditions that also have to be met. Thus, the statement would be translated into categorical form as "All people who can become president are people who are at least 35 years old." This captures in the right way the assertion that belonging to the predicate class is *a necessary condition* for belonging to the subject class. Similarly, "Having a clear voice is indispensable for success in the theater," becomes "All people who succeed in the theater are people who have clear voices."

In general, you should follow a three-step procedure for translating sentences into categorical form.

1. Decide what the sentence is about (what the S-class is) and what group it is being related to (the P-class).

2. Decide whether the sentence is about some or all of the subject class.

3. Decide whether a relation is being asserted or denied.

Consider, for example, "Not just any cat can catch mice." This does not fit any of the patterns already discussed, but we can recognize that (1) the sentence is about cats, and that cats are being related to the class of things that can catch mice; (2) it is only about some cats (it does not say that *all* cats can or cannot catch mice), and (3) it denies a relation between some cats and the predicate class. By looking at the list of standard forms, we arrive at "Some cats are not things that can catch mice."

Ambiguity can also be a problem with sentences containing the *indefinite article* "a" or "an." "A boy scout is trustworthy" can mean either "Some boy scouts are trustworthy people," or "All boy scouts are trustworthy people." This sort of statement is usually meant as a universal claim, and can be written as an (A) proposition, but you must rely on common sense and an understanding of the context to choose the correct interpretation.

We often make claims about individuals, either things or people, and refer to them by using proper names such as "Socrates" and "the Eiffel Tower." In these cases we transform the name of the individual into the name of a class, a class or category that contains at most one member. When using a name in this special way, we rewrite the sentences as follows:

2:3.   Norman Mailer is a writer = All *Norman Mailer* are writers.

Pegasus is not green = No *Pegasus* are green things.

The theory of relativity is difficult for the layperson to understand = All *theory of relativity* are things which are difficult for the layperson to understand.

The asterisks around the name remind us that we are talking about a class whose explicit label might be "things identical with Norman Mailer" or "things identical with Pegasus." These classes have at most one member. Therefore, anything that we want to say about an individual can be said about all the members of this new class, and any statement about an individual will be translated into an (A) or an (E) proposition about the entire S-class. Because the (A) and the (E) propositions do not commit us to there being any existing thing that actually belongs to the S-class, we can use this same device for the names of fictional characters, such as Pegasus, as well as for real individuals, such as the Brooklyn Bridge.

Each categorical statement has a **quantity** and a **quality**. Its quantity is either **universal** (about all members of the S-class) or **particular** (about some members of the S-class). Its quality is either **affirmative** or **negative**. By specifying the quantity and quality of a statement (e.g., "Some cats do not have tails," is particular and negative), we completely and uniquely characterize one of the four standard forms (in this case, an (O) proposition). The quantity and the quality of each type of categorical statement are given in the following table. Since many things depend on the quality and quantity of categorical statements, learn this table before reading further.

TABLE 2-2

NAME	FORM	QUANTITY	QUALITY
A	All S is P	Universal	Affirmative
E	No S is P	Universal	Negative
I	Some S is P	Particular	Affirmative
O	Some S is not P	Particular	Negative

Each categorical statement has a subject term and a predicate term. If the statement tells us about all the members of the class named by one of these terms, then that term is said to be **distributed** in the statement. If we are merely told something about some members of the class, then the term is **undistributed**. Each of the four types of categorical statement distributes its terms differently.

(A) propositions distribute their subject terms but not their predicate terms. Consider, for example, "All dogs are mammals." This tells us something about each dog, namely, that it is a mammal. But it does not tell us anything about each mammal since many mammals are not dogs.

An (E) proposition, such as "No person in this room is a carpenter," tells us something about each person in the room. It says of each of them that they are not carpenters. It also makes a statement about every carpenter, namely, that none of them is in the room. Thus, (E) propositions distribute both the subject term and the predicate term.

(I) propositions of the form "Some S's are P," tell us something about some members of the subject class, S, and something about some members of the predicate class, P, but nothing about all the members of either. Therefore, both the subject term and the predicate term are undistributed in (I) propositions.

Finally, there are (O) propositions such as "Some snakes are not dangerous reptiles." Clearly, this tells us something about some snakes, but not about all of them. Thus, the subject term is undistributed. But the sentence does tell us something about each and every dangerous reptile. Consider one of the snakes described by the sentence. Let us call it "Marigold." We now know something about each dangerous reptile, namely, that none of them is Marigold. Thus, the predicate term of (O) propositions is distributed.

Table 2-3 summarizes these results by underlining the terms that are distributed. The table shows that any universal statement (A or E) distributes its subject term, and that any negative statement (E or O) distributes its predicate term. In the section Rules for Valid Categorical Syllogisms of this chapter, the concept of distribution is used to formulate rules for valid categorical syllogisms.

TABLE 2-3

NAME	FORM	QUANTITY/QUALITY
A	All S̲ is P	Universal/Affirmative
E	No S̲ is P̲	Universal/Negative
I	Some S is P	Particular/Affirmative
O	Some S is not P̲	Particular/Negative

EXERCISES

For each of the following, (a) rewrite the statement in categorical form, (b) identify the form, (c) give its quality and quantity, and (d) underline the terms that are distributed.

1. Some people cannot sing.
2. Children are all noisy.
3. Wild tigers do not live in Africa.
*4. A coward will never die in a skydiving accident.
5. The sloth is a curious creature.
6. Only registered voters may run for office.
7. Mickey Mouse will never be president.
8. Everywhere that Mary went, the lamb was sure to go.
*9. Vandals left trash all over the campsite.
10. Not all logic books are dull.
11. Only wealthy people live in this neighborhood.
12. A marathon runner does not smoke cigarettes.
13. Millard Fillmore was not everyone's favorite president.

14. Nothing but the finest tuna is good enough for Starkist.

*15. I can stand anyone except a hypocrite.

16. Without the force of gravity, no object would remain on the Earth's surface.

17. The gods are angry tonight.

18. Tigers hunt only when they are hungry.

19. Four fifths of all trees are deciduous.

*20. It is untrue that all propositions can be put into one of the four forms of categorical statement.

Categorical Statements and Venn Diagrams

Now that we have defined the four basic forms of categorical statements and clarified their meanings, we can begin to explore their role in good reasoning. One way of doing this is to use **Venn diagrams**. Named after the British logician John Venn (1834–1923), who introduced them, these diagrams enable us to picture the information contained in a categorical statement or in a combination of such statements. Later we will use these diagrams to test the validity of categorical syllogisms. To represent a single categorical statement such as "All clowns are happy," we begin by drawing a box containing two intersecting circles.

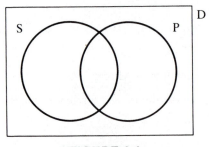

FIGURE 2-1

The box, D, represents the **universe of discourse**, the S-circle on the left represents the **subject class**, and the P-circle on the right represents the **predicate class**. The universe of discourse is a general category of things that includes both the S-class and the P-class. In our example, "All clowns are happy," D could be "people," or "things."

The entire area outside the S-circle but inside D, including the area inside P but outside S, represents non-S, the **complement** of S. The complement of S is the class of all the things that are not S, or things that are "non-S." The definition of non-S is relative to our choice of the universe of discourse. Thus, in our example, non-S could be either "people who are not clowns," or "things that are not clowns," depending on whether D is "people" or "things." It is important to re-member that non-S must contain everything that is outside S (relative to D). Thus, the complement of "white things" is "non-white things" (not "black things"); the complement of "people under five feet tall" is "people who are five feet or taller" (not "people taller than five feet").

Thus far we have not indicated on our Venn diagram which, if any, of the classes depicted have or lack members. There are two devices for representing class membership, the **asterisk** and **shading**. Putting an asterisk in a certain area means there is at least one actually existing object that belongs in that area. Shad-ing a particular area means the area is empty: there is no object that belongs to that set of categories. An unmarked area tells us nothing whatever. There might be things in the classes corresponding to unmarked areas, and there might not be. Here are Venn diagrams for the four standard forms of categorical statement.

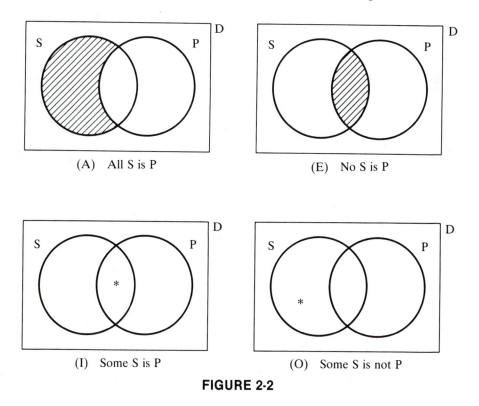

(A)   All S is P

(E)   No S is P

(I)   Some S is P

(O)   Some S is not P

FIGURE 2-2

To diagram the universal statements, an area is shaded out, indicating that nothing is in the category represented by the shaded-out area. To diagram the particular statements, an asterisk is used to indicate that at least one thing occu-pies the area in question. This feature of the diagrams reflects something we noted earlier—that (A) and (E) propositions do not commit us to the existence of any real objects in the S-class. They tell us only that whatever is in the S-class (if anything) must stand in a certain relation to the P-class. This leads to results that may seem odd. "All perpetual motion machines are revolutionary discoveries" is true, since there is nothing in the class of perpetual motion machines that falls outside the class of things that are revolutionary discoveries; but, "Some perpetual motion machines are revolutionary discoveries" is false, because that sentence claims that there is some real thing that is both a perpetual motion machine and a thing that is a revolutionary discovery. Since there are no perpetual motion machines, there is nothing that satisfies these conditions.

In general, one can diagram a statement by following three steps:

1. Use the quantity of the statement to determine what sort of marking to put on the diagram: universal statements require shading; particular statements need an asterisk.

2. Locate the area named by the subject term: the marking will go somewhere in this area.

3. Decide whether the marking goes inside or outside the part of the diagram designated by the predicate term: it goes outside that area if the statement is of the (A) or (O) form, inside if it is of the (E) or (I) form.

If we used these rules to help us diagram "No P are S," we would discover that the diagram is identical to the diagram for "No S are P." The area which is part of both the S-circle and the P-circle is shaded. This illustrates the fact that a Venn diagram can represent more than one categorical statement; in this case, the same diagram represents both "No S are P" and "No P are S." If two categorical statements have the same diagram, they are **logically equivalent**. Thus, "Some S are P" and "Some P are S" are logically equivalent to one another, whereas "All S are P" and "All P are S," which have different Venn diagrams, are not logically equivalent. Logically equivalent statements will be discussed in more detail in the section Immediate Inferences.

Following the general rules for Venn diagrams, we can also picture statements that contain complementary class terms such as "non-S" and "non-P." "Anything that is a non-S is a P" (e.g., "Anyone who has not paid his dues is delinquent") and "Some things that are non-S are things which are non-P (e.g., "Some people are neither rich nor famous") can be diagrammed as follows:

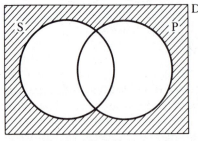
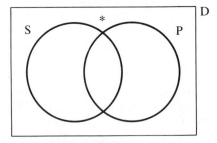

All non-S is P   Some non-S is non-P

FIGURE 2-3

Applying the rules given above to the statement just diagrammed, "All non-S's are P," we can see that (1) the diagram will have a shaded area, (2) the shading will go somewhere in the non-S area (i.e., outside the S-circle), and (3) the shading will also go outside the P-circle. For "Some non-S are non-P," the rules indicate that (1) we will put an asterisk on the diagram, (2) the asterisk will go in the non-S area, and (3) it will also be in the non-P area.

EXERCISES

I. For each of the statements in the practice exercises for the section Categorical Statements, identify its subject and predicate terms, and draw its Venn diagram.

II. Diagram the following statements.

1. All S's are non-P.

2. Some non-S's are P.

*3. Some S's are not non-P.

4. No non-S's are P.

5. All non-S's are non-P.

6. All non-P's are S.

7. Some non-S's are not P.

*8. No non-P's are non-S.

III. For each of the Venn diagrams for questions 1 through 5 in Exercise II, give a logically equivalent categorical statement—that is, one which is represented by the same Venn diagram—that has only S and P as its terms (as opposed to non-S or non-P). (Question 3 is answered in Appendix II.)

Immediate Inferences

With the help of Venn diagrams, we can discover more about the relations between statements. Starting from a statement in standard form, we can validly deduce the truth or falsity of several others. These are known as **immediate inferences**. Immediate inferences are based on the principle that an inference or argument is valid if its conclusion is **logically equivalent** to its only premise. As we will see, there are several ways of transforming statements into new but logically equivalent statements.

The method for deciding whether or not an immediate inference is valid is to draw the Venn diagram of the (single) premise and compare it with the Venn diagram of the (single) conclusion. If the diagrams are identical, then the statements are **logically equivalent**. If two propositions are logically equivalent, then (1) we can always validly infer the truth of one from the truth of the other, and (2) we can always validly infer the falsity of one from the falsity of the other. Also, (3) logically equivalent statements can be substituted for each other without any change in meaning.[2]

Let us begin with an (A) proposition, "All S's are P," and exchange the subject and predicate terms to get "All P's are S." For example, suppose we move from "All people who are child abusers are people who were abused as children" to "All people who were abused as children are child abusers." If we diagram these, we discover that they are quite different:

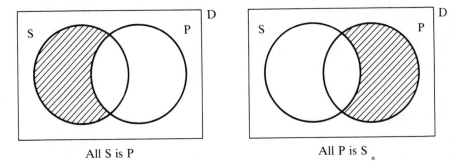

All S is P   All P is S

FIGURE 2-4

In effect, we have flipped the diagram over and produced something new. Since the diagrams are different, the propositions are not equivalent. Our transformation has produced a new sentence with a different meaning.[3] By contrast, we noted in the section Categorical Statements and Venn Diagrams that if we transform a sentence expressing an (E) statement in the same way—e.g., from "No dogs are cold-blooded animals" to "No cold-blooded animals are dogs"— the two sentences yield statements that have identical diagrams:

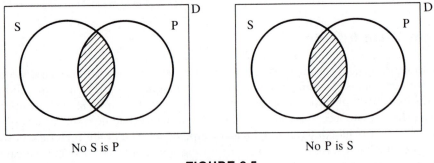

No S is P   No P is S

FIGURE 2-5

Since the diagrams are the same, the two statements are logically equivalent. Whenever we exchange the subject and predicate terms of a sentence, we construct the **converse** of the statement expressed by the original sentence. The diagrams we have just examined show that the converse of an (A) proposition does not yield an equivalent proposition. Thus, for (A) propositions, conversion is not a valid inference. On the other hand, an (E) proposition and its converse are equivalent, and thus we can validly infer one from the other. If we look at the other two standard forms, we see that the converse of an (I) proposition is also equivalent to the original statement, but the converse of an (O) proposition, like that of an (A) proposition, does not produce an equivalent statement.

To summarize, any (E) statement is equivalent to its converse, and so each can be validly inferred from the other and they can be used interchangeably; (I) statements are similar but the converse of an (A) or an (O) proposition has a different meaning, and hence cannot be validly inferred from the original statement or substituted for it.

TABLE 2-4

ORIGINAL	CONVERSE	EQUIVALENT?
(A) All S is P	(A) All P is S	NO
(E) No S is P	(E) No P is S	YES
(I) Some S is P	(I) Some P is S	YES
(O) Some S is not P	(O) Some P is not S	NO

A second type of immediate inference, **obversion,** is valid for all four sorts of categorical statement. Like conversion, obversion gives us a way of creating new statements; but unlike conversion, obversion yields a new statement, called the **obverse,** which is *always equivalent* to the original statement.

Obversion requires two steps:

1. Change the quality of the sentence. If the original is affirmative, change it to negative; if the original is negative, the obverse will be affirmative. The quantity—universal or particular—remains the same.

2. Replace the predicate term with its complement. The subject term remains unchanged.

In the following examples, the statements in each pair are obverses of one another, and hence equivalent.

TABLE 2-5

ORIGINAL	OBVERSE	EQUIVALENT?
(A) All S is P	(E) No S is non-P	YES
(E) No S is P	(A) All S is non-P	YES
(I) Some S is P	(O) Some S is not non-P	YES
(O) Some S is not P	(I) Some S is non-P	YES

In the first pair, since we started with a universal affirmative statement (A), the obverse remains universal, but becomes negative (E). The original predicate term is replaced with its complement. In the last pair, note that in the first sentence, the "not" is part of the sentence form, and the predicate term is P. In the second sentence, the form of the sentence has been changed from negative to affirmative, and the prefix "non-" is part of the predicate term "non-P," not part of the sentence form.

The rules for Venn diagrams covered in the section Categorical Statements and Venn Diagrams confirm the logical equivalence of categorical statements obtained by obversion. Thus, to diagram the statement "No S is non-P," we would shade out that portion of the S-circle that is also in the non-P area, that is, the portion of S that lies outside the P-circle. The resulting diagram is the one that is already familiar to us as the diagram that represents "All S is P." Similarly, to diagram "Some S is not non-P," we would have to place an asterisk in that portion of the S-circle that is outside the area representing the predicate term, non-P; the resulting diagram also represents "Some S is P."

The **contrapositive** of a categorical statement is obtained by (1) switching the subject term with the predicate term, and (2) taking the complement of each. The quantity and the quality of the statement remain unchanged. Thus, the contrapositive of "All S's are P" is "All non-P is non-S," and the contrapositive of "Some S is not P" is "Some non-P is not non-S." Contraposition yields an equivalent proposition only for (A) and (O) statements. The Venn diagrams in Figure 2-6

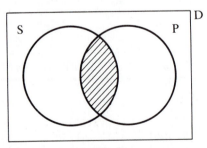

Some S is P

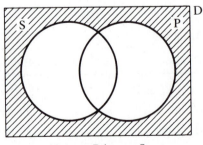

Some non-P is non-S

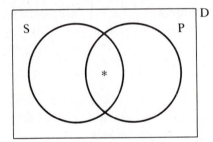

No S is P

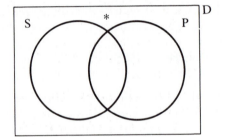

No non-P is non-S

FIGURE 2-6

shows that for (I) and (E) statements, the contrapositive differs in meaning from the original proposition.

The following table summarizes the information about contraposition.

TABLE 2-6

ORIGINAL	CONTRAPOSITIVE	EQUIVALENT?
(A) All S is P	(A) All non-P is non-S	YES
(E) No S is P	(E) No non-P is non-S	NO
(I) Some S is P	(I) Some non-P is non-S	NO
(O) Some S is not P	(O) Some non-P is not non-S	YES

When contraposition yields an equivalent proposition, as it does for the (A) and (O) forms, conversion does not; when conversion yields an equivalent proposition—for the (E) and (I) forms—contraposition does not.

Finally, we consider **contradiction**. To say that two statements are contradictory means that whenever one is true, the other must be false, and vice versa. If we look at the diagram of "All S is P," we see that the area in the S-circle that falls outside the P-circle is shaded in. This means that nothing is in that area. Thus, we can no longer put an asterisk in that area. If we first drew a diagram of "All S's are P" and then tried to represent, on the same diagram, the corresponding (O) proposition, "Some S's are not P," we would discover that this is impossible. The area in which the asterisk should go has already been shaded out. This tells us that whenever an (A) proposition is true, the corresponding (O) proposition must be false.

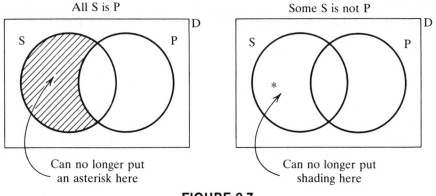

FIGURE 2-7

The same thing works in reverse. If we diagram "Some S's are not P" first, we place an asterisk in the area in which S and non-P overlap. Having done this, we can no longer represent "All S's are P" on the same diagram, since we cannot shade out an area (thereby saying that there is nothing in that area) that already contains an asterisk (which says that there is at least one thing in this area). Thus, the diagrams show that (A) and (O) propositions with the same subject and predicate terms are contradictory. The same relation holds between the other two forms. The contradictory of any (I) proposition is the corresponding (E) proposition, and vice versa. When the first of any such pair is true, the second must be false. When the first is false, the second will be true.

TABLE 2-7

ORIGINAL	CONTRADICTORY
(A) All S is P	(O) Some S is not P
(I) Some S is P	(E) No S is P
(E) No S is P	(I) Some S is P
(O) Some S is not P	(A) All S is P

Despite what you might think, (A) and (E) statements do not form contradictory pairs, nor do (I) and (O) propositions. In the first case, it is possible for both an (A) and the corresponding (E) propositions to be false, as in the following pair:

2:4. All college students are freshmen.

No college students are freshmen.

In the second case, it is possible for both an (I) proposition and the corresponding (O) proposition to be true at the same time:

2:5. Some dogs are beagles.

Some dogs are not beagles.

If we combine what we have learned about converses, obverses, contrapositives, and contradictories we can see that knowing one true statement (or one false statement) allows us to make inferences about other statements. For example, if we know that the statement "Some of the things in this room are antiques" is true, we can infer (1) that "No things in this room are antiques" must be false (it is the contradictory of a true statement), (2) that "Some antiques are things in this room" is true (it is the converse of an (I) proposition), and (3) that "Some of the things in this room are not nonantiques" is also true (it is the obverse of the original statement). Since we know that "No things in this room are antiques" is false, we also know that "No antiques are things in this room" and "All things in this room are nonantiques" must be false as well. It is good practice to take a categorical statement at random, one that you know to be true or one that you know to be false, and to see how many other statements you can validly infer to be true and how many statements you can validly infer to be false.

EXERCISES

I. For each of the sentences in the Exercises for the section Categorical Statements, (a) give the converse and state whether the converse is equivalent to the original, (b) give the contrapositive and state whether the contrapositive is equivalent to the original, (c) give the contradictory of the sentence, (d) give the obverse of the sentence, and (e) assuming that the original sentence is true, list two other statements that would also be true, and two that you can infer to be false. (Question 1 and 3 are answered in Appendix II.)

II. Use immediate inferences to show that the pairs of statements generated in Part III of the Exercises in the section Categorical Statements and Venn Diagrams are logically equivalent. (Questions 3 and 4 are answered in Appendix II.)

Categorical Syllogisms and Venn Diagrams

So far, we have considered only individual categorical statements, and what can be inferred from them. The next stage is to combine these statements into arguments with more than one premise, and to learn what makes such arguments valid or invalid. The most basic type of argument using categorical statements is the **categorical syllogism**. A categorical syllogism always has the following characteristics:

1. Exactly two premises and one conclusion. All three statements must be categorical statements.

2. Exactly three terms. One term is the subject term of the conclusion and appears in one of the premises. Another term is the predicate term of the conclusion and appears in the other premise. The third term occurs in each of the premises but not in the conclusion.

When writing out a syllogism (or any other argument) in standard form, we will begin each premise on a new line, and use a line to separate the premises from the conclusion.

Here are two examples of categorical syllogisms (one valid, one invalid):

2:6. Some taxes are inequitable things.

No inequitable things are acceptable proposals.

Some taxes are not acceptable proposals.

All mammals are warm-blooded animals.

Some pets are warm-blooded animals.

Some pets are mammals.

Each argument has exactly two premises and three terms ("taxes," "inequitable things," "acceptable proposals"; "mammals," "warm-blooded animals," "pets"), and in each case, one of the terms ("inequitable things," and "warm-blooded animals") occurs in both premises and not in the conclusion.

Just as we spoke of the subject and predicate terms of an individual sentence, we can refer to the terms of an argument. These are determined by looking at the conclusion. The subject term of the conclusion becomes the **subject term of the entire argument**, the predicate of the conclusion becomes the **predicate term of the argument**, and the term that occurs in both premises but not in the conclusion is known as the **middle term** (M).[4] Thus, the subject-term (S) of the first argument is "taxes," the predicate term (P) is "acceptable proposals," and the middle term (M) is "inequitable things." In the second argument S = "pets," P = "mammals," M = "warm-blooded animals."

To determine whether an argument is valid, we need to know if the truth of its premises guarantees the truth of its conclusion. If a syllogism is valid, then when both its premises are true, its conclusion must also be true. Since Venn diagrams represent what it is for a statement to be true, they give us a handy means of telling whether or not the conditions for a valid argument are met. The underlying intuition is that if we can picture both premises on the same Venn diagram, the resulting diagram will show what is true whenever both premises are true. That diagram then shows us whether the conclusion is already depicted, and hence whether its truth is guaranteed by the truth of the premises.

Since every categorical syllogism has three terms, we require a Venn diagram with three intersecting circles. To have room for all possible combinations, the circles are drawn this way:

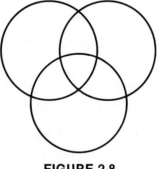

FIGURE 2-8

The circle that represents the subject term of the argument is always placed on the left, the circle representing the predicate term of the argument is on the right. The circle representing the middle term is at the bottom. For convenience, we refer to these as "the S-circle," "the P-circle," and "the M- circle," but we will also assign labels corresponding to the terms of specific arguments.

Now that we have the appropriate diagram, we can outline **the procedure for evaluating a syllogism:**

1. Put the argument into the proper standard form for syllogisms: write the premises and conclusion as categorical statements in standard form, using noun phrases throughout. If you wish, use letters as abbreviations of the noun phrases (but if you do so, avoid using "S", "P", or "M", which could lead to confusion). Write the conclusion last, separated from the premises by a line.

2. Identify the subject, predicate, and middle terms of the argument. Write the subject term (or the letter used to abbreviate it) next to the S-circle, the predicate term or letter next to the P-circle, and the middle term or letter by the M-circle at the bottom of the diagram.

3. Diagram each of the premises, in each case using the two appropriate circles in the diagram.

4. Imagine what the diagram of the conclusion would look like, and inspect the diagram of the two premises. If all the areas that would be marked in a diagram of the conclusion—either shaded out or with an asterisk—are already correctly marked that way in the diagram of the premises, then the argument is valid. If the areas are not marked, the argument is invalid. It does not matter if other areas in the diagram in addition to the ones needed for the conclusion are marked, but everything that would be needed for a correct diagram of the conclusion must be already shown if the argument is valid.

The aim of the procedure is to determine whether an argument is valid. If an argument is valid, then its conclusion must already be contained, implicitly, in its premises. A Venn diagram of the premises of a categorical syllogism displays this information explicitly. It reveals the content of both the premises taken together, and thus allows us to see whether the conclusion is already contained in them. If it is, the argument is valid. If it is not, the argument is invalid. Let us start with a simple example of a categorical syllogism:

2:7. Anyone in the room must be attending college, since everyone here is enrolled in this logic class, and only people who attend college can be enrolled in this class.

The first step is to transform the argument into standard form. The conclusion is "Anyone in the room must be attending college," so that will be written last. Each statement should be transformed into a standard categorical proposition, so, following the guidelines covered in the section Categorical Statements, we get the following:

All people in this room are people enrolled in this logic class.

All people enrolled in this logic class are people who attend college.

All people in this room are people who attend college.

At this stage it is convenient to introduce abbreviations for the various terms of the arguments. This makes it easier to write out the argument and to concentrate on its form. We shall abbreviate each single noun phrase with a different letter.

R = People in this room.

E = People enrolled in this logic class.

C = People who attend college.

With these abbreviations the syllogism can now be written:

All R's are E

All E's are C

All R's are C

The second step is to identify the subject, predicate, and middle terms of the argument. Still using the same abbreviations, we note that "R" is the subject of the conclusion, and so it becomes the subject term of the entire syllogism. Similarly, "C" can be identified as the predicate term of the argument, and "E," which occurs in both premises and not in the conclusion, is the middle term.

Next, we diagram the first premise. Since R is the subject term, and E is the middle term, we will be dealing with the S-circle, and the M-circle. Since the premise is an (A) proposition, we want to shade out all portions of the first circle that do not overlap the other; we want to show that anything that is in the S-circle must also be in the M-circle. The result is shown in diagram b:

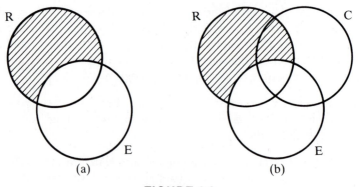

(a)   (b)

FIGURE 2-9

Since, in this example, the first premise involves only S and M, we have ignored the P-circle entirely. This is indicated in diagram a. We have, in effect, taken the Venn diagram of the first premise and rotated it until it matches the circles on the diagram. The second premise is diagrammed in much the same way, except that here we must shade out those areas of the M-circle that do not overlap the P-circle. Again, we can ignore the S-circle temporarily, to arrive at the following:

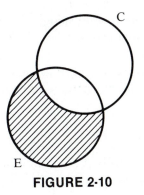

FIGURE 2-10

Putting everything together, we get the following diagram.[5] (When you are diagramming two universal premises, it is a good idea to slant the lines one way for the first premise, and another way for the second. This makes the diagram easier to interpret.)

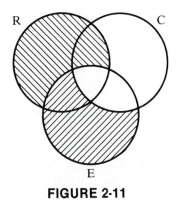

FIGURE 2-11

The final step is to check for the conclusion. We note that the conclusion is also an (A) proposition, and that it involves the S-circle and the P-circle. A diagram that includes this conclusion should have shaded out all the parts of the S-circle that do not overlap the P-circle. Once again, we ignore the M-circle. When we look at the diagram this way, we see that these areas are indeed shaded out, which tells us that the argument is valid.

You may have noticed that the upper part of the area shared by the S-circle and P-circle is also shaded out, and that this is not part of the conclusion. This does not affect the validity of the argument. It is permissible for the premises to contain more information than the conclusion does, just as long as the whole conclusion is also shown on the diagram.

Before considering more complicated cases involving particular premises and conclusions, let us look at an argument that is very similar to the previous one, but with one key difference:

2:8. Anyone in the room must be attending college, since everyone in the room has read Hamlet, and everyone who attends college has read Hamlet.

Using the abbreviations (R = people in the room, H = people who have read Hamlet, C = people who are attending college), our first two steps yield:

All R's are H   Subject term: R

All C's are H   Predicate term: C

All R's are C   Middle term: H

Step three, diagramming the premises, gives the following:

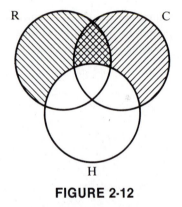

FIGURE 2-12

When we examine this diagram to see whether the conclusion is already shown, we discover an important difference. As before, a diagram of the conclusion would have all the areas of the S-circle that do not overlap the P-circle shaded out. Since the complete diagram of the conclusion is not already shown in the diagram of the premises, this argument is invalid.

The procedure for testing arguments with particular statements is exactly the same, but diagramming them can introduce a further complication. This is illustrated in the following syllogism.

2:9. Some S are M

All M are P

Some S are P

If we were to attempt to diagram the first premise, we would run into a problem. The diagram would have to show an asterisk in the intersection of the S-circle and the M-circle, but there are two areas that fit this description: one outside the P-circle, and one inside it. If we place the asterisk in the first of these areas, we are saying that there is something that is both S and M *and which is not P*, and this says more than our premise. Therefore, it is not an accurate representation. Similarly, if we place the asterisk in the other area, we are showing a situation in which there is something that is S and M *and P*, and this, again, is not what the premise says. There are two ways of dealing with this difficulty.

First, we can often avoid the problem by diagramming the universal premise first. In 2:9, once we have diagrammed the universal premise, our diagram looks like this:

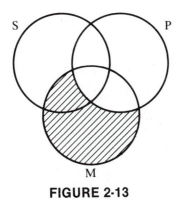

FIGURE 2-13

One of the two choices, the area outside the P-circle, has now been eliminated. The shading tells us that we can no longer put an asterisk in that area. So, if an asterisk is to go anywhere in the intersection of the S-circle and the M-circle (and our particular premise tells us that there must be such an asterisk), it will have to be placed in the area shared by all three circles. The completed diagram, then, looks like this:

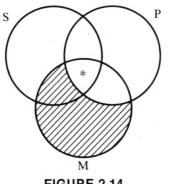

FIGURE 2-14

Since a diagram of the conclusion would require an asterisk in the intersection of the S-circle and the P-circle, and since such an asterisk is already on the diagram, the argument is valid.

Thus, when dealing with arguments that have a particular premise and a universal one, the moral is: *Always diagram the universal premise first.* But there are still some cases in which this strategy will not solve all of our problems, as shown by the following example:

2:10. All wealthy businessmen are conservatives, but some people who favor tax reform are not wealthy businessmen. Therefore, some conservatives favor tax reform.

Using the abbreviations (W = wealthy businessmen, C = conservatives, T = people who favor tax reform), 2:10 has the form:

All W's are C   Subject term: C

Some T's are not W   Predicate term: T

Some C's are T   Middle term: W

Diagramming the universal premise first, gives us the following:

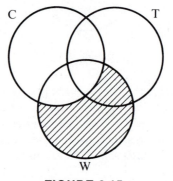

FIGURE 2-15

The particular premise directs us to place an asterisk in a portion of the P-circle that lies outside the M-circle. Once again, we have two areas that fit this description. Both of these areas lie inside the P-circle, but one overlaps the S-circle and one does not. Putting the asterisk in either of these areas conveys more information than we are entitled to. This time, diagramming the universal premise first did not solve the problem, so we must fall back on the second solution. We must diagram the premise in a way that leaves both possibilities open.

To show that (1) an asterisk must go in one of two areas, and (2) we are not sure which of the two it belongs in, we simply *put the asterisk on the line between the two areas in question.* It is as if the asterisk is "sitting on the fence," not having decided which of the two areas to fall into. In this example, we would put it on the line separating the two areas inside the P-circle, but outside the M-circle. This gives us the following diagram:

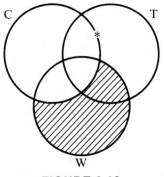

FIGURE 2-16

In interpreting this sort of diagram, remember that the asterisk is not committed to either of the two areas. The conclusion in this example asks us to look for an asterisk in the intersection of the S-circle and the P-circle. The asterisk that is shown on the diagram *might* be in that area, but it might not. Without a firm commitment, the truth of the premises does not guarantee the truth of the conclusion, and so the argument is invalid.

Let us summarize the procedure for syllogisms with particular premises. Always diagram the universal premise first. If the asterisk could still go into one of two areas, place it on the line between the two areas in question. Remember that an asterisk cannot possibly go into an area that has already been shaded out, so you would never put an asterisk in such an area, or on a line that separates a shaded area from an open one. If shading has eliminated one of the two possible locations, you can be sure that the asterisk must go in the only area left open.

We have been using Venn diagrams to test syllogisms for validity, but we can also use them to draw conclusions of our own. Whenever we have two statements that (a) can be translated into categorical statements and (b) have a term in common, we can diagram them both. The resulting diagram tells us whether any conclusion can be validly drawn from those two statements, and, if so, what it is. Here is an example:

2:11   Some people in this class have not read the material.

Only people who have read the material will pass the exam.

We first rewrite each sentence in standard form using, C = people in this class, R = people who have read the material, and E = people who will pass the exam. This yields:

Some C are not R

All E are R

R appears in both statements. Thus it is the middle term and will be represented by the bottom circle. But since we do not know yet what the conclusion is, we must arbitrarily assign C and E to the left and right circles at the top. Having done this, we diagram both premises as follows:

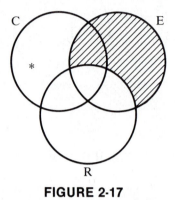

FIGURE 2-17

Inspection of the diagram reveals that we have an asterisk inside the C-circle and outside the E-circle, which is a picture of an (O) proposition. This tells us that, from the two statements given, we can validly infer "Some C's are not E," or in English, that some of the people in the class will not pass the exam.

Although this technique allows us to combine only two sentences at a time, we can deal with more statements by grouping them into pairs. Sometimes this leads to surprising results, as shown by the following example involving the testimony of four witnesses to a murder.[6]

2:12. Witness A: "All the women were playing cards."

Witness B: "Some of the victim's relatives were listening to the radio."

Witness C: "None of those who were playing cards were listening to the radio."

Witness D: "All of the victim's relatives were women."

Using abbreviations to put these statements into standard form (W = women, C = people playing cards, L = people listening to the radio, V = victim's relatives) we get the following:

a: All W's are C.

b: Some V's are L.

c: No C's are L.

d: All V's are W.

Since we know that we can draw a conclusion only from statements that have a term in common, we might try pairing a and c together (since C occurs in both) and also b and d, which both contain "V." Here are the diagrams for both of these pairs:

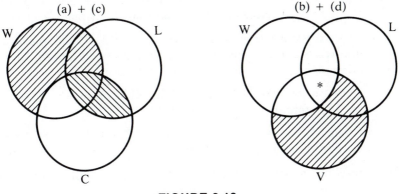

FIGURE 2-18

In the first diagram, the intersection between the L-circle and the W-circle has been completely shaded out. So from a and c we can infer "No W's are L" or, equivalently, "No L's are W." In the second diagram, an asterisk lies in the intersection of the two circles, which allows us to draw the conclusion that "Some L's are W" or, equivalently, "Some W's are L." But these two conclusions are contradictory. One must be true, and the other must be false. But if one of the conclusions is false, then one of the premises must be false, since one cannot validly infer a false conclusion from true premises. Thus, one of the witnesses must have been lying.

EXERCISES

I. In each of the following examples, decide whether or not the passage contains an argument that fits the definition of a complete syllogism. If it does, write the syllogism in standard form; if it does not, explain why not.

1. Anyone who favors increased welfare benefits is a liberal, but only incurable optimists are liberals. So those who favor increasing welfare benefits must be incurable optimists.

2. Mozart must have been a good man, since only the good die young.

*3. Not all ecosystems are well-balanced, since there are no predators in some ecosystems, and no ecosystem is both balanced and free from natural predators.

4. Fossil remains do not provide positive and absolute proof of the truth of Darwin's theory. Positive and absolute proof would justify the rejection of creationism, but fossil remains do not provide such proof. Thus, fossil remains fail to justify the rejection of creationism.

5. All ungulates are mammals, and some ungulates have horns, so some cows are mammals.

6. Reagan cannot be a true humanitarian, for he wants to cut aid to education, and no true humanitarian would want to do that.

*7. Either Reagan is a true humanitarian, or he will cut aid to education. Since he's not a true humanitarian, we can expect him to cut aid to education.

8. A good car is always reliable, but none of the cars in this lot are good cars. Therefore, none of them is reliable.

9. Of course Jimmy is a child of mine; I would only change the diapers of a child of mine, and I have changed Jimmy's diapers many times.

*10. I never met a man I didn't like, but not everyone in the room is a man. Thus, I don't like some of the people in the room.

II. For each of the complete syllogisms you found in Part I, (a) label the subject, predicate, and middle terms of the argument, (b) construct a Venn diagram of the argument, and (c) explain whether the diagram shows the argument to be valid or invalid. (Question 3 is answered in Appendix II.)

III. Using Venn diagrams, draw a conclusion from each of the following series of statements wherever possible. (Your argument should, of course, be valid). If more than two statements are given, continue drawing inferences until you have a chain that has used all of the statements on the list.

1. No syllogisms yield new knowledge. Any fruitful form of thought can yield new knowledge.

2. None of our products contain artificial preservatives. Some candy bars contain artificial preservatives.

3. No gem quality stone would be used for industrial purposes. Some diamonds are not gem quality stones.

4. George Washington was a U.S. president. He was also a general in the army. Not all of our folk heroes are U.S. presidents.

*5. Only factual statements provide a good reason for buying a product. Some advertisements rest on a simple appeal to vanity. Any advertisement is designed to sell a product. Nothing that rests on a simple appeal to vanity is a factual statement.

Rules for Valid Categorical Syllogisms

In this section, we examine a second method for determining whether or not a syllogism is valid. Since this method always gives the same results as using Venn diagrams, it can be used as a check on the latter. This method also aids in the construction of arguments, since it reveals what sorts of premises would be needed to reach a given conclusion. This allows us to determine, in cases in which we have one premise and a potential conclusion, what must be added to complete the argument. It even gives us a rough idea, starting from scratch, of what sorts of premises would be needed to validly infer a given conclusion.

Like the Venn diagram method, the **rules for a valid syllogism** work only for categorical syllogisms. So the first step is to make sure that what we have is a syllogism (two premises, three terms, etc.) and to put it into standard form. As with Venn diagrams, we should also identify the subject, predicate, and middle terms of the argument. Only then are we ready to check the argument against the following five rules. If all five rules are satisfied, the argument is valid. If one or more rule is violated, the argument is invalid.

Rules for Valid Syllogisms

1. The middle term of the argument must be distributed in at least one premise.

2. Any term that is distributed in the conclusion must be distributed in at least one premise.

3. At least one of the premises must be affirmative.

4. If one of the premises is negative, then the conclusion must also be negative.

5. A particular conclusion cannot be drawn from two universal premises.

To see how the rules are used to test for validity, consider two of our earlier examples, 2:7 and 2:10. Here are the two arguments in standard form:

2:7. All R's are E **2:10.** All W's are C

All E's are C Some T's are not W

All R's are C Some C's are T

In 2:7, we note that the middle term, E, is distributed in the second premise "All E's are C." Thus Rule 1 is satisfied. Since R is distributed in the conclusion, Rule 2 requires that it also be distributed in at least one of the premises. Since it is distributed in the first premise, Rule 2 is satisfied. We have an affirmative premise (Rule 3), and no negative premises (Rule 4). The conclusion is universal, not particular, and so Rule 5 is also satisfied. Thus, all five rules are satisfied, and so the argument is valid.

Let us now evaluate 2:10. This time, the middle term is W, and it is distributed in both premises. This is fine. Rule 1 requires that it be distributed at least once, and so having it distributed in both premises clearly satisfies the requirement. Rule 2 does not impose any restrictions on the premises in this argument, since neither term in the conclusion is distributed. The first premise is affirmative, and so Rule 3 is satisfied. But the second premise is negative and the conclusion affirmative. This violates Rule 4. So the argument is invalid.

Even though the violation of a single rule suffices to show that the argument is invalid, it is a good idea to check all five rules, since an invalid syllogism may violate more than one rule. This will give you a better sense of how the argument goes wrong and enable you to avoid those mistakes in your own reasoning. Thus, we complete our analysis of argument 2:10 by considering the last rule. It satisfies Rule 5 since it has a particular conclusion and a particular premise.

The rules also tell us precisely what has gone wrong in 2:10. In this case, the only problem is the negative premise with the affirmative conclusion. But we could not validly infer a negative conclusion from these premises, either: any negative conclusion (which would satisfy Rule 4) would distribute its predicate term. Since W is the only term distributed in the premises, Rule 2 would be violated. In short, there is no simple way of repairing this argument. In other cases, however, the rules may give us valuable clues about how to revise an invalid argument and make it valid.

EXERCISES

I. For each of the five rules, make up a syllogism that violates only that rule. (A syllogism that violates only Rule 1 is given in Appendix II.)

II. Test the following arguments for validity, using the rules. Go through all five rules for each argument.

1. Some conservatives do not like supply-side economics, since all wealthy businessmen are conservatives but some people who like supply-side economics are not wealthy businessmen.

2. Some of my pets are German shepherds, and every German shepherd is boisterous; so it follows that some of my pets are boisterous animals.

3. Some philosophers do no work of practical benefit, and this year only people who do work of practical benefit will get raises. Thus, some philosophers will get raises this year.

*4. Napoleon was not born in France, yet he was a French emperor. This shows that some French emperors were not born in France.

5. No adequate theory of ethics will be empirical, because any adequate ethical theory will yield principles that apply universally and with necessity, but no empirical study yields such principles. (From I. Kant, *Foundations of the Metaphysics of Morals.*)

6. Some tigers are fierce, for all man-eating animals are fierce, and some tigers are man-eaters.

*7. All the trees on Main Street are elms, and some elms have Dutch elm disease, so some of the trees on Main Street must have Dutch elm disease.

8. Teachers are underpaid public servants. Only victims of an unfair economic system are underpaid public servants. Therefore, a teacher is a victim of an unfair economic system.

Finding Missing Premises

In addition to their use in testing arguments for validity, the five rules can help us construct the missing premises of an argument. This skill is important, since people often leave some of their premises unstated when presenting an argument. We must be able to deduce what those unstated assumptions are. In other contexts, we may want to construct a valid argument for a given conclusion and would like to know what premises are required. In either situation, the rules for a valid syllogism can help.

First, let us consider an example of an argument with one of its premises left unstated. (The technical term for an incomplete argument like this is an **enthymeme**.) The object is to determine what must be added to produce a complete, valid argument:

2:13.   Only union members are eligible for this pension plan; therefore, some textile workers are not eligible for the plan.

We note that the conclusion is stated in the clause that follows "therefore," and both statements are categorical. We can put them in standard form this way (U = union members; E = people eligible for this pension plan; T = textile workers):

All E's are U

??????????????????

Some T's are not E

Since U does not appear in the conclusion, it must be the middle term of the argument. Because U is not distributed in the first premise, Rule 1 tells us that it must be distributed in the missing premise; the missing premise therefore cannot be an (I) proposition. T appears in the conclusion, but not in the premise we are given. It must therefore appear in the premise we are trying to formulate. So we are looking for a categorical statement other than an (I) statement which contains the terms U and T. This premise cannot be an (E) or an (A) proposition, since that would violate Rule 5. Thus it must be an (O) statement and, as we have already argued, it must distribute the middle term U. Thus, the second premise must be "Some T's are not U." Checking the other rules we verify that this premise does indeed result in a valid argument that satisfies all five rules: Rule 2 is satisfied, in that E is the only term distributed in the conclusion, and it is distributed in the first premise, Rule 3 is satisfied because the first premise is affirmative, and Rule 4 is satisfied because even though we have added a negative premise, the conclusion is also negative.

To discover the missing premise, we looked for a statement that would result in a valid argument. This is an instance of **the principle of charity**. When we evaluate someone's reasoning, the principle of charity directs that we should do so in the fairest possible way. Sometimes it will be obvious that a person is arguing badly, and then our reconstruction should reflect that. But in the absence of clear evidence to the contrary, we should assume that we are dealing with a valid argument. In example 2:13, the principle of charity tells us to supply a premise that will make the argument valid, since there is no evidence that this missing premise is not the one the arguer had in mind.

Some arguments require more work than others. Here, for example, is an argument that is often encountered in an abridged form:

2:14. Abortion is wrong, since the fetus is a separate and distinct individual starting from a point in time about 11 days after conception—before a woman even knows she is pregnant.

The conclusion here is clear. By rewriting it in standard form, we get "All abortions are wrong actions," or "All A's are W." But the reason given does not, by itself, imply anything about abortions or wrong actions, since it is about the status of the fetus. To connect this reason with the conclusion, we must supply the background information that abortion involves the removal and destruction of a fetus. This fact, combined with the reason that is stated, suggests that one of the unstated premises in the argument is "All abortions involve the destruction of a separate and distinct individual," or "All A's are D." (If you wish, you can treat this as a conclusion of yet another argument, involving the premises "All abortions involve the destruction of a fetus" and "Destroying a fetus is destroying a separate and distinct individual." This sort of argument chain is discussed further in the section Argument Chains.)

Now we have:

All A's are D.

?????????????

All A's are W.

By going through the five rules, we discover that the only statement that will result in a valid argument is "All D's are W," or in other words, "Anything that involves the destruction of a separate and distinct individual is wrong."

Here the value of reconstructing missing premises reveals itself. We now see that the argument depends on a premise that most people would think is false. Plants, insects, even bacteria, are "separate and distinct individuals," and yet very few people think that this makes it wrong to destroy them. If we had not reconstructed the missing premise, we might have remained unaware of the true nature of the argument. Here, of course, the principle of charity will be unable to save the argument. The only premise that will result in a valid argument is "All D's are W," and so the argument either relies on that premise, or it is invalid.

When using Venn diagrams to draw conclusions from pairs of statements, we noted that there are times when no conclusion can be drawn from certain pairs of statements. An analogous situation can arise in the reconstruction of unstated premises. With certain conclusions and premises, (e.g., a negative premise and an affirmative conclusion, or a premise that contains but fails to distribute a term that is distributed in the conclusion), nothing can be added to make the argument valid. Watch for situations like this; in these cases the reasoning cannot be saved.

The search for premises is not limited to the evaluation of someone else's reasoning. We often seek premises to support our own conclusions. In Chapter 1, for example, we learned to construct outlines of our own arguments. In these outlines there might be arrows running from a single reason to a conclusion. In cases like this, we have to discover what must be added to that reason to give a valid argument. The procedure is exactly the same as the one used here to reconstruct other people's unstated premises.

At times we may even start from scratch, with a statement that we would like to have an argument for, but for which we do not yet have any clearly formulated reasons. In cases like this, the five rules may not give us one definite argument, but they can supply helpful clues. Suppose, for example, that we wanted to construct an argument to support the following statement:

2:15. Some gun control laws would not be inconsistent with the U.S. Constitution (Some G's are not I).

We need a middle term, and so we try to think of something that would relate gun control laws to the U.S. Constitution. One possibility is the class of things that infringe on people's guaranteed rights (an idea that is often cited by opponents of gun control), which we can abbreviate as R. Since our conclusion is "Some G's are not I," we will have one premise that contains the terms G and R, and one that contains I and R. We also note that one of the premises must be affirmative (Rule 3), that the premises must distribute I (Rule 2) and R (Rule 1), and that one or the other must be particular (Rule 5).

We can start by rejecting all combinations consisting of only universal premises, or only negative premises, leaving us with the following: (A) + (I); (I) + (I): (I) + (O); (A) + (O). Since the first three pairs would not allow us to distribute two terms, the fourth pair, (A) + (O), is the correct combination to choose.

By taking distribution into account, and placing I and R in slots where they will be distributed, we come up with the following pairs of premises, any of which will lead to the desired conclusion. Any other combination will not distribute the proper terms, or will violate one of the other rules.

1: All I's are R.

Some G's are not R.

2: All R's are G.

Some R's are not I.

3: No R's are I (or No I's are R).

Some G's are R (or Some R's are G).

Translating back into English, we note that the second pair of statements fails to make sense. So we can eliminate that alternative. The third pair is rejected for the same reason. We certainly do not want to rely on a premise that says, in effect, that nothing which infringes on people's rights is inconsistent with the Constitution. The first pair, however, works well, and so we can argue as follows:

> Only things that infringe on people's guaranteed rights are inconsistent with the U.S. Constitution, but some gun control laws do not infringe on those rights. Therefore, some gun control laws are not inconsistent with the Constitution.

If we had been unable to find any premises that make sense and yield a valid argument, we would have had to reconsider the idea we were trying to argue for.

EXERCISES

Use the five rules to supply the missing premise, or to construct a pair of premises that would lead to the conclusion given. If no unstated premise would make the argument valid, explain why this is so. If more than one premise or set of premises could be used, you need only supply one.

1. Some jewels are not precious stones, so some jewels are not put to industrial use.

2. Not everyone supports the present policy of relaxing environmental protection standards, since some people believe in the need for conservation.

3. Not everyone supports the present policy of relaxing environmental protection standards; therefore some people believe in the need for conservation.

4. An historical novel should not be thought of as accurate history, because remaining within the historical evidence is not among the primary goals of such works.

5. No true communist would own private property.

6. Some curriculum requirements are needed to insure the value of a college education.

*7. Since no experienced surgeon is incompetent, it follows that not all competent surgeons are men.

8. Jenkins is not a logician.

Argument Chains

In Chapter 1, we noted that arguments can be organized into chains, with the conclusion of one argument serving as a premise in the next. Argument chains composed *entirely* of categorical syllogisms are called **sorites**. Even when they involve only categorical statements, not all argument chains are sorites, since they might also contain immediate inferences such as obversion and conversion.

Argument chains are often incomplete, with some premises or intermediate conclusions left unstated. In these cases, we need to reconstruct the missing premises and conclusions to analyze the reasoning.

One reliable indication of an argument chain is the occurrence of *four or more terms* in an argument. Remember that a syllogism must contain exactly three terms. Therefore, if four or more terms appear in a categorical argument, there must be more than one syllogism. Sometimes this complex situation has all of the premises and arguments made explicit, and sometimes missing pieces must be supplied. In either case, it is best to outline the argument that is given, and to start working from there.

Here is an example of an argument chain to be analyzed:

2:16. Only language users employ generalizations. No animals have a true language, yet some animals reason. Hence, some reasoning beings do not employ generalizations.

As a first step, we outline the argument.

[¹Only language users employ generalizations.] [²No animals have a true language] yet [³some animals reason.] {Hence}, [⁴*some reasoning beings do not employ generalizations.*]

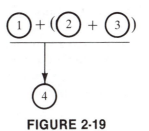

FIGURE 2-19

The parentheses around "2 + 3" remind us that the "yet" connecting these two statements in the original passage indicates that the two statements work together. Words like "and" and "but," and grammatical constructions—such as placing two clauses in the same sentence—perform a similar function. The next step is to transform all the sentences into standard categorical form. The numbers will correspond to those assigned originally (L = language users; G = things that employ generalizations; A = animals; R = reasoning beings):

1: All G's are L

2: No A's are L

3: Some A's are R

4: Some R's are not G

Following the clue given by the word "yet," we begin by diagramming 2 and 3, to see what **intermediate conclusion** can be drawn:

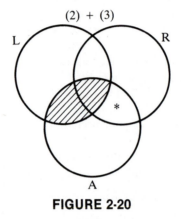

(2) + (3)

FIGURE 2-20

Since there is an asterisk in that portion of the R-circle that lies outside the L-circle, we can validly infer "Some R's are not L." Let us call this intermediate conclusion "(C1)."

At this stage, we have two alternative ways of proceeding. We want to get from (C1) to the final conclusion, "Some R's are not G." Either we could use the five rules to see what else is needed, or, since (C1) has a term in common with statement 1, we might choose to combine those two and see what follows. Either way is acceptable. They will both lead us to the same result. In this example we will take the first alternative. You should check that the other alternative leads to the same answer.

So we wish to discover the missing premise in the following syllogism:

Some R's are not L

??????????????????

Some R's are not G

The missing premise will contain L and G, G must be distributed (Rule 2), and the premise must be affirmative (Rule 3). The only statement that fits these criteria is "All G's are L," which is identical with statement 1 in the original passage. Thus, all the statements have been used, both syllogisms are valid, and we have arrived at the desired conclusion while remaining faithful to the organization and structure of the original passage. Since both parts of the chain are valid arguments, the whole argument is valid. Fully stated in standard form, the chain looks like this:

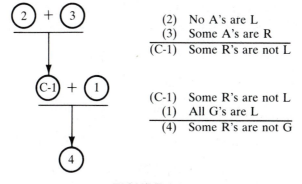

(2)	No A's are L
(3)	Some A's are R
(C-1)	Some R's are not L

(C-1)	Some R's are not L
(1)	All G's are L
(4)	Some R's are not G

FIGURE 2-21

In this example, there were two indications that we were dealing with an argument chain: the occurrence of four terms, and the use of more than two premises (a single syllogism has only two premises). In other cases, we may find four terms, but only two premises stated. This also indicates an argument chain, either a sorites with an implicit premise or an argument chain combining a syllogism with immediate inferences. Here is an illustration:

2:17. Jones must be a madman, for no sane person can be in favor of starting a nuclear war to protect commercial interests.

If we put these statements into standard form, using (J = persons identical with Jones; M = mad persons; S = sane persons; N = persons who favor starting a nuclear war merely to protect commercial interests), we get:

No S's are N

????????????

All J's are M

We cannot use the normal technique for finding a single missing premise, because we have four terms, not three. This signals a hidden argument chain rather than a single syllogism.

Before trying to construct a chain of syllogisms, we note that two of the terms, M and S, are complements of each other. In the section Immediate Inferences we learned that obversion changes the predicate term of any categorical statement into its complement. Thus, the stated conclusion "All J's are M," can be validly inferred from its (unstated) obverse, "No J's are S." Now we can look for the missing premise in the following argument:

No S's are N

????????????

No J's are S

Using the rules, we learn that the missing premise is "All J's are N." Putting the two inferences together, the whole chain looks like this:

No S's are N

All J's are N
_____
No J's are S

No J's are S
_____
All J's are M
(All J's are non-S; non-S = M)

Since the first step is a valid syllogism, and the second is a valid immediate inference, the whole argument chain is valid.

In general, when confronted with arguments containing more than three terms, check first to see whether some of the terms are complements of others. If there are such pairs, consider whether immediate inferences, including obverses, can be used to fill in the chain of reasoning. If there are no pairs of complementary terms, then we must rely on a series of syllogisms, of the sort illustrated in example 2:16.

If there are insufficient clues as to what organization the author intended, there may be several ways of reconstructing an argument chain. In these cases we can only follow the principle of charity in choosing between the alternative reconstructions.

Here is a summary of the steps to follow when analyzing an argument chain:

1. Outline the argument, and identify the final conclusion as well as any intermediate conclusions that are explicitly given.

2. Wherever necessary, rewrite statements in standard categorical form. If there are more than two premises, or more than three terms, you are dealing with an argument chain.

3. Look for complementary terms. Decide what immediate inferences are needed.

4. Use the outline, clue words such as "and" or "thus," sentence structure, and order of presentation to begin grouping parts together. Draw intermediate conclusions or supply missing premises using the rules or Venn diagrams.

5. When you run out of clues, start with the conclusion and work backwards. Find a statement in the argument that could serve as a premise in a syllogism that leads to the conclusion (i.e., a statement that contains a term in common with the final conclusion), and, if necessary, figure out what missing premise should be supplied.

6. Continue this procedure until all of the statements have been used.

7. Arrange all the immediate inferences and syllogisms in order, and check each one for validity. (If you have drawn a conclusion using a Venn diagram, or supplied missing premises by using the rules, some of this will have been taken care of already.)

By following these steps, you will be able to reconstruct and analyze quite complex chains of categorical reasoning. Using a similar procedure, and relying on the rules and Venn diagrams, you should also be able to construct complex argument chains of your own.

EXERCISES

I. Analyze the following argument chains fully. Put everything into standard form, supply any missing premises or conclusions, arrange the material into a series of syllogisms and/or immediate inferences, and indicate whether the argument chain is valid or invalid, and why.

1. All warlike countries are threats to world peace, but no member of the UN is a threat to world peace; therefore, all UN members are pacifists.

2. Darwin's theory of evolution denies that we are all descended from Adam and Eve, but anything that denies this is inconsistent with the Book of Genesis. Since only things that are consistent with the Bible are true, we must conclude that Darwin's theory should not be taught in our schools.

*3. You won't like Lucky's pizza unless you like anchovies. No one except a boor likes anchovies. Therefore, Steven is not a boor since he can't stand Lucky's pizza.

4. Only those who are misfits take any stock in Communism; but Jones cannot be that sort of person, for she repudiates the doctrines of Communism. Thus, since everyone except those who are misfits is eligible for office, Jones is eligible for office.

5. Lions are carnivores. Nothing that kills and eats baby gazelles is benevolent. Since lions kill and eat baby gazelles, carnivores are not benevolent.

II. Using the class terms provided, analyze the following arguments as valid argument chains. Begin by expressing the conclusion and the single explicit premise as categorical statements. Complete the argument chain in two steps, each of which is a valid categorical syllogism, by adding an appropriate implicit premise at each stage.

1. Alcoholics should not be allowed to run daycare facilities since drug addicts are unreliable people.

*2. Because sex acts between consenting adults are victimless crimes, consensual homosexuality should be legalized.

3. Some mammals are carnivores. Therefore, some vertebrates are not herbivores.

III. Go back and examine the outlines of arguments you developed in Chapter 1. Find at least two places on those outlines in which you rely on categorical statements, or claims that could be rewritten as categorical statements. For each of these, develop an argument chain (with nothing but valid arguments and immediate inferences) that makes explicit the connections indicated on your outline.

Notes

[1]There is an explanation for why confusions like this arise. In normal conversation, we often fail to distinguish between *what people literally say*, and *what they imply or suggest by saying what they do in the way they do*. The latter sorts of suggestions and implications are often referred to as **conversational implicatures**, and are discussed more fully in Chapter 6 the section What Is Suggested? In particular, we usually assume that a speaker is being "maximally informative," that she is conveying as much information as she has available. Thus, if someone says "Some S are P," we tend to assume that she does not know that all S are P, or that she knows that not all S are P. If she did know that all S are P, we would expect her to say so. But these are things we infer from the way something is stated, or things the speaker implies by using a certain form of statement; they are not part of the literal meaning of the statement. In logic, we focus solely on the meaning of the statement itself.

[2]Strictly speaking, two logically equivalent statements can be used interchangeably only if they are not "embedded" in a special context such as "John believes that . . . "

[3]Of course, when the subject and predicate terms mean exactly the same thing, the converse will always be logically equivalent: "All bachelors are unmarried males" is equivalent to "All unmarried males are bachelors." The logical equivalence here is a consequence of the special relation between the terms, not a consequence of the form of the statement.

[4]The predicate term of the argument is sometimes called the **major term**, and hence the premise which contains that term is called the **major premise**. Similarly, the subject term of the argument is also called the **minor term** and the premise in which it occurs is the **minor premise**. Traditionally, in a syllogism in standard form the major premise is always given first.

[5]For purposes of clarity, we have been drawing a new diagram at each stage. Normally you would not do this. Simply draw and label a diagram, diagram the first premise, and then go ahead and add the second premise to the same diagram.

[6]From Monroe Beardsley, *Practical Logic*, (Englewood Cliffs, NJ: Prentice-Hall, Inc., 1950), p. 342.

CHAPTER

3

Propositional Logic

In Chapter 2, we learned how to analyze and create categorical arguments. Unfortunately, not all arguments can be analyzed by rewriting them in standard categorical form. One reason for this failure is that some premises cannot be translated adequately as categorical statements because they are complex or do not express relations between classes.

Another limitation of categorical reasoning is its restriction to immediate inferences and syllogisms, that is, to arguments that have only one or two premises. Many arguments whose premises are complex statements cannot be reduced to syllogisms or to chains of syllogisms; their logical structure is more complex.

To deal with some of the arguments that defy categorical analysis, logicians have developed **propositional logic.** In this chapter, we study new forms for statements and arguments, and new methods for evaluating such propositional arguments. Despite this shift from categorical to propositional logic, we remain interested in deductively valid arguments, and the definition of validity remains the same. It is logically impossible for all the premises of a valid argument to be true and its conclusion false.

Truth-Functional Operators

Propositional logic is concerned with two sorts of logical relations between statements. The first, validity, concerns the relation between the premises of an argument and its conclusion. The second is the relation between the **truth values** of a complex statement (i.e., whether it is true or false) and those of the individual statements of which it is composed.

To analyze this second relationship, propositional logic constructs complex statements so that their **truth values** depend *entirely* on the truth values of their component statements and the definition of the connectives used to link them together. Connectives that allow us to create complex statements of this sort are called **truth-functional operators,** or **truth-functional connectives.**

The distinction between complex statements and their components is similar, but not identical, to the grammatical distinction between simple and compound sentences. As noted in Chapter 1, not all sentences express statements. In propositional logic, sentences that do express statements can be divided into two groups: the statements expressed are either **logically complex** or **logically atomic.** Logically complex statements are composed of logically atomic statements strung together using *only* truth-functional connectives. Roughly speaking, logically atomic statements are expressed by grammatically simple sentences such as "The sky is blue" and "Whole milk contains butter fat." More precisely, a logically atomic statement is any statement, however complex grammatically, that contains no truth-functional connectives.

Some grammatically complex sentences contain connectives that are not truth-functional. The difference between connectives that are truth-functional and those that are not is illustrated by examples 3:1 and 3:2, each of which contain the grammatically simple statements "The button was pressed" and "The bomb exploded":

3:1. The button was pressed *and* the bomb exploded.

3:2. The button was pressed, *which brought it about that* the bomb exploded.

Example 3:1 asserts merely that both events occurred. If it is true that the button was pressed and that the bomb exploded, then the complex statement must be true as well. In other words, the connective "and" in 3:1 is truth-functional. On the other hand, we need to know more than just the truth values of the two simple statements to determine whether 3:2 is true. Both events could occur, and thus both simple statements could be true, but if the button's being pressed did not *cause* the bomb to explode, 3:2 is still false. This feature of 3:2—that its truth value is a function not merely of the truth values of the grammatically simple statements of which it is composed—tells us that the connective, "which brought it about that," is not truth-functional. Grammatically complex statements that do not include truth-functional operators must be treated as (logically) atomic statements. Thus, as far as propositional logic is concerned, example 3:2 is an atomic statement despite its grammatical complexity.

The simplest truth-functional operator is **negation.** Whenever we take a sentence expressing a true statement and preface it with the phrase "it is not the case that," we create a new statement that is false. Similarly, negating a false statement creates a true one. To make it easier to write out propositional statements and arguments, we will use special symbols for each of the truth-functional operators.[1] The symbol for "it is not the case that" is a " ~ " (called a **tilde**); thus, " ~ p" means "it is not the case that p," or simply "not p." The lower-case letter "p" is a variable, or placeholder, which can be replaced by any statement. We will use the lower-case letters such as "p," "q," and "r," as statement-variables; later, we will abbreviate specific atomic statements with upper-case letters ("A," "B," . . .).

We can define truth-functional operators such as negation by using **truth tables.** A truth table is used to show how the truth value of a complex statement depends on the truth values of its component atomic statements. The truth table for negation is given in Figure 3-1.

p	~p
T	F
F	T

FIGURE 3-1

The "T" in a truth table stands for "true" and the "F" for "false." The first column in Figure 3-1, labeled "p," lists the various logical possibilities regarding p's truth value: it tells us that p might be true (the first row) or false (the second row). These truth values remain constant throughout the truth table in that, in all of the first row of truth table, in any column, p is true; across the second row, p has the truth value "false." The second column of our truth table shows what happens to ~p for each of the values of p defined in the first column. Thus, the first line of the truth table tells us that when p is true, ~p is false, and the second line says that when p is false, ~p is true. The truth table just given should make it clear that any pair of statements p and ~p are contradictory, in the sense defined in Chapter 2 in the section Immediate Inferences.

The English word "not" does not always negate an entire statement. For example, "Some dogs are beagles" and "Some dogs are not beagles" are not contradictories; "Some dogs are not beagles" does *not* mean "It is not the case that some dogs are beagles." The word "not" can be interpreted as a truth-functional operator only when it negates an entire statement.

The second truth-functional operator we consider is **conjunction,** which we symbolize with an **ampersand** (&). A complex statement such as "p & q" is called a conjunction; "p" and "q" are the **conjuncts.** A conjunction is true if both of its conjuncts are true; in all other cases, it is false.

To represent conjunction in a truth table, we must consider four different assignments of truth value: p and q could both be true, or they could both be false; p could be true while q is false, and p could be false while q is true. All of these possibilities are shown in Figure 3-2, which defines the truth-functional operator, &:

p	q	p & q
T	T	T
T	F	F
F	T	F
F	F	F

FIGURE 3-2

For the sake of consistency, we use the same truth-functional operator, &, to translate each of the connectives that follow this same pattern. Thus, whenever we encounter two statements joined by one of the terms on the following list, we write it in **standard form** as a complex statement of the form "p & q:"

p, but q	p, although q
p; q	p; also q
p, besides q	p; however, q
p, whereas q	p, despite q

In addition, sentences such as "Anna and Bob are engineers" can be translated as "A & B," where A = "Anna is an engineer," and B = "Bob is an engineer"; "Neither Anna nor Bob are engineers" can be translated into standard form as "~A & ~B."

If you are unsure of a translation, ask yourself "Under what conditions would this complex statement be true?" If it would be true only when both of its component statements are true, you can translate it into standard form using "&." Remember that propositional logic is concerned only with the truth-functional role of connecting terms. Words such as "but" and "although" often involve a contrast between statements (e.g., "Although it was Christmas Day, we went to the office as usual") as well as performing the same function as &. Propositional logic does not take into account these other aspects of the sentence.

Another useful truth-functional operator is **disjunction.** The result of connecting two statements with "or" or with "either . . . or . . . " is called a **disjunction;** each of the components is referred to as a **disjunct.** We must be careful when interpreting disjunctions, because "or" in English is used in two ways—**exclusively** and **inclusively.** When it is used exclusively, one or the other of the disjuncts is true, *but not both.* Statement 3:3 is an example in which "or" is used *exclusively:*

3:3. For dessert you can have either ice cream or sherbet.

At other times, the connective is *inclusive,* and means that one or the other disjunct is true, *or both* are true:

3:4. To fulfill the math requirement, you must take a course either in trigonometry or in calculus.

In statement 3:4, unlike 3:3, it is possible for both alternatives to be true, since one can take both trigonometry and calculus if one wishes.

In logic it is crucial to avoid ambiguity. We must, therefore, decide which of these meanings to assign to "or," and use that meaning consistently. Logicians have traditionally defined "or" inclusively, and we will follow that practice. The symbol for the inclusive "or" is the **wedge**. "p V q" always means "p is true or q is true or both are true." Figure 3-3 gives the truth table for a simple disjunction.

p	q	p V q
T	T	T
T	F	T
F	T	T
F	F	F

FIGURE 3-3

Usually it is easy to translate disjunctions into standard propositional form, since few English phrases involving "or" are ambiguous. "Either p or q" can be translated as "p V q," and "Neither p nor q" is equivalent to "~ (p V q)." Somewhat less obviously, "p unless q" is logically equivalent to "p V q." Thus, the statement "We will need to water the flowers unless it rains" can be translated as "Either it will rain or we will need to water the flowers." The order in which the disjuncts appear makes no difference to the truth value of the disjunction.

It is important to remember that we have defined or as inclusive. Therefore, in contexts in which an English sentence is clearly meant to describe two exclusive alternatives, we should not translate it as a simple disjunction. Consider example 3:5:

3:5. Either the jury must find the prisoner guilty, or the court must allow her to go free.

It would be misleading to translate 3:5 as "G V A" (where G = "The jury must find the prisoner guilty," and A = "The court must allow the prisoner to go free"). To capture its meaning properly, we should translate it as "(G V A) & ~ (G & A)," which says that either G or A is true, and it is not the case that both are true.[2] In this way, we can still express the exclusive sense of "or" by means of a complex statement using all three of the truth-functional operators we have discussed.

The final truth-functional operator we consider is the **conditional**, which is symbolized with an **arrow**. "If p, then q" is written in standard form as "p→q." The whole statement formed by connecting two statements with an arrow is called a **conditional**. The first part of the conditional (the statement between the "if" and the "then," or the statement that precedes the arrow) is the **antecedent** and the second part, the statement after the "then" or the arrow, is the **consequent**.

It is especially important in this case to remember that we are using "→" purely as a truth-functional operator, because in ordinary language we often use "if . . . then . . . " to assert a causal or logical link between the states of affairs described in the antecedent and consequent. As we stated at the beginning of this section, truth-functional relations concern only the way in which the truth value of the complex statement depends on the truth value of the components, and so propositional logic is forced to ignore these other factors.[3]

A conditional statement tells us that when the antecedent is true, the consequent is also true. When the antecedent is false, the consequent can be either true or false; the conditional is true in either case. This is the only way of capturing the truth-functional sense of the conditional without making it too strong. When we say "If p, then q," we are trying to convey the claim that you cannot have p without q too, or in other words, "~ (p & ~ q)." If we adopt this as our definition of the conditional by stipulating that "p→q" is logically equivalent to "~(p & ~q)," we arrive at the truth table in Figure 3-4.

p	q	p → q
T	T	T
T	F	F
F	T	T
F	F	T

FIGURE 3-4

Thus, as far as propositional logic is concerned, "If p then q" is false when p is true and q is false; otherwise it is true. Specifically, it is true whenever the antecedent is false, or when the consequent is true, or both. Given this definition of "if . . . then . . . ," we can see that each of the following statements is true:

If Jenny is a dog, then she is a mammal.

If guppies are dogs, then they are mammals.

If pigs have tails, then they are mammals.

If George Washington is the czar of Russia, then the moon is made of green cheese.

If 3 + 2 = 5, then Socrates was a philosopher.

As with the other truth-functional operators, we should learn to identify the many English phrases that are equivalent to "if . . . then . . . ." The following list contains some of the different ways of saying "p→q." Pay particular attention to the order in which p and q occur; it makes a difference. "And" and "or" are **symmetrical** relations, which means that the order of the terms can be reversed without changing the meaning; but this is not true for the conditional: "p→q" does not mean the same as "q→p." Here is a list of statements that can be translated into standard form as "if p, then q" or as "p→q":

if p, it would follow that q.

p implies q.

p entails q.

p only if q.

whenever p, q.

q, if p.

q, when p.

q can be inferred from p.

q follows from p.

q is a necessary condition for p.

p is a sufficient condition for q.

It is possible to define many more truth-functional operators, but "not," "and," "or," and "if . . . then . . . " are sufficient for our purposes. The operator "if and only if," for example, can be explicitly defined using "if . . . then . . . " and "and." Thus, "p if and only if q" is equivalent to "(p→q) & (q→p)." The operator is sometimes called the **biconditional** and given a special symbol "↔," the two-headed arrow. The biconditional is especially useful for giving definitions because it enables one to state both necessary and sufficient conditions for the term being defined. We have already used this operator in earlier chapters in defining concepts such as validity and soundness.

We gain even more flexibility when we combine operators, as we did in example 3:5. That sentence illustrates the fact that the variables in ~p, p & q, p V q, and p→q can stand for atomic statements, or statements such as "John goes to the movies," "Mary is very good at mathematics," and "All dogs are mammals," which contain no truth-functional operators, but they can also stand for complex statements such as "D & M," "~(A V C)→(~C & ~A)," and "If I have a pair of aces and I think the other players are bluffing, then I will raise the bet." Notice that in the second sentence, parentheses are used to avoid ambiguity. In English statements like the last example, sentence structure and punctuation usually indicate how the various parts of the statement should be organized.

We can now define the **standard form** for statements in propositional logic. To write a statement in standard propositional form:

1. Abbreviate each atomic statement with an upper-case letter.

2. When it is appropriate, add the symbols for the truth-functional operators.

3. If necessary, use parentheses to avoid ambiguity.

Thus, statements in standard form are either a single upper-case letter (if the statement is atomic) or some combination of letters and symbols for truth-functional operators; in the latter case, the statement may also include pairs of parentheses. A more formal definition of standard form, specifying the "legal" combinations of letters and symbols, could be given but is not really necessary here; just remember that the combination should make sense. To write a propositional argument in standard form:

1. Translate each premise and the conclusion into standard form for propositional logic.

2. List each premise on a separate line.

3. List the conclusion last, separated from the premises by a single solid line.

EXERCISES

I. Decide whether the following statements are logically complex or logically atomic. Write out the logically atomic components of the complex statements, indicating the truth-functional connectives and operators.

1. The river will flood only if yesterday's rainfall exceeded five inches.

*2. Smith will win the race unless Jones is entered.

3. Lyndon LaRouche is not a viable candidate.

*4. Aristotle believed that the earth is at the center of the universe.

5. Even a starfish is a complex entity whose neurological structure remains mysterious.

6. The river is flooding because it rained yesterday.

7. My dog has been well-behaved since I took it to obedience school.

8. Three people are campaigning for the nomination, but two of them will not get it.

*9. Regardless of whether taxes are raised or not, the budget deficit will not decrease unless Congress reduces the size of entitlement programs and eliminates waste and fraud in the Department of Defense.

10. Either Reginald will pass his exam or he will have to take it again, but only if the board agrees to give him a second chance and he does not leave the country.

II. Translate the following English sentences into standard truth-functional form, using capital letters to stand for atomic sentences, and indicating which atomic sentence each letter abbreviates.

1. If Jones lives in Albany, he lives in New York.

2. The ancient Greeks knew that the world was round, but Columbus often gets credit for that discovery.

*3. Unless taxes are raised, the deficit will grow even larger.

*4. Having a solid financial base is a necessary condition for starting a successful small business.

5. The strife in Lebanon will continue if the Syrians do not accept the new peace proposal.

6. A sibling has a brother or a sister.

7. A sibling is a brother or a sister. (Your translation should reflect the fact that these are exclusive alternatives.)

8. John will bet when he has three of a kind, but Jill will always win.

9. It is not the case that both Mildred and Harry will win prizes.

10. The fact that there is evil in the world is sufficient to show that either God is not benevolent or He is not omnipotent.

III. Write out each of the following propositional arguments in standard form.

1. John will quit unless he gets a better salary. He will not get a better salary. Therefore, he will quit.

2. Either I have a brother or I have a sister. I have a brother. Thus, I do not have a sister.

3. The budget will pass only if defense spending is increased. If the budget is not passed, defense spending will still be increased. Therefore, defense spending will be increased.

4. If 5 is an even number, then it is divisible by 2. Since 5 is not an even number, it is not divisible by 2.

*5. It is not the case that both of the following statements are true: Evelyn is in Paris; Fiona is not in Rome. Therefore, Fiona must be in Rome, since Evelyn is in Paris.

Using Truth Tables

The most important use of truth tables is to evaluate propositional arguments. By having a column for each premise of the argument, and one for its conclusion, we can determine whether it is logically possible for the conclusion to be false when all the premises are true. In other words, we can use truth tables to test the validity of propositional arguments.

Consider example 3:6 as an illustration of the general procedure:

3:6. If smoking is banned in the workplace, then smokers will consume fewer cigarettes; and, if smokers consume fewer cigarettes, then rates of lung cancer and emphysema will diminish. Thus, if smoking is banned in the workplace, rates of lung cancer and emphysema will be reduced.

The first step is to write out the argument in standard form. Let "B," "C," and "D" stand for the atomic propositions "Smoking is banned in the workplace," "Smokers will consume fewer cigarettes," and "Rates of lung cancer and emphysema will be reduced (be diminished)." This gives us the following:

$$B \rightarrow C$$

$$\underline{C \rightarrow D}$$

$$B \rightarrow D$$

Since this argument involves three atomic propositions (B, C, and D), we have to construct a truth table with eight rows to represent all of the logically possible combinations of their truth values. (In general, if n is the number of atomic propositions, our truth table will require 2^n rows.) To ensure that we have covered all the possible combinations of "T" and "F," we enumerate them systematically. In the first column, representing the possible truth values of atomic proposition B, we write T in the first four rows and F in the rest. In the next column, representing the truth values of C, we put two T's followed by two F's and then two more T's followed by two more F's. In the third column, representing D, we alternate T's and F's all the way down. This generates the entries in the first three columns at the left of the truth table in Figure 3-5.

B	C	D	(P-1) $B \rightarrow C$	(P-2) $C \rightarrow D$	(C) $B \rightarrow D$
T	T	T			
T	T	F			
T	F	T			
T	F	F			
F	T	T			
F	T	F			
F	F	T			
F	F	F			

FIGURE 3-5

We now add to our truth table a column for each premise and a column for the conclusion. To keep track of things, these columns in Figure 3-5 have been labeled "P1," "P2," and "C."

The next step is to complete the truth table by filling in the correct entries for each of the columns representing the premises and the conclusion. Consider column P1, which represents the premise "B→C." Since this is a conditional statement, it will be false only when its antecedent (B) is true and its consequent (C) is false. We read off the appropriate truth values of B and of C in each row from the B column and the C column at the left. We find that "B→C" is false only in rows three and four. In all the other rows it is true. Having completed the P1 column, we then repeat the procedure for the other two columns, P2 and C.

Finally, we inspect the truth table to see whether or not the argument is valid. It is important to be clear about the reasoning involved here. An argument is valid if and only if it is not *logically* possible for the conclusion to be false when all the premises are true. Thus, if the truth table of an argument contains no rows in which all the premises are true and the conclusion is false, it must be valid. Similarly, an argument is invalid if its truth table contains at least one row in which all the premises are true and the conclusion is false.[4]

It is not necessary to check every row to assess an argument's validity. Simply look at those rows in which the conclusion is false. If any of these rows are ones in which *all* the premises are true, then the argument is invalid. If none of these rows are ones in which all the premises are true, the argument is valid. In Figure 3-6, there are only two rows, the second and the fourth, in which the conclusion is false. But in each of these rows, one of the premises is false: in the second row, the premise (C→D) is false; in the fourth row, the premise (B→C) is false. So the argument is valid. In other words, by using a truth table we have discovered that it is logically impossible for all the premises of 3:6 to be true and its conclusion false. Thus, 3:6 is a valid form of argument.

B	C	D	(P-1) B → C	(P-2) C → D	(C) B → D
T	T	T	T	T	T
T	T	F	T	F	F
T	F	T	F	T	T
T	F	F	F	T	F
F	T	T	T	T	T
F	T	F	T	F	T
F	F	T	T	T	T
F	F	F	T	T	T

FIGURE 3-6

The same technique works for any propositional argument, regardless of the number of premises or how many atomic propositions it contains. Consider the following example:

3:7. If the president resigned yesterday, then the vice-president has become president. The president did not resign yesterday. So the vice-president has not become president.

Here, we have two premises but only two atomic propositions. If we let "R" stand for "The president resigned yesterday," and "B" for "The vice-president has become president," we get the following:

R → B

~R

~B

Its truth table is given in Figure 3-7.

R	B	R → B	~R	~B
T	T	T	F	F
T	F	F	F	T
F	T	T	T	F
F	F	F	T	T

FIGURE 3-7

In the third row, both premises are true, and the conclusion is false. This proves that 3:7 is an invalid argument.

When the premises or conclusion of a propositional argument are complex statements involving several truth-functional connectives, it is advisable to write down the intermediate steps leading to the final entries for a column, rather than try to do it all in one's head. In these cases we recommend that you execute the preliminary steps in separate columns, clearly marking the final columns that represent the premises and the conclusion. In this way you reduce the possibility of confusion when you later inspect the rows of the truth table to see whether the argument is valid. As an illustration, consider the truth table in Figure 3-8 of the following argument:

P → (Q V ~R)

R → (~P → Q)

P	Q	R	~R	Q V ~ R	~P	~P → Q	(P-1) P → (Q V ~R)	(C) R → (~P → Q)
T	T	T	F	T	F	T	T	T
T	T	F	T	T	F	T	T	T
T	F	T	F	F	F	T	F	T
T	F	F	T	T	F	T	T	T
F	T	T	F	T	T	T	T	T
F	T	F	T	T	T	T	T	T
F	F	T	F	F	T	F	T	F
F	F	F	T	T	T	F	T	T

FIGURE 3-8

In this truth table we have arrived at the entries for the premise column (P1) and the conclusion column (C) in three steps. First, we wrote the entries for ~R, then the entries for Q V ~R, and then, finally, the truth values of the single premise in the column labeled "P1." Similarly, three steps led up to the entries in the conclusion column, C. When we now assess the argument for validity, we look *only* at the columns labeled P1 and C. Since, in the seventh row, P1 is true and C is false, the argument form is invalid.

Another use for truth tables is in determining whether two statements are logically equivalent. Two statements are **logically equivalent** if they have the same truth value under all possible circumstances. In Chapter 2, we saw, for example, that each categorical statement is logically equivalent to its obverse, and that an (E) proposition is logically equivalent to its converse. We can also find many pairs of logically equivalent statements or forms of statements in propositional logic. If two statements have identical columns in a truth table, they are logically equivalent.

The simplest pair of logically equivalent sentence forms is "p" and "~(~p)." Compare the columns for these two statements in the truth table in Figure 3-9, and you will see that they are identical.

p	~p	~(~p)
T	F	T
F	T	F

FIGURE 3-9

Other pairs of equivalent statements may not be as obvious. Consider, for example, "p→q" and "~p V q." By comparing the truth table columns for these two statements in Figure 3-10, we can prove that they are logically equivalent.

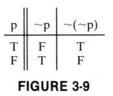

p	q	~p	p → q	~p V q
T	T	F	T	T
T	F	F	F	F
F	T	T	T	T
F	F	T	T	T

FIGURE 3-10

Truth tables have yet another useful application. They enable us to identify members of two special classes of complex truth-functional propositions: **tautologies** and **contradictions**. A tautology is a statement that is necessarily true; it is logically impossible for it to be false. A contradiction is the opposite of a tautology; it is necessarily false. We can use a truth table to prove that p V ~ p is a tautology, and that "p & ~p" is a contradiction.

p	~p	p V ~p	p & ~p
T	F	T	F
F	T	T	F

FIGURE 3-11

The third column of the truth table shows that "p V ~ p" is true whether p is true or false, whereas the fourth shows that "p & ~ p" is false in all possible cases. The number of different forms of tautology and contradiction is infinite. For example, "(p→q) V (q→p)" is a tautology; "(p→q) & (p & ~q)" is a contradiction. All tautologies are logically equivalent, as are all contradictions. Putting a tilde in front of a tautology always produces a contradiction; putting a tilde in front of a contradiction always produces a tautology.

EXERCISES

I. Use a truth table to determine which of the arguments in Practice Exercises III of the preceding section are valid. (The answer to problem 5 is given in Appendix II.)

II. Use a truth table to determine which of the following arguments are valid. If the argument is not already in standard form, translate it into standard form before you construct the truth table.

1. If matter exists, Berkeley was mistaken. If my hand exists, matter exists. Thus, either my hand exists or Berkeley was mistaken.

2. Either both Mars and Jupiter have moons or Neptune does. If Neptune has moons, then Jupiter does. Thus, Mars has moons only if Jupiter does.

3. It is false that life could have arisen in the primitive atmosphere of the Earth. For, if oxygen were in the primitive atmosphere, life could not have arisen because its chemical precursors would have been destroyed by oxidation; if oxygen were not in the primitive atmosphere, then neither would ozone have been, and if ozone were not present to shield the chemical precursors of life from ultraviolet light, life could not have arisen.

*4. In their paper, "Can Quantum-Mechanical Description of Physical Reality Be Considered Complete?" (*Physical Review* 47 (1935): 777–780), Einstein, Podolsky, and Rosen claim to have proven two things: first, that either the quantum-mechanical description of reality given by the wave function is not complete, or when the operators corresponding to two physical quantities do not commute, the two quantities cannot have simultaneous reality; second, that if the wave function does give a complete description of physical reality, then two physical quantities with noncommuting operators can have simultaneous reality. From these two results they then conclude that the quantum-mechanical description of physical reality given by the wave function is not complete. (P = "The quantum-mechanical description of reality given by the wave function is complete"; Q = "Two physical quantities with noncommuting operators can have simultaneous reality.")

5. "My contention is that understanding the meaning of any proposition is a necessary condition of justifying it. But this understanding can be achieved only by recognizing the relevance of cultural influences upon the context, construction, and statement of the proposition. Thus unless cultural influences are considered, no proposition can be justified." [From John Kekes, "The Context of Justification," in *The Heritage of Logical Positivism* (1985), p. 71.]

III. For each of the following pairs of statements, use truth tables to determine whether or not they are logically equivalent.

1. ~A & ~B; ~(A V B).

2. ~(A V B); ~A V ~B.

3. W → Z; Z → W.

4. ~Z → U; ~(Z → U).

5. A person can graduate only if he or she is a senior; a person cannot graduate unless he or she is a senior.

6. Taking the final exam is a necessary condition for passing the course; taking the final is a sufficient condition for passing the course.

7. A → (A V B); (A & B) → B.

8. A V (B & C); (A & B) V (A & C).

*9. (M → P) & ~P; ~M.

IV. Use truth tables to determine whether the following sentences are tautologies, contradictions, or neither.

*1. A → ~A.

2. E → (D → E).

3. E → (E → D).

*4. ~(~G V ~H) & ~H.

5. ((A V B) & (B V C)) → (~B → (A → C)).

Some Common Forms of Argument

There are several different ways of determining whether a propositional argument is valid or not. One of these methods relies on an aspect of valid arguments that was discussed in Chapter 1. If an argument exemplifies a valid form of argument, the argument is valid. Since many valid propositional arguments involve only a small number of valid forms, learning to recognize a few of these forms allows us to evaluate most of the arguments we are likely to encounter. An argument that has any one of the following forms is valid. Each of the argument forms we will learn has a name, and an abbreviation that will be given along with the form.

MODUS PONENS (MP)

$p \rightarrow q$

$\underline{p}$

q

MODUS TOLLENS (MT)

$p \rightarrow q$

$\underline{\sim q}$

$\sim p$

DISJUNCTIVE SYLLOGISM (DS)

$p \lor q$

$\underline{\sim p}$

q

HYPOTHETICAL SYLLOGISM (HS)

$p \rightarrow q$

$\underline{q \rightarrow r}$

$p \rightarrow r$

CONTRAPOSITION (CON)

$\underline{p \rightarrow q}$

$\sim q \rightarrow \sim p$

DILEMMA (DIL)

p V q

p → r

q → s
___

r V s

Note that these are all **argument forms,** not complete arguments. An argument results when we substitute statements (or capital letters, which are abbreviations for statements) for "p" and the other sentence variables. Obviously, when a variable occurs more than once, we must substitute the same statement for each occurrence of that variable. Example 3:8 is an argument that follows the DS form:

3:8. The president can sign the bill that has just been passed by Congress, or he will effectively veto it. The president did not sign the bill; therefore, he has effectively vetoed it.

As with the statements discussed in the section Truth-Functional Operators, we can substitute either atomic statements or complex statements for the variables. The following argument has the form MP (modus ponens); "~A" has been substituted for "p," and "B V C" for "q":

(~A) → (B V C)

~A
___

B V C

These argument forms can be used in two ways. They can help us determine whether an argument is valid, and they can also help us construct our own valid arguments. Thus, suppose I wish to argue for the following claim:

3:9. We should not teach creationism in our schools.

We can use the common argument forms to find premises that will lead validly to this conclusion. Because the conclusion is negative, it is natural to start thinking about a modus tollens argument, since in that form the conclusion is also negative. Modus tollens arguments have the following form:

p → q

~q
___

~p

Thus, we know that in the argument we create, the statement that is negated in the conclusion "We should teach creationism in our schools" should form the antecedent of a conditional. The consequent of the conditional must be something that we are willing to deny or negate in our second premise. This gives us the following partial argument:

If we teach creationism in our schools then ???

It is not the case that ???
_____

We should not teach creationism in our schools

One possible way of completing the argument is to question the status of creationism as a legitimate scientific theory deserving equal treatment with evolutionary theories. Thus, our completed argument might look like this:

3:10. We should teach creationism in our schools only if it is a legitimate scientific theory that deserves equal treatment with evolutionary theories. It is not such a theory; so we should not teach it in our schools.

With more complex substitutions, we can create more complicated arguments, but the principle is the same. In each case, we decide which argument form best suits our needs, and figure out what substitutions will give us the conclusion or premise we want to start with. After we have completed the substitution of our starting material—substituting those statements each time the appropriate variable occurs—we think of claims that will allow us to fill in the rest of the argument in an effective way. In many cases we may wish to rewrite our premises or conclusion in some form that is equivalent to the standard form but sounds more natural, as we did with the first premise in 3:10.

In using these common argument forms to test arguments for validity, we are relying on a fact discussed in Chapter 1: any argument that exemplifies a valid argument form is valid. Thus, if we can show that an argument exemplifies one of the six forms described here, we are sure it is valid. To determine whether or not it does exemplify one of the forms, we once again substitute statements for the variables in the form. Consider, for example, argument 3:11:

3:11. Either this is not a diamond or it will scratch glass. Thus, we know that it is not a diamond, since it does not scratch glass.

Letting D = "This is a diamond" and G = "This will scratch glass," we can put the argument into standard form:

~D V G

~G
_____

~D

You can easily see that if we were to start with the argument form DS and substituted "G" for "p" and "~D" for "q," we would arrive at an argument identical to this one, except that the order of the disjuncts would be reversed:

$$GV \sim D$$

$$\underline{\sim G}$$

$$\sim D$$

Since disjunction is a symmetrical relation, the order of the disjuncts is irrelevant. The argument in 3:11 does, therefore, exemplify the DS form, and hence it is valid. Just as some categorical arguments were incomplete, we may also encounter propositional arguments with some premises left unstated. Even if the second premise in 3:11 had not been supplied, once we recognized that the first premise and the conclusion are parts of a disjunctive syllogism, the DS form would tell us what the missing premise must be.

These valid forms of argument identify the most common valid arguments, but there are also invalid forms of argument that are quite prevalent. Learning to recognize the valid forms allows us to evaluate many arguments simply and quickly. Similarly, learning the most common invalid forms, also known as **fallacies,** often allows us to pick out invalid arguments efficiently. Before listing these fallacies, however, we should recall a point made in Chapter 1: a single argument can exemplify several different forms; showing that it exemplifies one valid form is enough to prove an argument is valid, but an argument can exemplify an invalid form, and still be a valid argument. Therefore, the fallacies we examine provide, at best, a general set of guidelines, not a foolproof test for invalid arguments. We can generally assume that an argument that has the form of one of these fallacies does not exemplify any valid form, and hence is an invalid argument, but we should always watch for exceptions to this rule. Similarly, if the statements substituted for the variables are logically related to one another in ways that are not reflected by the argument form, the resulting argument is valid as long as it is logically impossible for all the premises to be true and the conclusion false.

Here are some common fallacies to watch for:

FALLACY OF AFFIRMING THE CONSEQUENT

$$p \rightarrow q$$

$$\underline{q}$$

$$p$$

FALLACY OF DENYING THE ANTECEDENT

$$p \rightarrow q$$

$$\underline{\sim p}$$

$$\sim q$$

FALLACY OF CONVERTING THE CONDITIONAL

$\underline{p \rightarrow q}$

$q \rightarrow p$

FALLACY OF ASSERTING AN ALTERNATIVE[5]

$p \lor q$

$\underline{p \qquad}$

$\sim q$

Usually, an argument that exhibits one of these forms is invalid. Here are some examples:

> If the piece of paper in my wallet is a dollar bill, it is green. It is not a dollar bill; therefore, it is not green.
> Either my father has a son, or he has a daughter. Since he has a son, it follows that he does not have a daughter.
> If John passes his English class, then he will graduate, because passing that class is a necessary condition for graduation.

But some arguments are valid even though they exemplify the form of one of these fallacies. The following arguments are both valid, even though they both have the form of the fallacy of affirming the consequent:

3:12. $A \rightarrow (B \And \sim B)$

$\underline{B \And \sim B \qquad}$

A

3:13. If all college students are literate, then no college students are unable to read. No college students are unable to read; therefore all college students are literate.

Argument 3:12 is a valid argument because its second premise is a contradiction. Since this statement is always false, we can never have true premises leading to a false conclusion. In 3:13, the antecedent and the consequent are logically equivalent (one is the obverse of the other), and so the conclusion is also logically equivalent to the second premise. These situations do not occur very often, but they do prevent us from simply assuming that any argument that has a fallacious form is invalid.

We can now formulate a step-by-step procedure for determining whether a propositional argument is valid:

1. Write the argument in standard form, using only truth-functional operators.

2. Does the argument match one of the valid argument forms you have learned? (Be sure to check for complex as well as simple substitutions,

and for missing premises.) If it does, it is a valid argument. If it does not, go to step 3.

3. Does the argument commit one of the standard fallacies? If it does, and if it has no special factors that would make it valid anyway (e.g., a contradiction in the premises), the argument is invalid. If it does not commit any fallacies, proceed to step 4.

4. Decide whether the conclusion must be true if the premises are true. One foolproof method for doing this is to construct a truth table. If there are no rows in which the conclusion is false and all the premises are true, the argument is valid. If there is a row in which all the premises are true and the conclusion is false, the argument is invalid.

There are a few things to note about this procedure. First, the second and third steps are not strictly necessary; we could go directly from the first to the fourth. These steps are useful, though, because they often allow us to avoid having to construct a truth table. Second, the fact that an argument does not match one of the valid argument forms does not automatically make it invalid; we must continue the evaluation process to reach the correct judgment. Third, in the section Argument Chains and Variations we will encounter more complicated arguments that require some refinement of this procedure.

EXERCISES

I. If necessary, write each of the arguments in standard form. Identify the form of argument or the fallacy the argument exemplifies and determine whether the argument is valid or invalid.

1. If capital punishment really deterred criminals, it would be justifiable. We agree that it is justifiable; therefore, it must deter criminals.

2. Congress will act only if legislators put aside partisan concerns. Legislators will not put aside partisan concerns, and so Congress will not act.

*3. The jar will crack when the water inside it either freezes or boils. The water inside it has neither boiled nor frozen; thus, the jar has not cracked.

4. Either God chooses not to prevent evil, or He is unable to prevent it. If He chooses not to prevent it, He is not benevolent. He is unable to prevent evil only if He is not omnipotent. Therefore, either God is not omnipotent, or He is not benevolent.

5. Either God is not benevolent, or He is not omnipotent. He is benevolent; it follows from this that He is not omnipotent.

6. If traditional theism is correct, God is omnipotent. Thus, if God is not omnipotent, traditional theism is incorrect.

7. If antiabortionism required the perverting of natural reason and normal sensibilities by a system of superstitions, then the liberal could discredit

it—but it doesn't, so he can't. [From R. Wertheimer, "Understanding the Abortion Argument," in J. Feinberg, ed., *The Problem of Abortion*, 2nd ed. (Belmont, CA: Wadsworth, 1984), p. 54.]

*8. If determinism is true then all my actions are caused by events over which I have no control. But this means that determinism is incompatible with free will, since if I have no control over the events causing my actions, none of my actions is free.

II. Translate each of the following statements into standard form and then use it as a premise in an argument of the form specified in parentheses.

1. John will graduate if he passes this course. (MT)

2. Either the Democrats will win the election or the Republicans will. (DIL)

3. An independent candidate will never win a presidential election. (MP)

4. Acid rain will threaten our lakes unless stricter laws are enacted. (DS)

5. If church and state are to remain distinct, the government cannot dictate religious practices. (CON)

*6. Being a U.S. citizen is a necessary condition for registering to vote. (DS)

III. Translate each of the following statements into standard form and then use it as the conclusion of an argument of the form specified in parentheses. If no form is specified, you may use any form except MP.

1. John will not pass this course. (MT)

2. John will not pass this course. (DS)

3. Either this stone will scratch glass, or it is not a diamond. (MP)

4. Having hair somewhere on their bodies is a sufficient condition for whales being mammals. (CON)

5. Penguins are birds only if they have feathers.

*6. I am not an only child, but I do not have any sisters.

Argument Chains and Variations

In Chapter 2, we studied chains of arguments linking premises to a final conclusion. Such argument chains can also be constructed in propositional logic; 3:14 is one example.

3:14. If light rays are periodic waves (rather than consisting of streams of particles), then either the light waves are longitudinal pulses (like sound waves in air) or they are transverse vibrations (like ripples propagated along a rope). Phenomena such as interference fringes and diffraction show that light rays are periodic waves. Moreover, the fact that light rays can be polarized proves they cannot consist of longitudinal pulses. Thus, we can conclude that light rays are transverse vibrations.

Let W = "Light rays are periodic waves"; L = "Light waves are longitudinal pulses"; T = "Light waves are transverse vibrations." We can then translate the argument into standard form as follows:

W → (L V T)

W

~L

—————————

T

This does not match any of the standard valid argument forms; so, following the procedure outlined at the end of the previous section, we might construct a truth table to see whether the argument is valid. But there is a simpler alternative. We can show that a chain of valid arguments leads from the premises to the conclusion by filling in some missing steps:

1. W → (L V T)

2. W

—————————

C1. L V T

C1. L V T

3. ~L

—————————

C2. T

The first two steps in this chain are the first two premises given in the original argument. Modus ponens (MP) allows us to use these two statements to generate a valid argument with C1 as its conclusion. C1 and our last premise, statement 3, lead to the final conclusion, here labeled C2, by forming a disjunctive syllogism (DS). Each step of the chain is either a premise or something that follows from premises by means of a valid argument; so the entire chain is valid. In other argument chains, there may be missing premises that we must supply, with the guidance of the argument forms.

Many argument chains involve, among other things, the use of a **generalization** to support a conclusion about something more particular. Argument 3:15 is an example of such an argument:

3:15. Being at least 35 years old is a necessary condition for being a presidential candidate. Jones is not over 35. Therefore, he cannot be a candidate for president.

The conclusion is that Jones cannot be a candidate. We cannot use modus ponens to get to that conclusion, given the premises that are explicitly stated, since the conditional premise does not mention Jones at all. We need a procedure to derive specific claims from generalizations like this. The procedure to use is **substitution.** The rule govening substitution tells us that if (1) we have a generalization, and (2) we have a member of the class to which the generalization applies, then (3) we can create a new statement that is specifically about this member of the class by substituting the name of the member for the general class term. Thus, given the claim "If a person is a presidential candidate, that person is at least 35 years old," which we will abbreviate as "[C→O]," we can use substitution to infer that "If Jones is a presidential candidate, then he is at least 35 years old." The square brackets around "C→O" are a device for indicating that we are dealing with a generalization.[6] To show the substitution in our abbreviations, we add "J" (for Jones) to the statements into which his name has been substituted: "C-J→O-J." We can now complete the argument chain:

1. <u>[C → O]</u>

C1. C-J → O-J

C1. C-J → O-J

2. <u>~O-J</u>

C2. ~C-J

From statement 1 we can validly infer C1, using substitution. This, together with the second premise, gives us a valid modus tollens argument (MT) leading to C2, the conclusion that Jones is not a candidate. The result is an argument chain in which each component argument is valid; thus, the entire chain is valid.

So far we have been considering only arguments that concern straightforward factual or logical claims. In everyday life we encounter many other arguments in contexts that introduce new variations on this pattern, and so it is important to know how some of the most common variations affect arguments. The two most important variations are arguments with **qualifiers** or **hedging,** and **practical reasoning** about what we should do.

Often we find ourselves reasoning with premises that we think are true, but about which we may have some doubt. These doubts can be signaled by hedging the statement with words like "probably," "might be," or "possibly." This hedging affects how we reason. Consider the two statements in 3:16 as potential premises of an argument.

3:16.   It will probably rain today. If it rains today, then the picnic will be canceled.

We should not infer "The picnic will be canceled." The truth of the conclusion is not guaranteed by the truth of the premises because the first premise contains the term "probably." But it does seem reasonable to conclude that the picnic will *probably* be canceled. The difference between the two conclusions is that the former is left unqualified, while the latter is hedged in the same manner as the first premise. Alternatively, the conclusion might be more strongly hedged by asserting that there is *some chance* the picnic will be canceled. In general, the greater the expression of uncertainty about a proposition, the stronger the hedging.

You should have little difficulty in determining whether hedging has been carried through to the conclusion properly. The following list of hedging terms, arranges them more or less in order from weak (expressing very little doubt) to strong (expressing a great deal of doubt).

almost certainly
very likely
probably
possibly
maybe
perhaps
there is some chance that

A number of steps should be followed to determine whether or not an argument involving hedging is valid.

1. First write out the argument in standard form, putting each instance of hedging in parentheses to the left of the statement it modifies.

2. Determine whether **the underlying argument** is valid. (The underlying argument is the argument stripped of all the hedging terms.) If the underlying argument is invalid, then so is the original, hedged version.

3. If the underlying argument is valid, check to see that no more than one premise of the original argument is modified by a hedging term. If more than one premise is hedged, then the argument is invalid.

4. If only one premise is hedged, check to see whether it is an atomic proposition or the negation of an atomic proposition. If the hedged premise is logically complex (e.g., a conditional or disjunctive statement), then the argument is invalid unless a further condition is met. That condition is that the underlying argument would remain valid if the hedged proposition were replaced by a single letter throughout.[7]

5. Finally, compare the hedging of the conclusion with the hedging of the premise. If all the preceding steps are satisfied and the hedging in the conclusion is equal to or stronger than the hedging in the single premise, then the argument is valid.

If all the conditions in these five steps are satisfied, then the hedged argument is valid. Many hedged arguments turn out to be invalid, but you should not conclude from this that they are worthless. As explained in Chapter 4, invalid arguments can still be good ones if they are inductively strong. Our concern here is solely with validity.

The technique for assessing the validity of hedged arguments is illustrated by discussing the example in 3:17, given first in English, and then as it would be written in standard form:

3:17. Either the administration must cut spending, or the country will face an even larger deficit. The administration is very unlikely to cut spending. So we will probably have a larger deficit.

Let C = "The administration cuts spending," and D = "The country will have a larger deficit."

D V C

(very likely) ~D

(probably) C

The underlying argument is a valid disjunctive syllogism (DS), the single hedged premise is the negation of an atomic proposition, and the conclusion is more strongly hedged than the premise. Therefore, the argument is valid. (If only the first premise had been hedged, the argument would have failed the test of step 4 since the underlying argument would no longer be valid if "(D V C)" were replaced by "P" throughout.)

The last variation of propositional reasoning we consider here involves practical reasoning. As we noted at the beginning of Chapter 1, critical thinking also involves reasoning about what we should do. Any argument that draws a conclusion about what I (or some other person or group, or anyone) should do is an example of practical reasoning. Argument 3:18 is a typical example.

3:18. Energy conservation efforts are a necessary condition for reducing the amount of damage to the environment. Since we would like to reduce the amount of environmental damage, we should make an effort to conserve energy.

In most cases of practical reasoning, the truth of the premises cannot guarantee the truth of the conclusion. Too many other factors, not explicitly stated in the premises, can affect the truth of the conclusion. For example, if it were vital to our national interest that we produce more synthetic fuels from coal and if this cannot be done without huge investments of energy and damage to the environment, then it would no longer follow that we should try to conserve energy. Rather, we should expend even more energy to produce synthetic fuels. Note that in this case, the premises of 3:18 would still be true, but our desire to reduce the amount of environmental damage would be overriden by the more important goal of protecting the national interest. In the same way, although it usually makes sense to eat if one feels hungry, one should abstain from food and drink before undergoing surgery. The goal of minimizing risk overrides our desire to feel less hungry.

How, then, can we take into account the role of all these other factors? In many cases, the conclusion is not really meant to be unconditional, but should be understood as claiming "*Other things being equal,* we should. . . ." Thus, the conclusion does not simply ignore all the other factors that might affect our reasoning; it claims that if there are no factors that count against the proposed action, we should do it.

When the context makes it reasonable to interpret the conclusion as qualified in this way, we can evaluate the practical reasoning by means of the following steps:

1. Express the special elements of practical reasoning with prefixes (for the premises) such as "we want it to be the case that . . . ," "she wants it to be the case that . . . ," "everyone wants . . . ," and so on. The conclusion should have a matching prefix, such as "we should bring it about that . . . ," and the qualifier "other things being equal. . . ."

2. Write the rest of the argument in standard form to the right of the appropriate qualifiers.

3. Determine whether the underlying argument is valid, whether there is a "want" prefix in front of one premise and a "should" prefix in front of the conclusion, and whether the conclusion is properly qualified. If all three conditions are met, the argument is valid.

If the context of the argument in 3:18 makes it clear that the conclusion is only meant to be of the form "Other things being equal, we should . . . ," we could put it into standard form as follows:

$D \rightarrow I$

(We want . . .) D

(Other things being equal we should . . .) I

Since the underlying argument has the valid modus ponens form, and all the other conditions are met, the argument is valid.

Of course, in many other instances of practical reasoning, it is not appropriate, correct, or desirable to qualify the conclusion. In these cases, the open-ended nature of practical reasoning remains, and the arguments cannot be deductively valid. Such cases are discussed more fully in Chapter 9.

EXERCISES

Reconstruct and evaluate the following arguments: supply any missing premises; if there is an argument chain, break it down into its component arguments; identify and symbolize any substitution, practical reasoning, or hedging. In cases of practical reasoning, you may assume that the conclusion is intended as qualified or conditional, that is, as "Other things being equal, . . ." Finally, indicate whether the argument is valid, and explain your judgment.

1. Scientists often defend research on monkeys as a means of gaining knowledge to help humans. But if monkeys feel pain the same way humans do, it would be wrong to cause them pain. If they do not feel pain the way we do, the whole analogy between us and them breaks down. The experiments will yield knowledge that can help humans only if the analogy does not break down. Thus, whether monkeys feel pain or not, these experiments are unjustifiable.

2. Sally will get into medical school only if she gets an "A" in organic chemistry. Sally's doing well on the final exam is a necessary condition for her getting an "A" in that course. She wants to get into medical school; therefore, she should study for her exam.

3. If a person is in this course, he or she will have heard of modus ponens. Stanley has never heard of modus ponens, so he is not in this course.

4. It seems probable that if the governor applies pressure, the electric company will not raise its rates this year. So rates might go up since the governor refuses to apply pressure.

*5. Since the vast majority of neurosurgeons are men, it is very likely that if Jones is a neurosurgeon, Jones is a man. Similarly, since very few men have received formal medical training, it is very likely that if Jones is a man then Jones has received no formal medical training. Therefore, it is probable that if Jones is a neurosurgeon then Jones has received no formal medical training.

6. A necessary condition for eliminating poverty is to increase the wealth of each citizen above the poverty line. This can be done by giving every poor person enough money to bring him or her above the poverty line. Since we wish to eliminate poverty, we should give every poor person enough money to raise him or her above the poverty line.

7. Either the leaders of the Soviet Union were genuinely concerned about the safety of their athletes in Los Angeles or they had some other reason for boycotting the 23rd Olympic Games. It is unlikely that there was any serious threat to Soviet athletes at the Games, and so the Soviet leaders probably had some other reason for boycotting them.

*8. There is no smoke without fire. Huge clouds of smoke have been seen in the foothills of southern France. Therefore, there is probably a fire there.

Notes

[1]The symbols we choose are a matter of convention. Many logic books use the notation given here, but there are alternatives. Some people use a hyphen or a dash rather than a tilde as the symbol for negation; a dot is sometimes used in place of the ampersand for conjunction, and a horseshoe instead of an arrow for the truth-functional conditional.

[2]Notice that parentheses are used to ensure that the statement is unambiguous. In English, word order, punctuation, and other devices can be used to indicate how to group or organize the various parts of the complex sentence. When writing sentences in standard form, we must use parentheses to accomplish this.

[3]The truth-functional definition of the conditional is the weakest and the most basic of the many senses in which we ordinarily use the phrase "if . . . then. . . ." Other senses, such as those occurring in causal or subjunctive conditionals, can be regarded as the truth-functional connective plus other conditions of a nontruth-functional sort (e.g., that the states of affairs described in the antecedent and the consequent are connected in an appropriate way).

[4]Strictly speaking, what this shows is that the *form of argument* is invalid. As explained in Chapter 1, in the section Validity and Soundness, an argument is invalid only if it exemplifies *no* valid form of argument. Thus, showing that an argument exemplifies *one* invalid form does not guarantee that the argument itself is invalid *unless there is no valid form that it exemplifies.* This qualification should be understood throughout this section; it is discussed again in the following section Some Common Forms of Argument.

[5]This type of argument is invalid because the wedge stands for the *inclusive* "or." If the "or" were *exclusive,* the argument would be valid.

[6]The square brackets are necessary here because "C→O" by itself does not adequately translate the generalization "If anyone is a presidential candidate, then that person is over 35 years old." Strictly speaking, letters such as "C" and "O" should stand for determinate propositions, not expressions involving a variable such as "anyone." A proper formal treatment of generalizations requires expanding propositional logic to include predicate terms and quantifiers. Despite its limitations, one of the advantages of categorical logic is that it can handle such generalizations far more simply.

[7]Thus, the argument "Almost certainly (A ∨ B); (A ∨ B)→C; therefore, very likely C" is valid because the underlying argument would remain valid if "(A ∨ B)" were replaced by the single letter "P."

CHAPTER
4

Inductive Arguments

In the previous three chapters we have given rules for recognizing valid arguments and distinguishing them from those that are invalid. Only valid arguments can be sound, but this does not mean that all invalid arguments are worthless; for although the premises of an invalid argument cannot guarantee the truth of its conclusion, they still might make the conclusion highly probable. In an **inductive argument,** the goal is to supply premises that make it *probable* that the conclusion is true.

Any invalid argument in which the premises, if true, make the conclusion highly probable is **inductively strong.** If the premises do not make the conclusion highly probable, then the argument is either **inductively weak** or **worthless.** It will be **worthless** if the premises actually make it more probable that the conclusion is false than that it is true. If the premises do something toward making it more probable than not that the conclusion is true, but fail to make the conclusion highly probable, then we say that the argument is **inductively weak.**[1]

Inductive arguments are common in the empirical sciences and in everyday life. They typically occur when one is trying rationally to support a conclusion on the basis of evidence, even though the evidence does not logically imply the conclusion. In these situations probability is the best that one can hope for. The aim of this chapter is to help you recognize, classify, and evaluate inductive arguments.

Deductively Valid and Inductive Arguments Compared

In this and later chapters we refer to invalid arguments that are either inductively weak or inductively strong (but not worthless) as **inductive arguments.** Use of these terms can create the misleading impression that inductive arguments are a species of argument separate from the deductive ones. This impression is misleading because, *by definition, all inductive arguments are deductively invalid.* Thus, there are not two separate groups of arguments, the deductive and the inductive; rather there are deductively valid arguments and deductively invalid arguments. The invalid arguments can then be divided into those that are inductive (either strong or weak) and those that are worthless. With this important proviso about the meaning of the term *"inductive argument,"* we can compare inductive arguments with deductively valid arguments as follows:

1. In a valid argument all the information in the conclusion is already contained implicitly in the premises. In inductive arguments, the conclusion introduces new information that goes beyond the content of the premises. Because the conclusion of an inductive argument adds information, or amplifies the premises, inductive arguments are said to be **ampliative.** Of course, both inductive and valid deductive arguments can have conclusions that are *psychologically* surprising or express results that are new to us; but *logically,* the content of the conclusion of a valid argument cannot exceed the content of the premises, whereas the content of the conclusion of an inductive argument always does.

2. Because they are ampliative, inductive arguments always involve some risk. Even in the strongest inductive argument, there is always a chance that the conclusion is false even when all the premises are true. By contrast, in a valid deductive argument, the truth of the premises guarantees the truth of the conclusion. In a good inductive argument the premises strongly support the conclusion, but they do not guarantee its truth.

3. Valid deductive arguments are complete. If an argument is valid, then no matter what additional information is added to its premises, the argument remains valid. Inductive arguments are incomplete; adding information to the premises of an inductive argument often changes its strength. A good example of this is provided by arguments that draw conclusions about whether a particular person will die of a specified disease. The likelihood of John Doe's dying of cancer, given that he works with asbestos, is increased significantly when we add the further information that he smokes cigarettes.

4. Either a deductive argument is valid or it is invalid. There is no middle ground. By contrast, inductive arguments can vary in strength along a continuum from inductively weak to inductively strong.

There is an intimate connection between these four points of contrast. It is *because* inductive arguments are ampliative that they are incomplete and risky. Argument 4:1 illustrates these points:

4:1. All of the pizzas we have inspected from factory X have contained rodent hairs. The pizza you just purchased was made at factory X. Therefore, it will be similarly contaminated.

The conclusion of the argument goes beyond the content of the premises, since the first premise only tells us about the pizzas that have *already* been inspected. Thus, it is possible that the conclusion could be false even though the premises are true. Finally, new information (e.g., the fact that the pizzas we inspected were all manufactured six months ago, just before the factory made major changes in its sanitation policies, or that the pizza we just bought was from the same manufacturing lot as the ones inspected) can weaken or strengthen the argument.

Inductive arguments pose a theoretical problem: Can we justify the claim that the premises of any inductive argument really support the conclusion? In the history of philosophy, this question has become known as **the problem of induction.** Philosophers have been discussing this problem and proposing solutions to it since the time of David Hume. More than anyone else David Hume, a Scottish philosopher of the eighteenth century, pointed out the difficulty of justifying even the simplest of inductive inferences that we make in everyday life.

For example, we feel confident that taking two aspirin tablets will relieve our pain the next time we have a mild headache. When asked why we are so confident that aspirin will relieve our pain rather than intensify it, we appeal to our past experience. There is no *logical* necessity that aspirin will continue to relieve pain as it has in the past.

Thus, it would seem that there can be no deductive justification of induction.[2] On the other hand, if we try to justify inductive arguments inductively (by saying, for example, that such arguments have always worked in the past), we will have presupposed the very thing we set out to justify, namely, the reliability of induction. It is difficult to see how this kind of **circular reasoning** can justify anything. (For more on circular arguments see Chapter 5 in the section Responding to Arguments).

Many solutions to the problem of induction have been proposed, but there is still no consensus about which, if any, is correct.[3] Accordingly, in the following sections of this chapter we classify some major forms of inductively strong arguments without attempting to *prove* that they are strong.

EXERCISES

For each of the following arguments, supply any missing premises and decide whether the argument is best interpreted as deductively valid or as inductive.

1. No Muslims eat pork. So the next Muslims we meet probably will not have bacon for breakfast.

* **2.** It is well-known that copper conducts electricity. So this piece of copper tubing will conduct electricity.

* **3.** Only 20 percent of the oil that has been discovered in the Soviet Union is heavily contaminated with sulfur. Thus, there is an 80 percent chance that the oil deposits recently found in Siberia will yield oil low in sulfur.

4. A recent survey of 400 newly registered drivers revealed that those who had completed a driver education course had 15 percent more traffic accidents than those who had not taken such a course. Clearly, driver education courses do not improve driver safety.

5. Marcos is a crook. Therefore, anyone who knows Marcos knows at least one crook.

6. Far more people die each year from aspirin poisoning than from the side effects of birth control pills. Therefore, birth control pills are safer drugs than aspirin.

7. The chances of throwing any particular number with a fair die is 1 in 6. Therefore, the chances of throwing a double 2 with a pair of fair dice is 1 in 36.

8. Only three American presidents have been below the average height of American males at the time of their election. Thus, Melvin Short, who is 5 foot 2 inches tall, has only a remote chance of being elected president on the Communist Party ticket.

9. Every time I have brushed my teeth with powdered pumice, they have come out gleaming white. So I should brush with powdered pumice before my next job interview.

10. There are cases reported in the literature of men contracting toxic shock syndrome. So it is false that the use of superabsorbent tampons is the only cause of toxic shock syndrome.

Inductive Strength and Inductive Reliability

Despite the many differences between them, in one important respect the concepts of validity and inductive strength are similar—both are concerned solely with the *relation* between the premises and the conclusion, regardless of the status of the premises. Even if all the premises of an argument are false, it will still be inductively strong if the conclusion is highly probable *relative to* those premises. Whether the premises are actually true or false is irrelevant to an assessment of its inductive strength. The crucial issue is whether the conclusion would be highly probable if all the premises were true. Argument 4:2 is an example of an inductively strong argument in which the premises are false:

4:2.   Helium is a radioactive gas.

Argon is a radioactive gas.

Neon is a radioactive gas.

Radon is a radioactive gas.

The premises of 4:2 are false: helium, argon, and neon are not radioactive; but if they were, it is highly probable that radon and other elements in the same column of the Periodic Table (Column VIII, the so-called inert or noble gases) would share the same property. Thus, the argument is inductively strong despite the falsity of its premises. Another example illustrates the same point:

4:3.   Cheryl Tiegs eats eight big meals a day.

Cheryl Tiegs is obese.

As in argument 4:2, the premise in 4:3 is false, but if it were true, then it is highly probable that Ms. Tiegs would be obese. You might be tempted to think that she would not just probably be obese, but would definitely be obese if she ate eight big meals a day. In other words, you might consider turning 4:3 into a valid deductive argument by adding further statements to its premises. We could do this in a number of ways. One way is to add a premise that asserts "Anyone who eats eight big meals a day will be obese." But this does not help the argument; in fact, it makes matters worse. In 4:3 we were trying to decide whether Cheryl Tiegs's eating eight big meals a day makes it *probable* that *she* is obese. By adding our new premise, we would have to defend the assertion that *anyone* who ate eight big meals a day would *certainly* be obese. Our reason for expecting that someone who eats eight big meals a day will be obese is our past experience: we have seen that people who eat a great deal more than normal tend to be obese. In short, we rely on inductive reasoning.

Contrast argument 4:3 with 4:4:

4:4.   Zebras and horses belong to different species; therefore, they cannot interbreed and produce fertile offspring.

As in the previous example, we must decide whether to interpret this as an inductively strong argument (based on past observations of attempts to interbreed different species), or to reconstruct it as a deductive argument. To make this argument deductively valid, the missing premise would have to be "Animals of different species cannot interbreed and produce fertile offspring." This premise is true because it follows from the way species are defined; it does not require further inductive reasoning to establish its truth. For that reason, 4:4 should be reconstructed as a deductively valid argument, in contrast to the argument in 4:3.

Examples 4:1 through 4:3 also illustrate that inductive arguments do not always move from particular to general. Just like deductive arguments, inductive arguments can move from general to particular, from particular to particular, from general to general, and sometimes from particular to general.

Since inductive strength concerns solely the relation between premises and conclusion, it is useful to have another term for an inductively strong argument in which all the premises are true. We call such arguments **inductively reliable.** Mere inductive strength, by itself, is only half the story. Only when the argument is inductively reliable—that is, when it is inductively strong *and* all its premises are true—can we rely on the argument to establish the probable truth of its conclusion. If one or more of the premises are false, then the argument is **unreliable.** Just as strength is the inductive analog of validity, reliability is the inductive analog of soundness.

It should be obvious from the examples already given that not all inductive arguments are strong solely by virtue of their form. The strength of many, such as 4:3, depends crucially on the meanings of their constituent terms such as "obesity." Furthermore, these arguments work partly because of additional information, which does not appear explicitly in the premises, such as the generalization that overeating tends to cause obesity. In light of this, our project must inevitably be modest. The best we can do is to concentrate on those types of inductive arguments that do display a general form independent of their content; but even here, additional information, not explicitly stated but implicitly presupposed, plays a crucial role in determining inductive strength.

EXERCISES

Which of the following statements are true? If any of the statements are false, show this by giving a counterexample.

1. All inductively reliable arguments are inductively strong.

2. All inductively strong arguments are inductively reliable.

3. All inductively weak arguments are inductively unreliable.

4. All inductively unreliable arguments are inductively weak.

* 5. All inductively weak arguments have improbable conclusions.

6. No arguments with false conclusions are inductively strong.

7. No arguments with false conclusions are inductively reliable.

8. All inductively reliable arguments have true conclusions.

9. Any inductively weak argument can be transformed into a deductively valid one by adding appropriate premises.

*10. No inductively reliable argument can be weakened by adding further information to its premises.

Inductive Arguments from a Sample to a Population

One common form of inductive argument involves reasoning from premises about a sample of things (kinds of things, or persons) to a conclusion about the entire population of those things (kinds of things or persons). Such arguments are called **inductive generalizations.** In this section, we consider how such arguments work.

As one might expect, the most important factor in determining the strength of these arguments is the relation between the sample and the population. If the sample represents the population accurately, the generalization will be inductively strong. Thus, it is essential to pay close attention to the nature of this relation.

In analyzing an argument, it may be difficult to tell how the sample is related to the population, since this relation is often left unspecified. For example, only rarely does someone state that the sample is representative of the population, or that the sample was randomly selected. However, the strength of these arguments depends on what this relation is, and so a premise that states the relationship explicitly is necessary. The "**R-premise,**" as we will call it, fulfills this function: it describes the relation between sample and population.

Inductive arguments, therefore, are incomplete if they do not explicitly state an R-premise. In these cases, when the argument is put into standard form, we must treat the R-premise as a missing premise and attempt to reconstruct it using the principle of charity. The specific wording of the R-premise will vary from case to case, depending on the context and what we can reasonably infer about the author's intentions.

It should be emphasized that even when an R-premise is added explicitly, the resulting argument is still not deductively valid. Stating the R-premise explicitly is not a futile attempt to turn inductive arguments into valid deductive ones; rather, it asserts what the author is assuming to be the relationship between the sample and the population. This will help us later in evaluating inductive arguments, for if we can show that the R-premise is false, then the argument is unreliable.

Having seen the importance of the R-premise in any inductive argument, we are now ready to examine the two most common types of inductive generalizations: **universal generalization** (UG), and **statistical generalization** (SG). The principal difference between these is that a UG concludes that all members of a population have a certain property, whereas an SG concludes that a specified fraction or percentage of a population has a given property. In other words, the conclusion of a UG is a universal generalization; the conclusion of an SG is a statistical generalization.[4] Here is a schematic outline of the standard forms of UG and SG with the R-premise of each stated explicitly.

UNIVERSAL GENERALIZATION (UG):

Observed As all have property P.

The observed As stand in relation R to the entire population of As.

All A's have property P.

STATISTICAL GENERALIZATION (SG):

X percent of observed As have property P.

The observed As stand in relation R to the entire population of As.

X percent of all As have property P.

Several points should be noted about UGs and SGs when they are written in these standard forms. Although the sample in each case is described as being the class of "observed As," this talk about observation should not be taken too literally. Only rarely does the information about the sample come directly from visual observations. The important thing is that we have, by whatever means, obtained information about a subset of the population of As.

Second, there is no mention of time in these forms of argument. Presumably, all the information we have about the sample must have been collected in the past, up to and including the present. In both UG and SG, the conclusion is about the entire population of As—past, present, and future. Thus, although such arguments may seem to be from the past into the future, actually there is no temporal restriction on the scope of their conclusions. They draw conclusions about unobserved As in the present and past, as well as conclusions about (as yet) unobserved As in the future.

The inductive strength of a UG or SG depends on the specific wording of the R-premise. These inductive generalizations are inductively strong only if the R-premise specifies that the sample *closely resembles* or is *strongly representative of* the entire population. These or any other type of inductively strong argument are reliable if and only if all the premises, including the R-premise, are true.

To tell what the author thinks the relation between the sample and the population is, we must pay close attention to the context and how the argument is worded. If she has taken some pains to try to match the sample with the known properties of the population and asserts the conclusion in an unqualified way, then presumably she thinks the sample is strongly representative of the population. If, on the other hand, her sample is small, casually selected, and the conclusion strongly hedged, this is good evidence that the R-premise should state merely that the sample is representative or even weakly representative of the population. In reconstructing these arguments our aim is to reflect faithfully what the author had in mind.

For example, imagine we are faced with an argument in which the author expresses a strong conviction in the truth of an unqualified conclusion drawn from a sample *we* judge to be quite unrepresentative of the population. In such a case we should add an R-premise asserting that the sample is strongly representative of the population. Our evaluation would then be that the argument is strong but unreliable (since the R-premise is false). The alternative would be to add an R-premise stating that the sample is unrepresentative of the population. In this case the argument would be weak, even though its premises are now true. The first alternative is preferable because it comes closer to representing the argument that the author actually intended to give.

We can illustrate these points by considering how we would reconstruct the UG in 4:5:

4:5. The only safe recommendation we can make is that no "recovered" alcoholic should attempt to resume social drinking. All the programs that have attempted to teach former alcoholics to drink while keeping their drinking under control have been total failures.

This argument is a UG because it draws a conclusion about all former or recovered alcoholics from evidence about a property found in all members of a sample. To put the argument into standard form, we note that the sample consists of former alcoholics who participated in programs that attempted to teach them to drink in a controlled manner; the population is *all* former alcoholics. We assume that when the author refers to these programs as being "total failures," this means they failed to teach *any* of their participants to resume social drinking safely. Since the conclusion is hedged to some extent ("the only safe recommendation we can make"), this suggests that the author thinks the sample is representative of the population but not strongly representative. (It would have been different, if, for example, the passage had read "we cannot emphasize too strongly that . . .") Thus, in standard form, 4:5 would look like this:

Observed former alcoholics all have the property of being unable to safely resume social drinking.
Observed former alcoholics are representative of the entire population of former alcoholics.
All former alcoholics are unable to safely resume social drinking.

UGs are often used when there is reason to believe the population is uniform in some respect—that is, when its members are thought to have something significant in common. SGs often deal with populations that are arbitrary collections of objects (or persons) for which no theoretical reason exists to expect uniformity. For this reason, SGs usually have to rely on techniques such as random sampling to give some assurance that the sample is representative of the population. What particular percentage of As have property P must be determined empirically, and the exact figure can change with time.

Even when an exhaustive survey is physically possible (i.e., when the population is finite and reasonably accessible), it is often undesirable or prohibitively expensive. An example of the former case is taking a blood sample to infer the percentage of various gases in a patient's blood. We could remove all the blood from a patient's body for analysis, but this is highly undesirable for the patient. Here, as elsewhere, when reasoning inductively, we have to rely on our background knowledge. If we were interested in the gaseous composition of arterial blood being supplied to the brain, a sample of venous blood from the arm would not be representative.

The preceding remarks about reconstructing the R-premise of inductive arguments apply to both UGs and SGs. So far, we have focused our attention on UGs. Argument 4:6 is a simple example of an SG.

4:6. Based on a random survey conducted by telephone, pollsters predict that only 26 percent of registered voters will vote in local elections this year.

The conclusion of 4:6 indicates that we are dealing with an SG. The premise is not stated explicitly, but the reference to "a random survey" suggests the following reconstruction in standard form:

Twenty-six percent of the registered voters in a telephone survey indicated that they plan to vote in local elections this year.
The people surveyed were randomly selected from the entire population of registered voters.

Twenty-six percent of all registered voters will vote in local elections this year.

SGs are indispensable in business, economics, and government. Although the U.S. Constitution requires a census every 10 years, this sort of complete survey is costly, difficult, and not as accurate as one might think. The Census Bureau estimates that the 1970 census missed about 2.5 percent of the population as a whole, including 7.7 percent of all black Americans. For other sorts of information, including unemployment rates, voter registration, and living conditions, the government relies on SGs. In many situations (including inventories of large amounts of stock, or determination of royalties based on how many times a record is played) inductive arguments based on sampling are much cheaper and often yield conclusions that are nearly as accurate as, and sometimes more accurate than, obtaining the same information about the population by counting every item.

Given the differences between inductive and deductive arguments that were listed in the section Deductively Valid and Inductive Arguments Compared, it should be clear by now that there is no mechanical method for measuring inductive strength. To evaluate inductive arguments, we must first understand the goals of inductive reasoning and examine how those goals can be realized. After having studied the features that make arguments inductively strong, we can formulate guidelines for evaluating inductive arguments in general. These guidelines are discussed in the section Evaluating and Constructing Inductive Arguments. First, we must understand what makes an argument inductively strong.

The goal of both UGs and SGs is to learn about a large group—the population described in the conclusion—by examining a small portion of that group—the sample described in the premises. We use this sort of reasoning all the time; a simple example is tasting a spoonful of sauce (the sample) to tell whether the whole pot of stew (the population) needs more spice. This example can help us understand how generalizations can achieve their goal of gaining accurate information about the population on the basis of a sample.

We feel confident about judging the properties of our stew on the basis of a small taste because we believe the sauce in the spoon has the same ingredients in the same proportions as the rest of the sauce in the pot. We can try to increase our chances of getting a representative sample by stirring the stew before tasting it. This mixes the ingredients more thoroughly, so that we will be less likely to dip into an isolated area of more (or less) heavily spiced sauce. If our population is well-blended or **homogeneous,** we can be more confident that a small sample will have the same composition as all the other portions of the stew.

Other inductive arguments concern populations that are much less homogeneous and, unlike a stew, cannot be stirred. For example, if I am trying to draw a conclusion about students at a university, my population will include a great deal of variation within it: seniors and freshmen, men and women, people of different ages and majors, and so on. Any one student will be a member of several of these subgroups, and hence will not have the same general properties or makeup as all the other members of the population. Since I cannot blend my population the way I could stir the pot of stew, I must obtain a sample that is large enough and selected so as to include the variations that exist within the whole population. In the same way, if my stew contains many large chunks of different ingredients, I may want to include some sauce, a piece of meat, a chunk of onion, and so on, in my sample.

Our examples suggest there are two main ways in which inductive reasoning from a sample to a population might be unreliable. First, I may make a mistake in my observation of the sample; if I have just eaten something salty, I may not form an accurate judgment about the taste of my stew. This is an example of a **nonsampling error.** (Nonsampling errors are discussed further in Chapter 8 in the section Collecting Statistical Data.) If a UG or SG commits a nonsampling error, the first premise of the argument written in standard form will be false. Second, my sample might fail to be representative of the population perhaps because the sample is too small or because it was not randomly selected. This is an example of a **sampling error.** Depending on the wording of the R-premise, this might make the R-premise false. Even when the sample is reasonably large and randomly selected, its properties will generally not correspond *exactly* with those in the population. This kind of **random sampling error** is explored in the next section. The possibilities of both nonsampling and sampling errors must be considered when evaluating the strength of any inductive argument from a sample to a population.

EXERCISES

1. A retailer receives 20 boxes of oranges, packed four layers deep in each box. She examines the top layer of each box and finds that all the oranges in these layers are grade A quality. From this she concludes that all the oranges in the consignment are definitely of grade A quality. What kind of inductive argument is involved here? Write out the argument in standard form, adding the R-premise explicitly. Is the argument strong or weak? Explain your answer.

2. Concerned about the rapid decline in the population of blue whales (as reflected in diminishing catch rates), the International Whaling Commission tried to estimate their total number by several different methods. One of these methods involved first marking some whales by firing a foot-long blue metal cylinder into their blubber. Commercial whalers were then asked to examine all the blue whales they caught during the year to see how many of them were marked. Assuming that 50 whales were marked and the ratio of marked to unmarked whales in the year's catch was 1 to 19, explain how you would estimate the total number of blue whales in the ocean. How would your estimate be affected by each of the following factors? (a) Not all the metal markers that were fired at the whales actually stuck in their blubber, but some ricocheted off. (b) All the whales fired at were actually marked but the whalers missed some of the markers when they dismembered their catch. For further information on this topic, see Scott McVay, "The Last of the Great Whales," *Scientific American* 215 (August 1966): 13–21, and D. G. Chapman, "The Plight of the Whales," in J. Tanur et al. (eds.), *Statistics: A Guide to the Unknown,* pp. 105–112.

*3. The owner of a large warehouse has a stock of about 1 million spare automobile parts he wishes to inventory. He proposes that his staff count every single item. Why would this be a bad way to conduct the inventory? Describe a better method.

4. Laboratory tests for the toxicity of chemicals are always performed on special strains of animals, such as rats and mice, which are specially bred to be genetically identical. Why? Such tests also use a control group of animals who do not receive the chemical, randomly selected from the same initial population as the test group. Why?

5. A notorious fiasco in the history of sampling was the poll conducted by the *Literary Digest* to predict the winner of the U.S. presidential election of 1936. The magazine mailed out 10 million ballots to a sample of voters randomly selected from lists of automobile and telephone owners. Of these, over 2 million were returned. On the basis of this unusually large sample, the *Literary Digest* confidently predicted a sure victory for the Republican candidate, Alfred M. Landon. In fact, Franklin D. Roosevelt won, receiving more than 60 percent of the votes cast. What went wrong?

Statistical Generalizations Based on Simple Random Sampling

Imagine that we have a box containing 1,000 balls, of which 600 are white and 400 black. Obviously, "60 percent" is the correct answer to the question, "What is the percentage of balls in the box that are white?" Now, assume that we try to answer this question, not by examining every ball, but by taking a **simple random sample** of 100 balls. We are unlikely to observe *exactly* 60 white balls in our sample. Assume we find 56 white balls. If we were then to conclude, by SG, that 56 percent of all the balls are white, our conclusion would be wrong. Fortunately, since the sampling was random, we can estimate the size of the **random sampling error** by considering what we would get if we recorded the results of a whole series of such samplings.

Imagine that after taking our first sample of 100 balls, we return these balls to the box and thoroughly mix them up. We then randomly select another sample of 100 balls and, this time, we find that 62 percent of the balls in our sample are white. Again, we return the balls to the box, mix them up, and take another sample of 100. Each time we record the percentage of white balls observed in our sample. We repeat this procedure several hundred times and plot the values obtained in our samples against the number of times we obtain a particular value. The resulting graph is the **sampling distribution curve** for a sample size of 100. For a very large number of repetitions, this curve approximates the **normally distributed** curve shown in Figure 4-1.

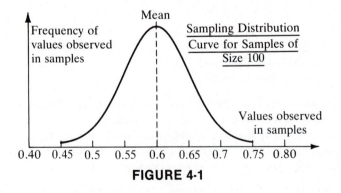

FIGURE 4-1

As we might expect, most of the values shown in Figure 4-1 cluster around 0.6, or 60 percent; but very low and very high values are possible. We want to know the probability that the fraction of white balls in any single sample of 100 balls will differ significantly from 0.6. We can estimate this probability from a knowledge of the **standard deviation** (SD) of the sampling distribution curve.[5]

The standard deviation is a number that describes how the curve spreads out from its central point. For any normal distribution, 68 percent of all the values under the curve lie within 1 SD on either side of the mean. (The mean is the average of all the values observed in the samples.) Ninety-five percent of all the values lie within 2 SDs either side of the mean; 99.7 percent lie within 3 SDs either side of the mean. These properties of all normally distributed curves are illustrated in Figure 4-2.

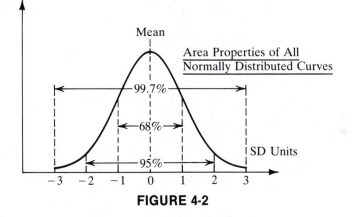

FIGURE 4-2

For a sample size of 100, the SD of a normally distributed sampling distribution curve is 0.05, or 5 percent. Thus, in our example, where we obtained a value of 56 percent in our first sample of 100 balls, there is a 68 percent chance that the true value lies within 1 SD of 56 percent. That is, there is a 68 percent chance that the true value lies within the range 51 percent (56 − 5) to 61 percent (56 + 5). Similarly, there is a 95 percent chance that the true value lies in the range 56 ± 10 percent. In other words, there is a 95 percent chance that the fraction of white balls in the box is between 46 and 66 percent. The reasoning behind this last conclusion is illustrated in Figure 4-3.

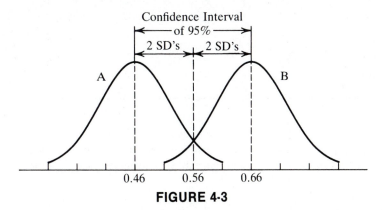

FIGURE 4-3

Our single sample of size 100 gave us a value of 56 percent. Assume that we want a 95 percent chance that our estimate of the true value for the population is correct. This is called a **confidence level** of 95 percent. We know that the true sampling distribution curve is normally distributed and that, for a sample of size 100, it has an SD of 5 percent. Though we do not know exactly where it lies on the x-axis, we can fix its lower and upper limits once we have decided to accept a confidence interval of 95 percent. It cannot lie any further to the left than curve A, whose mean is 46 percent (2 SDs left of 56%). Why not? If it did, there would be less than a 2.5 percent chance that we would have observed the value of 56 percent in our sample, and this falls outside the confidence level we have decided to accept. Similarly, the true sampling distribution curve cannot lie any further to the right than curve B. But it could lie anywhere between these two limits. Thus, the best we can do is to say that at the 95 percent level, the true value lies between 46 and 66 percent. In the long run, our conclusion that the true value lies in this range will be correct 19 times out of 20.

For most purposes a 95 percent confidence interval is sufficient. If we wanted to be 99.7 percent certain of including the correct value in our conclusion, then we would have to extend the range to 3 SDs (in this case, 15 percentage points) either side of the value observed in our sample.

Table 4-1 gives approximate 95 percent confidence intervals for cases in which we have observed a property in 30 to 70 percent of the sample. (When the observed frequency in the sample is close to 0 or 100 percent, the figures in Table 4-1 are no longer reliable.)

TABLE 4-1

SAMPLE SIZE	SD	95% CONFIDENCE INTERVALS
10	15%	±30%
25	11%	±22%
50	7%	±14%
100	5%	±10%
250	3%	±6%
500	2%	±4%
1000	1.5%	±3%
1500	1%	±2%

In the light of the preceding discussion, we can formulate a more sophisticated version of the inductive argument SG when this is based on simple random sampling:

STATISTICAL GENERALIZATION BASED ON SIMPLE RANDOM SAMPLING (SGRS)

X percent of As in sample S have property P.
Sample S, of size N, was randomly selected from the entire population of As.

The fraction of As having property P in the entire population is X ± D, at the Z percent confidence level.

One important moral of simple random sampling is that the accuracy of one's estimates depends only on the absolute size of the sample, *not* on its size relative to the size of the population. The bigger the sample, the smaller the SD of the sampling distribution curve, and thus the smaller the confidence interval. In part this reflects common sense. If you want a more precise estimate of the fraction of Americans who support ratification of the ERA, you should increase the size of your sample. But it also means that regardless of whether the population contains several thousands or several millions, if you want to have a 95 percent chance of getting within 3 percentage points on either side of the correct value and your population is greater than 1050, your sample should include at least 1000 people.

Finally, a word of caution. This analysis applies only to simple random sampling. Most government surveys and national opinion polls use more sophisticated techniques such as **stratified random sampling** and **cluster sampling**. Stratified sampling is another important technique for making sure that the sample matches the total population as closely as possible. You may remember that we used the example of tasting a stew to illustrate the principle underlying inductive generalization from a sample. We also noted that if the total population is not homogeneous, but contains many different subgroups, we should attempt to select a sample that reflects these variations accurately. In stratified sampling, we deliberately choose the sample to ensure this. If we want to survey college students, and know that 21 percent of all college students are seniors, 24 percent juniors, and so on, we can select a sample of 100 people and deliberately choose 21 seniors and 24 juniors to be part of our sample. (Which seniors are among the 21 included in the sample can be determined by random selection.)

These more elaborate methods have several important advantages over simple random sampling. They are more economical. Imagine the expense and difficulty of obtaining a list of the names of all U.S. residents, numbering them, and then contacting a sample randomly selected from that list. Stratified and cluster sampling are more efficient in reducing sampling error and they allow us to get significant results with a smaller sample. Finally, they give more precise information about subgroups within the population such as racial minorities and households at different levels of income.

To construct a good stratified sample, we need accurate information about the composition of the total population, and we must also know which variations will be relevant to the conclusion. In the example just mentioned, we must decide whether to stratify the sample of college students with respect to gender, major, or grade point average; these variations may be relevant to some conclusions but not to others. Once we have decided which variations are relevant, we must have accurate information about the population as a whole. If we cannot satisfy these conditions, we will have to fall back on a simple random sample.

A 95 percent confidence interval for surveys using these sampling techniques differs from those in Table 4-1 and must be obtained from the relevant organization. Nonetheless, all reputable polls and surveys cite the confidence level (almost always the 95% level) or sampling error when promulgating their conclusions. For example, if the results of a poll are reported as "45% with a sampling error of 5%" without any further explanation, this means that there is a 95 percent chance that the true value lies between 40 and 50 percent. Without such information about its reliability, an SG based on a sample cannot be evaluated properly.

EXERCISES

*1. Assume that SAT scores are normally distributed with mean 500 and standard deviation 100. Though scores of 800 or higher are reported as 800, this does not imply a perfect performance. What percentage of scores are 800 or higher? What SAT score is at the 16th percentile? (The nth percentile of a set of numbers is a value such that n percent fall below it, and the rest above.)

*2. Hermione claims that my lucky nickel is biased toward heads. To prove her point, she tosses the coin 100 times and gets 58 heads and 42 tails. Does this result show that my lucky nickel is not a fair coin?

3. Comment on the following report, which appeared in *The Washington Post National Weekly Edition* (February 27, 1984, p. 38):

    Morale among federal employees is good and as high as it was before President Reagan took office, according to a survey recently released by the Federal Office of Personnel Management. OPM director Donald J. Devine said that the 1983 Federal Employee Attitude Survey showed that 76% of the nation's 2.7 million nonmilitary employees indicated that they were "satisfied with their jobs." 85% "liked working" for the government. Those results were nearly identical to the findings of OPM's 1979 employee attitude survey, Devine said. Federal unions and several members of Congress reacted to the findings with skepticism, including Rep. Patricia Schroeder (D-Colo.), chairman of the House Post Office and Civil Service subcommittee on civil service and a frequent critic of Devine. The survey was mailed to a random cross section of 28,120 employees, and 72%, or more than 20,000 employees, responded, Devine said.

4. Most market research is based on samples of households drawn randomly from telephone directories and then contacted by phone. What groups of people does this procedure omit and what effect might this have on the conclusions reached? How might one include those with unlisted phone numbers?

5. Assume that in a poll of 1000 voters, 52 percent say they will vote for Senator Black. If the margin of error is 3 percentage points, explain why

the election is too close to call. Would this still be true if the poll was an exit poll (i.e., a poll in which people are asked how they voted as they leave the election booth area) rather than a preelection poll?

6. The following report appeared in the Calgary *Herald* (June 28, 1980) concerning a poll taken by the Gallup organization for the Canadian Institute of Public Opinion: "About one in three Canadians attend a church service during the first week of May. This is down slightly, but not significantly from the 37% who reported attendance a year earlier. Results are based on 1042 personal, in-home interviews with adults 18 years and over, conducted during the first week of May. A sample of this size is accurate within a four percentage point margin, 19 in 20 times." What is the standard deviation of the sampling distribution curve? Why is the difference in church attendance found in the two polls not "significant"? If the sample size in 1980 had been larger (3000, say) with the same 1 in 3 of those interviewed reporting church attendance, might the difference from the previous year be significant? Explain.

Other Common Types of Inductive Argument

In the section Inductive Arguments from a Sample to a Population we considered inductive arguments based on samples whose conclusions are either universal or statistical generalizations about *all* objects of the same type. Many inductive arguments are less ambitious. They draw a conclusion not about an entire population of objects (past, present, and future), but about a single individual or a restricted class of such individuals. The simplest type of such arguments is an **induction to a particular** (IP). Argument 4:7 is an example of such an argument:

4:7. We will have at least one snowfall in Indiana this January, since it has snowed here in January every year for which we have a record of the weather.

This is an example of IP because we reason from an observed sample (previous years for which we have records) to a particular case that is not included in the sample (this coming January). Here is the standard form for (IP):

INDUCTION TO A PARTICULAR (IP)

Observed As all have property P.

Observed As stand in relation R to this as-yet unobserved A.

This as-yet unobserved A has property P.

IPs can be quite strong, especially in the sciences, where relation R often involves a sample containing several members of a species, genus, or kind of thing to which the case in the conclusion also belongs. Argument 4:2 is an example of this type of inductive reasoning. Its R-premise states that helium, argon, neon, and radon are all inert gases belonging to the same column of the Periodic Table.

A type of inductive argument that reaches a more general conclusion than an IP is known as an **induction to the future** (IF):

INDUCTION TO THE FUTURE (IF)

As observed in the past have all had P.

As observed in the past stand in relation R to As that will be observed in the future.

All As that will be observed in the future will have P.

An IF is more general than an IP because its conclusion concerns all future instances of a certain kind of thing, not just a single case. If example 4:7 had concluded that it will snow every January from now on, it would have been an IF rather than an IP. IFs differ from UGs in that their conclusions are only about instances that will occur in the future. In a UG, the conclusion makes a claim about *all* instances of a population, past, present, and future, including those mentioned in the first premise.

It may have occurred to you that we really do not need all these different forms of inductive argument. If we first had a UG to the conclusion "All As have property P" we could then use that generalization as a premise in a second deductive argument that would lead to a conclusion about this A or As that will be observed in the future. We could work this way, but the more specialized forms often give us a stronger inductive argument than we could get with a UG. In an IP, for example, we can focus on the need for a sample that is representative of only the instance about which we want to draw our conclusion; we need not worry about a sample that is representative of all As. Similarly, an IF can pay particular attention to changes over time that might make our sample less representative of future instances.

The last two forms of inductive arguments we consider exhibit a somewhat different pattern. The first of these, **arguments from analogy** (AA), may look similar to IPs, but instead of beginning with a premise about a group of instances, they compare one thing with a similar thing. Here is an example:

4:8. Senator Jones has consistently opposed affirmative action legislation, argued that abortion should be illegal, and voted against the ERA. The Moral Majority supports his candidacy. Senator Smith also opposes affirmative action legislation, thinks that abortion should be illegal, and voted against the ERA. We can, therefore, expect him to receive the support of the Moral Majority.

In 4:8, a conclusion has been drawn about a single case, Smith, from premises asserting that he shares a number of characteristics with another case, Jones.

Both IPs and AAs draw conclusions about single cases. In an IP, however, the premises must identify a number of observed instances belonging to a specified category (in standard form, the class of As), and the single case mentioned in the conclusion must belong to the same category. In AAs, on the other hand, the premises mention only two cases, and neither the premises nor the conclusion need specify a category or class. This means that AAs are particularly useful when we have no clearly defined categories to which the cases can be assigned.

Here is a schematic outline of the standard form for arguments from analogy, with the R-premise made explicit:

ARGUMENT FROM ANALOGY (AA)

A has properties P, Q, R, S, and T.

B has properties P, Q, R, and S.

Properties P, Q, R, and S, establish that A stands in relation R to B.

B has property T.

The specific wording of the R-premise depends on the example. Typical versions of the R-premise might specify that "A is similar to B," "A and B are somewhat similar," or that "A is very similar to B." Only when A is very similar to B in the right way is the argument inductively strong. Being similar in the right way means, roughly, that the properties (P, Q, R, S) A and B share are *relevant* to the possession of the further property, T, mentioned in the conclusion.

The number of properties involved in AAs varies from case to case. In general, the truth of the R-premise in AAs depends on (a) the number of shared properties mentioned in the premises, (b) the relevance of those properties to the property, T, mentioned in the conclusion, and (c) dissimilarities between A and B that are relevant to the possession of T. The greater the number of relevant shared properties, the more likely it is that A and B are similar in the right way. If we can point to relevant dissimilarities between A and B, this weakens the support for the R-premise. Any irrelevant properties, whether shared or not, have no effect on the status of the R-premise.

The last common type of inductive argument we will consider is **statistical syllogism** (SS). These arguments draw a conclusion about a particular case from premises that supply statistical information about a group to which the particular case belongs. The group described in this premise is called the **reference class.** For example, people often reason as follows:

4:9. Ninety-five percent of all Americans do not speak French fluently. Jake is an American. Therefore, Jake does not speak French fluently.

The inductive strength of an SS depends on the relevance of the reference class to the property mentioned in the conclusion. In 4:9 the reference class is "Americans"; the property mentioned in the conclusion is "not speaking French fluently." Choosing the most relevant reference class makes an SS inductively strong, but if a less relevant reference class is picked, a weaker argument results.

Deciding which reference classes are relevant is a matter of background knowledge and available information. Presumably, the fact that Jake has brown hair and is left-handed has no relevance to the chances that he speaks French fluently. So we would not need to consider this information, even if it were available. Other available information should be included if it is likely to affect the probability of the conclusion. When we make the assumption about relevance explicit in the R-premise, the standard form of statistical syllogisms is as follows:

STATISTICAL SYLLOGISM (SS)

X percent of all Fs are Gs.

A is an F.

Reference class F is relevant to A's being a G.

A is a G.

The degree of relevance of the reference class mentioned in the R-premise varies from case to case. F will be **the most relevant reference class** for A's being G if (1) the defining characteristics of F are relevant to property G, and (2) F is the **most narrowly specified reference class** that is relevant to A's being G for which information is available.

Obviously a necessary condition for SSs to be inductively strong is for X to be as close as possible to 100 percent. But this alone does not suffice to make an SS reliable; its R-premise must also be true. To understand the meaning of the R-premise and its role in assessing SSs consider argument 4:10 about the same individual mentioned in 4:9, Jake. For the sake of this illustration, we assume that both 4:10 and 4:9 have true premises.

4:10. Ninety-five percent of all Americans who have been educated in France speak French fluently. Jake is an American who was educated in France. Thus, Jake speaks French fluently.

The conclusion of 4:10 contradicts the conclusion of 4:9, and 4:10 clearly seems to be by far the stronger argument. Since we are assuming that both arguments have true premises, the explanation of the superiority of 4:10 must lie in the unstated R-premise. If we know both that Jake is an American and that he was educated in France, we should assign him to the more specific, relevant reference class of French-educated Americans rather than to the broader class of Americans in general. Given all the available information about Jake, the most relevant reference class is the one mentioned in 4:10.

We can summarize our discussion as follows. An SS is inductively strong if and only if two conditions are satisfied: (a) X is close to 100 percent; and (b) the individual case, A, has been assigned to the reference class, F, that is most relevant to A's being G based on the available information.

EXERCISES

For each of the arguments in questions 1 through 8 (a) decide which of the types (IP, IF, AA, and SS) it fits most closely; (b) reconstruct the argument by writing it in standard form and adding the R-premise explicitly. Be careful to distinguish the inductive argument from any deductive arguments with which it may be associated.

   1. The earth–moon system, the satellites of Jupiter, and the satellites of Saturn are all examples of planetary systems in which a satellite moves in the gravitational field of a much more massive body. All of these satellites move in ellipses. Therefore, the moons of Uranus will move in ellipses, too.

   2. Compare a human fetus at any stage of pregnancy with a young pig. Apart from the obvious difference in the species to which they belong, both have the same morally relevant properties to roughly the same degree: they have similar levels of rationality and awareness, and possess the same capacity to feel pleasure and pain. Since the value we place on a pig's life is quite low, we should place a similarly low value on the life of a human fetus.

   *3. Ninety-eight percent of all Chinese restaurants use substantial quantities of monosodium glutamate (MSG) in preparing their meals. Therefore, since Lisa is allergic to MSG, she should not eat lunch at "The Golden Dragon."

   4. When consumed in large quantities, saccharine causes liver cancer in rats. Therefore, saccharine causes liver cancer in humans.

   *5. All colonial empires of which we have historical knowledge have crumbled as a result of the crippling cost of maintaining military bases and financing wars in distant lands. The Roman empire and the British empire are two good examples. Thus, it is likely that all future colonial empires will suffer a similar fate.

   6. The days of democracy in the United States are numbered. All democracies in the past have succumbed to factious disputes between competing groups of special interests coupled with gross inefficiency, waste and corruption in government, and decadence in society at large.

   7. According to the mortality tables published by my life insurance company, fewer than 10 percent of all American males live beyond the age of

80. Since I am now 33, this means that I will almost certainly be dead 47 years from now.

8. Whenever I have been told that an exotic meat dish "tastes just like chicken," it has always turned out to be lizard, rattlesnake, iguana, or something equally disgusting. So when Ricardo tells me that his *pollo Neapolitana* "tastes just like chicken" I fully expect to be chewing on reptile flesh.

Evaluating and Constructing Inductive Arguments

We are now in a position to offer general guidelines for evaluating inductive arguments. The strength of the most common types of inductive argument depends on two factors: the relation specified in the R-premise and the nature of the claim advanced in the conclusion.

In evaluating any inductive argument from a sample to a population, the first step is to examine the relation between them. How likely is it that the sample provides a representative picture of the population mentioned in the conclusion? Choosing a sample that does not match the population will result in an inductively weak argument; this is known as a **sampling error.**

Sampling errors are of two sorts: **random sampling errors** and **nonrandom sampling errors.** Roughly speaking, a selection from a population is random when each member of the population has the same chance of being selected. Random sampling errors are present in all surveys and studies that use random sampling, however well designed. Fortunately, as we saw in the section Statistical Generalizations Based on Simple Random Sampling, the size of these errors can be accurately estimated.

Nonrandom sampling errors can be harder to detect. One source of such errors is the use of a sampling method that, despite appearances, is not truly random. This type of bias can be eliminated by using statistical techniques such as tables of random numbers to select the sample. Nonrandom sampling error can also arise even when the sample is random if it is selected from a subgroup of the target population. This is often a problem when households are randomly selected from telephone directories since, in some areas, many families have unlisted phones. A stratified sample can be subject to error if the information used to design the stratification is inaccurate or incomplete.

To sum up, other things being equal, an inductive argument is strong if the R-premise asserts that the sample is representative of the population mentioned in the conclusion. The sample is likely to be representative if it avoids the errors described in the previous two paragraphs. In some cases, as in 4:11, common sense and background knowledge will help us identify sampling errors.

4:11. A survey of 500 students questioned at random from 10:00 to 11:30 A.M. outside the Memorial Union building revealed that 30 percent of all Purdue students plan to vote in the next election.

The sample will contain only those students who were in one area of the campus at one particular time. It will miss part-time students who take classes only in the evening, veterinary or agriculture students whose classes are in other parts of the campus, and anyone else who is unlikely to be at the Union. Our general knowledge tells us that these students make up a substantial portion of the population mentioned in the conclusion, and hence we can tell that the argument contains a serious nonrandom sampling error. Therefore, it is inductively weak.

In other cases—reading a newspaper, for example—we may not be able to assess the quality of the sample directly, simply because we lack the relevant information. In such cases, we must rely on the integrity and reputation of the source. Polls conducted by the Gallup or Harris organizations, for example, are usually well designed. Evaluating such sources of information is discussed in greater detail in Chapter 7.

The second major factor that determines the strength of an inductive argument is the nature of the claim advanced in the conclusion. Consider example 4:12:

4:12. In all cases in which the gas gauge of my car has been observed to read "empty," the car has failed to start. Therefore, it is always the case that being out of gas prevents my car from starting.

The conclusion of 4:12 makes a claim about a causal connection between being out of gas and my inability to get the car started. The premise merely describes an observed correlation between a reading on the gas gauge and my car's failure to start, and this is weaker than a causal connection. (For more about causal reasoning, see Chapter 10.) Similarly, the argument in 4:5 would have been stronger if it had predicted the failure of future programs to teach former alcoholics to resume social drinking; the conclusion would then have been closer to the observations cited in the premise.

Other things being equal, an inductive argument is stronger if the conclusion is about a property that has been demonstrated in the sample; it is weaker if it draws a conclusion about something only suggested by observation of the sample. Thus, 4:12 would be stronger if it concluded merely that "It is always the case that my car will fail to start when the gas gauge reads 'empty.'"

If the conclusion diverges too far from the observation described in the premise, the argument is weak or even worthless. One common mistake is to draw a conclusion that the premises may not make probable. Consider the argument in 4:13:

4:13. All the Nissans we have tested so far have been fuel efficient.

This new Nissan will be a good car too.

In 4:13, the premise reports a presumed fact dealing with an objective property, fuel efficiency; but the conclusion makes a value judgment about the new

Nissan being a good car. What makes a car good is open to debate. Fuel efficiency may be one factor, but there are also considerations of safety, reliability, and price. Thus, there is no reason to expect that 4:13 is inductively strong.

So far, we have noted that two factors determine the inductive strength of arguments: the representativeness of the sample, as described by the R-premise, and the connection between the property mentioned in the conclusion and the property observed in the sample. Thus, we can evaluate the inductive strength of an argument by assessing the relation specified in the R-premise and examining the relation of the claim advanced in the conclusion to the properties observed in the sample.

Since our ultimate concern is the **reliability** of inductive arguments, we must also ask whether their premises are true. The truth of the R-premise depends on whether the relation asserted in that premise actually obtains. For example, is the sample representative of the population?

Even when the sample *is* well-chosen, we must still make sure that the information we acquire about it is accurate and that the other premise is true. This means we must be careful to avoid **nonsampling errors.** As the term suggests, nonsampling errors are not the result of sampling but might be present even in an exhaustive census. Such nonsampling errors often play a role in opinion polls and other surveys of human subjects. They range from missing data and mistakes in processing information to subjects giving false or misleading answers and the effects of the methods used to collect the data (e.g., the race and sex of the interviewer, the timing of the poll, whether the poll is based on personal interviews or on questionnaires sent by mail.) Avoiding bias from nonsampling errors is discussed further in Chapter 8 in the section Collecting Statistical Data.

We also noted earlier that all forms of inductive argument are open-ended. When we are trying to assess the inductive reliability of an argument, it is often helpful to take advantage of this open-endedness. Thus, if we can think of many things not included in the argument as stated that would make it stronger, the argument itself may be unreliable. On the other hand, if there are few facts that would make the argument stronger than it already is, the argument is likely to be quite reliable. We speak here of "reliability" rather than just inductive strength because many of the considerations we discover using this technique cast doubt on the truth of the R-premise by showing that the sample may be unrepresentative.

To see how this technique works, consider the argument in 4:14, which someone might give to justify the purchase of a new Nissan Sentra:

4:14. All Nissan cars that were tested three years ago were fuel efficient.

Nissan cars that were tested three years ago are representative of this new Nissan Sentra.

This new Nissan Sentra will be fuel efficient.

(Note that, despite the use of the future tense in the conclusion, this argument has the IP, not the IF form.) We can think of many facts that, if added to this argument, would make it quite weak. Nissan produces many different types of cars, and some of their high-performance and luxury models are not very fuel efficient. Nissan has changed its line considerably in the past several years, and so data about cars manufactured three years ago will not tell us much about new models. Thus, we must conclude that the argument, as stated, is unreliable because the R-premise is false.

We could improve the argument in 4:14 considerably by changing it to make these additional considerations irrelevant. One way of accomplishing this is to restrict the premises to a class of objects that is more representative of the one referred to in the conclusion. Thus, compare 4:14 with 4:15:

4:15. All Nissan Sentras that have been tested this year have been fuel efficient.

Nissan Sentras that have been tested this year are representative of this new Nissan Sentra.

This new Nissan Sentra will be fuel efficient.

In discussing statistical syllogisms, we noted that we should assign the subject of the conclusion to the most specific reference class about which we have reliable information. With a more detailed reference class, there is less likely to be other factors that would count against the conclusion. The principle is the same here: by specifying a narrower sample, we have reduced the chances that other factors could be introduced to weaken the argument. The more this is done, the more reliable the argument will be.

Like deductive arguments, inductive arguments can be varied slightly by introducing hedging qualifiers such as "possibly" or "probably." These are handled in a similar way here. If a qualifier appears in a premise, the conclusion must be made even weaker, if the inductive argument is to retain its strength.

Our survey of inductively strong arguments in the sections Statistical Generalizations Based on Simple Random Sampling and other Common Types of Inductive Argument is far from complete. One important class of inductive arguments is discussed later, in Chapter 10. These arguments are used in the sciences and in everyday life to test and reason about causal hypotheses.

The comments on evaluating inductive arguments also serve as guidelines for constructing arguments: choose the appropriate sample, avoid bias, and so on. We can expand on this, to some extent, by identifying two sorts of cases in which one might want to construct an inductively reliable argument.

The first case is one in which we have some information about a sample, and we want to know what sort of conclusion we should draw. We can determine a range of possible conclusions by recalling the standard forms of the inductive arguments described in the sections Inductive Arguments from a Sample to a Population and Other Common Types of Inductive Argument.

If our information tells us about some property observed in a sample (e.g., "According to a study completed by the American Lung Association, people who smoked more than two packs a day were at a much higher risk of developing lung cancer"), we can use this as a premise in a UG, SG, IP, IF, or SS. All of these arguments begin with that kind of premise.

The guidelines for evaluating inductive arguments tell us two things about how we should formulate the conclusion. First, our conclusion should be about a population of which the sample is representative. Thus, our inductive argument would be stronger if we drew a conclusion about Americans alive today who smoked two packs of cigarettes a day, weaker if it were about smokers in general. Second, we should pay close attention to the property actually observed in the sample. Thus, concluding that someone who smoked more than two packs a day would be more likely to develop lung cancer would give us a stronger argument, based just on this information, than the conclusion that smoking *causes* lung cancer.

Alternatively, we may want to justify an assertion by showing that it is the conclusion of an inductively reliable argument. In this second type of case, we have already picked out the conclusion, so we must (1) decide which form of argument to use and (2) determine what sort of premises we will need and whether such facts are available.

Suppose we are trying to justify our prediction that eating this particular hamburger will give Sam an upset stomach. The specific nature of the conclusion allows us to narrow our choice of argument forms to IP, SS, or AA. To construct an IP argument, we would need good information about a sample of the class to which this hamburger belongs, for example, "All hamburgers from the Greasy Spoon All-Night Diner Sam has eaten in the past have given him an upset stomach." If we do not have such information, we might try an argument from analogy, based on a comparison of properties of this hamburger (its fat content, its spiciness, its containing raw onion, etc.) with some other food that caused Sam to have an upset stomach. Which of these arguments we decide to give will depend on the information we can acquire for our premises.

EXERCISES

I. For each of the following inductive arguments, identify its form (if it is one of the standard types), state the R-premise explicitly, and explain your judgment about its reliability. (For this set of exercises, assume that the factual information in the premises is true.)

1. Nearly all expatriate Irishmen deplore the violence in Northern Ireland. Therefore, Pat Feeny, who recently emigrated from Ireland, will strongly disapprove of the latest IRA bombings in Belfast, even though he has two previous convictions for terrorist activity.

*2. Sixty-six percent of male alcoholics are married. Therefore, the chances of a married man becoming an alcoholic are double those of a bachelor.

3. A TV evangelist encourages his viewers to write to him if they think that homosexuals and "other sinful perverts" should be allowed to teach in public schools. He receives an avalanche of mail (4500 letters), 98 percent of which is against permitting homosexuals to teach in public schools, or in any other kind of school. From this evidence he concludes that "the overwhelming majority of Americans are opposed to the recognition of gay rights in our public schools."

4. American families worry more about paying for health care than about any other domestic issue. This was the conclusion reached by a survey sponsored by the National Association of Extension Home Economists. The survey, conducted by mail, asked the extension service's home economists throughout the United States and some overseas territories to list what they thought were the three issues of greatest concern to families in their areas. Responses came from 547 of some 4000 association members. The overwhelming majority of those responding were married, under 40 years old, and working in rural counties. More than 46 percent were from the South.

5. Since 1980, the U.S. Food and Drug Administration (the FDA) has advised pregnant women to limit their caffeine intake on the grounds that caffeine causes birth defects in rats. The warning followed an FDA study in which pregnant rats were force-fed massive amounts of caffeine—the human equivalent of up to 24 cups a day of strong coffee. Some of the offspring of these rats were born with missing toes.

6. Growing food for local consumption receives low priority from many governments of African nations. In 1983, drought devastated millet production in the northern provinces of Upper Volta, yet farmers in the south—with bumper surpluses of millet to sell—were discussing planting cotton instead. The reason is simple. The farmers know that cotton for export will be quickly collected and paid for by the government. Thus, cotton production has shot up over 20 times since independence while yields of sorghum and millet, the major food crops for the region, have stagnated.

   The trend is typical for many African countries. In Mali, during the great drought between 1976 and 1982, while food production plummeted, cotton production increased by 400 percent. During the drought of 1973–74 in Tanzania, sales of maize fell by a third while the output of tobacco continued to grow. Both crops need about the same amount of rain. The difference comes in inputs available and the incentives to growers. Sixty-two percent of money loaned by the Tanzanian Rural Development Bank between 1978 and 1979 went for tobacco and only 19 percent for maize. [Adapted from Tony Jackson and Paula Park, "Nature Pleads Not Guilty," *New Internationalist,* September 1984; reprinted in J. Rohr, ed., *Problems of Africa: Opposing Viewpoints* (St. Paul, MN: Greenhaven Press, 1986).]

II. Assume that the following statements are true. In each case, construct an inductively strong argument using the given statement as a premise.

1. At every Thanksgiving dinner I can remember, the turkey has been over-cooked.

2. Saccharin causes bladder cancer in mice.

3. No previous attempt to stop the fighting in Lebanon has succeeded.

*4. Cats, dogs, cattle, and horses are all color-blind, whereas lemurs, monkeys, apes, and human beings all have good color vision.

5. Twenty-six percent of the marbles drawn from this urn have been red.

III. For each of the following claims, construct an inductively reliable argument to support the claim. If an argument form is mentioned in parentheses, use that form for your argument.

1. Smith's dog is vicious. (AA)

2. Smith's dog is vicious. (IP)

*3. The birthrate in the United States will continue to decline.

4. Gold conducts electricity very well.

5. Selling arms to Iran will not bring a halt to the taking of American hostages in Lebanon.

Notes

[1] This way of regarding the strength of inductive arguments pays no attention to the concept of *increase in probability* that often underlies our intuitions about confirmation. Thus, if we acquired some evidence that raised the probability of an hypothesis from 0.1 to 0.3, for example, we might judge that the evidence confirmed the hypothesis because its probability had been increased. But since the hypothesis still has only a probability less than 0.5 (and thus, even with that evidence, the hypothesis is still more likely to be false than true), the associated inductive argument using the hypothesis as conclusion and a statement of the evidence as its premise is, in our terms, worthless.

[2] The basic point here is explained in the discussion of example 4:3 in the section Inductive Strength and Inductive Reliability. To construct a deductively valid argument to justify an inductive inference, we would have to add to our statement of the past evidence premises that are at least as uncertain as the inference we are trying to justify.

[3] For clear discussions of the major proposals, see Brian Skyrms, *Choice and Chance: An Introduction to Inductive Logic* (Belmont, CA: Dickenson, 1966), and Wesley Salmon, *The Foundations of Scientific Inference* (Pittsburgh: University of Pittsburgh Press, 1967). Hume's own skeptical conclusion in his *Treatise of Human Nature* (1739) was that there is *no* rational justification of induction at all!

[4]The same phrases, *universal generalization* and *statistical generalization,* are used to describe forms of statement and types of inductive argument. To avoid possible confusion we use the abbreviations UG and SG to refer to arguments. When we refer to types of statement, we will write the phrases out in full.

[5]Since this is not a course in statistics, we have not explained how the standard deviation (SD) is defined and calculated. For a clear introductory account, see Chapter 5 of David S. Moore, *Statistics: Concepts and Controversies.* Very briefly, the SD of a group of numbers is the positive square root of their variance. The variance of a group of numbers is the mean of the squares of their deviations from their mean. The mean and other sorts of "average" are discussed in Chapter 8 in the section Percentages and Averages.

CHAPTER 5

Arguments in Context

In this chapter we deepen our understanding of how arguments are used by applying the general principles of reasoning to longer and more complex examples. In the first section we examine how different types of arguments can be combined to form **mixed argument chains.** In the next section we introduce a new form of argument, the **reductio ad absurdum,** a common means of proving a statement is false. The next two sections deal with the problem of identifying and evaluating the extended argument chains contained in lengthy passages. Finally, other factors relevant to the task of responding to and criticizing arguments are discussed in the section Responding to Arguments.

Mixed Argument Chains

Since many statements can be written in either propositional or categorical form, it is quite common to find chains with a propositional argument whose conclusion, restated in categorical form, becomes a premise in a categorical argument. It is also possible to have a categorical argument whose conclusion becomes a premise in a propositional argument. Example 5:1 contains three pairs of equivalent statements, one categorical and one propositional:

5:1. All diamonds are things composed of carbon.

If something is a diamond, then it is composed of carbon.

No person in this course is a person who is confused about validity.

Either a person is not confused about validity, or else that person is not in this course.

It is not the case that if you are an American citizen, then you are eligible to vote in national elections.

Some American citizens are not people who are eligible to vote in national elections.

It is easy to find argument chains in which statements like these link two different types of arguments. Argument 5:2 is one example:

5:2. All people in this class are people who have studied Chapter 1.

No person who has studied Chapter 1 is a person who is confused about validity.

No person in this class is a person who is confused about validity.

Either a person is not confused about validity, or that person is not in this course.

Either Martin is not confused about validity, or Martin is not in this course.

Either Martin is not confused about validity, or Martin is not in this course.

Martin is confused about validity.

Martin is not in this course.

One can also construct argument chains that combine deductive and inductive arguments. In these cases, the most common order is an inductive argument with a conclusion that becomes a premise in a deductive argument. For example, universal generalization can yield a conclusion that may be useful as a premise in a categorical argument.

5:3. All senators from my home state who have expressed their views publicly have been unsympathetic to the idea of a nuclear freeze.

Senators from my home state who have expressed their views publicly are representative of all senators from that state.

All senators from my home state are unsympathetic to the idea of a nuclear freeze.

All senators who are unsympathetic to a nuclear freeze are people who will vote against the proposed amendment.

All senators from my home state are senators who are unsympathetic to the idea of a nuclear freeze.

All senators from my home state are people who will vote against the proposed amendment.

When you are trying to develop chains of reasoning, do not hesitate to combine different types of arguments. For each step, choose the form that best fits the ideas you are working with. Here are some general rules of thumb:

1. If you have information about a pattern, and you want to extend that pattern, try some form of **inductive argument.**

2. If you are comparing two things that have many properties in common, try an **argument from analogy.**

3. If your argument involves classifying things under different labels or into different categories, try a **categorical argument.** This is especially true of claims about some members of a class (particular statements), which are often hard to put into standard propositional form.

4. If the premises you are working with have connectives such as "unless," "and," "if . . . then . . . ," or refer to necessary or sufficient conditions, you will probably have to use a **propositional argument.**

5. If you want to eliminate alternatives, try a **disjunctive syllogism.**

6. Arguments that involve looking at the consequences of different alternatives can often be written as **dilemmas.**

7. Arguments that combine conditional with atomic statements can often be written as **MT** or **MP** arguments.

These rules can also help you reconstruct mixed argument chains encountered in your reading. Consider, for example, 5:4, taken from paragraph 3 of Extended Argument 7 (Extended Arguments are found in Appendix 1. For ease of reference, the paragraphs in each of the Extended Arguments have been numbered).

5:4. If this characterization of murderers [as generally being otherwise law-abiding citizens] were accurate, banning handguns would seem an appealingly simple means of reducing domestic and acquaintance homicide. Most killings are not, however, perpetrated by the average noncriminal citizen whose law-abiding mentality (it is believed) would induce him to give up handguns in response to a ban. Refuting "the myth that the typical homicide offender is just an ordinary person" with "no previous criminal record," Professor Gary Kleck of Florida State University's School of

Criminology notes FBI figures showing two-thirds of all murderers to have previous felony conviction records.

You may find it necessary to start by outlining the argument, but whether you do so or not, you should notice that the last sentence contains an argument for one of the claims made earlier: "Most killings are not perpetrated by the average noncriminal citizen." This argument starts by describing a pattern in a sample (the group of crimes for which the FBI has statistics), and generalizes it. Following the suggestion in the preceding Rule 1, we might try to reconstruct it as an inductive argument. We can also see that other parts of the argument concern the relation between different groups of people: murderers, people who are (or are not) law-abiding, and people who would give up handguns in response to a ban. If we follow Rule 3, and reconstruct this portion of the chain as a categorical argument, we can arrive at the following:

Two-thirds of the murderers observed by the FBI were people with previous felony conviction records.

(The murderers observed by the FBI are representative of all murderers.)

Approximately two-thirds of all murderers are people with previous felony conviction records.

Some murderers are people with previous felony conviction records.

No people with previous felony conviction records are ordinary law-abiding citizens.

Some murderers are not ordinary law-abiding citizens.

Only ordinary law-abiding citizens are people who would give up their handguns in response to a ban = All people who would give up handguns in response to a ban are ordinary law-abiding citizens.

Some murderers are not ordinary law-abiding citizens.

Some murderers are not people who would give up handguns in response to a ban.

This example illustrates one drawback to mixing different arguments in standard form. Many claims can be expressed in one form but cannot be translated completely into another form. Thus, particular categorical statements have one term, "some," that must cover all cases between 0 and 100 percent. We must, therefore, keep track of the fact that in 5:4 "some" actually means "approximately two-thirds," and should be interpreted that way throughout. Thus, the conclusion in 5:4 is meant to refer to a sizable majority of murderers, not just one or two.

Even with mixed argument chains, the same principle of evaluation applies—

that is, for the chain to be strong, each of its arguments must be deductively valid or inductively strong. The reasoning is reliable only if each component is deductively sound or inductively reliable.

EXERCISES

The following questions pertain to Extended Argument 5.

1. Reconstruct the argument by which the author criticizes the "community standards" test of obscenity. (See paragraphs 3, 7, 8, and 9.) Include only those premises that are relevant, paraphrasing when necessary. Add any implicit premises you think are essential to the argument.

2. Reconstruct as two separate valid syllogisms, Okruhlik's criticisms in paragraph 10 of the claim that material should be censored if and only if it causes disgust in the average member of the community. Use the following class terms: F = Things that cause feelings of disgust in the average member of the community; H = Things that harm some members of the community; C = Things that should be censored. Clearly indicate the role of each conclusion in the overall criticism. In the light of the implicit premises (one in each argument), what is Okruhlik assuming here to be a necessary and sufficient condition for something to be censored?

*3. Using categorical reasoning, reconstruct the argument in paragraph 11 using the following class terms: T = Things that can be taken off the streets; D = Things that are deemed obscene; S = Things that are on the streets. (Note: This involves adding the implicit conclusion.) Is the syllogism valid?

The following questions pertain to Extended Argument 6.

4. By adding appropriate implicit premises, reconstruct as deductively valid the argument in the first three sentences of paragraph 3 by which Stich tries to establish that knowledge is an intrinsic good (has intrinsic value).

5. Reconstruct as deductively valid the argument in paragraph 8 for the conclusion that, there being some knowledge we ought not to acquire, it is consistent with the enlightened view.

*6. In light of your answer to question 5, and bearing in mind paragraph 9, reconstruct Stich's argument in paragraph 15 for his conclusion concerning recombinant DNA research. Is his argument intended to be valid or merely inductively reliable?

Reductio Ad Absurdum Arguments

The Latin phrase *reductio ad absurdum* means "reduction to absurdity." It describes a very useful and powerful form of argument. A **reductio ad absurdum**

argument, or more simply, a **reductio argument,** is an argument about another argument, which we will call "**the target argument.**" If we can show that the target argument, also referred to as "T," is deductively valid and that it has a false conclusion, then we know at least one of the premises of T is false. This follows from the definition of validity, since it is logically impossible for a valid argument to have all its premises true and its conclusion false. In the special case in which the conclusion of T is a contradiction, we can be certain that it is false, but reductio reasoning works equally well when the conclusion of T is an empirical statement, just as long as it is false.

Reductio reasoning is usually directed against a specific premise of the target argument. For the sake of uniformity in reconstructing examples of reductio reasoning, we will always write this statement as the *first* premise of the target argument. If, in addition to T's being a valid argument with a false conclusion, all its premises except the first are true, then we can validly conclude that premise 1 of T is false. Thus, in our reconstruction, all reductio arguments will have the same form, R.

REDUCTIO ARGUMENT, R

(1) Target argument, T, is valid.

(2) The conclusion of T is false.

(3) All the premises of T, other than the first, are true.

(4) The first premise of T is false.

When written out in this form, all reductio arguments are valid. Whether a particular reductio argument is also sound depends on whether each of its three premises are true, that is, on whether the claims made by R about the target argument, T, are true. Since the target argument varies from case to case, to decide whether R is sound we need to specify what T is. Consider example 5:5:

5:5. Many people believe that intelligence, as measured by standard IQ tests, is entirely hereditary—that two people with identical genetic structure will always have the same IQ. Since identical twins have the same genetic structure, they should always have the same IQ. However, careful testing of twins raised in different environments shows a wide discrepancy. So one of these assumptions must be false. By definition, identical twins have the same genetic structure; therefore, IQ is not entirely hereditary.

When we reconstruct the target argument in standard form, its first premise should be "IQ is entirely hereditary," since the rest of the argument is designed to show that this statement is false. To construct a sound reductio argument showing that this statement is false, we need to combine it with other, true, premises in a way that will allow us validly to deduce a conclusion that is known to be false. In this example, the conclusion of the target argument is "All identical twins have the same IQ," which we are told is refuted by careful tests of identical twins raised in different environments. Thus, the target argument can be reconstructed as follows:

TARGET ARGUMENT, T

    (1)   IQ is entirely hereditary.

    (2)   If IQ is entirely hereditary, then all people with the same genetic structure have the same IQ.

    (3)   All identical twins have the same genetic structure.

    (4)   All identical twins have the same IQ.

We would then complete the reconstruction by writing out the reductio argument, R, in exactly the same way as before. Since all reductio arguments are valid, the key issue in evaluating R is to decide whether it is sound. In other words, are all the premises of R true? The first premise of R asserts that the target argument, T, is valid. We can see that T is valid by analyzing it as a **mixed argument chain.** The first step of the chain involves propositional reasoning. From premises 1 and 2 of T we get, by modus ponens, the intermediate conclusion, "All people with the same genetic structure have the same IQ." The second step involves categorical reasoning. Taking this intermediate conclusion together with premise 3 of T yields a valid categorical syllogism with 4 as its conclusion. Thus, the first premise of R is true; T is valid. We have already dealt with the second premise of R; T's conclusion is false. The third premise of R is true since premises 2 and 3 of T are true solely by virtue of the meanings of the terms "entirely hereditary," "identical twin," and "same genetic structure." So R is a sound argument, and thus premise 1 of T is false.

In analyzing the argument in 5:5, we reconstructed an example of reductio reasoning in which the target argument had already been supplied. We can also construct our own reductio arguments to show that a claim is false. The key is to find a target argument that has the claim in question as its first premise and validly leads to a false conclusion. If all the other premises of our target argument are true, then we will have shown, by reductio reasoning, that the original claim is false. For example, if we want to show it is false that no mammals lay eggs, 5:6 would be an appropriate target argument:

5:6.   (1)   No mammals lay eggs.

        (2)   All platypuses are mammals.

        (3)   No platypuses lay eggs.

This argument is a valid categorical syllogism. Its second premise is true because female platypuses are vertebrates who have milk-secreting glands for feeding their offspring. The conclusion is false: there are well-documented cases of individual platypuses laying eggs from which their offspring hatch. Thus, 5:6 is an appropriate target argument for a sound reductio showing that premise 1 is false.

Reductio arguments are common in logic and mathematics, in which they are sometimes referred to as "indirect proofs." Typical examples from mathematics are the proof that the square root of 2 is irrational, and the proof that the number of primes is infinite. Because all logical and mathematical statements are either necessary truths or necessary falsehoods, a reductio argument in logic or mathematics establishes not merely that the first premise of the target argument is false, but that it is necessarily false.

EXERCISES

1. The following argument is taken from Richard Jeffrey, "Valuation and Acceptance of Scientific Hypotheses," *Philosophy of Science* 23 (1956) p. 237. He is criticizing an earlier paper by Richard Rudner. "The form of Rudner's reasoning is hypothetical: *if* it is the job of the scientist to accept and reject hypotheses, *then* he must make value judgments. Now I shall argue that if the scientist makes value judgments, then he neither accepts nor rejects hypotheses. These two statements together form a *reductio ad absurdum* of the view that Rudner presupposes, that scientists accept and reject hypotheses." Let P = "Scientists accept and reject hypotheses," and Q = "Scientists make value judgments." Using propositional logic, reconstruct Jeffrey's reductio argument by making P the first premise of the target argument.

*2. Using propositional logic, reconstruct Stich's reductio argument in paragraph 14 of Extended Argument 6. (Hint: Let the first premise of the target argument be the generalization, "If it is logically possible that doing X will lead to disaster, then we ought not to do X.")

3. Reconstruct as a reductio argument one of the arguments in Extended Argument 8 by which Hormats seeks to establish that it is false that Soviet forces have used a wide variety of chemical and biological weapons in Southeast Asia and Afghanistan.

4. Reconstruct the reductio reasoning in the following passage, adapted from A. J. Ayer, *Language, Truth, and Logic*, pp. 66–67.

   The problem of induction is, roughly speaking, the problem of finding a way to prove that certain empirical generalizations which are derived from past experience will hold good also in the future. There are only two ways of approaching this problem on the assumption that it is a genuine problem, and it is easy to see that neither of them can lead to its solution. One may attempt to deduce the proposition which one is required to prove either from a tautology or from an empirical statement. In the former case one commits the error of supposing that from a tautology it is possible to deduce a proposition about a matter of fact; in the latter case one simply assumes what one is setting out to prove. . . . Thus it appears that there is no possible way of solving the problem of induction, as it is ordinarily conceived. And this means that it is a fictitious problem, since all genuine problems are at least theoretically capable of being solved. (Hint: Let the first premise of the target argument be, "The problem of induction is a genuine problem.")

5. Construct an appropriate target argument to show that it is logically impossible for a barber to exist who shaves all and only those men who do not shave themselves. (Hint: Let the first premise of the target argument be the generalization, "The barber shaves X if and only if X does not shave himself.")

6. Show by reductio reasoning that it is impossible to move a rook from one corner of a chessboard to the corner diagonally opposite so that it passes through every square exactly once.

Thematic Outlines of Extended Arguments

Most of the arguments we have discussed thus far have been relatively short and clearly defined. Unfortunately, much of what we read and hear does not come to us in this form. Therefore, to apply the techniques of critical reasoning, we must learn how to deal with extended arguments as they appear in essays, editorials, and speeches. This requires four main steps:

1. Identify and isolate relevant portions of the argument.

2. Organize these elements into a coherent order that accurately reflects the author's intentions.

3. Make crucial arguments explicit by identifying their type and supplying missing premises.

4. Determine, to the best of your ability, whether the arguments are sound or reliable.

In Chapter 1, we carried out the first two steps by means of an outline. Outlining works well for fairly short passages in which we can recognize statements that are not a part of the argument. These statements are omitted from our outline. In Extended Argument 2, for example, the first three paragraphs do not form part of the argument at all. The first paragraph supplies some background information, paragraph 2 identifies the issue (Who should make these decisions?), and paragraph 3 leads into the actual argument. Thus, if we plan to outline the argument, we should begin by bracketing statements in paragraph 4.

How do you tell which statements should be bracketed and which do not contribute to the arguments? There is no easy formula to apply, but it helps to remember that, in order to be relevant to the task at hand, a statement must form a premise in an argument that eventually leads (perhaps as part of a chain) to the main conclusion. For that reason, it is important to get a clear idea of what the final or main conclusion is as soon as possible. Sometimes the conclusion is obvious, but at other times getting a good, precise statement of the conclusion is a matter of gradual refining.

In Extended Argument 2, for example, it is tempting to look for the conclusion in the last paragraph, that sounds as if it is summing up the main point. However, the claim that these decisions are an individual matter is rather vague, and much of the previous discussion has been more specific. We are on the right track, but need to get a more precise formulation of the point of this editorial. If we remind ourselves that we are dealing with the question identified in paragraph 2 (Who should make these decisions?), we can recognize that the main conclusion is that parents, with the help of doctors, should be allowed to decide. This claim is contained in paragraph 5, but since reasons and conclusions are run together, it is better to state the conclusion in our own words.

Having identified the conclusion, we can see that the information contained in the first three paragraphs neither supports nor discredits the conclusion. By setting aside this portion of the editorial, we can focus on, and outline, the remainder:

5:7. [¹It's hard for any of us to know until we're in that situation,] and [²until we've been advised by those who know best.] [³Those of us isolated from the situation in the cold and separate chambers of judges and juries can't decide.]

[⁴Rather, let it be decided by those closest to and most deeply involved in the pain of it, the parents—those who are in the midst of every hope, every disappointment.] And, [⁵let the doctor help guide the decision.] [⁶He is the expert few of us shall ever become.] [⁷By granting him a license under the conditions above, we accept his decision.]

[⁸Medicine has grown since the time those words were written, perhaps more so than its authors ever dreamed.] [⁹It now has the flexibility to decide when the living can die and when the dying can live.] [¹⁰Yet, as the legal community deals with medicine, it insists on using rigid standards carved in stone.]

[¹¹It simply can't.] [¹²The situation is too complex and involved to fit a ready-made scheme.] [¹³It's a highly individual matter,] and [¹⁴can only be dealt with on that basis.]

As usual, we can begin by outlining smaller chunks of the argument, as shown in Figure 5-1.

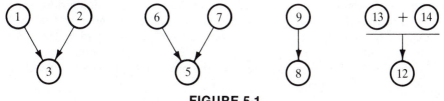

FIGURE 5-1

The completed outline in Figure 5-2 reveals three main strands in the argument. The first emphasizes the need for involvement, not isolation, the second focuses on the rigidity of the legal system, and the final one combines the first two to reach the positive conclusion.

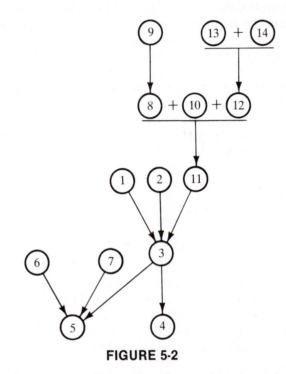

FIGURE 5-2

Notice that we could have achieved a similar analysis of the editorial by simply **labeling its main themes.** The first **theme** that is introduced concerns involvement: parents are involved, judges, juries, and most other people are not. We come next to the paragraph containing the conclusion, which we will label "parents/doctors." The last two paragraphs can be grouped under the label "flexibility." If we do this in the margins, we can write the labels at the appropriate points; if we are working on a separate sheet of paper, we should indicate the paragraphs in which each of the arguments or claims occur. Numbering paragraphs, as we have done with the Extended Arguments, is a useful method of identification.

We also want to make note of the conclusion. It is generally better to formulate the conclusion in your own words. If you have difficulty doing this, it may help you to consider first the topic of the passage, the issue under discussion. In Extended Argument 2, the editorial is about decisions regarding Infant Doe cases, involving the life of a deformed newborn child. Our notes would then look something like this (the numbers now refer to the paragraphs, as given in Extended Argument 2 in the Appendix.):

Topic: Who should make decisions about treatment in "Infant Doe" cases?
Conclusion: Parents, guided by doctors, should make the final decision in cases like that of Infant Doe.
Involvement: 4, 5.
Parents/doctors: 5.
Flexibility: 6, 7.

Labeling themes in this way is simpler than outlining, and this is both an advantage and a disadvantage. The disadvantage is that the list has little detail—we have not, for example, identified specific premises—and it does not show the relation between the parts. The advantage is that its simplicity makes this method easier to work with in analyzing longer arguments. This editorial approaches the limit of arguments that can be analyzed efficiently by means of an outline, but labeling themes can be used to analyze essays that are many pages long.

To overcome some of the disadvantages of this system, we can supplement our list by stating in our own words the focus of each theme. This statement will usually turn out to be an important premise in one of the main argument chains. By putting these ideas in our own words, we can often cut through some of the obscurity or verbiage of the original passage. For Extended Argument 2, our analysis might look like this:

Conclusion: Parents, guided by doctors, should make the final decision in cases like that of Infant Doe. (The decision should not be made by the legal system.)
Involvement: 4, 5. (The people most closely involved are in the best position to make these decisions.)
Parents/doctors: 5. (Parents are the people most closely involved, and doctors have the special expertise.)
Flexibility: 6, 7. (Medicine and medical decisions require flexibility that is lacking in the legal system.)

This analysis is not intended to be a complete summary of the entire argument, but it does indicate the main threads of the reasoning leading to the conclusion, and prepares us for the next step, evaluating individual arguments.

Before we move on to evaluation in the next section, let us label the themes in a longer example, Extended Argument 1. Before reading further, you should turn to that argument, identify the conclusion, and work out an analysis of the sort just given for Extended Argument 2.

The **topic** of the essay is how to ensure that teachers are competent. The **conclusion** is basically negative: that the most popular proposals are no good. It is important to be as precise as possible in stating the conclusion. We should therefore take account of the fact that Shanker rejects many proposals because they single teachers out for special treatment; in some cases, he also argues that a method does not work. The various themes introduced in support of the argument can then be broken down as follows (you will probably have assigned different labels, but the general picture should be similar):

Conclusion: Many proposals to ensure competence in teachers are unfair or ineffective.

Protection: 4. (Tenure does not give teachers more protection than professionals in other fields have.)

Quality: 5. (Abolishing tenure does not improve quality of teaching.)

Recertification: 6, 7. (Recertification is unfair to teachers.)

Retesting: 8, 9. (Retesting is unfair to teachers.)

Abuses: 10. (Currently available measures such as adequate salaries, initial testing, and selective tenure are not properly used.)

Thematic outlines can also be used as a first step in constructing your own arguments. Their advantages and disadvantages compared to the outlines discussed in Chapter 1 in the section Constructing Arguments are similar to those that affect their use in analyzing other people's arguments. They identify broad themes to be developed, but provide little detail about the content of specific premises and arguments. Because thematic outlines do not usually specify many premises or intermediate conclusions, it is harder to develop fully worked out arguments to fill in a thematic outline than it was to develop arguments to complete the sort of outline presented in Chapter 1. On the other hand, for a longer argument whose details we have not yet formulated, a thematic outline with its lack of specificity may be the most appropriate first step.

EXERCISES

Develop a thematic outline for Extended Arguments 3, 4, 5, and 8. (Appendix II contains a thematic outline of Extended Argument 8.)

Evaluating Extended Arguments

After constructing a thematic outline of a passage, the next step is to evaluate its constituent arguments: to determine whether its constituent arguments are valid or inductively strong, and whether the premises of those arguments are true or plausible. To some extent our approach should be tailored to the length of the passage and the depth of the analysis desired. To illustrate the **different levels of analysis and evaluation,** we give examples of two extremes: first, a very broad and general evaluation, and then a more detailed and fully developed account of the same passage. Drawing on the analysis provided in the section Thematic Outlines of Extended Arguments, we will consider Extended Argument 1.

In giving a **general evaluation** of a passage, we need not reconstruct each individual argument. We are trying only to establish an overall sense of its strengths and weaknesses. By skimming the list of themes presented in Shanker's editorial, we can see that all but one of the arguments rely on premises about fairness; the arguments in paragraphs 4, 7, and 8 all invoke arguments to the effect that other professionals (doctors, lawyers, pharmacists, and dentists) are not subject to treatment of the sort proposed for teachers and singling out teachers would therefore be unfair. The further premise that we should not adopt an unfair practice is implied but not stated.

Even when the arguments are sketched in this way, we can see how their soundness can be judged. Are the premises true? In the argument in paragraph 4, Shanker claims that other professionals enjoy job security equal to or better than the protection afforded by tenure. Although this is true in some cases, it does not apply as widely as he suggests. This is an example of a common pitfall in arguments: sweeping generalizations that go too far. It is true that some other professions have a great deal of job security, but it is false to claim that *all* professionals have protection equivalent to tenure.

We should also note that the claim that the proposals would "single out" teachers does not automatically lead to the conclusion that the proposal is unfair, or that it should not be adopted. Additional premises must be supplied, something Shanker does not do. This does not mean that we can reject these arguments out of hand, since a little thought will tell us what the missing premises must be. A claim like "We should treat teachers in the same way that we treat other professionals" would do nicely. Because such a premise is not obviously true, it would require further supporting arguments. We can see, however, that Shanker's argument is incomplete in this area.

We can summarize the results of this very sketchy evaluation. Some of the premises involve **overgeneralizing,** although Shanker does supply a fair number of examples in which other professionals are treated better than teachers would be under the proposed regulations. Moreover, no connection has been established between the assertion that a proposal singles out teachers and the conclusion that the proposal should be rejected.

Note that we did not wind up with a claim such as "Overall, this is a good (bad) argument." In rare cases, we find examples of extended reasoning in which all the arguments appear to be sound, or all unsound, but most of the time we encounter arguments some of which appear to be strong and some weak. In these latter cases, we should *not* try to balance the strong arguments against the weak ones in order to assign a label of "good" or "bad" to the entire piece of reasoning. Each argument or argument chain for a given conclusion must be assessed on its own merits. A single good argument (either sound or reliable) suffices to establish its conclusion. Many weak arguments for the same conclusion are just that— weak arguments. They do not "add up" to a strong argument, nor can the virtues of a good argument compensate for the defects in a bad one.

A detailed evaluation of Shanker's editorial would give us a more precise understanding of its strengths and weaknesses by forcing us to reconstruct individual arguments rather than sketch them in vague terms. In a detailed evaluation, we must decide for each argument whether it is inductive or deductive. If we think it is deductive, we must decide whether it is best reconstructed as a propositional or a categorical argument. Once we have made these decisions, we should rewrite the argument in standard form, and determine whether it is deductively valid or inductively strong, using the methods discussed in Chapters

2, 3, and 4. We must also decide whether we are justified in accepting each of the premises as true. If the premises are true and the argument is deductively valid or inductively strong, we should accept its conclusion. To evaluate a complete argument chain, we must follow this procedure with each of the arguments in the chain. This complete evaluation of an extended piece of reasoning requires considerable time and effort.

If we plan to evaluate completely an extended piece of reasoning, we can choose any starting point we wish. We can begin with the first theme and work through the argument in order, proceed in order of apparent importance, or simply group similar arguments together. If we are trying for something less than a complete analysis, we should start with either the central argument or the one(s) that seem most likely to involve difficulty. We will evaluate Shanker's arguments in the order in which they appear in his essay, the order in which we have listed them in the preceding section.

The first argument occurs in paragraph 4. We labeled it the "protection" argument. To evaluate it, we must first decide what sort of argument it is, and write it in standard form.

Since the argument seems to move from a discussion of some groups of professionals (doctors, dentists, etc.) to a conclusion about another group, teachers, you might be tempted to reconstruct this as an inductive argument. It looks as if it might be the sort of argument that identifies a pattern in a sample group and extends that pattern in the conclusion by applying it to another member of the same class, which is the hallmark of an inductive argument (IP). However, the goal in this argument is not to establish that teachers have a certain property, but to show that a property we already know them to have (the protection afforded by tenure) is not unique. For this reason, it is best reconstructed as a propositional argument. Argument 5:8 is one possibility:

5:8. If tenure gave special protection to teachers, then other professionals would not have similar sorts of protection.

Other professionals do have similar protection.
_____

Tenure is not a form of special protection for teachers.

Argument 5:8 is an accurate reconstruction of the argument in paragraph 4. It does not lead directly to the conclusion that tenure should not be abolished, but that argument is never explicitly stated here. As noted earlier, an implicit appeal to fairness runs throughout the editorial, and might justify the further conclusion that tenure should be retained. Since Shanker does not supply many clues, there are several ways of constructing the argument. The best is to try to formulate the missing assumption that would allow us to link the point about special privilege to claims about abolishing or retaining tenure. The arguments in 5:9 are two attempts to link the argument in paragraph 4 to the main conclusion.

5:9. If tenure gave special protection to teachers, then it would be unfair and should be abolished.

Tenure does not give special protection to teachers.

Tenure should not be abolished.

Either tenure is a form of special protection, or there is no reason to abolish it.

Tenure is not a form of special protection.

There is no reason to abolish tenure.

The first attempt produces an invalid argument; it commits the fallacy of denying the antecedent. The second is deductively valid, but the first premise is highly doubtful, since there might be other reasons for abolishing tenure. There are other ways of trying to construct the argument based on different ways of formulating the premise dealing with special protection, but each seems to result in either an invalid argument or a premise so contentious that it needs further defense.

The main argument in paragraph 5 can be reconstructed as follows:

5:10. If abolishing tenure would improve teaching, then Mississippi and Texas should have superior educational systems.

Mississippi and Texas do not have superior educational systems.

Abolishing tenure does not improve teaching.

Consider how one might justify the first premise: "If abolishing tenure would improve teaching, then Mississippi and Texas should have superior educational systems." It appears to be a simple substitution argument:

5:11. If abolishing tenure improves teaching, then a state without tenure should have a superior educational system.

If abolishing tenure improves teaching, then Mississippi and Texas should have superior educational systems.

As noted in Chapter 3, substitution is a legitimate step in propositional arguments. Since Texas and Mississippi are states without tenure, they can be substituted for the phrase "state without tenure." But we should be careful about the exact meaning of the original statement, so that we can spot any alterations that might be caused by careless substitution. When the general statement refers to "superior educational system," a contrast is implied, but a contrast with what? The only legitimate contrast would be with the same state with tenure, or with a state similar in all other respects; otherwise too many other factors might also affect the quality of educational systems. Thus, our general rule, when made fully explicit, would dictate the slightly different substitution in 5:12:

5:12. If abolishing tenure improves teaching, then a state without tenure should have an educational system that is superior to the system it would have had with tenure (or superior to that of states similar in all other relevant respects).

If abolishing tenure improves teaching, then Mississippi and Texas should have educational systems superior to the systems they had with tenure (or superior to that of other states similar in all relevant respects).

When worded this way, it is less clear that Shanker's statements in the last part of paragraph 5 are appropriate. To decide whether or not the argument is sound, we need to know more about the evidence he refers to.

Paragraphs 6 and 7 contain the following arguments:

5:13. If we are justified in requiring recertification for teachers, we should also require it for other professionals.

We do not require it for other professionals.

We should not require recertification for teachers.

5.14. If we are justified in requiring recertification for teachers, the justification for doing so is to minimize the damage caused by deteriorating performance.

If the justification for recertification is to minimize damage caused by deteriorating performance, we should require it for doctors, dentists, and others.

If we require recertification for teachers, we should also require it for other professionals.

Argument 5:14 provides support for the first premise of 5:13, but it also directs our attention to a feature of 5:13 that deserves closer scrutiny. All of 5:14, and hence the first premise of 5:13, deals with justification and what we should do. The second premise of 5:13 should therefore read "We should not require recertification for other professionals"; otherwise the argument is invalid. Although it is clear that we do not require recertification for all professionals, 5:14 might well be taken as part of an argument chain for the claim that we should do so, thus undercutting the second premise of 5:13.

In paragraphs 8 and 9, we find a similar line of argument:

5:15. If we are justified in retesting teachers, the justification would be based on the need to keep up with the "knowledge explosion."

If the justification is based on the need to keep up with the "knowledge explosion," we should also require retesting in medicine, dentistry, and pharmacy.

If we are justified in retesting teachers, we should also require retesting in medicine, dentistry, and pharmacy.

5:16. We can justifiably retest teachers only if they are not singled out = If we can justifiably retest teachers, then they are not singled out.

Teachers are singled out (under the proposal to require retesting.

We cannot justifiably retest teachers.

Here, 5:16 parallels the argument in 5:13, with one important difference. In the earlier argument, the shift from talk about what we *should* do to what we *actually do* took place in the middle of 5:13; here the switch occurs in the move from the conclusion of 5:15 to the first premise of 5:16. In both cases, though, we can see that Shanker has failed to establish his conclusion.

The detailed evaluation leads to a better understanding of the reservations we encountered in our brief overview. In many cases, the brief overview suffices, and in many others we can give a detailed evaluation of selected portions of the argument chain without going through every component. However, the procedure will be a more limited version of the one just illustrated: identify the individual arguments, reconstruct them, test for inductive strength or deductive validity, and examine the premises critically. As before, we often cannot summarize these findings into a simple decision that the argument as a whole is good or bad, but that is not our goal. We now can see exactly where Shanker has provided sound arguments, what the conclusions of those arguments are, and where and how his other arguments fail to support their conclusions.

EXERCISES

1. Give a detailed evaluation of one of the Extended Arguments for which you have prepared a thematic outline in the section Thematic Outlines of Extended Arguments.

2. Take a topic that interests you, prepare a thematic outline, and then construct from it an extended piece of reasoning that argues cogently for a clearly stated conclusion. You will probably want to work through several drafts, applying the techniques you have learned to criticize and improve successive versions. Do not throw the drafts away. Hand them in with your final version, explaining where you made changes and why.

Responding to Arguments

In Chapter 1 we emphasized that "arguments," in the technical sense, are not always disagreements between people or differences of opinion. Nonetheless, we often encounter arguments whose conclusions we disagree with, arguments whose premises strike us as dubious, or arguments to which we want to respond in some way. In this section, we discuss two ways of responding to an argument: arguing that it is deductively unsound or inductively unreliable, or arguing that it is ineffective.

The first method, showing that an argument is unsound or unreliable, is the approach we have emphasized up to this point. If an argument is sound, its conclusion must be true, and if it is inductively reliable, it is highly probable that the conclusion is true. Either way, it would not be rational simply to reject the conclusion as false.

To justify rejecting the conclusion, we must either produce a demonstrably sound **counterargument** to show that the conclusion is false, or demonstrate in some other manner that the argument is unsound or unreliable. If we can show that an argument uses a false premise, or that it is invalid and inductively weak, that argument no longer provides sufficient reason to accept the conclusion.

Proving that the conclusion of an argument is false, that one or more of the premises is false, or that the argument is invalid and inductively weak are all strategies used in the first method of responding to arguments. Let us examine each of the strategies in more detail.

One way to prove that a conclusion is false is to produce a **counterargument,** that is, a new argument with a conclusion that is **inconsistent** with the statement we are trying to disprove. Statements that are inconsistent with each other are called **contraries.** Two contrary statements cannot both be true; so if one of them is true, the other must be false. **Contradictory statements,** which were discussed in Chapters 2 and 3, are a special case; two contradictory statements cannot both be true, *and* they cannot both be false: they always have opposite truth values. The statements "All cats are black" and "Exactly three cats are white" are contraries but not contradictories: they cannot both be true, but they might both be false. Each statement has only one contradictory, but many statements can be inconsistent with it.

The technique of disproving a statement by producing a counterargument works when we are trying to disprove *any* statement; it is not limited to criticisms of the conclusions of arguments.

For example, Argument 5:7 might be given to prove that the conclusion of 5:6 is false:

5:17.   All the animals in this cage are platypuses.

Some of the animals in this cage lay eggs.

Some platypuses lay eggs.

In Chapter 2 we learned that "Some S's are P" is the contradictory of "No S's are P." So, if 5:17 is sound, the conclusion of 5:6 must be false. The conclusion of the argument in 5:17 is a **counterexample** to the general claim that no platypuses lay eggs. Not all arguments designed to disprove a statement work by offering a counterexample, but the technique is often worth trying.

When we produce a counterargument, this shows only that *one* of the arguments, either the original or the counterargument, is unsound. Thus, if an audience is convinced that the premises of the original argument are true, and the truth of the premises of the counterargument is doubtful, we will not have succeeded in casting doubt on the statement we are trying to disprove. Consider the pair of arguments in 5:18:

5:18. It is wrong to force people to accept situations that threaten their well-being.

Making abortion illegal forces some women to accept situations that threaten their well-being.

It is wrong to make abortions illegal.

The fetus is an innocent human being.

If abortion is made legally permissible, then we permit the killing of fetuses.

It is wrong to permit the killing of innocent human beings.

It is wrong to make abortions legally permissible.

This pair of arguments gives us a situation parallel to the arguments in 5:6 and 5:17, since the conclusion of the second argument in 5:18 is inconsistent with that of the first. Nonetheless, the second argument does not compel us to reject the conclusion of the first unless it is sound. Since the premises of both arguments are subject to much question and debate, it is unlikely that proponents of either argument will agree that the other is sound. Either we need to add additional arguments to support the controversial premises or we must try a different approach.

This first strategy—constructing a counterargument—involves a direct attack on the claim one is trying to disprove. Other strategies involve undermining the support for the claim, either by showing that the supporting argument is deductively invalid or inductively weak, or (the third strategy) by casting doubt on its premises. To employ either of the latter two approaches, we must first identify the argument that is under attack. It is not enough merely to cite its conclusion.

As an illustration of the third strategy in action, suppose someone were to offer the argument in 5:19 in favor of performing so-called eugenic abortions. (This example is adapted from Paul F. Camenish, "Abortion: For the Fetus's Own Sake?" *Hastings Center Report,* April 1976, pp. 38–41.)

5:19. A fetus diagnosed as malformed will lead a life of suffering. We should always try to eliminate avoidable suffering for the sake of the being who would suffer; therefore, we should allow eugenic abortions for the sake of the fetus.

We can reconstruct 5:19 as the categorical syllogism in 5:20. Let A = Abortions of fetuses diagnosed as severely malformed; M = Actions that are morally right; B = Actions that benefit a being who would otherwise suffer.

5:20.   (1)   All B are M.

(2)   All A are B.

(3)   All A are M.

In his paper, Camenish attacks premise (2) of 5:20 by arguing that it makes no sense to talk about benefits in the absence of a beneficiary. His reasoning is reconstructed in 5:21:

5:21.   If an action benefits a being, then that being must exist to enjoy the outcome.

If eugenic abortions benefit the fetus, then the fetus must exist to enjoy the outcome.

If eugenic abortions benefit the fetus, the fetus must exist to enjoy the outcome.

In eugenic abortions the fetus does not exist to enjoy the outcome.

It is not the case that eugenic abortions benefit the fetus.

The conclusion of argument 5:21 contradicts the second premise of 5:20. Thus, if Camenish's argument is sound, his opponent's argument is unsound.

Finally, we can criticize an argument by trying to show that it is invalid and inductively weak. The techniques discussed in Chapters 2, 3, and 4 provide a variety of methods for doing this.

It is important to remember that even if an argument is unsound, its conclusion might still be true. Thus, when we attack an argument by showing that it is unsound, we may succeed in undermining our opponent's reasons for holding a certain thesis, but we would not be justified in concluding *on that basis alone* that the conclusion is false. This is true whether we undermine the argument by showing it to be invalid or by attacking one of its premises.

As noted in the beginning of this section, showing that an argument is unsound (or showing that it is inductively unreliable) is one of two general ways of responding to arguments. The second is to show that the argument is *ineffective*. To do that, we must consider the context of the argument and the reasons for offering it.

In Chapter 1, we noted that good arguments show us what it is rational to believe; they convince us that the conclusion of the argument is true. Thus, when a speaker or writer presents an argument, she is usually trying to convince her audience to believe her conclusion. To achieve this goal, she must offer arguments that her audience will *recognize* as deductively sound or inductively reliable. As example 5:18 illustrated, one's audience will be unconvinced by any argument with premises that it believes are false. This suggests that an **effective argument** must satisfy two conditions:

1. The audience to which it is addressed will accept it as inductively reliable or deductively sound.

2. The argument is capable of rationally leading the audience to believe something it did not previously believe, or increasing the confidence with which it believes the conclusion.

Because the first condition has to do with what the audience will accept, it is possible to have effective but unsound arguments, if an audience will believe a false statement. Although it is important to give effective arguments, effectiveness alone is not enough for critical thinking.

Circular arguments are extreme examples of arguments that are likely to prove ineffective. In an argument that is blatantly circular, the conclusion merely repeats one of the premises or a part of a premise. More generally, we can characterize circular arguments as follows:

A circular argument is one in which it is rational to believe that all the premises are true only if one already believes the conclusion is true.

Argument 5:22 is an example of an obviously circular argument:

5:22. Jones is not a liar.

Jones always tells the truth.

In 5:22, the conclusion merely repeats the premise, using slightly different words. Because it is circular, it does not satisfy the second condition for an effective argument—it cannot add to anyone's store of beliefs.

It follows from the definition of validity that many circular arguments are valid. For example, if the conclusion makes the same statement as one of the premises, it is impossible for the conclusion to be false when all the premises are true. A circular argument can, therefore, also be sound. Nonetheless, it will be ineffective. If members of the audience already believe the conclusion, no additional argument is needed to convince them. If they do not believe the conclusion, they will not believe the premise, which is repeated in the conclusion, either, and consequently they will not recognize the argument as sound. The circular arguments in 5:23 illustrate this:

5:23. Nixon is not a crook; therefore he did not knowingly do anything illegal in connection with the Watergate scandal.

Human beings are nothing but complicated physical mechanisms.

There is no such thing as an immortal nonphysical human soul.

The circularity of the first argument in 5:23 is easy to see: we must accept the conclusion—that Nixon did nothing illegal in connection with Watergate—*before* we would agree to the premise. In the second argument, the circularity is more subtle. Nonetheless, since one must reject the existence of a nonphysical human soul before one can believe human beings are *nothing but* physical mechanisms, this argument is also circular.[1]

Because we are not always aware of how we could know a statement, or how it is possible to come to know or believe a premise, it is possible to make mistakes about circularity. Thus, someone might think that an argument is circular when it is not. Alternatively, it is possible not to notice that an argument is circular, if one fails to notice that one must already believe the conclusion in order rationally to accept one of the premises.

To understand the second way in which an argument can fail to be effective, we must first discuss the concept of a **presupposition**. When we accept a statement, X, as true, we **presuppose** another statement, Y, if Y must be true in order for X to be true. We can also say that statement X presupposes Y if and only if X logically entails Y. For example, if we believe that Mars is the fourth planet in our solar system, we presuppose that Mars is a planet. Someone who claims "Abortion is a form of homicide" presupposes "Fetuses are human beings."[2]

Accepting any statement involves many presuppositions, including any statement logically equivalent to the original. Usually we are not aware of everything we presuppose, and if we have not considered our beliefs with sufficient care, we may even presuppose statements that we think are false. Some of these presuppositions can render an argument ineffective.

The premises of arguments are statements, and accepting those premises as true—believing them—implies accepting their presuppositions as well. If we reject some of the presuppositions—believe that they are false—we must, rationally, reject the relevant premises as well. Thus, we will believe that any argument in which those premises occur is unsound; for us, the argument will be ineffective.

Suppose we criticize an argument by pointing out that one of its premises, X, presupposes another statement, Y, and then prove that Y is false. In doing this, we have proven that X also is false (since, by definition, X cannot be true if Y is false), and hence that the argument is unsound; that is, we have gone back to the first major strategy for responding to arguments. However, sensitivity to presuppositions can also allow for the more limited claim that an argument is ineffective. Consider argument 5:24:

5:24. Deception is *always* wrong, and espionage involves deception; therefore, the United States should not engage in espionage.

The first premise presupposes many things, including "Deception cannot be justified by showing that it leads to desirable consequences" and "Many experiments in psychology which involve deception are wrong." We may not be prepared to argue that these presuppositions are clearly false, but we may not be convinced that they are true, either. In this case, it is rational to reserve judgment on the presuppositions. But we cannot both reserve judgment on the presuppositions and believe that 5:24 is sound. Once we decide to reserve judgment, the argument becomes ineffective because it fails to satisfy the first condition for an effective argument: we are not prepared to accept the argument as sound.

Example 5:24 shows how attention to presuppositions can be used to show that an argument is ineffective. In general, if we can show that a premise presupposes a statement that the audience is not prepared to accept as true, we will render the argument ineffective.

Giving an argument whose premises presuppose something one's audience would not accept is always a bad idea. A specific version of this fault even has a special name: **begging the question.** Begging the question means that, in arguing for a conclusion, one has presupposed a statement that one's audience believes to be false.[3]

It follows from this definition that an argument may be question-begging in one context and not in another. Argument 5:25 is an example of such an argument:

5:25. The evil and suffering we observe in the world must all be necessary for some ultimate good purpose, because God is omnipotent and benevolent, and thus He would not allow unnecessary suffering.

The first premise in this argument chain, "God is omnipotent and benevolent," presupposes that God exists. This presupposition would be acceptable only to people who believe in the existence of an all-powerful, all-good deity. The argument could be used effectively if one wanted to convince such an audience to accept the existence of suffering without complaint, but one would be guilty of begging the question if one proposed this argument to an atheist.

We can summarize the results of this section by noting that one can criticize an argument either by showing that it is unsound or inductively unreliable, or by showing that it is ineffective in the context in which it is offered. The first option requires an argument to show (1) that the conclusion is false, (2) that one or more of the premises is false, or (3) that the argument is deductively invalid and inductively weak. The second option involves identifying premises that require prior acceptance of the conclusion, or presuppositions that the intended audience would not accept as true. By showing that a premise requires prior acceptance of the conclusion, we show that the argument does not add to our beliefs in a rational way. By identifying problematic presuppositions, we show that the audience may not be prepared to accept the argument as reliable or sound.

This section has emphasized the analysis of arguments proposed by others, but it also suggests important guidelines for constructing good arguments. We have already emphasized the need to construct sound or reliable arguments in Chapters 2, 3, and 4; we can now add the advice to construct effective arguments. As noted earlier, not all effective arguments are sound, so this new advice does not supersede the concern with sound or reliable arguments, but it will help you construct more useful arguments.

To construct effective arguments, determine what is presupposed by your premises, and ask whether your audience will believe those presuppositions are true. If you think your audience might be neutral about a presupposition, or is likely to reject a presupposition as false, you should try to provide an argument to show it is true. If you cannot do this, you should abandon your argument in favor of a different one.

Using an outline to plan your argument, as described in Chapter 1 in the section Constructing Arguments, can help you carry out these recommendations. Pay particular attention to those statements that occur at the beginning of a line of reasoning, those that have no arrows pointing to them. Try to predict (perhaps by imagining arguments for the opposite conclusion) which of these statements are most likely to be challenged or doubted by your audience, and extend your outline to provide support for any which are questionable.

EXERCISES

*1. Construct a response to argument 5:21.

2. Suppose that someone offers the following inductive argument for the conclusion that the mass of planet A is smaller than that of planet C. "Planet B is known to have a mass much greater than C's. The mass of a planet is the product of its volume times its average density. Planet A is smaller than planet B, and its average density is less. Thus, it is highly probable that A's mass is less than C's." Respond to this argument by trying to show it is inductively weak.

3. In light of your answer to question 2, respond to Stich's argument (Extended Argument 6, paragraph 15) that you were asked to reconstruct in question 6 in the section Mixed Argument Chains.

The following questions pertain to Extended Argument 7.

4. Reconstruct and respond to Kates's argument in paragraphs 24 through 26, for his conclusion that it is false that the absence of handguns would lower the death and injury rate in confrontations with criminals and that, in fact, the rate would increase. In answering this question, assume that, of the estimated 120 million guns in private hands (in 1978), about one-quarter are handguns; the rest are shoulder weapons such as shotguns and rifles. All studies agree that about half of all the guns confiscated by the police have been stolen from their legal owners.

5. Reconstruct and respond to Kates's argument in paragraph 11 for his conclusion that gun ownership deters burglars. Does the following information support or weaken his argument? "The burglar is shot and wounded or killed by the intended victim in 2 out of each 1000 cases of home burglary reported to the police. Ninety percent of all home burglar-

ies occur when no one is at home. The overall chances of a burglar ending up in jail for the crime are about 2 in 100."

6. Reconstruct and respond to Kates's argument in paragraphs 12 and 13 for his conclusion that gun ownership decreases the likelihood of injury and death from burglars (i.e., the rates of injury and death of householders caused by burglars would be higher if no householders owned guns).

Notes

[1]Notice that the definition of a circular argument involves the relation of *priority:* in a circular argument one cannot rationally believe that all the premises are true without *first* believing that the conclusion is true. This element of priority is crucial. Without it, any valid deductive argument would be circular, since it would be irrational to believe the premises of such an argument without also believing its conclusion. However, many deductively valid arguments are effective, and any argument recognized as circular will be ineffective.

[2]Some people speak of the presuppositions of *arguments,* but our definition deals only with the presuppositions involved in accepting *statements.* If we think of such presuppositions, by analogy with the definition given here, as other statements that must be accepted for the argument to be valid or inductively strong, the "presuppositions of arguments" are simply unstated premises. Instead of calling them presuppositions, one should identify them as implicit or missing premises.

[3]Many people use the terms **circular argument** and **begging the question** in ways that make them equivalent. We believe it is useful to distinguish flaws that are intrinsic to the argument from those that are relative to the audience and purpose. Based on the definitions given here, an argument is circular or not regardless of author or audience; but an argument may be question-begging in one context and not in another.

CHAPTER

6

Words, Meanings, and Definitions

Clarifying what words mean is often a vital step in understanding and evaluating arguments. It can affect our judgments about the truth of an argument's premises and conclusion, as well as our verdict on its validity or strength. In this chapter, we explore how determining what words and statements mean contributes to the evaluation of arguments.

Analytic and Synthetic Statements

Some statements are true (or false) *solely* by virtue of the meanings of the words and symbols used in the sentences that express them. These are called **analytic statements**. In theory, we can tell whether an analytic statement is true or false without knowing anything beyond the meaning of all the terms used to express it. (In practice, some analytic statements, especially those in mathematics, are so complex that we may have great difficulty in deciding whether or not they are true.) Argument 6:1 contains examples of analytic statements:

6:1. 2 = 2.

No odd number can be divided by 2 without leaving a remainder.

All bachelors are unmarried.

Some squares have three sides.

"$\sim pVq$" is logically equivalent to "$p \rightarrow q$."

All bachelors are bachelors.

Unlike the other statements in 6:1, the claim that some squares have three sides is false. But as in the other cases, its truth value depends entirely on the definitions and meanings of the terms used.

Tautologies and **contradictions** are important classes of analytic statements. These statements are true or false solely by virtue of their logical form. Thus, the last two statements in 6:1 are both logical truths. One does not even have to know what the word "bachelor" means to know that "All bachelors are bachelors" is true, since any statement of the form "All A's are A's" must be true. Tautologies are also called **logical truths**, and contradictions are also referred to as **logical falsehoods**.

The truth values of analytic statements that are neither tautologies nor contradictions depend on the definitions and meanings of their nonlogical terms. Examples are "All bachelors are unmarried," "All triangles have three sides," and "No odd numbers are exactly divisible by 2." To determine whether these claims are true, we need only to understand the meaning of the words; we do not have to examine bachelors, triangles, or odd numbers to see if they have the relevant properties.

Any statement that is not analytic is **synthetic**. The truth value of a synthetic statement, such as "Some chairs are green," depends partly on empirical facts about the world. Because they convey factual information, synthetic statements are also called **empirical statements**. All synthetic or empirical statements are contingent, which means that their truth value is *not* a matter of logical necessity: it is *logically* possible that an empirical statement could be false.

Deciding whether a statement is analytic or synthetic can play an important role in evaluating arguments. Consider, for example, the argument in 6:2:

6:2. Computers may solve complicated math problems and manipulate huge amounts of data, but they cannot truly think. Thinking requires creativity and imagination, and by definition, creativity cannot be captured by a set of rules and mechanical procedures.

The last premise, "Creativity cannot be captured by a set of rules and mechanical procedures" is presented as true "by definition," which is a way of claiming that it is analytic. Someone who presented this argument could be expected to reject any example of computer-generated poetry or music by claiming that, since it was generated by a rule-governed mechanical procedure, it could not possibly be evidence of creativity. But there is good reason to be suspicious of this sort of definition of creativity—or indeed any definition that refers to the way in which a creative process is carried out. After all, we do not know much about how human beings manage to be creative. If creativity is defined, instead, as an ability to produce new and interesting things, any premise such as the one we are discussing will turn out to be synthetic, not analytic.

Thus, in 6:2 a premise that might seem to be analytic turns out to be synthetic. It is important to identify such statements correctly, since how one argues for or against them depends in large part on whether they are synthetic or analytic. In the former case, it is relevant to offer factual evidence. In the latter case, we have to assess the definitions on which the analytic claim is based or the logical form of the statement.

In other cases, a statement that seems at first to be empirical is, in reality, analytic. Consider example 6:3:

6:3. All actions, however altruistic they may appear on the surface, are at bottom selfish. This is because whenever a person acts, her action is always prompted by her own motives and desires, not by those of anyone else. Thus, each person is always pursuing her own ends and trying to satisfy her own desires.

At first, it appears that the author is addressing an empirical question, but on reflection we can see that she is assuming a definition of "selfish" which makes her conclusion analytic. In standard English, a selfish action is one that is done out of self-interest rather than to benefit others. But in this passage, the adjective "selfish" is being used to mean "prompted by the desires and motives of the person who acts." Given this nonstandard meaning of "selfish," it becomes an analytic truth that all acts, even those of heroic self-sacrifice or altruism, are selfish. The empirical question as to whether people always act to benefit themselves is not addressed.

It is helpful, in cases like this, to remember that it is impossible to deduce a synthetic statement from only analytic premises. We cannot settle questions of physical existence or other empirical matters by definition alone.

Example 6:3 illustrates the need to watch for arguments in which an analytic claim masquerades as an empirical one. For example, if someone claims that a tree falling in an uninhabited forest makes no sound, he might seem to be making a factual assertion. But if he is using the word "sound" to mean "an aural sensation experienced by a human being," his claim is really analytic. One test for this sort of hidden analyticity is to ask whether there is any possibility of a counterexample, or whether counterexamples are ruled out as impossible by the very meaning of the words involved.

EXERCISES

For each of the claims given here, decide whether it is analytic or synthetic. Explain your judgment.

1. Whales are fish.

2. The gestation period of a whale is longer than that of a human.

3. A "Saturday night special" is a cheaply made handgun.

4. No true libertarian would endorse a policy of mandatory retirement.

5. Parallel lines never intersect.

6. The sum of the interior angles of a triangle is 180 degrees.

*7. Neanderthal man is a hominid.

*8. Neanderthal man is an ancestor of *Homo sapiens*.

9. All effects have causes.

10. All events are caused.

What Is Said?

Whether we are dealing with analytic or synthetic statements, we must be sure that we correctly understand their meaning. What a statement means depends on (1) what the person making the statement intends to say, and (2) the generally accepted conventions for the correct use of language. The first condition makes it possible for one person to call a weapon "good," meaning that it is effective, while another person might call the same weapon "bad," meaning that its use would be immoral. Because of the second condition, a person should not use the term "murder" to refer to an act of killing unless it is believed to be unlawful or lacking moral justification.

Most of the time, understanding the meaning of a statement does not pose a problem. Familiarity with the rules and vocabulary of English determine a large portion of the interpretation of a statement, and the context within which the statement occurs usually does the rest. When told "Andrew hit Charles with the bat," we know, on the basis of English syntax, that Andrew was performing the action, and that Charles was the one being hit. The context should tell us whether "bat" should be understood as referring to a baseball bat, a cricket bat, or a small flying mammal.

Like all natural languages, English contains many terms that are easy to apply to paradigm cases but that are subject to dispute when associated with borderline examples. Even with a word as simple as "red," there are occasions when we are simply unsure whether a color can properly be called red. In other cases, as with "bat," a word can have more than one meaning.

In this section, we explore some of the problems that may arise when we try to determine what a word, phrase, or statement means. As we shall see, a word may be so **vague** as to render the truth value of a premise moot; it may be **ambiguous** or it might be used in an **idiosyncratic** way, so that it misses the point of the argumentative context.

The first potential problem we will consider is **vagueness**. Although it may be difficult to decide how to apply a term in borderline cases, most words have many paradigm cases in which they apply unproblematically. Having "fuzzy boundaries" in this way does not mean that a term is vague.

A term is **vague** when it is *often* unclear whether it can be applied correctly to a given situation. Obviously, vagueness in this sense admits of degrees. When we say that a term is "clear" or "not vague at all," we mean that in most cases a competent speaker of the language can decide whether the term is correctly applied, and that legitimate doubt will exist in relatively few cases. Thus, "red" is not vague, since we can look at most objects and decide quite easily whether they are red. Vaguer terms have fewer clear cases, and more doubtful ones. The term "literature," for example, clearly applies to *Moby Dick* and a great many other works. But there is an equally large area of doubt. Are comic books literature? Science fiction and mystery novels? The word "literature" is, therefore, somewhat vague. A term that is very vague lacks clear-cut applications, even in central cases.

To the extent that we cannot specify what a vague term means, a statement containing it does not say much; it has very little real content. Such vagueness can tempt us into reading more into the statement than we are entitled to. For example, advertisements that tell us a certain cigarette is "richer-tasting" or an appliance is "built with quality" or simply that Brand X is "better than" its competitors, are all vague. Vagueness often occurs in incomplete claims: we are told that something is better, bigger, lasts longer, or is 99 percent pure, but someone has neglected to tell us what the product is bigger or better than, and never answers the question "99 percent pure what?" The remedy is to be as precise as possible when making claims and to avoid assuming too much when interpreting claims made by others.

Vagueness often results from using **obscure** language. A string of polysyllabic terms can disguise the fact that very little is actually being said, as in the passage in 6:4:

6:4. Extant organizational structures, including infrastructures, shall make all appropriate effort to ensure that any parameters adopted by one unit interdigitate with previously approved protocols in a synergystic manner.

Using **buzz-words** can also produce vagueness. **Buzz-words** are words or phrases that are calculated to elicit a positive or negative attitude *without providing an objective reason for that attitude*. The word "natural," for example, occurs in recommendations for everything from breakfast cereal to rat poison, but it guarantees nothing about wholesomeness, nutrition, or taste. "New" and "improved" are two classic buzz-words. These words arouse reactions in us that have nothing to do with any objective claim about the quality of the item being touted. Cars are described as "exciting," whisky is sold by appeal to "self-confidence" and "pride," political opponents are derided as "fuzzy-headed," "weak," "uncaring," "warmongers" or "peaceniks." These claims often seem substantive, and audiences may react as if something definite were being asserted. Closer examination reveals that they are vague and contain little or no information.

Not all positively or negatively charged terms are buzz-words. Someone can present an argument containing words like "genocide" or "a national hero" without being guilty of relying on buzz-words if the negative or positive judgment implicit in those terms is adequately justified. Something becomes a buzz-word only when it is used as a substitute for reasons. In passage 6:5, for example, highly emotional terms are used to arouse feelings, but few reasons are given to justify their use.

6:5. Swiftly and gracefully, propelled by their flippers, the harp seals begin their two-thousand-mile journey south . . . to their breeding grounds, *and to a fateful rendezvous with human greed and vanity.* . . . For decades now, humankind has placed a higher value on the wearing of that baby fur and the profits to be made from its sale than on the survival of infant harp seals. As a result, while two centuries ago harp seals and their young literally covered the ice floes at breeding time, since then, *the most protracted infanticide ever inflicted on any wild animal anywhere* has been committed. . . . If you are angered and revolted by this incredible obscenity, you are among a world majority. . . . (Advertisement for the Animal Protection Institute of America.)

What information does this passage convey? It tells us that for some period of time, people have been killing baby seals for their fur, but it does not give reasons to support the implicit claim that this action is morally wrong. For example, 6:5 does not assert that harp seals are an endangered species, despite the contrast between "covering the ice floes at breeding time" and "protracted infanticide." Instead, it relies on buzz-words such as "greed and vanity," "infanticide," and "incredible obscenity," which produce a negative reaction without conveying much information or providing an argument. There are, of course, other issues that might be relevant to this topic (for example, the pain associated with the way the seals are killed, and questions about what would morally justify the killing of wild animals), but these issues are not addressed in 6:5.

Thus, the major difficulty with any variety of vagueness, whether the problem is simple vagueness, buzz-words, or obscurity, is that vague statements seem to convey more information than they actually do. Since information is essential to good reasoning, vague statements can leave us without the material necessary to reach a reasonable conclusion.

On the other hand, it is important not to exaggerate concerns about vagueness. We should not demand more information than is appropriate or necessary, or level a charge of "vagueness" against any statement that does not supply a complete description. Thus, it would be incorrect to say that the statement "Johnny ate all the cookies" is vague, just because it does not tell us how many cookies there were, or what kind of cookies he ate. "Cookies" is a broad term— it covers many kinds of cookies—but it is not vague. Similarly, technical terms should not be rejected as obscure if they occur in an appropriate context, and, as noted before, not all positively or negatively charged terms are buzz-words.

Vague terms play a crucial role in a special sort of bad reasoning known as **slippery slope arguments.**[1] Slippery slope arguments rely on the reasonable premise that if two cases are similar in relevant ways, conclusions about one of them should extend to the other. For example, if we believe that heroin should not be sold to children, and if we establish that selling cocaine to children is similar in all relevant respects to selling heroin to children, it follows that we should not allow the sale of cocaine to children either. This premise is perfectly legitimate, and its use does not make the argument fallacious, or a slippery slope. One gets a slippery slope argument when one exploits this premise by using a vague term to blur the distinction between dissimilar cases. The argument suggests that if a term clearly applies to case A, then it must also apply to case B, and if it applies to B, then it must also cover C, and so on. The vaguer a term is, the harder it will be to articulate differences between A and C that might be relevant to the conclusion, but are obscured by the difficulty of deciding to which cases this vague term really applies. Consider the slippery slope argument in 6:6:

6:6. Some people defend euthanasia by suggesting that someone who is terminally ill and would like to be allowed to die should do so. But what of the terminally ill patient who has not expressed his wishes one way or the other? Allowing him to die, or even actively bringing his death about, is also euthanasia. And then there are the severely defective infants; withholding food and medical support from them also counts as euthanasia. So if we decide that euthanasia is morally permissible, we will be condoning the killing of individuals who do not wish to die. That is, we will be condoning murder.

The slippery slope is generated because the term "euthanasia" clearly applies to some cases (allowing someone to die who wishes to do so), and clearly does not apply to others (killing a healthy individual who desires to go on living), but there are many cases that fall between these extremes and thus there is some doubt about how far the term "euthanasia" extends. Argument 6:6 is fallacious because the real issue is whether there is a relevant difference between allowing someone to die who wishes to do so and actively killing someone who has not expressed such a wish. Unless the two sorts of case are relevantly similar, permitting euthanasia in the one implies nothing about the morality of the other.

Because almost all words and statements have some degree of vagueness, we should not simply dismiss any claim we suspect is vague. When we evaluate a claim or argument, we must use the context, further investigation, and our background knowledge on the correct use of the language to develop an interpretation precise enough to be useful. In making claims or constructing arguments, we should try to be as precise as the situation warrants.

A second obstacle to the correct understanding of what a statement means is **ambiguity**. Statements that can be interpreted in more than one way are ambiguous. Ambiguity should not be confused with vagueness. An ambiguous statement or term can be understood in two (or more) different senses, but each sense, taken on its own, may be quite precise. Vague terms or statements do not usually have two *distinct* interpretations; we simply cannot determine with any precision how to interpret them. A statement is rarely both vague *and* ambiguous. Consider, for example, statement 6:7:

6:7. It is unethical for a doctor to bring a public charge of malpractice against a colleague.

Someone who asserted 6:7 might be saying that it would be *morally wrong* for a physician to act this way. But the terms "ethical" and "unethical" can also refer to *actions that are recommended or prohibited by a professional code of conduct* (such as the one imposed by the American Medical Association). In this latter sense, ethical behavior is not necessarily moral. Because the word "ethical" has two different meanings, its use here is ambiguous.

In many cases, the context makes it clear which sense of an ambiguous word or phrase is meant. In Extended Argument 7, for example, the term "use" in Paragraph 24 is ambiguous: it could mean either "carry" or "inflict injury with." The subsequent argument (paragraphs 25 and 26) makes it clear that "use" must mean "inflict injury with."

Some authors draw a distinction between **ambiguity**, which involves a word or phrase having two or more meanings, and **amphiboly**. The latter term applies to sentences that can be interpreted in two different ways, even though each individual word is clear enough. Amphiboly is usually a result of sloppy syntax (e.g., "I drove past the building where the Declaration of Independence was signed every afternoon at 5 o'clock"), but this is not always the case, as 6:8 illustrates:

6:8. My brother, Lloyd, and I went to the baseball game.

Does 6:8 tell us that three people went together, or that my brother, whose name is Lloyd, attended the game with me? Amphiboly, like ambiguity, can make it difficult to understand what a sentence really means.

It is probably impossible to eliminate all ambiguity from our language, but it is important to check the meaning of statements carefully. In particular, many advertisements make use of subtle ambiguities to seem to say one thing when they actually are saying something quite different. Thus, an automotive company might be perfectly justified in claiming that its cars have the best average gas mileage of the Big Three, but that does not mean that any given model will have better gas mileage than the models of equivalent size made by its competitors. If we calculate the average gas mileage of all the cars it sells, we arrive at a lower figure for one company than for the others. But this difference may merely reflect the fact that this manufacturer has a higher percentage of small cars in its total sales. As we will see in Chapter 8, the term "average" has several meanings; therefore, not specifying which sort of average one means results in ambiguity.

Another problem that stems from ambiguity is **equivocation.** A person is said to equivocate when she switches from one meaning of an ambiguous word to another. Some philosophers label this **the fallacy of equivocation**, since equivocating in an argument almost always makes the argument unsound. Consider example 6:9:

6:9. The Constitution guarantees that "all men are created equal," but since Sally is not a man, she is not necessarily entitled to equal rights under the Constitution.

In the first premise the term "men" is used generically, meaning "people" or "human beings." In the second premise its meaning has shifted, and now refers only to males. The argument is therefore invalid; if we reconstructed it as a categorical syllogism, it would have four terms.

A final problem that may occur in interpreting what someone says is the **idiosyncratic** use of a word or phrase. A word is used idiosyncratically when the speaker departs from the word's accepted meaning. This is usually done to make a statement or argument seem more reasonable than it really is. Consider 6:10, a quotation from an interview with Phyllis Schlafly:

6:10. Family Circle: Does sexism exist? Schlafly: If by sexism you mean that women *as a group* have been oppressed, mistreated, and discriminated against, no. I don't think that's true of this country. Now, some women have been discriminated against. (*Family Circle,* 9/18/79, p. 62.)

By defining "sexism" as she does, Schlafly discounts cases of discrimination against individual women as evidence of sexism. Ambiguity and vagueness both invite idiosyncratic interpretations, since it is easier to use one's own definition if the term is open to misinterpretation. But the use of a vague or ambiguous term is not always idiosyncratic, and a clear and univocal term can also be used idiosyncratically.

We can summarize our remarks about the meaning of statements in this warning: *It is essential to formulate and interpret statements carefully in order to avoid misunderstanding or uncritical position taking.* In the examples discussed so far, we have considered statements in isolation, but the same warning applies to arguments as well. Buzz-words can conceal the lack of any real argument, or make an argument appear stronger than it really is. Ambiguity can introduce further difficulties in an argument; we have seen one example of that, and will explore the topic further in the section What Is the Issue? Vague statements in arguments carry with them all the problems discussed in relation to vague claims in isolation, and they also afford the possibility of a slippery slope.

EXERCISES

For each of the following, explain in your own words what is being said. Eliminate buzz-words. If a statement is vague, show how it is vague, and suggest a more precise reformulation. If there is an ambiguity, indicate the different ways of interpreting the statement. If you think a word is being used idiosyncratically, explain.

1. The average student misspells four words in a five-page essay.

2. The movement to ban abortion deserves your support because it is pro-life.

3. Crispettes cereal is full of the good, wholesome ingredients that will start your day off right. It's the smart choice for breakfast.

*4. The interest payments on our new line of trucks is only $98 a month until December 31.

5. Unlike race or sex discrimination, sexual harassment is a hard-to-define term which is in part related to natural sex urges. What some women perceive as harassment, others may perceive as desirable attention.

6. The advocates of gun control legislation, including the YMCA, are the ones whose action is coercive and smacks of intimidation. If I own something (e.g., a gun) and somebody takes it away from me by force (gun control legislation), I am being coerced.

*7. Everybody should have tax relief, but special breaks for couples are only tax "bandages." We should not penalize either the married or the single taxpayer. But special breaks do not eliminate bias. They only bias the system against someone else.

8. Well-meaning but sentimental animal lovers have suggested that we need more bureaucracy to police research involving animals. Their naive protests ignore the multitude of medical advancements that were possible only because of such research. Besides, no reputable scientist would waste animals unnecessarily; experiments involving animals are always designed to be as humane as possible, consistent with achieving valid results.

9. In a Volvo, good gas mileage is standard. But it's not the sole attraction. Volvos come with much more important things. Like superior braking, handling, performance, and construction which protect you and your passengers. And give you superior value for your money.

10. Reagan is far from a good Conservative. If he were, he would not advocate interference by the government in the private concerns of its citizens.

What Is Suggested?

The preceding section dealt with a statement's literal meaning. When a person utters or writes a statement, however, he often suggests something that goes beyond this literal meaning. In Chapter 2, for example, we saw that an (I) proposition suggests that there are some S's that are not P, even though it literally means only that at least one S is P. What is suggested, rather than stated explicitly, is often important in interpreting a claim or an argument.

The philosopher H. P. Grice has provided a framework within which we can better understand this phenomenon.[2] It can also help us to specify what is being suggested in a given context. Grice's central idea is that we follow certain basic **maxims** or rules when we engage in conversation. We assume that other people follow these maxims, and interpret their statements as if they were doing so. We also expect *our* statements to be interpreted in the same way. Grice uses the term **conversational implicature** for information that is conveyed in this way without being part of the explicit or literal meaning of a statement. The implications of a statement, or what the statement suggests, are the further claims generated by interpreting the statement in light of these maxims.

The maxims identified by Grice fall under four general headings: **quality, quantity, relation**, and **manner**. We have paraphrased the maxims as follows:

Quantity: Make your contribution as informative as is appropriate.
Quality: State only things that you believe to be true and for which you have adequate evidence.
Relation: Respond to questions and remarks in a way that is relevant to the question or comment to which you are responding.
Manner: Be clear, brief, and orderly.

Grice's maxims attempt to capture the assumptions that we all make in interpreting another person's claims. Underlying all of this is the presupposition that discussion or conversation is a cooperative effort: the speaker and the audience are trying to work together to accomplish something. Thus, if I ask a question, I assume that the person who answers is trying to help me get the information I am seeking; this entails that she will not deliberately mislead me, that she will supply the information I seek if she can do so, and that she will not distract me with information that is irrelevant. These assumptions are made explicit in Grice's maxims of quality, quantity, and relation, respectively.

These rules governing normal conversation explain why we infer "Some S's are not P" when someone tells us that some S's are P. If *all* S's were P, the maxim of **quantity** would direct me to say so; if I say, instead, that some S's are P, this suggests that it is not the case that all S's are P or, in other words, that some S's are not P. The maxims also make us aware of more subtle implications, as in 6:11:

6:11. The brave pioneers crossed the prairie with their wives and all their worldly possessions.

In light of the maxim of manner, we notice that 6:11 mentions both "brave pioneers" and "their wives," rather than just "brave pioneers." Assuming that the person who made this statement is being as brief as possible, the **implication** is that the wives were not themselves brave pioneers.

The maxim of relation can help us uncover the implication in the exchange reported in 6:12:

6:12. A: "Did you hear that Smith's warehouse burned to the ground last night?"

B: "I'm not surprised. He was heavily insured, and his business was doing poorly."

In trying to see how B's remarks might be relevant, we realize he is suggesting that the fire was arson. Similarly, ads that show someone using a particular brand of toothpaste, and then suddenly getting a date with the man of her dreams, suggest that using this toothpaste will make one sexually attractive. (Suggestion often introduces elements of sexuality, power, or status.)

Grice's maxims also explain how **slanting** can suggest attitudes and judgments that go beyond what is explicitly claimed. In one type of slanting, **buzzwords** with a strong positive or negative connotation are used to evoke attitudes, either favorable or unfavorable, without giving objective reasons for them. In more subtle cases of slanting, neutral terms are used to disguise something that, by its very nature, ought to be described negatively. Hitler's euphemism "The Final Solution" for his policy of genocide is a grim example. The rhetoric of war is replete with further examples: terms like "pacification," "incursion," "protective air strikes," and "incontinent ordnance" (all used in reporting actions during the Vietnam War) *sound* better than "killing," "invasion," "bombing," and "bombs that went off-target."

Since Grice's maxim of quality tells us to make claims only if we have good evidence for them, we are tempted to assume that there are good reasons to support the positive, negative, or neutral appraisal conveyed by the language used. But unless the context or our background knowledge indicates what those reasons might be, we should refrain from accepting those appraisals uncritically. This is especially important when slanted language expresses prejudice and stereotyping. Calling a man "aggressive" while labeling a woman who behaves similarly "pushy" or "bitchy" is an example of using slanted terms to reinforce sexist attitudes. Even the use of an otherwise neutral term such as "girl" introduces slanting (by conveying the message that one is not talking about an adult) when it is applied to a woman.

Although we sometimes single out a statement as being "suggestive," it is important to remember that we normally assume people are following Grice's maxims. Therefore, most remarks suggest certain attitudes or beliefs that go beyond what is actually said. This is not normally a problem; in fact, it usually makes conversation more efficient. Consider the following exchange:

6:13. A: Do you know where Smith is?

B: He is not in his office.

Since we naturally assume that B is following the maxims, A will probably come to believe that Smith is not in his office, that B does not know where Smith is or does not think that it is relevant. Of course, B could have added: "Smith is not in the office, and since I assume you want to see him on business, any other information about his whereabouts is irrelevant," or "Smith is not in his office and I don't know where he is," but the conversational implicature of his answer makes such additional comments unnecessary.

Thus, in most cases, suggestion is a common and useful feature of language. However, we should make it a practice to consider carefully what is suggested by a statement, especially a premise in an argument we are constructing or evaluating. In particular, we need to make sure of the following:

1. That we do not convey (or accept) attitudes that should be examined more carefully. For example, we should avoid slanting and using negative stereotypes.

2. That beliefs about relevance are well founded. Failing to do this may lead one to overlook important information. In Extended Argument 3, the author correctly points out that the extent of the UN's actual powers is relevant to claims about what it should or should not do. The editorial he is criticizing did not adequately assess its own judgments about what was relevant to the issue.

3. That we do not employ assumptions based on Grice's maxims when it is inappropriate to do so. As noted earlier, the assumption that the maxims are being followed is based on the model of conversation as a cooperative enterprise. Not all uses of language fit this model. Advertisements, for example, are designed to sell products, not just to convey helpful information; it would therefore be naive to expect an advertisement to contain all the available information that might be relevant to assessing the quality of a product. The same is true of other uses of language in which the primary goal is something other than the cooperative sharing of information.

EXERCISES

In each of the following, explain what is suggested by the statement, using Grice's maxims. If slanting is present, identify the terms or phrases responsible for the slanting, and suggest more appropriate alternatives.

1. Buy Jif peanut butter. It contains no cholesterol.

*2. Teaching is no longer seen as a woman's job. Teaching is seen as a tough, exciting place where things are happening.

3. When asked to comment on a presentation to the Board of Trustees of

arguments in favor of divestment, the president of the Board said "We listened to them and thought they did a very nice, competent job."

4. Smith is vacationing somewhere in England.

5. Senator Jones is pro-family; she opposes the ERA.

6. Smith has impeccable credentials for his new post at the Treasury. He has a BA in psychology, a successful car dealership, and has never been indicted for fraud.

*7. I see little difference between someone in Florida harvesting oranges and someone in northeast Newfoundland engaging in the seal hunt.

8. Ms. Robbins is industrious and honest; I recommend her highly for a position as a secretary or receptionist.

9. Decisions about wartime policy should not be in the hands of the squeamish; we cannot afford to let the realities of war blind us to the goals of democracy and freedom for which we are fighting.

10. This airline is extremely safety-conscious. It has not had an in-flight emergency in over six months.

What Is the Issue?

Interpreting a word or a phrase correctly is often a crucial step in understanding an issue, determining what a debate is really about, or responding appropriately to an argument or claim. Consider the exchange in 6:14:

6:14. Smith: Alcoholism is a disease.

Jones: That's the wrong way of looking at it. The alcoholic chooses to drink, and the only "cure" is deciding not to drink.

We may know many facts about alcoholism but still be unsure whether Smith's claim is true or whether Jones's objection is relevant, if true. We must know more about how the term "disease" is being used—about the meaning of the concept of disease—to be able to evaluate this exchange. The disagreement in 6:14 is about what makes something a disease rather than the symptoms or characteristics of alcoholism. For these reasons, "disease" is a **key word** in this debate.

Key words in debates, exchanges, and arguments are terms open to more than one interpretation and occur in statements whose truth depends on which interpretation is adopted. The careful analysis of key words is often an important step in clarifying debates and exchanges. A complete reconstruction of an argument containing a key word should include an analytic statement about the term among its premises.

Not every term central to an argument or debate is a key word. If its main concepts are unambiguous, or if the intended audience agrees on their correct interpretation, an argument may not have any key words, in the sense defined here. Moreover, the key words in a debate are not always its principal focus.

We should ask three questions about key words in arguments and debates:

1. In what way is the meaning of the term relevant to the issue?

2. What does the speaker or writer mean when she uses the word?

3. What is the best way of interpreting or defining the word?

The third question is the main focus of the section What Should a Word Mean? in this chapter. Right now we are concentrating on the first two.

We do not have enough background information about 6:14 to determine why Smith and Jones are arguing about alcoholism, but we can imagine several contexts in which their debate might arise. They might be interested in whether it is appropriate to blame alcoholics for their condition. Alternatively, they might wonder whether medical insurance should cover the cost of treatment and counseling. Or they might be evaluating social programs for the prevention of alcoholism. In each case, the conclusion that alcoholism is or is not a disease might be relevant to their deliberations.

Neither Smith nor Jones tries to define the term "disease," but since Jones has given reasons for his position, we can infer something about what he means by the term. Jones claims that an alcoholic can simply choose to drink or not to drink. Therefore, he thinks that a disease is not the sort of thing we can choose to have or not have, something we can get rid of simply by deciding to do so.

Understanding these assumptions will put Smith in a better position to respond to Jones. He could, for example, point out that "choosing to drink" is not the same as "choosing to be an alcoholic," since alcoholism is not merely a matter of how much someone drinks. More important, he can then tell why the issue of whether or not alcoholism is a disease is relevant, if it is relevant at all. For example, whether something is a disease in Jones's sense is not too relevant to the question of medical insurance policies, but it might be crucial to decisions about what sorts of programs would be most effective in preventing alcoholism.

Example 6:15 reveals even more clearly why it is important to understand how a speaker is using a key word:

6:15. Poverty is ineradicable. As the proverb says, the poor are always with us, and they will always be. As long as anyone is free to accumulate a little more of the world's goods than others, there will always be people at the bottom of the scale: these are the poor. Even if you move them up the scale of wealth by charity, they will only leave someone else at the bottom.

What conclusion may be drawn from this? That all this talk of raising the standard of living is utopian folly—and utter nonsense. For it follows that some people must always be poor.[3]

The final conclusion, stated in the second paragraph, follows from the intermediate conclusion that poverty cannot be eradicated. The other two statements in the first paragraph supply reasons for this intermediate conclusion. By looking carefully at those two statements, we realize that what "poverty" and "the poor" mean is crucial to the argument. If we reconstruct the first of these arguments in categorical form, we get the following:

All times when there are inequalities of wealth are times when there will be people at the bottom of the economic ladder.

???

All times when there are inequalities of wealth are times at which the poor will be with us.

The missing premise is "All times when there will be people at the bottom of the economic ladder are times at which the poor will be with us." This indicates that "poverty" is being taken to *mean* "being at the bottom of the economic ladder." Poor people are being identified as those who are the least wealthy *as a matter of definition*. It is certainly true that poverty, in this sense, cannot be eliminated in any society in which people have unequal wealth. But the argument does not end here. The final conclusion deals with the futility of trying to raise the standard of living. We must "shift gears" at this point. Attempts to raise living standards do not aim at eliminating all economic inequality; rather, they try to remedy situations in which people lack basic necessities such as food, shelter, and health care. Nothing in the argument shows that poverty in *that* sense cannot be eliminated. We can easily imagine that even the people at the bottom of the economic ladder have access to these goods.

The most charitable evaluation of this argument is that it shows some welfare systems may be futile, but it offers no reasons that would discredit the majority of systems which strive to provide a minimum standard of living. Because the meaning of "poverty" does not shift in the middle of the argument, we cannot accuse the author of presenting an invalid or unsound argument. The best course of action is simply to refuse to be misled about the very limited and idiosyncratic nature of the only justifiable conclusion.

There is another reason for paying careful attention to the meaning of key words. It sometimes happens that people disagree because they are using a key word in two different ways. Consider the dispute between Smith and Jones in 6:16:

6:16. Smith: Locating hazardous waste sites close to populated areas poses an unjustifiable risk to society. People have made it clear that they will not tolerate such threats to their well-being.

Jones: Such a site poses no more risk than many other accepted features of modern life. The probability of dying as a result of living near a hazardous waste facility is no greater than the probability of dying in an automobile accident.

Jones's mention of probability tells us that he is speaking of "objective risk," which can be defined as "the measure of the probability of occurrence and the severity of negative effects." Smith, on the other hand, is concerned with "subjective risk," which is a measure of people's attitudes toward a potential risk, an attitude that is affected by a number of factors that do not enter into the calculation of objective risk (for example, how familiar and well understood the danger is, whether exposure to risk is voluntary, whether effects are immediate or delayed, chronic or catastrophic).[4] Obviously they will not be able to reach a reasonable conclusion until they agree on what sort of risk they are discussing.

As noted earlier, not all arguments have key words. Indeed, if we think of key words as terms whose meanings are especially important and stand in need of careful and precise interpretation, it is easy to understand why we should not think of "being a key word" as an all-or-nothing affair. Sometimes the validity or soundness of the entire argument hinges on the correct interpretation of a single word, whereas in other cases the role of a key word is less dramatic, though still important. Whenever an argument does contain a key word, it should be used correctly and consistently.

EXERCISES

I. Find the key word(s) in each of the following examples. Explain why that term is important, and how it is being used.

1. Despite all the renewed interest in basic skills, most high school graduates are still illiterate. They can pass tests, but cannot read well enough to enjoy and appreciate the great works of literature.

2. Evolution is only a theory; it cannot be proven on the basis of the fossil evidence. Since scientific creationism is also a theory about how animals and plants came into existence, a person should be able to choose which of these theories to accept. Thus, schools should present both options in a balanced way.

3. It is a biological fact that the fertilized ovum is a human life form. It is also a biological fact that human life begins in the male with the manufacture of sperm and in the female with the production of the ovum. Though few, if any, would argue that the sperm and ovum are persons, some individuals claim that these life forms become people at the moment of conception. The facts distinguish between human life forms and persons. The tendency to equate the two has no biological justification.

4. Although our cars cost a bit more, they are the best economy cars on the market. All the things you would pay extra for on a cheaper model are

standard, giving you much more value for your money. Isn't that what economy is all about?

*5. Although we claim to oppose totalitarian governments, our citizens are subject to a tyranny that is as pervasive as one can imagine; that is the tyranny of a majority rule that can and does override individual rights. As long as the wishes of the majority determine our laws without sufficient safeguards against the erosion of individual freedom, we live in tyranny.

6. In the broadest sense, it may be argued that all crimes are political crimes, inasmuch as all prohibitions with penal sanctions represent the defense of a given value system, or morality, in which the prevailing social power believes. Taking this to the very extreme, even a bank robbery, a shoplifting, or a rape is a political crime.[5]

II. Each of the following exercises identifies a key word in one of the extended arguments in the Appendix. Thus, "unfair" (1, 7) refers to the use of the term "unfair" in Extended Argument 1, paragraph 7. Read the relevant portion of the argument, and explain how the author is using that term and why it is a key word.

1. "Unfair" (1, 7).

2. "Involved" (2, 5).

3. "Erotica" (5, 5).

4. "Liberal" (5, 32).

5. "Scientific knowledge" (6, 3).

6. "Self-defense value" of gun ownership (7, 11).

7. "Crime deterrence value" of gun ownership (7, 11).

What Should a Word Mean?

In previous sections of this chapter, we have explored the role that the meanings of terms and statements play in critical thinking. Since our ability to communicate would disappear if each person decided for himself what words mean, we need standards for using them correctly and appropriately. This section surveys some of the considerations relevant to these judgments.

Although we are concerned with using words correctly, we neither try to give an exhaustive analysis of **definitions** nor focus exclusively on that topic. There are several reasons for this. First, it is extremely difficult to define precise methods and standards for good definitions. Second, the quality of a definition depends a great deal on context: something that is a good definition in one context may be useless in another. Most important, being able to evaluate a definition requires that we first clarify how a word should be used, and it is really the latter skill that is relevant to critical thinking. For that reason, we concentrate directly on the problem of deciding what a word should mean, or deciding when words are being used correctly.

In most cases, the correct use of a term is the one accepted by speakers of English. Thus the first standard is a good dictionary. This may seem too obvious to deserve special mention, but many arguments can be criticized for failing this test. In 6:10, for example, the claim that sexism does not exist in this country depends on a definition of sexism that differs from standard usage. A survey of dictionaries reveals that "sexism" usually means "the domination of one sex by another (usually the domination of women by men) or discrimination against a person on the basis of sex." Thus, it is fair to object that Schlafly has not shown that sexism, as usually understood, does not exist.

Other things being equal, statements and arguments should rely on **lexical definitions**. These are the standard, common, uses of a word or phrase reported in dictionaries and accepted by competent speakers of the language. An argument that employs lexical definitions can presuppose agreement about the meaning of a certain term to justify its application to a given case. Unless its author indicates otherwise, one should assume that an argument is relying on lexical definitions.

Sometimes words are used incorrectly. As noted previously, one possible flaw is to use words idiosyncratically. Argument 6:17 illustrates a different problem:

6:17. If theism is a religion, then atheism must also be a religion, for a belief that God does not exist must be founded on the same sort of faith as the belief that He does exist.

The word "religion" is difficult to define; for example, one can debate whether or not belief in a divine power is necessary for a religion. Nonetheless, even a minimal definition of religion will contain a condition such as "a particular system of faith and worship."[6] Since atheism is simply the rejection of a belief, without necessarily involving a system of positive beliefs, or worship, it would violate standard usage to call it a religion.

When a word is applied to something that would not be included under a standard lexical definition, the usage is **too broad**. The opposite problem, denying that a word applies to something that is included under the correct lexical definition, is using the word in a manner that is **too narrow**. These two ways of misusing a term, together with **idiosyncratic definitions**, are the most common mistakes associated with lexical definitions.

There are times when the ordinary English usage may not be adequate or appropriate. An English word may be ambiguous or too vague, in which case a good argument explicitly offers or implies a more precise meaning. In some cases, English usage may not capture a distinction that is important to a particular argument. In such cases, we may need a **stipulative definition**, in which it is declared that the speaker or author proposes to use the term this way.

Stipulative definitions often occur in contexts in which an ordinary, somewhat vague, term must be made more precise. Thus, a university might stipulate that "full-time student" means "a student having a course load of twelve credit hours or more." Another reason for using a stipulative definition is that ambiguity or confusion about what a term really means might hinder attempts to reason clearly and carefully about an issue.

How do we decide whether a definition is stipulative or simply an incorrect lexical definition? If the author *intends* to follow standard usage, a lexical definition is being assumed, and it is fair to criticize a use that does not conform to accepted definitions. If the author deliberately chooses to offer a new definition for some specific purpose, we must, instead, evaluate the appropriateness and usefulness of the proposed stipulative definition.

The author's intentions can often be determined by what she says she is trying to do. In other cases, the context might provide a clue: a law or regulation, for example, might be expected to offer stipulative definitions of terms that are, in ordinary English, imprecise, while someone who is describing an event would normally rely on lexical definitions. Finally, we should be guided by the principle of charity. Thus, consider example 6:18:

6:18. So-called ape-languages which involve teaching gorillas or chimps to produce sentencelike strings of signs are really not languages at all. They are merely the result of complex stimulus–response training, and lack the creativity necessary to any true language.

The only reason one would normally give such an argument is to try to show that what the apes are doing does not count as a language *in the normally accepted sense*. It is hard to imagine the point of simply arguing on the basis of a stipulative definition. Thus, unless there is evidence to the contrary, the principle of charity dictates that we take the author of 6:18 to be working with a lexical definition of "language."

A stipulative definition can help us avoid misunderstanding and prepare the way for a more precise statement of a position or an argument. An example of this can be found in Extended Argument 5 ("Pornography and Censorship") in paragraph 5. By stipulating a definition of "pornography," the author is able to distinguish pornography from erotica, and thus narrow the scope of her argument.

As this discussion of stipulative definitions suggests, we should not simply choose to use words in a new way for no good reason. An argument that uses language well either respects the ordinary usage and lexical definitions of terms or gives some reason to justify its use of a stipulative definition. Sometimes this reason is made explicit, while in other arguments it is implied. Thus, Extended Argument 5, paragraph 5, implies that the distinction between erotica (sexually explicit material) and pornography (explicit depictions of sexual behavior that portray women in a degrading and demeaning way) is crucial to the justification of censorship. The remainder of the article reveals why the distinction is important, since its main argument rests on the harm done to women by the special characteristics of pornography.

Why is it fair to criticize an argument for using or presupposing a stipulative definition for no good reason? At the very least, departures from the accepted meanings of words in these cases create unnecessary confusion and complexity. More important, arguments that do this run the risk of missing the point. Consider the argument in 6:19:

6:19. Some vegetarians object to raising and killing animals for food on the grounds that these practices inflict pain on animals simply for our trivial gastronomic pleasure. But scientists have recently discovered that plants feel pain too: trees emit distinctive chemicals when damaged, and houseplants reveal increased electrical activity when their leaves are burned or torn. So the vegetarian might as well recognize that we have to cause pain to something to survive.

The author of this argument uses "pain" to refer to any sort of reaction to damage. This is much broader than the accepted meaning of the word, which emphasizes a certain kind of sensation normally associated with specific sorts of physiological states, behavior indicative of distress, and a desire to avoid the sensation. The author's shift in the meaning of "pain" renders the argument pointless; for we have no reason to think that "pain" in the broader sense *matters*, that it is morally relevant. We have strong intuitions that "pain" in the accepted sense does matter and that we should not inflict it without justification. The vegetarian attempts to use that intuition in opposing the raising and killing of animals for food. Because 6:19 does not talk about this sense of pain, it does not discredit the vegetarian's position.

As we saw in the preceding section, in some cases a word may have more than one accepted meaning (or its meaning may be unclear), and offering a correct interpretation may be necessary to understand what the issue is. What standards should we use in such cases?

To focus on the specific example of the public policy debate over the disposal of hazardous waste (6:16), should we rely on the subjective or on the objective meaning of "risk"? The best guideline is to *choose the meaning that is most closely tied to features that are relevant to the issue*. Since public policy in the United States is supposed to reflect the democratically expressed will of the people, it follows that we should use the sense of "risk" most closely tied to the values and preferences people express. Thus, subjective risk is a better choice than objective risk and is, in fact, the one required by the Congressional Research Office.

By contrast, if a loan officer must decide which of two (risky) business enterprises to support, his arguments should rest on the objective financial risks involved, not his subjective preferences and values.

EXERCISES

For each of the following exchanges, identify the key terms involved, decide whether the definitions being used are lexical or stipulative, and evaluate them.

*1. A: The Eighth Amendment to the Constitution forbids "cruel and unusual punishments." Capital punishment is unusual since, unlike all other punishments, it cannot be varied in severity to fit the magnitude of the crime and, by its very nature, it precludes the possibility of correcting errors. It is also cruel since it deprives the condemned person of a basic human right—namely, the right to life.

B: In most societies, including our own, capital punishment is the usual penalty for the worst crimes. It is the only punishment that fits the crime of murder. Electrocution is admittedly barbaric, but being put to death by a lethal injection is not cruel, it is painless.

2. A: State lotteries are a bad way of raising revenues, since they are a form of legalized gambling.

B: But you don't object to people playing the stock exchange or taking out life insurance policies. Aren't those "forms of legalized gambling"?

3. A: Keeping track of statements made by people who claim to predict the future allows us to expose them as charlatans. Their predictions are either so vague that something is bound to satisfy them or their success rate is no better than one would obtain by chance. Either way, such people portray themselves as having a power they simply don't possess.

B: Although *some* of them may be charlatans, most of them sincerely believe that they have such powers. Thus, even if their beliefs are false, they are not charlatans.

4. A: Drunk drivers who kill while intoxicated are not guilty of murder because they do not intend to kill their victims.

B: That's false. If an arsonist sets fire to a building knowing that there's a significant chance that the people inside will be burned to death, then he's guilty of murdering anyone who dies in the fire. Just like the drunk driver, the arsonist is acting with reckless disregard for human life. They are both murderers.

5. A: There is no moral difference between the terrorist who detonates a bomb in a crowded airport and the head of state who orders the bombing of a military installation in a crowded city. Both end up killing and maiming innocent civilians and children. Both are terrorists.

B: You misunderstand the distinction between terrorism and a justified military action. The air strike is directed against a military target in pursuit of legitimate political goals. Every effort is made to avoid killing civilians. The terrorist acts with the intention of killing as many civilians as possible.

6. A: Affirmative action programs are nothing but reverse discrimination. They are unjust because they involve favoring certain groups of people on the basis of race or sex. They are unfair to the people who are being discriminated against.

B: Affirmative action programs are not unjust since they are being employed in situations in which discrimination already exists. They are trying to bring about a fairer society by working against present injustices. "Reverse discrimination," as you call it, is not unjust if it means counteracting the unfair advantages enjoyed by traditional majorities.

7. A: It is obvious that a normal person possesses free will. Most of us are capable of deliberately choosing one action over another and acting in accord with that choice. In acting in accord with our own choices, we act freely.

B: We may be able to act in accord with our own choices, but the picture of choosing from among equally possible alternatives is a sham. Our previous conditioning, cultural influences, and even genetic makeup make it inevitable that we will choose one way rather than another. Since the choice itself is not free, neither is the action resulting from that choice.

8. A: The foreign policy of the United States should be governed by the same moral principles that apply to individuals. It is hypocritical to adopt a double standard, to condemn selfishness in individual persons and yet always to put our nation's interests first.

B: It is not hypocritical to act in accordance with one's moral duty. Governments have a responsibility to serve the interests and happiness of the citizens they represent. It would be immoral for the U.S. government *not* to put the welfare of its own country above that of other nations.

9. A: "Euthanasia" simply means "a good death" or "dying well." As such, it is something we all hope for but it is not a suitable subject for legislation.

B: The term "euthanasia" has changed in meaning over the years. Now it primarily refers to the means or act of achieving a good death. Our current laws make it difficult for terminally ill patients to die without unnecessary suffering and loss of dignity.

*10 A: Most medical malpractice suits are not really about malpractice at all since, usually, the physician or surgeon is not guilty of incompetence or negligence. Rather, the patient is the unfortunate victim of a risky procedure for which no one is to blame.

B: A physician is negligent if she fails to adequately inform her patient of the risks involved when obtaining the patient's consent. If the patient would not have consented had he been adequately informed, the physician is guilty of malpractice regardless of whether the outcome is successful or not.

Notes

[1]Slippery slope arguments are sometimes presented as one of *two* different types of "wedge" arguments. In our analysis, slippery slope arguments are the "logical version" of wedge arguments, since they assume that there are no relevant differences between cases that fall under the same vague term. The "consequentialist version" of wedge arguments need not involve the use of vague terms or statements but rests on the predicted impact on society of a given practice. The following is an example of a consequentialist wedge argument "Even though there are relevant differences between letting a person die at his request and killing him without his consent, society will eventually become insensitive to this distinction. Therefore, if we permit the former, our decision will lead to the approval of the latter." For a more detailed discussion, see Tom L. Beauchamp and James F. Childress, *Principles of Biomedical Ethics*, 2nd ed. (New York: Oxford University Press, 1983), pp. 120–124.

[2]H. P. Grice, "Logic and Conversation," in *The Logic of Grammar*, Donald Davidson and Gilbert Harman, eds. (Encino, CA: Dickenson, 1975), pp. 64–153.

[3]Adapted from Monroe Beardsley, *Practical Logic*, p. 60.

[4]Example 6:16, the definition of "objective risk" and the discussion of subjective risk, are adapted from Anne L. Hiskes and Richard P. Hiskes, *Science, Technology, and Policy Decisions* (Boulder, CO: Westview Press, 1986), pp. 100–106.

[5]Stephen Schafer, "Power and the Definition of 'Crime,'" in *Philosophy for a New Generation*, 3rd ed., A. K. Bierman and James A. Gould, eds. (New York: Macmillan, 1977), p. 390.

[6]*Oxford English Dictionary*, 1971.

CHAPTER
7

Evaluating Sources
of Information

In previous chapters, we surveyed different methods for forming and supporting beliefs with good arguments. But in many cases we do not know if a claim is true or not, and so we are unable to judge the soundness or reliability of an argument that uses it as a premise. Consider Extended Argument 8: few people could simply read that article and determine whether its arguments are sound or reliable on the basis of their own knowledge.

In cases like this, we have to consult additional sources of information. Since not all sources of information are equally good, we need guidelines for evaluating them. That is the topic of this chapter. More specifically, we will investigate two of the most important sources of information: **testimony** and **factual reporting**.

The distinctive characteristic of **testimony** is that the source of information is regarded as **an authority** on the topic under consideration. We ask someone to form an opinion or judgment because he or she has the appropriate expertise. For that reason, we sometimes call the person[1] serving as the source of information "the authority"; using such testimony is called an **appeal to authority**.

Unlike testimony, **factual reporting** does *not* require specialized knowledge or information. Factual reports tell us what happened, who did what, and other things we could have learned directly if we had been present at the appropriate place and time. In theory, factual reporting should not involve interpretation or drawing inferences; it should be an "objective" account of what the reporter observed. Newspaper stories are obvious examples of factual reporting. Reporting also makes up a significant portion of history texts, biographies, and the premises of some arguments.

Appropriate Subjects for Testimony

If you are trying to decide when using testimony is appropriate—that is, when it would be a good idea to appeal to authority—it helps to ask why anyone would want to take someone else's word for something rather than find out for herself. To see why, consider the questions in 7:1:

7:1. *Arthur's Britain*[2] is an interesting book which argues that King Arthur was a genuine historical figure. Is its main thesis true, and is its description of preconquest Britain accurate?

Most people do not know enough about English history to answer these questions on the basis of their own knowledge. Answers could be obtained in several ways, not all equally good. First, we might consult an historian or archeologist who specializes in that period, and ask her opinion of the book. Alternatively, we might consult a reference work we know to be reliable, and compare it to *Arthur's Britain*. Finally, we might just look at several other books on the same topic and try to discover the points on which all or most of them agree.

Because we lack the knowledge or expertise to form an opinion that is based on good reasons, we have to rely on the judgment of an authority—someone who is in a better position than we are to form a reliable opinion. This is the essence of testimony: if, through lack of knowledge or training, you cannot make a reliable judgment yourself, consult someone else who can.

One of the dangers with testimony or appeals to authority is the temptation to overuse them, to expect an authority to do your thinking for you, and to make decisions that are not merely the result of applying the special knowledge that justifies the use of testimony in the first place. A medical doctor, for example, may be an authority on the subject of fetal development, and we might for that reason rely on her testimony about the age at which fetuses become viable; that piece of information, in turn, might enter into a debate about the morality of abortion. But questions such as "Under what circumstances is abortion morally permissible?" and "Should fetuses be treated as human beings?" cannot be answered *solely* on the basis of *medical* knowledge; therefore, it would be a misuse of testimony to appeal to a doctor's authority to decide these questions.

Debates about the morality of abortion illustrate another factor one should keep in mind when judging whether testimony is appropriate: even when the issue, as a whole, cannot properly be decided by an appeal to authority, you may still want to use testimony as a source of relevant information.

Questions 7:2 contain examples of questions that could appropriately be answered by an appeal to authority. Contrast these with those in 7:3, which illustrate cases in which testimony would be inappropriate:

7:2. Is the Sabin vaccine as effective as the Salk vaccine in preventing polio? Is it as safe?

Are the current containment facilities for nuclear wastes liable to be damaged by earthquakes?

Is there any proof that vitamin C prevents colds?

Is the Stealth bomber capable of evading detection by Soviet radar?

These questions cover a wide variety of topics, but they have one thing in common: a good answer to any one of them requires background knowledge, technical training, or expertise that most people do not have. Possible sources of testimony for answers to these questions include individual scientists, reference works, government agencies, and independent testing services or laboratories. A combination of sources might supply the best testimony. To answer the second question in 7:2, we might want to consult a geologist and an engineer.

Many questions cannot be answered solely on the basis of expert knowledge. Some concern matters that we should be able to make informed judgments about for ourselves. Others involve an element of personal taste or choice. Still others involve elements of decision making that go beyond matters of purely factual and technical judgment. Questions 7:3 contain examples of the sorts of questions for which an appeal to an authority is *not* the best way of obtaining an answer. In all of these cases, we may still choose to ask other people for their opinions, but it would be wrong to take those opinions as expert testimony.

7:3. Is *Arthur's Britain* a book that a nonhistorian might find interesting?

Are the risks to health posed by nuclear power plants justified by their economic advantages?

Which car should I buy?

Is a birth control method that is free from side effects but only 75 percent effective better or worse than one that is 98 percent effective but is known to cause side effects in a small percentage of the people taking it?

Is euthanasia ever morally permissible?

None of these questions can be answered appropriately by appealing to authority because good answers to them are not solely a function of specialized knowledge and training. Of course, some of the questions, such as those about birth control or nuclear power, may require additional information that is best obtained from an authority. Thus, I may wish to know what side effects are associated with the more effective birth control method, how serious they are, and whether they are more prevalent in some groups of identifiable high-risk users. But even here, the information obtained through testimony does not automatically lead to an answer, and at best serves as premises of arguments in support of a conclusion.[3]

EXERCISES

I. For each of the questions or problems listed here, state whether you think it is the sort of question that should be answered by using testimony and explain why.

1. Is unrefined sugar better for one's health than refined sugar?

2. Do stricter gun control measures reduce the number of violent crimes?

3. Is abortion ever justified?

*4. Can regular exercise reduce my chances of getting a stroke?

5. Will a tax cut reduce the rate of inflation?

*6. Would taking a computer science course be a good idea for me?

7. Does passive smoking increase a nonsmoker's risk of getting lung cancer?

8. Should the cessation of brain activity be adopted as a legal criterion of death?

9. Which of the current models of compact car has the best fuel economy?

10. Is "creation science" really a science

II. Take two of the questions in Section I that you decided could not be answered simply by an appeal to authority. Can you think of some more limited questions that are appropriate subjects for testimony that could help answer the broader question?

Choosing Authorities

We use testimony to get an opinion or judgment based on technical knowledge and expertise we ourselves lack. Since we are probably dealing with a topic we know little about, it will be difficult for us to evaluate this opinion or judgment by examining any arguments the authority might offer in its support. So in deciding whether or not a piece of testimony is reliable, we must evaluate its source, the authority from which it comes. We need criteria for choosing and recognizing the right kinds of authority.

The criteria for choosing authorities are suggested by our goal in seeking testimony in the first place. What we are after is a judgment based on special knowledge that represents the careful, fair, and considered opinion of someone who is in a position to know. So we should first ensure that the testimony is really based on the sort of special knowledge necessary for making an informed judgment.

Three factors—relevant expertise, agreement among experts, and impartiality—are the principal criteria to use when choosing authorities and when evaluating testimony and appeals to authority.

The first thing to check is the **legitimacy of the authority**. Is it true that the person or source providing the testimony has special knowledge or training in the appropriate field? In the case of testimony from individuals, we assess their legitimacy by asking the following sorts of questions: (a) Is the person in the relevant field? What is he trained in? (b) Does the person have the kind of background, education, and experience that would make him an expert? (c) What is the person's status in his field? Is he eminent or respected by other experts in the same area? If the testimony derives from a group or organization, we look for similar factors, with special emphasis on the last questions. When testimony relies on printed matter such as a book, we must try to assess its author. In the case of works which, like encyclopedias and reports, have no single author and may contain unattributed material, we must rely on the reputation of the work as a whole and the credentials of the organization that produced it. (In a library, the research librarian is often a good source of information about this sort of thing.)

Because the legitimacy of an authority is essential to the reliability of testimony, it is important to show that the authority in question *is* legitimate. Consider the use of testimony in 7:4:

7:4. I'd like to go on record as being in favor of nuclear power, based on what I have learned from reading some expert opinions. . . . Dr. Peter Beckman of the University of Colorado has written very favorably about nuclear power being the cleanest, safest, and cheapest. In an article written for *Review of the News* magazine, he states that the Three Mile Island incident was proof of the effectiveness built into a nuclear plant. (Letter to the Editor, *Indiana Rural News*)

When we try to decide whether Dr. Beckman is a legitimate authority on nuclear power, we run into a problem because we are given very little useful information about him. The facts that he is associated with the University of Colorado and has either written an article for a nontechnical magazine or been cited in such an article do not tell us anything about his credentials as an expert. In short, we simply cannot tell from the letter whether he is an expert or not.[4]

To get reliable testimony about a new vaccine, we would like our authority to be a medical doctor who does research in that area or is familiar with its technical aspects. Ideally, she should also be prominent and respected by her colleagues: perhaps in a position of stature at a major medical research center, the holder of awards in her field, or a trusted consultant on policy committees. The type of special credentials we insist on depends on the kind of technical knowledge required. Any doctor is (one hopes) enough of an expert in the field of medicine to know what the effects of a common antibiotic are, but we should consult a specialist if we wish to learn about some experimental drug in the early stages of testing.

When trying to select a legitimate authority, we should be careful to avoid two common errors. The first mistake is to be impressed by credentials that do not mean very much. The second mistake is to be misled by **crossover**, which occurs when someone who is an authority in one field is relied on for testimony in a different (perhaps related) field.

There are many ways of trying to foster the appearance of authority. Someone who wishes to cite testimony about the doctrine of special creationism might, for example, mention that the "authority" is a Ph.D., a scientist, someone who has devoted years to the study of these issues, or "the author of many books." But if the person's degree is not in biology, the fact that he is a Ph.D. or a scientist in some other field does not make him a legitimate authority on evolutionary theory. Similarly, the fact that he has published several books does not guarantee expertise, since there are many firms that publish any book for a fee (so-called vanity presses) and several others that publish anything that argues for the position the firm is promoting.

Such testimony, then, would rest on the word of someone who has not been established as a legitimate expert in the relevant field. Some television ads go even further in exploiting the mere appearance of expertise by having an actor in a white coat, stethoscope in pocket, extolling the virtues of a particular sort of painkiller; an uncritical viewer is supposed to assume "white coat, therefore doctor, therefore authority."

Closely related to testimony from someone who, despite appearances is not an authority is testimony from someone who is an authority in a different but related field. This is called **crossover**, because the authority being appealed to crosses from one area into another in which he does not have any special expertise. Linus Pauling may be a great chemist but still not be an expert on the effects of megadoses of vitamins; a race-car driver is not an authority on the best motor oil for a family car; a nuclear engineer has no special knowledge that enables him to decide whether we *need* more nuclear power plants.

Some cases of crossover are difficult to identify. If a famous tennis player appears in advertisements endorsing a bank or a camera, is that crossover? Probably not. A famous person in an advertisement can perform two different functions. The first is to act as an expert, recommending a product on the basis of expertise. A tennis player endorsing tennis rackets and a model selling makeup are good examples. The second function is merely to attract our attention, to make us notice the ad. Actors advertising credit cards or pizza and football players selling beer fall into this category. The important difference between the two functions is that advertisements in the latter category do not ask us to accept a certain judgment just because X says so. Unless we are asked to accept a judgment or opinion ("This tennis racket will improve your game") primarily because of the authority of its source, we do not have an instance of testimony, and hence are not confronted with the danger of crossover.

Of course, one can find genuine examples of crossover in ads. Athletes who tout Wheaties as the "Breakfast of champions" or "What the big boys eat" are trading on their reputation as physically fit persons, but this does not make them experts on nutrition. An actor who is also well-known as a race-car driver may endorse a family sedan, but his expertise in racing does not make him an authority on cars in general. The important thing to remember is the reason for insisting on legitimacy: an authority should have some special knowledge, training, or experience that allows her to make correct judgments more reliably than the average person.

The second major factor to consider when trying to use testimony is the presence or absence of **consensus** among authorities. Do the experts in the field agree with each other on the issue in question? The reason for insisting on consensus is that in many areas experts have honest and important differences of opinion, in which case the opinion of any one expert cannot be evaluated by itself. One psychologist's judgment that the victim of a kidnapping was brainwashed is likely to be balanced by an equally eminent psychologist with the opposite opinion. Supreme Court justices disagree about the correct interpretation of the Constitution, engineers disagree about the safety of power plants, and so on. In these cases, an appeal to authority is not a reliable means of getting to the truth, because the absence of consensus warns us that possession of expert knowledge in the field is not enough to reach a true judgment. After all, if two people with the same expertise give contrary opinions, one of them must be wrong, despite the special knowledge possessed by both.

The testimony cited in 7:4 does not fare well when we consider the second criterion, consensus. Many experts disagree about the safety of nuclear power plants at the present time, and about the lessons to be learned from the accident at Three Mile Island. This lack of consensus undercuts the reliability of any testimony on this issue, including the one advanced here.

We are sometimes advised to get a range of opinions when using testimony, but that advice can be misinterpreted. Checking a piece of testimony by consulting a second authority is a good idea, because consensus is a necessary condition for the reliability of an authority. Conflicts between the two sources may reveal an absence of consensus which, in turn, tells us that an appeal to authority will not guarantee reliable information. But we are not looking for a smorgasbord of different opinions from which to choose one that suits our taste, because we would have no rational basis for deciding which is correct. We would be choosing arbitrarily or on the basis of personal prejudice—not a good way of uncovering the truth. Consulting a number of sources is useful primarily for the purpose of ascertaining whether there is consensus of the sort needed for reliable testimony. That is why one strategy suggested in connection with 7:1 was to look at several history books to see if they agree.

The third factor to keep in mind when looking for good testimony is the

trustworthiness of the authority. Having a vested interest in presenting testimony of a certain sort, or in a certain way, will undermine an authority's trustworthiness. A testing service run by Chrysler Motors has an interest in concentrating on those tests in which Chrysler cars do well; the Soviet news agency Tass may have an interest in reporting a good wheat harvest but not the poor corn harvest; a college public relations office may report an increase in enrollment and leave out the fact that admissions standards were lowered. Industry-sponsored research, advertisements, books written to persuade, magazines that depend on advertising for support all have at least a prima facie interest in the facts they report, and this raises the possibility of this interest leading to a distorted report. These distortions might take the form of selective reporting and editing, or perhaps redefining terms, rather than statements that are actually false. Such distortions can be hard to spot. The best defense against them is to choose an authority who has nothing to gain personally by convincing you of one view or the other.

In applying the final criterion to the example in 7:4, we have the same problem we encountered with the first criterion: lack of information. No potential source of bias is indicated—as far as we know, Dr. Beckman does not work for a power company with a vested interest in nuclear power—but it would be better if we had specific evidence of his impartiality.

When judging the trustworthiness of a piece of testimony, we are trying to identify and eliminate extraneous factors that might affect the authority. This is consistent with the possibility that the source has a strong opinion on the issue. We should not summarily reject testimony by saying something like "Yes, but your information about the salaries of men and women in the same job comes from the National Organization for Women, and everyone knows that they are always looking for cases of discrimination." NOW's testimony about salaries may reflect a concern about discrimination against women, but this concern is based on a consideration of the available facts; it is not merely a bias that grows out of a personal interest.

You should not be afraid to use a particular authority just because it has definite views on a particular topic. You should be concerned only about considerations of self-interest that might lead an authority to offer a distorted or slanted judgment. In fact, most testimony involves asking an authority to render a judgment or offer an opinion or evaluation; testimony is not limited to consultation about purely factual claims. It would not make sense to dismiss testimony with the overused rejoinder "That's just his opinion." Not all opinions are created equal; some are better than others because they are supported by more knowledge, training, skill, or thought. When we use testimony, we accept someone else's opinion because we think that our authority's judgment is better than most people's on this question.

Thus, we want an objective evaluation, but "objective" does not mean "without an opinion"; rather, it means not being influenced by factors that are irrelevant to the truth of the claim being advanced. This point is closely related to another important aspect of using testimony: our overall purpose is not to present "both sides of the issue," but to learn which side is correct. In cases that require expert knowledge, we cannot decide this simply by hearing both sides. If we cite a reliable authority to show that all the available scientific evidence supports evolutionary theory over scientific creationism, and are satisfied that there is consensus among the experts on this question, we are not obliged by any demands of "objectivity" to find someone who supports creationism to represent the other side. As long as the authority relies on an unbiased assessment of the data, the judgment is objective.

To sum up, once we have a question that is best decided by the use of testimony, we should look for three characteristics in a potential source: (a) the legitimacy of the authority, (b) consensus among the experts, and (c) trustworthiness.

EXERCISES

I. Choose two of the questions you identified in the exercises for the first section of this chapter as being appropriately dealt with by testimony. Locate an example of reliable testimony on the subject in the library. Explain why you think the authority is a good one, referring to the three criteria for good testimony.

II. For each of the following sources of information, indicate a field or topic for which you might legitimately consult that source and another topic for which the source would be less appropriate.

1. The National Rifle Association.

2. A local veterinarian.

3. *Webster's New Twentieth Century Dictionary*.

4. *Consumer Reports*.

5. A Catholic priest.

6. A cardiologist.

7. Department of Defense publications on U.S. weapons.

8. *The Congressional Record*.

9. A college catalog.

10. Planned Parenthood.

Recognizing and Evaluating Testimony

The criteria for choosing an authority discussed in the preceding section can also help us to evaluate someone else's use of testimony. But before doing that, we must first learn to recognize *when* someone is relying on testimony. Then we can consider whether it is appropriate to do so and how well the authority cited satisfies the three criteria.

Let us examine several different claims that seem to be appeals to authority.

7:5. Cocaine abuse is a serious and growing health problem in the U.S. The Drug Abuse Warning Network (DAWN) of the National Institute on Drug Abuse reported a 300% increase in the number of cocaine-related emergency room visits between 1976 and 1981, and a 400% increase in cocaine-related deaths in the same period. [Adapted from J. Zonderman and L. Shader, M.D., *Drugs and Disease* (New York: Chelsea House Publishers, 1987), p. 67.]

7:6. Every day, 63 Americans are killed by handguns. There are now 50 million privately-owned handguns in America, most of which are useful only for killing people. (From an article by Senator Edward Kennedy, *Family Weekly*, August 4, 1979.)

7:7. Pilot error may garner more attention in coming years as the demand for pilots outstrips supply. Deregulation and the subsequent proliferation of airlines and flights created an insatiable appetite for more pilots. At the same time, says James Luck at the Future Aviation Professionals of America, the number of pilots available from the traditional source—the military—is shrinking. For one thing, the pilots trained during the Vietnam war are reaching retirement age. Moreover, "since Vietnam, there's been a dramatic cutback in [pilot] training by the military, and the military is trying to retain the ones they train," Mr. Luck says. . . . "We're right at the tip of a pilot shortage," says Henry Gasque at the Air Line Pilots Association. (*The Christian Science Monitor*, July 21, 1987.)

The first thing to decide in each of these examples is whether we are, in fact, dealing with a case of testimony. Remember that "testimony" is being used in a technical sense here. It is not merely any second-hand fact, or someone attesting to something, but rather a fact or judgment that we are asked to accept *because* it comes from a reliable authority or expert. In 7:5, determining the increase in the number of medical emergencies and deaths related to cocaine use is not an easy thing for most of us to do directly, on the basis of our own experience; we are instead asked to accept the figure because it comes from an agency in a special position to know—namely, the Drug Abuse Warning Network.

Statement 7:6 is somewhat different. No authority is cited, so this is not really a case of Senator Kennedy using testimony to persuade us of the accuracy of his claims. If someone else were to repeat the statistics in an argument of his own, citing Kennedy as an authority on gun control as his source, that would be testimony. But Kennedy is not asking us to accept the figures because they come from an authoritative source.

Statement 7:6 makes factual claims, but the source of the information is not identified. When information is readily available, it is common not to mention any specific source. In these cases, we can choose simply to accept the claim as true, perhaps on the grounds that it would be foolish to make up or misrepresent statistics that can be easily verified. But since people do sometimes lie, forget, or simply get confused, independent verification is advisable if the data are important. In this particular example, statistics on deaths caused by handguns are fairly easy to check, but experts differ widely on their estimates of the number of handguns in private hands.

Finally, in 7:7 we have another case of testimony. We are asked to believe that there will be an increasing shortage of experienced pilots on the basis of the statements made by the authorities cited.

Once we have identified a statement as testimony, the next step is to check whether such an appeal to authority is appropriate. In all of the cases just quoted, we can see the need for testimony, but testimony is often abused by being relied on when it should not be—for example, citing an authority to tell us that a proposed bill would outlaw sex-segregated public restrooms, rather than quoting or paraphrasing the actual bill.

Once we have decided that testimony is being appropriately used, we then ask how reliable is the information? How much trust it is reasonable to place in the claim? The three criteria discussed in the preceding section are also used to evaluate the authority cited by someone else. These criteria are (1) the **legitimacy** of the authority, (2) **consensus** among authorities, and (3) **trustworthiness** or lack of bias. Only 7:7 will be discussed here; you should try to apply the same criteria to the other examples and form your own judgment about the adequacy of the testimony.

In 7:7, the authorities are the spokespersons for the Future Aviation Professionals of America and the Air Line Pilots Association. These professional organizations are clearly in a position to have accurate information about the growing shortage of pilots. Therefore, they are legitimate sources of testimony. There is no evidence of disagreement among them, and so consensus can be presumed. Finally, there are no other motives that might affect the trustworthiness of their testimony, especially since they are revealing facts that might cause public alarm about the safety of the airlines their members work for. All things considered, this is a good use of an appeal to authority.

One last point should be kept in mind when evaluating someone else's use of testimony. You will sometimes encounter cases that look very much like testimony but do not mention any specific source. In such cases, the testimony is clearly unfounded and unreliable. Here are some common "pseudoauthorities":

The printed word: "See, it says so right in this book"; "I read it somewhere."

Popularity: "More people choose Bayer aspirin than any other brand"; "Don't be left out"; "But everyone does it"; "Everyone knows that . . ."

Technology: "Our computers have determined . . . "; "Extensive research with the most modern equipment shows . . . "; "Your phone company uses lasers to give you the best service."

Nature: "The all-natural cereal"; "Nature's way."

Experience: "I've been in business for twenty years, and I know that won't work."

"They": "They say you can catch AIDS from sharing a toothbrush"; "They say that in Poland people have to stand in line for six hours to buy a loaf of bread."

The main reason to reserve judgment about these claims is that the anonymous or vague references do nothing toward establishing a legitimate authority. Hence, it is impossible to point to any good reason for accepting the claims being put forward.

In evaluating someone's use of testimony (and in choosing an authority to use in your own reasoning), it is important to keep a sense of perspective. The best we can hope for is to find testimony that it would be reasonable to accept, given the circumstances. We should not insist on perfection. The circumstances will determine how strict our standards should be: the testimony used in a letter to the editor of a local newspaper should not be judged as stringently as, for example, the use of testimony by an official who is arguing in Congress for a multibillion-dollar government project. The ultimate goal in evaluating testimony, as in everything else we have discussed, is not to see how many holes we can poke in someone else's claim; that is an unproductive exercise. What we would like to do is to be able to reach a rational decision, based on the available evidence and common sense, about how much credence to give to a claim—how reasonable it would be to accept or believe it.

EXERCISES

I. In each of the following examples, decide whether testimony is being relied on. If it is, identify the authority, and state the claim the appeal to authority is supposed to support.

1. The U.S. Department of Transportation measured gas mileage for a typical 4000-pound car and found that it traveled 11.08 miles per gallon at 70 miles per hour, 13.67 miles per gallon at 60 miles per hour, 16.98 mpg at 50 mph, and 14.89 mpg at 40 mph. [Sylvia Porter, *Sylvia Porter's Money Book* (Garden City, NY: Doubleday, 1975)]

*2. After analyzing the 84-page bill, the National Rifle Association said it found it repressive and obviously designed to make handgun ownership so difficult it will discourage lawful ownership. . . . The NRA said a major anti-gun organization privately claimed it had written most of the bill. (*Lafayette Journal and Courier*, December 23, 1979)

3. There is no longer any doubt that lives can be saved by lowering cholesterol levels in the blood, but can this be achieved just by improving diet? If so, would healthier eating habits benefit all Americans? According to Columbia University cardiologist Robert Levy, who directed the study [in which cholesterol levels were lowered using drugs] the answer is yes on both counts. Says Levy: "If we can get everyone to lower his cholesterol 10% to 15% by cutting down on fat and cholesterol in the diet, heart-attack deaths in this country will decrease by 20% to 30%." (*Time*, March 26, 1984)

4. In Velikovsky's case we're lucky because his book caused so much furor that a number of refutations have been written. The most recent of these refutations is the published proceedings of a symposium held in 1973 by the American Association of the Advancement of Science (AAAS). . . . Velikovsky claimed flatly that hydrocarbon-based manna fell upon the Israelites during their desert wanderings. Yet the National Aeronautics and Space Administration (NASA) space probes have turned up no evidence of hydrocarbons in the atmosphere of Venus. (James Trefil, "A Consumer's Guide to Pseudoscience," *Saturday Review*, April 29, 1978)

5. An overwarm freezer can radically shorten the storage life of frozen foods. Frozen beef, for instance, can keep nicely for 13 or 14 months at 0°, but will lose quality after only five months at 10°. (*Consumer Reports*, January 1987)

6. The [South African] authorities say that the emergency decree, the second to be imposed in less than a year, has pacified some areas. But they assert that a "revolutionary climate" persists, justifying harsh tactics. Asked to comment on the charges of abuse, the Bureau for Information, the sole source of authorized news about the emergency decree, said in a telexed statement: "A charge concerning the incarceration of a person in a deep-freeze is presently being investigated." (*New York Times*, December 11, 1986)

*7. The father of Pakistan's nuclear program, A. Q. Khan, has finally made it official: Islamabad has the bomb. At least that's what he told a prominent Indian journalist in an interview published last week by London's *Observer*. The charges and countercharges flew quickly after that. Pakistani authorities repudiated the interview. Said one indignant Pakistani: "It was unbelievable that Dr. Khan or anyone else would choose to issue a statement confirming the existence of a Pakistani bomb, to an Indian journalist of all people." Then a leading Pakistani journalist, Mushahid Hussain, editor of *The Muslim*, stepped forth to say he had witnessed the exchange. "For too long the government here has been trying to deny what is obvious to most," Hussain said, suggesting that his countrymen should be proud of Pakistan's "Islamic Bomb." The next day Hussain's telephone was cut off while he was talking to a reporter. After his paper printed a statement saying Khan's remarks had been faked, Hussain resigned.

The interview brought to critical mass the evidence that Pakistan has become the latest member of the world's nuclear-arms club. Last year, according to Reagan administration and academic sources, Islamabad's Kahuta facility managed to enrich uranium past the 93 percent threshold needed to make a bomb. "Pakistan has all of the key components for their first nuclear device and a couple of components they have not manufactured but readily could," said Leonard Spector, a leading U.S. authority on nuclear proliferation and a senior associate at the Carnegie Endowment for International Peace. "For all intents and purposes, they're over the hump. . . ." At House hearings last week, Rep. Stephen Solarz asked U.S. Deputy Secretary of State Robert Peck if the U.S. government would be able to certify that Pakistan is not developing a bomb. "I don't think we could," Peck replied. (*Newsweek*, March 16, 1987)

8. "I am a retired foreign service officer who was involved in negotiations on a treaty banning chemical weapons between 1977 and 1981, and who thus became caught up in the controversy over the reported use of chemical weapons in Southeast Asia and Afghanistan. In 1980 and 1981 I was the U.S. Representative to the Committee on Disarmament, and in that capacity I was in charge of the U.S. delegation in the First Committee of the United Nations General Assembly when the issue of a UN investigation of the possible uses of chemical weapons was first debated.

Hence this response to Peter Pringle's article ["Political Science," *Atlantic Monthly*, October 1985]. I was interviewed by Mr. Pringle when he was doing his research, but I detect only a bare whiff of my views in the end product. Some of my disagreements relate to specifics, and some to the article's overall thrust.

To begin with, there is the concentration on vegetation containing yellow spots as the principal physical evidence. . . . "Yellow rain" is a convenient shorthand for describing chemical warfare in Southeast Asia, not a definition. Several types of agents and delivery techniques have been reported by eyewitnesses, as would be expected in this kind of military operation.

The medical evidence for toxin poisoning gets short shrift in the Pringle article. Pringle says, for example, that no Western doctor has examined, or even seen from a distance, the body of a victim reported to have died from chemical attack. In fact Western doctors have examined many of the victims and in several instances performed autopsies on those who have died. . . ." (Letter to the editor by Charles C. Flowerree, *Atlantic Monthly*, January 1986)

In his reply (published in the same issue of *Atlantic Monthly*) Pringle writes:

"Flowerree disputes my assertion that 'no Western doctor has examined, or even seen from a distance, a body of a victim reported to have died from chemical attacks.' He says, 'In fact Western doctors . . . have performed autopsies on those who have died.' Doctors have examined *living* refugees in Thai camps, and they have presented widely differing reports on what they found. Some believe that the sores and other symptoms could have been caused by toxic chemicals; some offer natural explanations. And, I repeat, no Western doctor has examined the body of a person independently reported to have died from chemical-agent poisoning. One soldier who died after he said he was exposed to yellow rain was given a postmortem. This is the only postmortem whose results have been made public, and the doctors involved could not agree on the reason for his death. American doctors, including one from the CIA, concluded that the soldier had died from mycotoxin poisoning, but a Canadian military doctor said it appeared that he had died from blackwater fever."

II. For each of the examples of testimony that you identified in Section I, evaluate the testimony, using the three criteria of legitimacy, consensus, and trustworthiness discussed in this chapter. Remember that the goal is to decide how much credence to give the information, not merely to be as critical and skeptical as possible.

III. Find at least three examples of testimony in magazine articles, newspapers, advertisements, or other sources. Evaluate the effectiveness of their use of testimony.

IV. The following numbers refer to paragraphs in the Extended Arguments: "4-7," for example, refers to Extended Argument 4, paragraph 7. Evaluate the use of testimony in each of the paragraphs cited. You should consider other relevant information contained in the Extended Argument as well as information contained in the specified paragraph.

1. 4-7

2. 5-7

3. 5-24

4. 7-3

5. 7-13

6. 8-5

7. 8-14

Factual Reporting

At the beginning of this chapter, we noted that testimony is one of two cases in which we evaluate information primarily by examining the source of information.

The second is **factual reporting**. The distinction between these cases is that testimony requires someone with special expertise; factual reporting also conveys second-hand information, but it is information that could have been obtained by any observant person who was in the appropriate place at the appropriate time. Because of these differences, we must apply different criteria in evaluating the two cases.

Factual reporting is a common means of obtaining information: a friend may tell you about what happened in yesterday's chemistry class, a television newscast may report a riot in London, a newspaper covers the visit of a well-known public figure, or a history book informs you about life in seventeenth-century France. Since we get so much of our knowledge of what went on in the world from factual reports, it is important to know how to evaluate them.

Testimony concerns information that requires special expertise; therefore, our evaluation was limited to considering the source of information. Reporting, on the other hand, deals with more readily accessible information; hence, we can use common sense to evaluate the substance of the report as well as the source. A report that seems wildly implausible, or conflicts with other things we know, should be evaluated with extra caution. This internal evidence cannot totally replace an evaluation of the source of the report, but it is a useful place to start.

Thus, the first step in evaluating a factual report is to consider its content. We should ask whether the information contained in the report is the sort of knowledge a reporter or observer could obtain and look for clues that indicate how it was gathered. Consider the report in 7:8:

7:8. At his Haifa summit meeting with Menachim Begin, Anwar Sadat took aside his close friend Israeli Defense Minister Ezer Weizman and asked him to "look after Begin." The Israeli Premier's health is indeed precarious: now 66, he has survived a heart attack, and is still recovering from a mild stroke he suffered last July. Worries over Begin's well-being could be an important factor in Sadat's determination to move forward on the peace agreement with Israel as soon as possible. (*Time*, September 24, 1979)

How could the reporter know what Sadat said to Weizman? It is highly unlikely that he was in a position to overhear a private remark, and he is clearly not quoting part of Sadat's official statement to the press. No other source of information is identified, or even alluded to as "an unnamed source" or "a source close to Sadat." The most plausible explanation is that this is a bit of background chosen to illustrate the general point that Begin's health was a topic of concern, not a literal quotation.

Because factual reporting is intended to convey information about what happened at a specific time and place, good reporting starts with a reporter *observing* the event. There should also be a reliable route by which the information moves from the original observation to the final report. A report that satisfies these standards is said to be **authentic**.

Two factors determine a report's degree of authenticity. The first is *the pro-*

portion of observation to inference. An **eyewitness report** based on what the reporter actually saw and heard is more authentic than one in which someone guesses at what happened. The second is *the strength of the connection between the observation and the report*, or how likely it is that information has been passed along accurately, without distortion.

Internal evidence often provides clues about the authenticity of a report. We may know that the reporter was at the appropriate place and can see that the report is limited to the sort of information that the reporter was in a good position to gather. Examples of this sort of direct report include your friend telling you about events in yesterday's chemistry class. Other examples of this very direct reporting are a newspaper story written by a reporter who attended a public event or the diary of an eighteenth-century officer a historian might consult as a **primary source**. In each case, we have a single person relating what he believes happened at a particular time and place.

Direct reports are based on eyewitness information—information that the reporter obtained by actually being on the scene and observing what took place. If, by contrast, the reporter is relaying information she got from someone else, there is the risk of distortion at each successive retelling, and the report becomes increasingly less accurate and authentic. Whenever a person hears a piece of information, she interprets it, understands it in a certain way, emphasizes some details and forgets others, draws some inferences, and generally changes the story at least a little. If there are no independent checks on accuracy (note this qualification: it becomes important in the more complex cases), the further away from the original event the reporter is, and the more intermediate reports are involved, the more distorted the information will be.

Even eyewitness reports may not be totally accurate. The main problems that arise with eyewitness reports are that (a) even someone who is on the scene can make mistakes about what he thinks he sees, and (b) even an eyewitness can conflate what he sees with what he infers, and these inferences may be wrong. Thus, an observer may think he saw a rock being thrown, when there was only an arm gesture, may think there were more people at a riot than there were, may think he heard shots when there were none, and so on. Alternatively, he may see a gun being fired, and assume that it was done deliberately, or he may see two people talking loudly, and assume that they are fighting. Blurring of what is actually seen is especially problematic in the "you are there" style of reporting sometimes encountered in news magazines and some history books. A wealth of information is supplied in order to make the reader feel as if she is getting a complete inside picture of an event or situation, but the small details are often the result of inferences, imagination, informed guesswork, or dramatic flair. It is difficult to tell from the manner of presentation what is observation and what is inference, but a careful reader can often recognize that a detail or description is one a reporter is unlikely to have been able to observe directly or accurately.

In many other cases, we cannot evaluate authenticity quite this simply. Because of the complex nature of current events, and the larger number of events that one might wish to report on, it is unrealistic to expect all reporting to work on the model of eyewitness reporting. An historian writing about life in Athens in 450 B.C. cannot have been an eyewitness to the events she describes, nor can she be expected to rely solely on first-hand, eyewitness sources (primary sources). Many of the stories in local newspapers come from an agency such as the Associated Press (AP) or United Press International (UPI). A television broadcast often relies on the same agencies or on national network reporting. News magazines print stories that have gone through several stages of retelling, from the local "stringer" to area coordinator, and on up. In each case, the time and distance involved make it practically impossible to limit oneself solely to eyewitness reports.

By giving up the immediacy of eyewitness reports, we also give up a source of assurance about authenticity. Alternative methods must therefore be employed to ensure accuracy. This is usually done by double-checking at each new stage: ascertaining the reliability of one's sources, using independent verification of the information where this is possible, and generally being cautious about accepting information of unknown accuracy. You, the ultimate "consumer" of the report, usually have no way of telling from the report how often or how carefully this was done. In most cases, therefore, the best guide is the general reputation of the source, its general record for reliability. A good reputation is not an iron-clad guarantee of reliable information and careful self-policing, but it does provide one of the few guidelines that most of us are in a position to use.

There are other clues to authenticity. A report may reveal its reliance on other sources by the extensive use of quotations and citations. If it is done carefully, this can enhance its authenticity, but sometimes a careful reader can recognize that the sources quoted are not terribly reliable or accurate. A special instance of this is the history book that relies almost exclusively on **secondary sources** (works by other historians), but any sort of report can reveal inadequacies in this way.

Another source of information used in reports, especially in newspapers, is the "official press release." Everyone from presidents to labor unions to garden clubs issues press releases, and in many cases these are published without question. News stories obtained in this way get very low marks for authenticity, since the reporter/writer has not gathered or checked the facts directly at all. Other factors also make press releases a suspect source of information: the person writing the press release has some direct interest in the situation being reported, which means there is a potential for biased reporting, one-sided interpretation, inaccuracy, and distortion. A vivid example of this can be found by comparing the press releases of the incumbent administration with those of the opposition party dealing with a matter of current concern, such as the economy: the two sides offer very different accounts of the same situation.

Even more problematic, and potentially less authentic, than the official news release is the report based on unidentified sources. All the same problems that afflict the official press release apply here, too, with the additional complication that since no one's name is tied to the original information, no one can be held responsible for any inaccuracies. Phrases like "informed sources," or "inside informants" do not allow the reader to judge whether the source of information is in a position to give an authentic report.

Thus, two factors determine the authenticity of a report. The first is the way in which the information was originally obtained. Other things being equal, the best reports come from someone who was in a good position to see what was going on, and who is careful to be accurate and to separate observation from inference. The second is the route by which the information moves from original source to final report. If the same individual observes an event and writes the report, there is little room for distortion, other than misunderstanding or failure of memory.

Reputation can help us in assessing both of these factors. A student newspaper may rely on reporters who are poorly trained and lack experience; they are more likely to quote someone out of context, misunderstand the significance of an event, or simply lack the training in good note-taking that will enable them to recall what they observed. These problems occur much less frequently at well-respected newspapers such as *The Los Angeles Times* and *The Christian Science Monitor*. Weekly publications such as *Time* and *Newsweek* have more time to check facts and verify their reporters' sources.[5]

As was suggested in the discussion of press releases, even the most accurate or authentic report in the world is of limited value if it contains only part of the story or tells the story in a distorted or biased way. For that reason, we cannot use authenticity and reputation as the sole criteria for a good factual report. We should also check to see whether the report is complete enough to be **adequate**. A report is adequate if it contains the information the reader needs to form an accurate picture of the event being reported.

Adequacy is especially important in forming an opinion or judgment based on a factual report. To put the point crudely, if we know only part of a story, we do not usually know enough to make a careful and informed judgment—additional information may give us a totally different perspective.

Put less crudely, there are many ways of giving less than the full story that can affect the reliability or usefulness of the facts. Simply omitting facts often makes it hard to use the information that is given. The statement that Texaco makes only three cents profit on every gallon of gas it sells at the pump may be true, but unless we know how much that adds up to, and what percentage of their total income is pure profit, we cannot evaluate the significance of the original data.

Self-censorship is another reason for omitting data; a reporter may feel that information about missiles, nuclear power plants, or diplomatic treaties should not be made public and sometimes consciously refrains from publishing information he thinks should be kept secret. Quite apart from the constraints of military censorship, many British and American war correspondents who witnessed atrocities committed by Allied troops during World War II failed to report them because they believed such revelations would harm the war effort.[6]

Alternatively, the report may be incomplete because the reporter is trying to distinguish his report from others on the same general topic: an author wants to present a new and original perspective, an investigator desires to contribute something important that was not previously known, and a newspaper chooses to focus on what is *news*, which usually means what is *new*. A riot may be new, and hence news, but the social and economic conditions that gave rise to it may be long-standing, and thus judged insufficiently "newsworthy" to be discussed in the report.

When we assess the adequacy of a report, we again rely partly on internal clues, partly on our own background knowledge, and partly on the reputation of the source. We should also keep in mind that adequacy is not purely a function of a report's content; it also depends on its intended use. For example, most newspapers and magazines have a section that contains very brief overviews, highlights, or summaries of national and international events.

The final criterion for a good report is **objectivity**. Reports are intended to convey objective, factual information, not to express opinions or value judgments. This is another way in which reports differ from testimony. Slanted language, descriptions that reinforce biases, even sensational headlines that do not match the actual content of the report all lessen the objectivity of a factual report. Finally, relying on sources of information that have an interest in presenting their own case affects objectivity. Consider the pair of reports in 7:9:

7:9. **BACKSLIDING IN MANILA: AQUINO STRUGGLES BETWEEN THE ARMY AND THE LEFT**

> Corazon Aquino was back to her old self last week: waffling and unsure. Days after she sacked her truculent defense minister, demanded resignations from the rest of her cabinet and signed a cease-fire accord with communist insurgents, the president began backing away from the policy "recommendations" delivered last month by Armed Forces Chief of Staff Fidel Ramos as the price of staving off a military coup. . . . (*Newsweek*, December 15, 1986)

ANXIETY ON THE EVE OF A CEASE FIRE: THE NATION GETS READY FOR A TRUCE WITH THE COMMUNISTS

> Being the woman President in a country known for the macho style of its politics has been a special burden for Corazon Aquino. . . . Aquino spent a good part of the week cleaning up the mess after the firing of another man who had underestimated her, former Defense Minister Juan Ponce Enrile. Having dismissed Enrile a fortnight ago after accusations that he was plotting against her, she was now slowly revamping her cabinet at the urging of her armed forces Chief of Staff Fidel Ramos and other military leaders. . . . The military's role will be particularly crucial starting this week, when a 60-day truce with Communist rebels goes into effect. The army has been suspicious of possible Communist moves during the cease-fire and has been making contingency plans to counter them. (*Time*, December 15, 1986)

The second report maintains a high degree of objectivity. The first uses terms like "backsliding," and "waffling and unsure" to portray President Aquino as weak and ineffective. Such judgments go beyond objective reporting and offer evaluative conclusions that should not be part of a factual report.

To sum up, the three criteria for a good factual report are **authenticity, adequacy,** and **objectivity.** We can determine how well a report satisfies these criteria by using internal evidence, background knowledge and common sense, and the reputation of the source of information.

These criteria are meant to apply *only* to factual reports—objective descriptions of events or phenomena as they were observed. It is important to keep this in mind because many of the things we read combine factual reporting with other things, such as explanations, interpretations, or evaluations. A history book will often attempt to explain why something happened and why it was significant, as well as to tell us it happened. A factual report of the results of a scientific experiment may be combined with arguments designed to show that these results confirm or refute a hypothesis. An article in a news magazine might include predictions about what will happen as a result of the events on which it is reporting.

Because factual reporting often occurs in this sort of context, it is important to distinguish the parts of an article or book that are reports from those that are generalizations, causal accounts, explanations, or inferences about motivation. The former can be evaluated according to the criteria discussed in this section. The latter must be judged on the basis of the reasons that support them, that is, by determining whether the arguments that support them are sound.[7]

EXERCISES

Evaluate the following examples. For each passage (a) identify the portions that are factual reports, distinguishing them from testimony; (b) comment on the authenticity, adequacy, and objectivity of the factual reports; (c) identify those elements of the report that you think are likely to be fairly reliable; and (d) point out those portions you think are unreliable.

*1. M. de Corny, and five others, were then sent to ask arms of M. de Launay, Governor of the Bastille. They found a great collection of people already before the place, and immediately planted a flag of truce, which was answered by a like flag hoisted on the parapet. The deputation prevailed on the people to fall back a little, advanced themselves to make their demand of the Governor, and in that instant, a discharge from the Bastille killed four persons of those nearest the deputies. The deputies retired. I happened to be at the house of M. de Corny, when he returned to it, and received from him a narrative of these transactions. On the retirement of the deputies, the people rushed forward, and almost in an instant, were in possession of a fortification of infinite strength, defended by one hundred men, which in other times had stood several regular sieges, and had never been taken. How they forced their entrance has never been explained. They took all the arms, discharged the prisoners, and such of the garrison as were not killed in the first moment of fury;

carried the Governor and Lieutenant Governor, to the Place de Grève [the place of public execution], cut off their heads, and sent them through the city, in triumph, to the Palais royal. [From "The Autobiography of Thomas Jefferson," in *The Life and Selected Writings of Thomas Jefferson*, edited by A. Koch and W. Peden (New York: Random House, 1944), pp. 101–102.]

2. Thanks to two centuries of Jacobinic propaganda and romantic literature, the Storming of the Bastille has become the most distorted and celebrated event in French History. Actually, on July 14, 1789, the stronghold with its eight round towers, standing formidably at Porte St. Antoine, in the east end of Paris, inspired fear as a citadel and arms depot, not as a prison.

At that time, guarding munitions was of greater concern than the seven prisoners, including one volunteer, who were confined in the relatively comfortable fortress. . . .

On that hysterical day, the arsenal-prison was guarded by 82 retired soldiers and 32 Swiss. Its governor was 49-year-old Bernard Launey, a civilian who had held the post since 1776 and been reputed as one "who always treated prisoners committed to his charge with every degree of leniency and humanity." (Guest columnist, Maurice Ross, *Lafayette Journal and Courier*, July 14, 1980)

3. Before we knew it it was winter, and the winter in 1944–1945 was the coldest in Europe for twenty-five years. For the ground troops conditions were unspeakable, and even the official history admits the disaster, imputing the failure to provide adequate winter clothing—analogous to the similar German oversight when the Russian winter of 1941–1942 surprised the planners—to optimism, innocence, and "confidence":

Confidence born of the rapid sweep across Europe in the summer of 1944 and the conviction on the part of many that the successes of Allied arms would be rewarded by victory before the onset of winter contributed to the unpreparedness for winter combat.

The result of thus ignoring the injunction "Be Prepared" was 64,008 casualties from "cold injury"—not wounds but pneumonia and trenchfoot. The official history sums up: "This constitutes more than four 15,000-man divisions. Approximately 90 percent of cold casualties involved riflemen and there were about 4,000 riflemen per infantry division. Thus closer to 13 divisions were critically disabled for combat." We can appreciate those figures by recalling that the invasion of Normandy was initially accomplished by only six divisions (nine if we add the airborne). Thus crucial were little things like decent mittens and gloves, fur-lined parkas, thermal underwear—all of which any normal peacetime hiker or skier would demand as protection against prolonged exposure. But "the winter campaign in Europe was fought by most combat personnel in a uniform that did not give proper protection": we wore silly long overcoats, right out of the nineteenth century; thin field jackets, designed to convey an image of manliness at Fort Bragg; and dress wool trousers. We wore the same shirts and huddled under the same blankets as Pershing's troops in the expedition against Pancho Villa in 1916. Of the 64,008 who suffered "cold injury" I was one. During February 1945, I was back in various hospitals for a month with pneumonia. I told my parents it was flu. [Paul Fussell, "My War," in *Paul Fussell, The Boy Scout Handbook and Other Observations* (New York: Oxford University Press, 1982), p. 260.]

*4. Ivan III, more clearly than any of his predecessors or followers on the grand princely throne of Moscow, knew precisely where he was going. He knew his goal, the means at his disposal, the obstacles to be encountered. He never over-estimated his own strength or under-estimated that of his enemies. His cold reasoning told him just how far he could abuse the freedom of his subjects and tamper with the sanctity of religious institutions. . . .

Seldom can a man have reigned for so long and achieved so much, and left so little impression on his contemporaries. Almost nothing is known of his personal qualities or of his private life. [J. L. I. Fennell, *Ivan the Great of Moscow* (New York, 1962), pp. 18 and 354, quoted in David Fischer, *Historians' Fallacies*, p. 200.]

5. A battlefield strewn with corpses and the burned hulks of Soviet-built equipment testified to a major clash between Angolan troops and rebel forces along the banks of the Lomba River in southeastern Angola that reportedly has resulted in a government retreat from one of the major battles of the 10-year-old conflict.

Rebels of Jonas Savimbi's National Union for the Total Independence of Angola claim that they turned back the major assault just north of the key town of Mavinga and 150 miles from UNITA's bush headquarters at Jamba, which Angola claimed two weeks ago that Savimbi had abandoned in the face of the government's two-month-old campaign. The rebels' claims became apparent when a group of foreign correspondents visited the scene of battle last week and saw evidence of Angolan losses.

The corpses of Angolan soldiers and destroyed armored cars and big Zil troop carriers, supplied by the Soviets, littered the flat bush country. UNITA is known to possess antitank weaponry capable of inflicting such damage.

The reporters saw the wreckage of a big Soviet-built Mi25 helicopter gunship, one of five UNITA claims to have shot down. It was clear that a considerable amount of expensive Russian military hardware had been destroyed in the battle.

Trees had been smashed by heavy vehicles and stripped by shells, and there were hundreds of foxholes, slit trenches and underground bunkers, making the scene reminiscent of a World War I battlefield.

It was obviously a major conventional battle in what until now has been a guerrilla war. (*The Washington Post National Weekly Edition*, October 21, 1986)

6. (The following letter appeared in the correspondence section of the British science journal *Nature*. The author is Sir Brian Pippard, Cavendish Professor of Physics, University of Cambridge, UK.)

Sir—On Tuesday, 3 August, shortly after 4:00 p.m., the Cavendish Laboratory and the surroundings were struck by lightning several times during an exceptionally intense storm. No structural damage ensued, but immediately after one of the discharges a ball of light was seen by a number of observers. Their descriptions are not entirely consistent but certain features are agreed upon well enough to enable a broad description to be given. The discharge apparently responsible struck near the centre of the Bragg Building, which runs east-west. An observer on the ground floor of the Mott Building, whose back was to the window, saw his room momentarily lit as if by a very bright object moving past rapidly towards the west, between the Bragg and Mott buildings. Another observer on the first floor saw the space between the buildings filled with a luminous haze at least to the first floor level, and on looking to the west noticed a blue-white light that he thought at first was a warning light on a distant tower. He apparently noticed no motion, but his companion in the same room must have seen it an instant earlier for she had the impression that it was moving past and away, and possibly expanding as it went, being about the size of a grapefruit when first seen. Three people who saw it after that, as it moved over the ground to the west, agreed it looked about the size of the moon, was blue-white in colour, very bright, and was visible for some 4–5 seconds before suddenly vanishing.

To this reasonably well attested observation must be added that while an assistant in the duplicating room, on the ground floor, was closing a small window she was startled by a noise that made her think the window had been knocked in; a bright sparkling object, resembling the lights thrown out by expensive rockets, entered by her head, rebounded from a machine and left as it came. The window was in fact undamaged, and when examined next morning entirely unmarked. Both assistants who were there at the time are convinced something came into the room. (*Nature*, Vol. 298, 19 August 1982, p. 702.)

7. (The following passage is excerpted from testimony by Robert White before the House Subcommittee on Western Hemisphere Affairs, February 2, 1984. Robert White was the U.S. Ambassador to El Salvador during the Carter administration.)

The administration of President Carter classified ex-Major Roberto

D'Aubuisson, accurately, as a terrorist, a murderer, and a leader of death squads. As ambassador, I denied him access to the United States embassy and succeeded in having him barred from our country.

Shortly after President Reagan took office, this administration overturned this policy and began the process of rehabilitating ex-Major D'Aubuisson. The Reagan administration granted D'Aubuisson a visa to enter the United States, made him an honored guest at our embassy and saw to it that he met regularly with Congressmen. The legislators were, of course, unaware of the strength of evidence against D'Aubuisson.

Primarily as a result of the Reagan administration's acceptance of D'Aubuisson, his reputation and effectiveness increased. No longer was he a pariah but a legitimate political leader, well and favorably known to the United States embassy. The fortunes of ARENA soared. D'Aubuisson emerged from the March 1982 elections President of the new Constituent Assembly and his country's strong man. In a very real sense, the Reagan administration created Roberto D'Aubuisson the political leader.

Yet from the first days in office the Reagan White House knew—beyond any reasonable doubt—that Roberto D'Aubuisson planned and ordered the assassination of Archbishop Arnulfo Romero. In mid-November of 1980, a particularly brave and resourceful American diplomat made contact with a Salvadoran military officer who had participated in the plot to kill Archbishop Romero. This officer was present at the March 22nd meeting which resulted in the death of Archbishop Romero on March 24.

According to this eyewitness account, Roberto D'Aubuisson summoned a group of about twelve men to a safe house, presided over the meeting, announced the decision to assassinate the Archbishop and supervised the drawing of lots for the "honor" of carrying out the plot. The Salvadoran officer informant was disappointed that the luck of the draw had not favored him. He gave bullets from his gun to the officer selected in order that he might participate vicariously in the murder of the Archbishop.

The officer who "won" the lottery was Lt. Francisco Amaya Rosa, a D'Aubuisson intimate. Amaya Rosa chose a military hanger-on and sharpshooter named Walter Antonio Alvarez to fire the single bullet which ended the life of Archbishop Romero as he said Mass in the orphanage of the Good Shepherd. . . . [Reprinted in Gary E. McCuen, ed., *Political Murder in Central America: Death Squads and U.S. Policies* (Hudson, WI: Gem Publications Inc., 1985), pp. 65–67.]

8. Reports of the giant kangaroo of South Pittsburg, Tennessee, made it all the way to the pages of New York's daily newspapers. During mid-January of 1934, a kangaroo spread terror among the Tennessee hill farmers. This extremely atypical 'roo was reported to have killed and

partially devoured several German Shepherd police dogs, geese and ducks. The Reverend W. J. Hancock saw the animal and described it as fast as lightning, and looking like a giant kangaroo as it ran and leapt across a field. Another witness, Frank Cobb, quickly came upon more evidence of the kangaroo's activities. The head and shoulders of a large police dog were all that remained. A search party tracked the 'roo to a mountainside cave, but the prints disappeared. Loren Coleman, *Mysterious America* (Boston: Faber & Faber, 1983), p. 121.

II. Find two different reports of the same incident, fact, situation, or event. These may be accounts in two history books, a newspaper that quotes two different eyewitnesses, articles from two different news magazines about the same thing, or other reports. (Remember that a report can be about an event or some other factual information, such as the result of a scientific study.) Compare the two reports, and discuss how each measures up against the standards for a good report.

Notes

[1] It is convenient to think of the source of information as a person, since much of the testimony we are familiar with does have a single person as the identified source. But appeals to authority can also involve sources such as books (especially reference works), committees, and organizations.

[2] Leslie Alcock, *Arthur's Britain* (Middlesex, England: Penguin Books, 1971).

[3] Some people regard philosophers as authorities on moral questions such as euthanasia. Some committees or panels that make policy decisions may even include a philosopher as an "ethicist." Insofar as philosophers have had more training and experience in evaluating arguments than most people, this makes sense, but the judgments offered in these contexts should be evaluated by trying to determine whether the arguments in their favor are sound. It would not be appropriate simply to ask the philosopher to render a verdict and accept it on the grounds that "she is the expert."

[4] We must be careful in our evaluation here, and not conclude hastily that Dr. Beckman is not a legitimate authority. In such cases it may be appropriate to find out about the credentials of a source of testimony. In the complete absence of such information, we should simply reserve judgment.

[5] For a good account of the scrupulous checking procedures at *The New Yorker*, see Judith A. Hennessee, "The Annals of Checking," reprinted from *[MORE]* magazine in Richard Pollak, ed., *Stop the Presses, I Want to Get Off!* (New York: Random House, 1975).

[6] See Philip Knightley, *The First Casualty* (New York: Harcourt Brace Jovanovich, 1975). Similarly, during the Vietnam war, American correspondents were reluctant to describe the massacre of civilians and other racist atrocities committed by American soldiers. When such stories were filed, they were often suppressed by the editors of American

newspapers who judged them to be too harrowing for American readers. Several war correspondents who published their accounts in European newspapers had their visas revoked and were unable to return to South Vietnam.

[7]For a more detailed discussion of how to evaluate such arguments, see David Hackett Fischer, *Historians' Fallacies: Towards a Logic of Historical Thought* (New York: Harper & Row, 1979).

CHAPTER

8

Statistics
and Probability

Long lists of numbers can be difficult to work with, and it is hard to identify patterns or trends in them simply by looking. Summarizing numerical data in **statistical statements** makes it easier to see and understand the information that we are interested in. For example, suppose a university has a total enrollment of 33,682 students; 16,167 are women and 10,105 receive financial aid. It is easier to see the significance of these figures when they are summarized as "48 percent of the students are female, and 30 percent of all the students receive financial aid." Notice that this ease of interpretation comes at a price: statistical statements usually omit some of the data (in this case, the total number of students) used in their calculation. Evaluating statistical claims correctly depends on knowing what they mean and how they have been calculated.

Probability theory is the study of that part of statistics dealing with randomness and randomization. From the information in the previous paragraph we can deduce that, if a student is selected at random, there is a 0.52 chance that the student will be male and a 0.3 chance that he or she is on a scholarship. These **probabilistic statements** follow deductively from the preceding statistical ones.

Collecting Statistical Data

Statistical reasoning can be thought of as divided into three stages: first one collects data; then one organizes and describes that information in a meaningful and useful way; last, one draws appropriate conclusions.

Most statistical claims are about populations of things or people. They are arrived at either by taking a census of the entire population or by making an inductive inference from a sample. In either case, the original data results from testing each member of a group to see whether it has the property under investigation. For example, if I want to know how many students in my class are from outside the state, I can simply ask each one in turn.

Even though the collection of this sort of data may seem straightforward, it is still subject to error. First, people (and even machines) can make mistakes in counting, especially if the population (or sample) to be tested is large. That is why the loser of a close election, for example, usually demands a recount, to determine whether errors or omissions have been made in the initial tally of the votes. The likelihood of errors in counting large populations explains why carefully constructed statistical generalizations can yield conclusions that are more accurate than those obtained from an imperfect census.

The second factor to consider in collecting data is how one detects the property that is being studied. To determine to the nearest inch the heights of a group of people, it suffices to measure the height of each person with a crude measuring stick. For greater accuracy, we need a measuring stick that is divided into finer increments, since the accuracy of the resulting data cannot exceed the accuracy of our measuring device. In either case, this would be a **direct test** for the property being investigated.

If we cannot directly observe or measure the property being reported, we must rely on an **indirect test**, and this introduces a new source of potential error. List 8:1 contains examples of indirect tests:

8:1.   Measuring a child's intelligence by his performance on an IQ test.

Determining a person's beliefs by his answers to certain questions.

Testing a student's mastery of a subject by his answers on an exam.

If the test is poorly designed, or the questions on the opinion poll are badly written or poorly administered, the information we gather may not accurately measure the properties in which we are interested.

The **accuracy** (or what is often called the **validity**) of a test should not be confused with its **reliability**. (This use of the terms "validity" and "reliability" should be distinguished from the very different concepts of validity and reliability as applied to arguments.) A test is valid or accurate if it actually measures the property we are interested in; a test is reliable if it gives the same (or very similar) results each time it is applied to the same group. Assuming that the property in question does not change during the testing, a valid test is also a reliable one, but a test can be reliable without being valid. Merely pointing out that a student obtains closely similar scores when she takes the same kind of test several times does not, by itself, establish that the test actually measures what it is claimed to measure.

Even without a detailed knowledge of statistics, we can often estimate the validity of an indirect test. Consider example 8:2:

8:2.   Based on answers to five questions dealing with dating and interpersonal relationships, a recent study of college students revealed that 75 percent of all the fraternity men who were surveyed rated themselves "above average" in attractiveness to members of the opposite sex.

In 8:2 the property being studied is attractiveness, and the indirect test relies on answers given about oneself. Common sense tells us that a person's self-image is often distorted, and that even when people have accurate knowledge they may be reluctant to give honest answers. The information we receive may be distorted, either deliberately or unconsciously, by the people surveyed. Sometimes people tailor their answers to what they think they ought to say: they claim to watch less television than they really do; they overestimate the amount of exercise they get and underestimate how much they drink or smoke. Psychological factors can also affect a test's reliability. Drug studies on human beings, for example, are often performed double-blind to eliminate the placebo effect. In a double-blind study, neither the subjects nor the experimenters know who was given the drug and who received the placebo until the experiment is over.

One problem that can undermine the validity of opinion polls is the **slanted question,** or a question whose phrasing makes one kind of response more likely than another, regardless of a person's actual views on the issue in question. Thus, "Do you favor legalized abortion, the killing of an unborn child, even for trivial reasons?" and "Do you agree that a woman should be the one to decide whether she wishes to continue an unwanted pregnancy?" are likely to elicit different answers, even from the same group. There is a similar flaw in the question described in 8:3, a question that was used by the Center for Media and Public Affairs (and criticized by Barry Sussman in *The Washington Post Weekly Edition,* October 14, 1985):

8:3.   "Recently there has been a great deal of discussion about racial discrimination in South Africa. Some people say that American corporations should not be allowed to invest money there and that corporations already having investments there should be forced to sell them. Other people say that American corporations should be allowed to remain in South Africa so that they may use their influence to help promote equality for black people. Which of these two positions comes close to your own?"

When this question was put to 600 randomly selected blacks nationwide, 74 percent said that corporations should stay in South Africa and only 26 percent supported disinvestment. As Sussman points out, not only is the question much longer than those normally used by pollsters, but it contains loaded phrases: "should not be allowed," "should be forced," and "to help promote equality." When the same question was put to 105 black leaders, 59 percent favored disinvestment. Far from showing that "black leaders may be out of step with the rest of black America" (the conclusion drawn by the Center for Media and Public

Affairs), the difference was probably due to the fact that most black leaders have settled views on the disinvestment issue and are less likely to be swayed by the question's wording.

To determine whether or not a question is slanted, we must know how it is worded. Unfortunately, in a final report of the results of a poll, we may never see the original question. In evaluating the information gathered by means of an opinion poll, then, it is important to see the original questions and check for slanting.

A properly formulated question in an opinion poll should deal with a single issue, and if alternatives are presented, they should be mutually exclusive and exhaustive. "Should we be satisfied with current gun control measures or should we ban all handguns?" is a poor question because the answers would not accurately reflect the opinions of those who favor other possibilities, such as stricter registration requirements or banning armor-piercing bullets while allowing people to own handguns. Responses to earlier questions can influence answers to later ones: we can expect a larger percentage of people to favor job-related drug testing on a survey in which prior questions asked them how serious they think the drug problem is. Once someone has indicated that he thinks drugs are a serious problem, he will be less likely to say he is opposed to drug testing.[1]

The problem of obtaining reliable data is compounded if we cannot (or choose not to) take a census of the entire population. In such cases, we must examine a sample of the population and rely on inductive reasoning to lead us to a conclusion about the whole group. In addition to the nonsampling errors just discussed, we now have to worry about random and nonrandom sampling errors.

Random sampling errors have already been treated at some length in Chapter 4. Remember that random sampling errors are an inevitable consequence of the sampling procedure, since there is always a chance that even the most scrupulously selected sample will differ from the population to some degree. If our sampling procedure is not truly random, we will obtain a less representative sample, thereby weakening our inductive argument.

As noted in Chapter 4, a sample may be **stratified** to overcome some of the difficulties just described. There are also statistical tests that can be used to detect sampling errors and to compensate for them. When we are not told how a statistical conclusion was arrived at, the best we can do is to assess the source of the information. Gallup and Harris polls have a much better reputation for accuracy, and are more likely to produce reliable statistical data, than, for example, a small issue-oriented group that produces its own survey. Relying on the authority of the information-gathering source is not foolproof, as example 8:3 indicates, but it may be the only alternative open to us. The guidelines discussed in Chapter 7 are relevant.

In evaluating any statistical claim about a population, then, we should, if possible, first discover whether the claim is the result of a census, and is merely using statistics to summarize and organize the findings, or is the result of examining a sample and then using inductive reasoning. In either case, we must consider the reliability and adequacy of the information-gathering process, and in the latter case we must also consider how strong or weak the inductive reasoning is.

EXERCISES

1. If you were asked to collect statistical data on the following questions, would you use a direct or an indirect test? What would the test look like, and how would you attempt to ensure its accuracy? Explain your answer.

*(a) How many Americans subscribe to public television?

 (b) How many pets are owned by apartment dwellers in Manhattan?

 (c) How many drivers who passed through a given intersection between 8 A.M. and 4 P.M. were wearing seat belts?

 (d) How many people in District 21 with a college education voted for Senator Smith?

 (e) During the last year, how many Americans have driven an automobile while being legally drunk?

2. What is wrong with the following indirect tests? How could they be improved?

 (a) The average price of houses sold in 1986 is determined by looking at the prices advertised in the newspaper supplement.

 (b) The literacy rate of a population is calculated by finding out how many people have completed sixth grade or its equivalent.

 (c) The availability of health care is estimated by calculating the ratio of M.D.s to patients.

 (d) Attitudes toward mandatory drug testing are surveyed by asking the following question: "If your employer wanted to test all employees to determine if they had used illegal drugs recently, would you be willing to be tested, or would that be an unfair invasion of your privacy?"

*(e) The number of Americans who filed fraudulent tax returns in a given year is estimated from the number of taxpayers caught in IRS audits.

3. Evaluate the statistics cited in Extended Argument 7, paragraph 25, as support for the claim that "in the majority of cases, a criminal denied access to a handgun will turn to a sawed-off shotgun or long rifle."

4. Comment on the use of statistics in the following passages.

 (a) According to a survey conducted by Target Systems Inc., of Arlington, Virginia, 87 percent of smokers refused to participate in the Great American Smokeout of November 1986 and most do not want any advice on their habit. The telephone survey of 906 smokers in six major cities was conducted in the three days following the November 20 Smokeout, an annual event sponsored by the American Cancer Society which asks people to stop smoking for one day. Ninety-one percent of the smokers surveyed said they were aware of the event but 87 percent said that they did not participate, according to Philip Morris U.S.A., which funded the study. According to the tobacco company's survey, 87 percent of respondents believed adults who choose to smoke do not need advice on their habit, and 73 percent said antismoking groups are too extreme. (Reported in *The Purdue Exponent,* December 11, 1986.)

(b) "Most medical students develop the symptoms of hypochondria—fear of disease or the false belief that one is sick—at some point during school, studies show. Many people assume, therefore, that the condition is more prevalent in medical schools than elsewhere. But a new study of hypochondriacal concerns—the first to compare medical students with another group—proves this assumption false. Psychiatrist Robert Kellner of the University of New Mexico, Albuquerque, gave 30 medical students and 30 law students questionnaires aimed at detecting hypochondriacal tendencies. It asked, for example, whether the students avoided unhealthful foods, are afraid of death, and worry that they may have cancer. To Kellner's surprise, hypochondriacal fears surfaced in just 8 percent of each group, suggesting that among medical students, at least, such concerns are temporary. If most of these students exhibit symptoms of hypochondria at some point during their schooling but just a small percentage have them at any one time, says Kellner, 'the concerns can't last long.'" (Reported in *Science Digest,* August 1986, p. 74.)

(c) A survey conducted for *Time* magazine by Yankelovich, Clancy, Shulman (one month after the Surgeon General's report on AIDS urging sex education in schools) revealed that 86 percent of the respondents favor sex education in public schools and 76 percent believe that such courses should teach 12-year-olds about how men and women have sexual intercourse. Only 34 percent of mothers and 21 percent of fathers answered "yes" to the question "Have you ever told your 8- to 12-year-old children how men and women have intercourse?" The report, published in *Time* (November 24, 1987), gives the following information: "The survey of 1,015 Americans 18 years or older was conducted by telephone Nov. 10 to 12, 1986. The potential sampling error is plus or minus 3% for the entire population. Among the smaller group of 150 parents, the potential error is larger."

Percentages and Averages

Statistical claims that use percentages tell us what proportion of a specified group of things has a certain property. If we examine a class of 75 students, and discover that 25 of them are seniors, we can easily determine that 25/75 of them, or 0.33 are seniors; in other words, approximately 33 percent of the class are seniors. We could have obtained a figure that looks more precise by extending the calculation to further decimal places—33.333 percent, for example—but the appearance of increased precision would be misleading, given the size of the group from which is was obtained.[2]

Assuming that the calculations have been performed correctly, the only factors that can affect these simple percentages are (1) the accuracy of the test used to decide which members of the group have the property in question, and (2) the proper description of what is being reported. The latter point is sometimes overlooked. Consider the claim made in 8:4:

8:4. Thirty-five percent of the students in a course rated it as excellent on a course evaluation.

We need to know whether that figure represents 35 percent of the total number of students, or 35 percent of the students who filled out the evaluation. On the basis of a mail-questionnaire, for example, a politician might announce that 80 percent of his constituents oppose gun control. But if this means that 80 percent of the people who responded were against gun control, that tells us nothing about the views of the constituents as a whole. Generally, the response rates to such questionnaires are very low, and they tend to overrepresent people who have strong feelings about the issue. In the next section we will see that the question "What is this a percentage of?" is even more important when percentages are used to compare two or more groups of things.

Another familiar way of presenting statistical information is to summarize the data in terms of an "average." There are actually three commonly used sorts of averages: the **mean,** the **median,** and the **mode.** Although any one of these figures may be cited as "the average," it can give us a very different picture of the information which is summarized. Consider, for example, Table 8-1, which lists the annual salaries, in dollars, for ten employees of a small company:

TABLE 8-1

EMPLOYEE	ANNUAL SALARY ($)
1	65,000
2	50,000
3	31,000
4	30,000
5	30,000
6	22,500
7	22,500
8	22,500
9	20,000
10	18,500

The **mean** annual salary is computed in the way most commonly associated with averages: we total all the salaries ($312,000) and divide by the number of employees (10) to arrive at $31,200. This figure shows how misleading a mean can be. If a job-hunter were told that the mean salary was over $31,000 he might expect that his salary might be near that figure. But half the employees make at least $8500 less than that. The mean is always distorted by extreme variations at either end of the scale, and here the two very high salaries have inflated the average in a misleading way.

The **median** is another figure that is often given as the average. One calculates the median by first ranking all the figures in order, from highest to lowest. (This has already been done in Table 8-1. Note that if a figure occurs more than once, it must be included each time it occurs: we should not, for example, enter $22,500 only once.) The median is simply the midpoint of this list, the number that occurs halfway down. If, as in this example, the midpoint falls between two figures (here, between $30,000 and $22,500) the median is halfway between them. In our example, this would be $26,250. This median value tells us that exactly as many employees make more than $26,250 a year, as make less. Unlike the mean, the median is relatively insensitive to extremes. Thus, if employee 1 had earned $100,000 and employee 10 had earned $12,500, the median would remain unchanged.

Because it is unaffected by a few very high and very low values, we prefer the median to the mean as a picture of the average whenever we wish to ignore the effect of extremes. Thus, the average price of housing is usually reported as the median, not the mean. Although the sale of a few multimillion dollar mansions will raise the mean significantly, we are not particularly interested in that very small segment of the market. The median is also the most appropriate figure to use if we want to know where a particular instance falls within the range of the total population. If a student wishes to know whether she ranks in the top half of her class, she should compare her grade to the median. When test scores are reported in terms of percentiles, the median is the 50th percentile.

The **mode** is the third kind of average. It is simply the number that occurs most frequently. In Table 8–1, the mode is $22,500. Although the mode is less informative than the mean or median, it is the only appropriate figure to use if we are dealing with nonquantifiable values, or values that should not be combined. If we ask "Which of the following problems facing the administration do you think is the most important?" and give a choice of five responses, the mode will tell us which response was chosen by the most people. Since the responses themselves cannot be ranked, it would not make sense to try to calculate the median or mean.

The mean, median, and mode together can provide a more detailed picture of how the values in a population are distributed. This is illustrated by the two graphs in Figure 8-1:

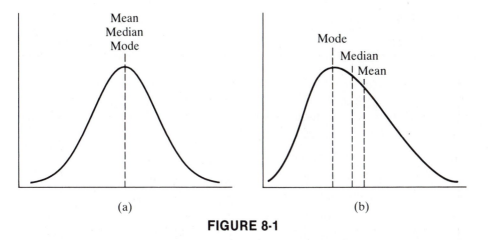

(a)   (b)

FIGURE 8-1

If the curve is symmetrical, as in Figure 8-1a, its mean, median, and mode will coincide. When these values are different, as in Part b, we can determine the direction in which the distribution is **skewed**. Notice that the median falls between the mode and the mean in a distribution like that in Part b, and it always divides the area under the curve in half. Even if we did not have a graph of curve b, but knew only its mean, median, and mode, we could deduce that the group contained a few extreme values that have skewed the curve toward the high end of the scale.

EXERCISES

1. What is the most plausible meaning of the term "average" in the following statements?

(a) The average American household has two television sets.
(b) The average car owner spends $785 a year on gasoline.
(c) The average West German family has 1.28 children.
(d) The average smoker buys four or more packets of filtered cigarettes a week.
(e) On a customer survey, more than half the owners of "Easy Rider" motorcycles rated their durability and performance as "above average."

2. You are about to buy a camera, and learn that the mean price for this model is $150, the median is $170, and the mode is $185:

(a) What can you tell about the general distribution of prices?
(b) Why is the median higher than the mean?

3. Use the information in the following table to answer questions a through d.

TABLE 8-2

STUDENT	YEAR	FIRST TEST	SECOND TEST
1	Senior	75	80
2	Senior	65	85
3	Sophomore	90	90
4	Junior	85	60
5	Sophomore	80	85
6	Junior	85	90
7	Senior	70	75
8	Sophomore	90	95
9	Freshman	100	65
10	Senior	85	90

(a) Calculate the mean, the median, and the mode for the first test.
(b) Compare the mean, median, and mode of the first test with that of the second. Can you explain some of the differences?
(c) Do seniors tend to score higher than average or lower than average on the first test? Use all three kinds of average, and then explain which figure is the most informative.
(d) What percentage of students raised their grade? What percentage of freshmen raised their grade (i.e., scored higher on the second exam than they did on the first)? What does this show about misleading uses of statistics?

*4. Information was gathered about 1000 recently graduated economists who obtained jobs in either teaching or industry. Two hundred had Ph.D.s; the rest did not. Of the economists with doctorates, 150 went into teaching at an annual salary of $20,000 each; the remaining 50 earned $40,000 a year in industry. Of those without doctorates, 50 received teaching positions at an annual salary of $15,000; the remaining 750 received $31,000 a year in industry.

(a) Who earns more in the teaching profession, economists with a Ph.D. or economists without it?
(b) Who earns more in industry, economists with a Ph.D. or those without it?
(c) What is the mean salary of the economists with Ph.D.s?
(d) What is the mean salary of the economists without Ph.D.s?
(e) Explain the difference between your answers to parts a and b and your answers to parts c and d.

Comparisons, Rates, and Correlations

Some statistical claims concern rates and trends. Consider the claim in 8:5:

8:5. The annual per capita crime rate has risen 25 percent in the decade from 1975 to 1985.

This statement means that the number of crimes recorded in 1985 divided by the total number of people in the population in 1985 is 5/4 of the corresponding figure for 1975. To evaluate this claim, as with any statistical claim, we need to know what it means, how it was calculated, and what data it was based on.

The main thing to watch for in evaluating statements about rates and trends is that the claim should be comparing *comparable* things. For example, if the crime rate for 1975 included misdemeanors as well as felonies, and if the 1985 rate includes only felonies, any comparison between the two is meaningless. The definition of "unemployment" often varies, too, resulting in illegitimate claims about the rise and fall of unemployment rates. Less obvious differences can also affect the legitimacy of a comparison. Suppose, for example, that over the last ten years, changes in public attitude have encouraged more rape victims to report the crime to the police. If the number of reported rapes increased during this period, this does not imply that the incidence of rapes has increased.

Because inflation decreases the value of money, any changes in the price of a commodity over time should be expressed in **real** (or **constant**) **dollars,** not in **nominal** (or **current**) **dollars.** Unlike nominal dollars, real dollars are adjusted for inflation. Thus, while the nominal price per barrel of crude oil rose continuously from 1972 to 1980, the real price, expressed in terms of 1972 dollars, actually fell in 1974, 1976, 1977, and 1978.[3]

When evaluating any comparison we should also ask whether the data being used are appropriate. If, for example, we want to compare the fuel economy of two cars, we would do better to look at their respective "mpg" ratings than at how far they can go on a tank, which may hold different amounts of gas; yet advertisements often stress the latter figure when claiming that a certain car is more fuel-efficient than its competitors. Similarly, federal and state budgets are better measured and compared in terms of (real) dollars spent *per capita* than by the total amount expended. The comparisons in 8:6 all involve inappropriate bases for judgment:

8:6. (1) The safety of an airline: the percentage of the total number of airline accidents that involved the company.
(2) The value for money of detergents: their price per fluid ounce.
(3) The efficiency of traffic control: the number of speeding tickets handed out.

(4) The effectiveness of educational reforms: improvements in S.A.T. scores.

Comparison (1) fails to recognize that a small airline may fly a great deal less than others, and thus it may have a small percentage of the total number of accidents simply because it has fewer flights. Airline safety is better measured by comparing accident rates, that is, the number of accidents per flight-hour. (Why is this better than comparing the number of accidents per passenger-mile flown? What do you think is wrong with the other examples?)

These are but a few examples of comparisons based on inappropriate data. Whenever you encounter a comparison you should ask, "What is the basis for comparison?" (What data are being used to calculate relative differences?) and "Is that basis appropriate to the claims being advanced?"

Similar questions arise when one evaluates the calculations involved in such comparisons. We must be sure that we understand what is being compared to what, and how changes in the basis of comparison can affect the final figures. Consider a very simple case. If your salary is lowered by 10 percent, and then raised by 10 percent, you do not wind up with the same salary you had before. If you earn $20,000 a year, a pay cut of 10 percent reduces that to $18,000. A raise of 10 percent would result in a salary of $18,000 + $1800 = $19,800. The difference of $200 arises simply because the first calculation involved 10 percent of $20,000, and the second involved 10 percent of $18,000, a difference that might be overlooked, for example, in an offer by a manufacturing company to offset a pay cut of 10 percent by adding fringe benefits equivalent to 10 percent of the workers' new salary.

The importance of identifying the basis of comparison and the items being compared is shown in the following claim made by a British politician:

8:7. Fifty percent more teachers considered that educational standards had fallen rather than risen over the previous five years.

The first thing to note is that "50 percent more" is not the same as "50 percent of all teachers." When we ask "50 percent more than what?" we discover that the survey on which this claim was based found that 36 percent of the teachers thought that educational standards had fallen, 24 percent believed they had risen, 32 percent thought there was no significant change, and 8 percent had no opinion. Thus, the group that thought standards had fallen is 50 percent larger than the group that thought standards had risen—which is what 8:7 says—but this ignores 40 percent of the total responses.[4]

A more complicated form of comparison occurs when we are interested in whether two or more properties are *correlated*. To begin with a simple example, we may want to know whether high-school graduates are more likely to vote for a certain candidate than are people with less education. Statement 8:8 shows one way of expressing that information:

8:8. A survey reveals that 59 percent of the high-school graduates in the city plan to vote for the Democratic candidate, while only 35 percent of the voters who have not completed high-school are in favor of the same candidate.

In other cases, we may want to discover whether men are more likely to be cigarette smokers than women, whether city dwellers are more likely to have ulcers than rural dwellers, or how salary affects job satisfaction. In each of these cases, we are really trying to determine whether two properties, A and B (candidate preference and education, gender and smoking habits, etc.), are correlated.

The easiest method of answering this question involves two steps. First, we determine the proportion of Bs that are A (in 8:8, this would be the fraction of high-school graduates who favor the Democratic candidate) and the proportion of non-Bs that are A (the fraction of people who did not graduate from high school who favor the Democratic candidate). By comparing these two figures, we can determine whether A is **positively correlated** with B, **negatively correlated** with B, or whether A and B are **uncorrelated**.

To prevent confusion, it is helpful to think of correlations as represented by a chart like the following:

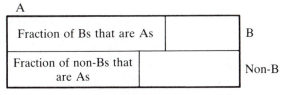

FIGURE 8-2

In determining the **strength of the correlation** between A and B, we need to know the fraction of As in each of the two classes, B and its complement, non-B. As we will see in the section Calculating the Odds, the calculation of strength of correlation follows the same pattern as the calculation of the probability of A given B, and the probability of A given non-B.

In the case described a few paragraphs earlier, the property of favoring the Democratic candidate is positively correlated with being a high-school graduate because the fraction of people within the group of high-school graduates who favor the Democratic candidate is higher than the fraction of people within the other group. In general, A is positively correlated with B if the fraction of As among the Bs is higher than the fraction of As among the non-Bs; similarly, A and B are negatively correlated if there is a higher fraction of As among the non-Bs than there is among the Bs. Finally, if there is no correlation between A and B, the fraction of As will remain relatively constant, whether we survey Bs or non-Bs. Example 8:9 illustrates how statistical data can be used to calculate the degree of correlation.

8:9. We are told that 66 percent of all male alcoholics are married, as if this were evidence that marriage contributes to drinking problems. But if we take into account the fact that 75 percent of all men are married, and the alcoholism rate among men generally is about 10 percent, we can see that just the reverse is true.

The question addressed here is whether (restricting the inquiry to the class of adult males) being married (property A) is positively or negatively correlated with being an alcoholic (property B). To determine this, we must divide the population into two classes, men who are alcoholics and men who are not, and compare the fraction of married men in each class. We are given the information about the first: the fraction of Bs that are A is 0.66. To determine the strength of correlation, we must take into account (a) that 34 percent of all alcoholics are bachelors and (b) that bachelors comprise 25 percent of the total population. If we imagine a matrix representing a group of 1000 men, we can fill in the information we have, and then calculate the rest; this is done in Figure 8-3.

	Married men (75% of 1000 = 750)	Bachelors (25% of 1000 = 250)
Alcoholics (10% of 1000 = 100)	66 (66% of 100)	34 (100 − 66)
Nonalcoholics (1000 − 100 = 900)	684 (750 − 66)	216 (250 − 34)

FIGURE 8-3

We now have all the information to construct the chart in Figure 8-4, which illustrates the strength of correlation between being married and being an alcoholic.

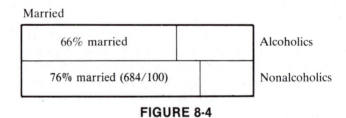

FIGURE 8-4

We calculate the strength of correlation between A and B by subtracting the fraction of non-Bs that are A from the fraction of Bs that are A. In the example just analyzed, the strength of correlation between being married and being an alcoholic is (0.66 − 0.76) = −0.10, a negative correlation, which indicates that a married man is less likely to be an alcoholic than a bachelor is.

Similarly, the data in 8:8 can be expressed as a correlation: there is a correlation of $+0.24 = (0.59 - 0.35)$ between acceptance of the Democratic candidate and graduating from high school. If, on the other hand, we discover that 20 percent of all philosophy students go on to make a salary of $20,000 or more, while 78 percent of all the students in other fields make that much, we can say that there is a negative correlation between making at least $20,000 and studying philosophy. The strength of correlation will be $(0.20 - 0.78) = -0.58$, showing a high negative correlation between the two properties.

The highest possible positive correlation is $+1.0$, meaning that all Bs have A, and no non-Bs have A; analogously, the lowest possible negative correlation is -1.0, and no correlation at all will yield a figure of 0. (If the fraction of non-Bs that are A is exactly the same as the fraction of Bs that are A, subtracting the first number from the second gives zero.)[5]

The strength of correlation is easy to calculate, but its use is limited to simple all-or-nothing properties such as being an alcoholic or having graduated from high school. In cases where the properties A and B vary continuously on a quantitative scale of measurement, (e.g., height, income, number of cigarettes smoked per day), it is better to calculate the **coefficient of correlation,** also called the **degree of correlation.** Although we will not discuss the actual calculation here, the idea behind it is readily grasped by imagining the data plotted on a scatter diagram such as the one in Figure 8-5.

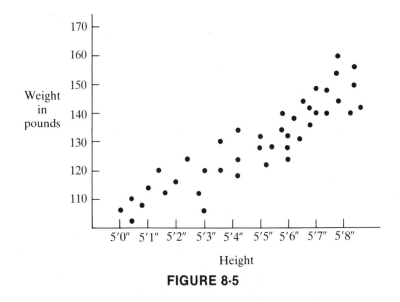

FIGURE 8-5

In this figure, each point on the diagram represents the height and weight of one person measured. We can imagine a line drawn through the middle of the cluster. The fact that most of the points lie fairly close to the line indicates that the coefficient of correlation is high, and the fact that the line runs from the lower left to the upper right tells us that the correlation is positive. The coefficient of correlation is expressed in the same way as the strength of correlation, with $+1.0$ being the highest possible positive correlation, -1.0 being the highest possible negative correlation, and 0.0 no correlation at all.

Using scatter diagrams to represent the coefficient of correlation allows us to take full advantage of the data we have. If we had used only the simpler strength of correlation, we would have been forced to simplify the data by organizing the cases into categories—for example, those taller than 5 feet 10 inches and those 5 feet 10 inches and under.

The other advantage of the coefficient of correlation is that it is perfectly *symmetric*: given the same data, the coefficient of correlation between A and B is always the same number as the coefficient of correlation between B and A. As one can see from example 8:9, this is *not* true of the strength of correlation. The strength of correlation between being married and being an alcoholic (-0.10) is not the same number as the strength of correlation between being an alcoholic and being married (-0.048). In general, if A is positively (or negatively) correlated with B, then B will be positively (or negatively) correlated with A, but the numerical value of the strength of correlation will not be the same. Thus, both the coefficient of correlation and the strength of correlation are *qualitatively* symmetric, but only the coefficient is *quantitatively* symmetric.

Correlation is not the same as causality. We should not infer from the mere fact that A is positively correlated with B that A *causes* B. For one thing, we have just seen that correlation is qualitatively symmetrical, so if A is positively correlated with B, then B must be positively correlated with A. But clearly we cannot infer *both* that A causes B *and* that B causes A. Also it is possible that there is no direct causal connection between A and B at all; the correlation between them might be the result of a third factor, C, which is the **common cause** of both. For example, there is a positive correlation between schoolboys' shoe sizes and the legibility of their handwriting, but neither is the cause of the other. Older boys, being larger, tend to have bigger feet, and being older, they have more legible handwriting. The use of correlations to test causal hypotheses is discussed in Chapter 10.

EXERCISES

1. The Republic of Ruritania adopts a five-year plan to double its annual output of iron and steel from 50 million tons to 100 million tons. At the end of five years, the actual output is 70 million tons. The President of Ruritania reports that the country has achieved 70 percent of its goal. The opposition party claims that the country has achieved only 40 percent of its goal. Who is correct and why?

2. The manufacturer of Sparkle toothpaste conducts a five-year study of a group of 1000 children using its product, and asserts that this group had "33% fewer cavities." Explain what this comparison might mean and

whether it can be used as evidence that using Sparkle reduces the likelihood of cavities.

3. You have discovered that the tendency to condone or engage in violence toward women is positively correlated with the amount of time spent reading or viewing pornographic material. Give three possible explanations for this correlation.

*4. Sixty percent of the women students at Dixie College are currently studying a foreign language, while only 15 percent of the male students do so. There are 200 students at the college, equally divided among men and women.

(a) What is the strength of the correlation between studying a foreign language and being a woman?

(b) What is the strength of the correlation between being a woman and studying a foreign language? (Hint: First calculate the total number of students of both sexes who are studying a foreign language.)

5. An experiment is performed to see whether a newly discovered hormone promotes growth in plants. Twenty plants are divided into five groups of four. Each plant in the first group receives 1 gram of the hormone, in the second group each receives 2 grams, and so on. At the end of six months, the height of each plant is measured. The results are as follows, with the height of plants given in inches: 1 gram (8.7, 8.2, 6.8, 6.9); 2 grams (8.1, 7.8, 6.9, 6.5); 3 grams (7.5, 7.2, 6.8, 6.3); 4 grams (7.1, 7.3, 6.5, 6.0); 5 grams (7.2, 7.0, 6.1, 5.5).

(a) Plot the information on a scatter diagram. What is the qualitative correlation between hormone dosage and plant height?

(b) Calculate the strength of correlation between growing to a height of 7 inches or more and receiving a hormone dose of 3 grams or more.

(c) Explain the difference between the answers to questions a and b.

6. Explain how you would gather reliable information about how many violent crimes (rapes, robberies, and assaults) are committed each year, regardless of whether they were reported to the police.

Understanding Probability Statements

A **quantitative probability statement** assigns a number between 0 and 1 to the chances that an event of a specified type will occur (or has occurred), or to the probability that an object (or person) has a specified property. Instead of using numbers, **qualitative probability statements** express the chances of an event by means of qualitative phrases such as "highly probable," "probable," "more probable than not," and "quite unlikely." The following list contains typical statements of both kinds of probability statement:

8:10. The chances of getting a 5 on one roll of a fair die is 1/6, or about 0.17.

There is a probability of 0.5 of throwing a head on one toss of a fair coin.

It is highly unlikely that an effective vaccine against AIDS will become available in the next year.

It is more probable than not that the Democrats will win the next presidential election.

Although qualitative probability statements are often unavoidable, especially in nonmathematical contexts, an effort should be made to make them as precise as the context allows. For example, when one reads that the election of a Democrat as the next U.S. president is "more probable than not," this presumably means that the probability of this event is reckoned to be greater than 0.5. Phrases such as "highly probable," "probable," and "quite unlikely" are more difficult to interpret. Some authors use the term "probable" to describe any probability greater than half. Others have a higher figure in mind. One has to rely on one's common sense, background information, and the context.

Regardless of whether they are quantitative or qualitative, it is important to distinguish **subjective** probability statements from **objective** ones. Suppose that we ask a nuclear engineer and a layperson to tell us what each thinks is the probability of a nuclear meltdown at a power plant. Both the layperson and the expert have subjective degrees of belief, which they express in probability statements. These probability statements indicate how confident each is that the proposition "a nuclear meltdown will occur" is true. But we rely on the expert's testimony because the informed judgment of an expert about the objective value of this probability is more likely to be correct than the uninformed guess of a layperson. Whenever we think a probability statement *merely* expresses a person's subjective degree of belief, or when there is no reason to believe it accurately reflects an objective probability, we refer to the probability in question as being "subjective." It is in this sense that Stich uses the phrase "subjective probability" in paragraph 11 of Extended Argument 6.

In the rest of this section we concentrate on quantitative probability statements and treat them as objective. Although the standard form of such statements is "The probability of X is P," where $0 \leq P \leq 1$, there are several common variations, some of which are illustrated in 8:11:

8.11. The chance of rolling a 7 with a pair of fair dice is 1 in 6.

There is an 80 percent chance of precipitation tomorrow.

The odds against being dealt three of a kind in a five-card poker hand are about 49 to 1.

The first two statements in 8:11 can easily be converted into standard form: divide 6 into 1 to get 0.17 (rounding off to two significant figures); divide 80 by 100 to get 0.8. The only example likely to cause trouble is the third. Odds of A to B against an outcome means that the probability of that outcome is B/(A + B). In the third example, this means that failing to get three of a kind happens about 49 times as often as succeeding at it, or that 1/50 of the poker hands will contain three of a kind. This "odds" talk should not be confused with locutions such as "1 in 6." The latter means simply a probability of 1/6.

There are several ways of interpreting the meaning of objective probability statements. We will discuss just two of the more common ones: **the classical, a priori approach,** and **the empirical, relative frequency approach.**

The classical, a priori approach is the simplest and most natural way of analyzing games of chance (e.g., roulette, dice, and cards) in which only a finite number of **equipossible** alternatives are involved. Consider throwing a single die. What is the probability of throwing a 5? Obviously, the answer is 1/6. Dividing the number of favorable outcomes by the total number of possible outcomes gives us the desired probability.

In the classical approach to probability theory, it is vital that the alternatives involved be **equipossible,** which is to say that the probability of one alternative occurring is the same as the probability of each of the others occurring. Although it may be impossible to give a complete and noncircular definition of this concept, it is intuitively clear, for example, that my driving home safely tonight and my being killed in a car wreck are not equipossible; therefore, it would be a mistake to judge that my chances of arriving home are 0.5. The importance of judging equipossible alternatives correctly is illustrated by the famous error made by Jean-le-Rond D'Alembert (French mathematician, 1717–1783) in his analysis of the game described in 8:12:

8:12. Two players, Primo and Secundo, toss a coin twice. If heads appears on either toss, Primo wins. If heads appears on neither toss, Secundo wins. D'Alembert argued that there are three possibilities. Either (a) heads shows on the first toss and Primo wins or (b) the first toss is tails and Primo wins on the second toss or (c) the first toss is tails and Secundo wins on the second toss. Since two of these three cases are favorable to Primo, D'Alembert concluded that the probability of Primo winning is 2/3.

D'Alembert was mistaken. In fact there are *four* equipossible alternatives to consider (HH, TT, HT, TH) of which three favor Primo. The correct answer is 3/4. One way of exposing D'Alembert's error is to realize that his three cases are not equipossible; they are not *equiprobable* alternatives. Schematically, we have the following:

(a) (H, −)	P wins	Prob = 1/2
(b) (T,H)	P wins	Prob = 1/4
(c) (T,T)	S wins	Prob = 1/4

Listed in 8:13 are some examples for which the classical approach is inadequate because we do not have a finite number of equipossible alternatives:

8:13. This biased coin has a 0.57 probability of turning up tails.

The probability that a Purdue student is on a scholarship is 0.3.

The chance of a 60-year-old American male dying of cancer within the next five years of his life is 0.39.

The most natural way of interpreting these probability statements is through the **empirical** or **relative frequency approach.** This approach also has the merit of being able to cover all the situations usually handled on the classical conception of probability.

The **empirical approach** regards all probability statements as expressing the limit of a relative frequency in an infinitely long series of repetitions of some experimental setup or sampling procedure. The basic idea can be illustrated by considering the claim that there is a 0.5 probability that a fair coin will turn up heads when tossed. Imagine that we toss the coin 100 times. Even though the coin is fair, this does not mean we will always obtain exactly $n/2$ heads on n tosses. In fact, when n is an odd number, this is logically impossible! Let us assume that we obtain 52 heads on our 100 tosses. The relative frequency is the number of successful outcomes divided by the total number of trials. In our example, the relative frequency of heads on 100 trials is 0.52. The empirical approach claims that as the number of trials is increased, the relative frequency of heads gets closer and closer to 0.5; thus, in an infinite number of trials the relative frequency would reach the limiting value of 0.5.

Strictly speaking there is no such thing as *the* probability of a fair coin's turning up heads when tossed. The probability of heads depends not only on the coin but also on the details of the tossing mechanism. From now on, we will take care to specify the situation or context in which a given probability is defined. For any probability statement, we will want to specify the **reference class** as well as the **attribute class**. For a biased coin that has a probability of 0.43 of showing heads when tossed, the reference class, R, is the set of all tosses of the coin (where the tossing mechanism is specified). The attribute class, A, is the subset of these tosses which have the additional property, or attribute, of having heads as their outcome. We can represent any quantitative probability statement, defined in this way, on a Venn diagram such as the one drawn in Figure 8-6. The reference class, R, is assigned an area of one unit; the area of the attribute class, A, is set equal to the value of the probability, in this case 0.43. In other words, the value of the probability is equal to the ratio of the area of A (representing the attribute class) to the area of R (representing the reference class). Since it is difficult to draw these diagrams to scale, we simply write in the numerical value of the area of A relative to the unit area assigned to R, as illustrated in Figure 8-6.

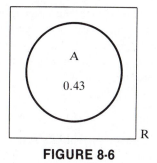

FIGURE 8-6

Common sense and one's background information are often vital in deciding on the most plausible meaning of a probability statement. When we read, or hear, that there is a 60 percent chance of precipitation tomorrow, the reference class is presumably the set of days relevantly similar to tomorrow. The relevant similarities in this case are specified by our best meteorological theories and would include such things as the prevailing wind patterns, current direction of the jet stream, atmospheric pressures and temperatures, and precipitation during the preceding week. The fact that tomorrow is the anniversary of D-Day or the last Friday of the month is irrelevant.

When the reference class is not specified, we should try to infer the most plausible reference class. Consider the information in 8:14:

8:14. There is a 52 percent chance of a Purdue student's being male. There is a 0.1 percent chance of a Purdue student's being a Rastafarian ballet dancer.

With no further information being provided, it is reasonable to presume that the reference class for the first statement is the class of all Purdue students; the probability statement then follows deductively from the statistical statement that 52 percent of all Purdue students are male. It is also reasonable to assume that in the second statement the reference class is still the set of all Purdue students, and the attribute class is the subset of Purdue students who are both Rastafarians and ballet dancers. This is the most reasonable guess. But it is logically possible, though highly implausible given our background information about the Purdue student body, that the probability in question was derived from the percentage of Rastafarian students at Purdue who also happen to be ballet dancers. (Why is this highly implausible?)

Finally, there is the **problem of the single case.** Often we encounter or make statements such as "The probability of getting a head on the next toss of this coin is 0.43." This statement is about a single case, namely, the next toss of a particular coin. How can we interpret this kind of statement with the empirical approach? The reference class and the attribute class are the same as those drawn in Figure 8-6. We are still referring, implicitly, to the limit of a relative frequency in an infinite sequence of trials. In addition we are supposing that the next toss is randomly selected from the reference class. Imagine that you are blindfolded and then stick a pin into the Venn diagram at random. There is a 0.43 chance that the pin will land inside the A circle, representing the tosses that turn up heads. If we were to repeat this process an infinite number of times, in the limit our success rate of correct guesses would be 0.43.

EXERCISES

I. Classify each of the following probability statements as being quantitative/qualitative and subjective/objective. If the probability statement is objective explain which approach, classical or empirical, gives the best interpretation.

*1. If I choose a page of the local newspaper at random, it is more probable than not that it will contain at least one typographical error.

2. There is a 1 in 4 chance that the Soviets will have a space station on the moon by the year 2000.

3. Given that 1 person in every 500 carries a recessive gene for trait T, the chances of finding a married couple both of whom carry the gene for T are 4 in 1 million.

*4. In any group of more than 23 people, the odds are better than even that at least two people have the same birthday (same day and month).

5. Because most coins wear unevenly, the actual probability of a tossed coin landing heads up is 0.48.

II. What is the probability of each of the following events? How did you arrive at that figure? When an exact calculation requires information you do not have, explain how you would arrive at the probability in question.

1. The probability of drawing a spade from a shuffled deck.

2. The probability of randomly selecting a black ball from a box containing 40 white balls and 10 black ones.

3. The probability that the next president of the United States will be a woman.

*4. The probability that Ronald Reagan was elected president in 1984.

*5. The probability of a 30-year-old man surviving through the year 2000.

Calculating the Odds

From any group of quantitative probability statements such as $Pr(A) = 0.4$ and $Pr(B) = 0.7$, we can use the rules of probability theory to deduce further probability statements. (In a mathematical treatment, these rules are the axioms of the so-called **probability calculus.**)

The simplest type of deduction is the calculation of the probability that an event will not happen, or the chances that an object or person does not have a given attribute. For example, if the probability that a randomly selected American has been immunized against polio is 0.99, then the chance that he or she has not been immunized is 0.01. Similarly, if the probability of throwing a tail on a coin toss is 0.57, then the probability of *not* throwing a tail on a toss of the same coin is 0.43. In all cases, the probability that an event will happen (or an object or person will have a given attribute) plus the probability that the same event will not happen (or an object or person will not have that attribute) must sum to 1. This gives us the **Negation Rule**:

Negation Rule

$$\Pr(\text{not-A}) = 1 - \Pr(A)$$

In Figure 8-7, Pr(not-A) is proportional to the shaded area outside the A circle but inside the R rectangle. Since we always assign the reference class a probability value of 1 (since it is certain that anything selected from R will be a member of R), the negation rule is satisfied. This is illustrated in Figure 8-7.

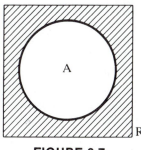

FIGURE 8-7

It is important that both of these probabilities be defined with respect to the same reference class, R. For example, if R is the set of all outcomes of tossing a coin on to a level surface, the chance is very small that the coin will land vertically on its edge, and thus be neither heads nor tails. Only if we exclude this possibility in our definition of R can we identify the set of outcomes that are not tails with the set of outcomes that are heads.

The next two rules concern the probability of disjunctive statements of the form "(A or B)." For example, we may wish to calculate the probability of the complex event of getting either a 4 or a 6 on the roll of a die. Assuming the die is fair, there is a 1/6 chance of getting any particular number. Thus, the probability of rolling a 4 (A) is 1/6, and the probability of rolling a 6 (B) is 1/6. The probability of rolling either of these two numbers (A or B) is simply the sum of these probabilities, or 1/3. In this example, the alternatives are *exclusive*; the attribute circles on the Venn diagram in Figure 8-8 do not overlap.

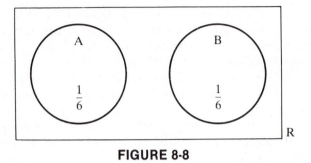

FIGURE 8-8

The probability of getting either A or B is simply the sum of the areas of the A circle and the B circle. This is expressed in the **Limited Alternation Rule**:

Limited Alternation Rule

$$Pr(A \text{ or } B) = Pr(A) + Pr(B)$$

The Limited Alternation Rule applies only when the alternative outcomes are exclusive. In cases in which the alternatives are not exclusive, we have to use the **General Alternation Rule.** For example, "What is the probability of getting either an ace (A) or a heart (B) when we draw a single card from a randomly shuffled deck of 52 cards?" When we draw the Venn diagram in Figure 8-9, we see that the A circle and the B circle overlap, since it is possible that the outcome is a card that is both an ace and a heart. The alternative outcomes of getting either an ace or a heart are not exclusive. If we were simply to add the area of the A circle (4/52) to the area of the B circle (13/52), our answer (17/52) would be too large. Because the circles overlap, they cover a smaller area of the Venn diagram, as shown in Figure 8-9.

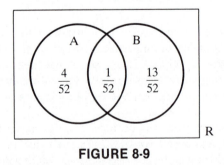

FIGURE 8-9

To get the right answer we have to subtract the area of intersection corresponding to the complex event of drawing the ace of hearts (1/52). Thus, the correct answer is 16/52 = 4/13. This is an application of the **General Alternation Rule:**

General Alternation Rule

Pr(A or B) = Pr(A) + Pr(B) − Pr(A and B)

The Limited Alternation Rule is really just a special case of the General Alternation rule, since when the alternatives are exclusive, Pr(A and B) = 0.

Next we consider ways of determining the probability that two events, A and B, will both occur. As in the previous cases, we must keep in mind the relationship between the two events. Instead of worrying about whether the two events are exclusive (if they are, we would not have to calculate the probability that they both occur), we must ask whether they are **dependent** or **independent** events. In general, two events are **statistically independent** if the occurrence of one has no effect on the probability that the other will occur. For example, getting heads on the first toss of a fair coin has no effect on the chances of getting heads on the second toss.

If we have statistically independent events, the probability of their conjunction is just the probability of the first multiplied by that of the second. This is the **Limited Conjunction Rule**:

Limited Conjunction Rule

Pr(A and B) = Pr(A) × Pr(B)

The Limited Conjunction Rule works only when the outcomes are statistically independent. In the case of getting two heads in a row, Pr(H1 and H2) = Pr(H1) × Pr(H2) = (1/2) × (1/2) = 1/4. But in the case of drawing two aces in a row from a shuffled deck of cards, the outcomes are not independent. If the first card drawn is an ace, then 51 cards are left, of which 3 are aces. The first outcome changes the probability of the second. For this case we have to use the General Conjunction Rule, explained later.

It is important to remember, when we apply the Limited Conjunction Rule, that if we know event A has already occurred, Pr(A) = 1. Thus, although the probability of drawing the ace of diamonds from a shuffled deck twice in a row is (1/52) × (1/52) = 1/2704, the chance of doing it again after having done it once is just (1) × (1/52) = 1/52. If the events in a series are indeed statistically independent of each other, then the probability of any one of them happening is unaffected by the occurrence of the others: when shells are falling randomly on a battlefield, a fresh shell hole is no safer than any other spot; even after a long unbroken run of heads, if the coin is fair, the probability of getting heads on the next toss is still 1/2; carrying aboard one's own bomb does not decrease the chances that a (second) bomb is on the plane; and so on.

To formulate the General Conjunction Rule, which is used to calculate the probability of two statistically dependent events occurring together, we need to refer to the probability of one event, A, given that the other, B, has already occurred. This is called a **conditional probability statement**, and is written as Pr(A/B).

Imagine that someone has drawn a heart from the deck but does not tell us whether or not the card is an ace. What is the probability that the card is an ace (A) given that the card is a heart (B)? Obviously the answer is 1/13, since only one of the 13 hearts is also an ace. In terms of our Venn diagram, we can now regard the B circle as our reference class, and the area of intersection corresponding to the complex event (A and B) as our attribute class. The value of the conditional probability Pr(A/B) is just the area corresponding to (A and B) divided by the area corresponding to B. Thus, we get $(1/52)/(13/52) = 1/13$. We can write this as follows:

Pr(A/B) = Pr(A and B)/ Pr(B)

Conditional probability statements sometimes lead people astray. Remember that Pr(A/B) means "the probability of A given B." Thus, when we are told in example 8:9 that 66 percent of male alcoholics are married, this means that Pr(M/A), the probability of being married given that one is an alcoholic, is 0.66. Assuming that all unmarried males are bachelors (not-M = B), the Negation Rule gives us that Pr(B/A) = 0.34. But from these figures alone we cannot validly draw any conclusion about the value of Pr(A/M), the probability of being an alcoholic given that one is married, or about the value of Pr(A/B), the probability of being an alcoholic given that one is a bachelor. As explained later, the calculation of Pr(A/M) from Pr(M/A) requires additional information and the use of Bayes's theorem.

If we now rearrange the formula for conditional probability, we get the **General Conjunction Rule**:

General Conjunction Rule

Pr(A and B) = Pr(A/B) × Pr(B)

In other words, the probability of the complex event (A and B) is the probability of B times the conditional probability of A given B.

A common mistake is to use the Limited Conjunction Rule when one should be using the General Rule, in other words, one commits the error of assuming that events are statistically independent when in fact they are not. This often results in an estimate for the probability of the complex event (A and B) that is either too low or too high. Consider the chances that a person chosen at random is a cigarette smoker and has heart disease. Since rates of heart disease are higher among smokers than among nonsmokers, the probability of being a smoker with heart disease is greater than the product of the (unconditional) probability of being a smoker times the (unconditional) probability of having heart disease. Similarly, the chances of a randomly selected person being a long-distance runner and having heart disease are lower than the product of the unconditional probabilities. As a general rule, whenever the probability of a complex event is calculated by simply multiplying a string of unconditional probabilities, it is wise to stop and consider whether the events or properties in question are really independent. If they are not, the calculation might be wildly in error.

By rearranging variations of the General Conjunction Rule, we obtain a version of **Bayes's theorem** (named after the English clergyman, the Reverend Thomas Bayes, c. 1702–1761):

Bayes's Theorem

$$Pr(A/B) = [Pr(B/A) \times Pr(A)]/ Pr(B)$$

Bayes's theorem is very useful. It can be used to calculate conditional probabilities from their inverses if we also know the values of the unconditional probabilities in the formula. Example 8:15 gives a real-life case that illustrates the rules we have been discussing.

8:15. A test for a rare disease is positive 99 percent of the time when the disease is present and negative 95 percent of the time when the disease is absent. If the rate of occurrence of the disease is 0.01, what is the probability of having the disease, given that the test is positive?

The information given in 8:15 is typical of how the accuracy of diagnostic tests is reported in the medical literature. The **true-positive rate** (or sensitivity) of the test is $Pr(Pos/D) = 0.99$; its **true-negative rate** (or specificity) is $Pr(Neg/not-D) = 0.95$; where D = "Having the disease," not-D = "Not having the disease," Pos = "The test is positive," and Neg = "The test is negative." The true-positive rate is obtained from performing the test on patients who are already known to have the disease, usually from a pathological examination of their tissue. Similarly, the true-negative rate comes from running the test on subjects who are known to be free of the disease. For this reason, some authors refer to these rates as specifying the retrospective accuracy of the test. What we are being asked to calculate is $Pr(D/Pos)$, which is one component of the predictive accuracy of the test. In other words, if we do not yet know whether a patient has the disease, what is the probability that she has it if her test has come out positive? As we shall see, the predictive accuracy of the test depends on the frequency of occurrence of the disease in the population from which the patient has been randomly selected. To avoid confusion, we refer to the predictive accuracies, $Pr(D/Pos)$ and $Pr(not-D/Neg)$, which are of crucial diagnostic importance, as the inverse true-positive rate and the inverse true-negative rate, respectively.[6]

First, we calculate $Pr(Pos)$, the *unconditional* probability of getting a positive test result. Either a person gets a positive result and has the disease (Pos and D) or she gets a positive result but does not have the disease (Pos and not-D). These are the only two possible conditions for a positive result, and the alternatives are exclusive. Using the General Conjunction Rule, we know that

$$Pr(Pos \text{ and } D) = Pr(Pos/D) \times Pr(D)$$

and

$$Pr(Pos \text{ and } not-D) = Pr(Pos/not-D) \times Pr(not-D)$$

Since the alternatives (Pos and D) and (Pos and not-D) are exclusive, we can use the Limited Alternation Rule to get

Pr(Pos) = Pr(Pos/D) × Pr(D) + Pr(Pos /not-D) × Pr(not-D)

We already know the values of Pr(D) and Pr(Pos/D). We can calculate Pr(not-D) and Pr(Pos/not-D) from Pr(D) and Pr(Neg/not-D) using the Negation Rule:

Pr(not-D) = 1 − Pr(D) = 1 − 0.01 = 0.99

Pr(Pos/not-D) = 1 − Pr(Neg/not-D) = 1 − 0.95 = 0.05

Remember that the test is negative 95 percent of the time when the disease is absent, and so Pr(Neg/not-D) = 0.95, the rate of true negatives. Whenever the test is not negative, it is positive, and so Pr(Pos/not-D) = 0.05. Thus,

Pr(Pos) = (0.99 × 0.01) + (0.05 × 0.99)
       = 0.0594

If we now plug all of these values into Bayes's theorem we get

Pr(D/Pos) = (0.99 × 0.01)/(0.0594)
         = 1/6

Thus, when a person has a positive test result there is only a 1 in 6 chance that she actually has the disease! This is fairly typical of diagnostic screening tests for rare diseases. These tests are usually inexpensive and noninvasive. They are designed to yield a very low number of false negatives; that is, if the test is negative, the chances are very good that you do not have the disease. In this particular example the inverse false-negative rate, Pr(D/neg) = 1/9406 = 0.00011. (Thus, the inverse true-negative rate Pr(not-D/Neg) is very high.) Few people with the disease are missed by the test, but the inverse false-positive rate, Pr(not-D/Pos) = 5/6 = 0.83, is high. (Thus, the inverse true-positive rate Pr(D/Pos) is low.) For this reason, persons with positive test results are given further tests such as X-ray studies or biopsies before any positive diagnosis is made. Five out of every six persons who showed positive on the first test are subsequently found to be free from disease.

Though it is not a separate rule, since it can be deduced from the others, the **At Least One Rule** is often useful in calculating the probability of getting at least one out of a set of outcomes.

At Least One Rule

Pr(At least one of A, B, . . . , G) = 1 − Pr(not-A and not-B and . . . and not-G)

We can illustrate this rule by considering the wager with which the Chevalier de Méré, a French gamester of the seventeenth century, won a considerable amount of money. The Chevalier bet at even money that he could get at least one 6 in four rolls of a die. Since the probability of not getting a 6 on any roll is 5/6, the chances of failure four times in a row are (5/6) × (5/6) × (5/6) ×

$(5/6) = 625/1296$, or about $13/27$. Thus, the chances of the Chevalier winning his bet were $1 - (13/27) = 14/27$. In other words, the odds favoring his bet were 14 to 13, or slightly better than even. In a long series of bets at even money this wager was a sure winner for de Méré.

EXERCISES

1. In a deck of 20 cards, 6 are red, 5 blue, 4 yellow, and 5 green.

(a) What is the probability that a card drawn at random is either red or green?

(b) If three cards are drawn at random without being replaced, what is the probability that the first is blue, the second red, and the third blue?

(c) If three cards are drawn at random without being replaced, what is the probability that at least one of them is green?

2. There are 100 passengers on a cruise ship. Twenty are French, and the rest are Swedish. Of the passengers who speak English, 64 are Swedish and 5 are French.

(a) What are the chances that a passenger selected at random is Swedish?

(b) What are the chances that a passenger selected at random either speaks English or is French?

(c) If two passengers are selected at random, what is the probability that they have the same nationality?

(d) You overhear a passenger speaking English. What is the probability that she is Swedish?

3. A serious accident, X, at the Peaceable Kingdom Chemical Plant can arise in only three ways: (a) a serious mechanical failure, (b) a minor mechanical breakdown followed by employee incompetence, or (c) gross negligence. A serious accident will result from possibility a, b, or c occurring by itself, or from any combination of these three possibilities, which are not mutually exclusive.

(a) By drawing a Venn diagram, show that $Pr(X) = Pr(A) + Pr(B) + Pr(C) - Pr(A \& B) - Pr(B \& C) - Pr(A \& C) + Pr(A \& B \& C)$.

(b) Use the rules of probability to prove the same result. Begin by writing $Pr(X)$ as $Pr[A \lor (B \lor C)]$. Hint: $[A \& (B \lor C)]$ is logically equivalent to $[(A \& B) \lor (A \& C)]$.

4. Cystic fibrosis is an incurable genetic disorder, unique to whites, which occurs with a frequency of 1 in 2000 among white infants. It results from a child inheriting two c genes, one from each parent. Since the disorder is always fatal, both of the parents have a Cc genotype, where C is the "normal" gene. Thus, the parents are both heterozygous or "carriers" with respect to the c gene. The affected child, with a genotype of cc, is homozygous.

(a) If the frequency of heterozygotes in the white population is 1 in n, what is Pr(M), the probability of two heterozygotes mating? Assume that the population is very large and that mating behavior is unrelated to possession of the c gene.

(b) In sexual reproduction, the chances that any particular parental gene is transmitted to the offspring is $1/2$. Given that two heterozygotes mate, what is Pr(F/M), the probability of their producing an affected child?

(c) Combining your answers to Questions a and b with the information given in the description, what is the value of n (as used in a)?

5. Suppose a clinician's practice is to have an X-ray mammogram performed on all of her female patients who have an abnormal physical examination. The frequency of cancer in such women has been found to be about 8 percent. In one series of mammograms in this population, a true-positive rate of Pr(Pos/C) = 0.92 and a true-negative rate of Pr(Neg/not-C) = 0.88 were obtained. The physician now has a patient who she feels is representative of this sample population; that is, Pr(C) = 0.08. She orders a mammogram and receives a positive result from the radiologist.[7]

(a) What is the probability Pr(C/Pos) that this patient has cancer, given the positive result?

(b) If the result had been negative, what would be the probability Pr(not-C/Neg) that this patient does not have cancer?

*6. A murder has been committed and there are only two suspects, one male and the other female. On the basis of the evidence then available, it is judged that the female is four times more likely than the male to have committed the crime. Then a sample of skin from the assailant is found. An histological examination of a skin sample (the Barr body test) can determine the sex of the donor with the following retrospective accuracies: if the donor is female, the detection of Barr bodies is 80 percent likely; if the donor is male, it is 95 percent probable that no Barr bodies will be found. Suppose that the test of the skin sample shows no Barr bodies. Does the test result now make it more probable than not that the man is the murderer? (Use Bayes's theorem to calculate Pr(M/Neg), that is, the probability the murderer is male given that the test is negative.)

7. A number of proposals have been made to require AIDS antibody screening as a condition of receiving a marriage license. Assume that the prevalence of seropositive individuals in the (low-risk) marrying population is 1 in 100,000, and that the ELISA test (which detects antibodies associated with the AIDS virus) is 93.4 percent sensitive and 99.8 percent specific.

(a) What would be the inverse false positive rate, Pr(not-D/Pos), if the ELISA test alone were used to screen marriage license applicants?

(b) What would be the inverse false positive rate if the test were used on a high-risk population in which the chance of infection is 1 in 10?

> For further information see Kenneth R. Howe, "Why Mandatory Screening for AIDS Is a Very Bad Idea," in Christine Pierce and Donald VanDeVeer (eds.), *AIDS: Ethics and Public Policy* (Belmont, CA: Wadsworth, 1988), pp. 140–149.

Drawing the Correct Conclusion

In the preceding sections we have discussed what statistical and probability claims mean, how they should be evaluated, and what it is reasonable to conclude from them. Since such claims can be misleading even whey they are true, it is worth reviewing some of the points made earlier. It is also useful to draw attention to the ways in which the presentation of statistical claims can affect how we interpret them.

When confronted with a statistical claim, the first step is to decide what kind of claim is being made and to ask how it was arrrived at. If the claim describes a population, did it result from a census, or was it based on an inductive inference from a sample? In either case, it is important to consider possible sources of nonsampling error, such as the validity of any indirect tests used to gather the data. If the statistical claim is the result of an inductive argument, we must also consider the size and selection of the sample, and the sampling error.

In evaluating the significance of the figures we are given, we should also understand how they were calculated. Looking at discussions of "average," for example, we must determine whether the mean, median, or mode is being given, and should try to imagine how these figures might give a misleading picture of the whole population. Background information is useful here, as example 8:16 illustrates:

8:16. The mean price of new cars in Hollywood is $28,924; in Ottumwa, Iowa, the mean price is $12,425. Therefore, if you are looking for a new car, you are likely to get a better price in Iowa.

We know that the mean is affected by extremely high or low values, and common sense tells us that the group of cars sold in Hollywood will probably contain some very expensive ones, which would bring up the mean. Example 8:16 also illustrates another flaw: it uses a comparison that probably does not involve comparable things. To determine which city (or dealership) offers the best prices for a car, we must compare the prices for the same model. Thus, we should look at the mean prices for the same model car, comparably equipped.

If we are trying to draw a conclusion on the basis of percentages, we must know what the figures are percentages of, and how different populations might yield different figures. As just noted, in the case of comparisons, we want to be sure that we are comparing comparable things, and that we are comparing them in an appropriate way.

Conclusions based on probability statements must also be carefully assessed. We should ask whether the probability statement is merely subjective or intended to be objective. When calculations are involved, we must also be sure that the appropriate rules have been followed; in particular, that nonexclusive alternatives and dependent events have been handled correctly.

Statistical claims do not appear in a vacuum. They are usually part of an attempt to persuade, convince, or woo an audience. How a claim is presented can aid in these endeavors. The mode of presentation can make a statistical claim seem more dramatic or important than it really is. So when you evaluate a statistical claim, you should also consider the way in which it is presented.

First, the choice of figures can be dictated by the writer's own point of view. We saw earlier that one could present very different pictures of the average, depending on whether the mean, median, or mode is given. Similarly, there are cases in which a percentage figure seems more dramatic or startling than the actual numbers (especially when the numbers are small and the percentage high), and sometimes it is to the writer's advantage to use numbers rather than percentages. To avoid being misled, you should try to find out both figures—the percentages (of what population?) and the numbers.

Another way to present accurate statistics in a misleading way is to leave out information that detracts from the position being defended. If a person argues that people with professional training earn higher salaries than nonprofessionals, he may cite figures for doctors and lawyers, but simply omit statistics on less well paid professions. Similarly, in the debate over the effectiveness of family-planning clinics that counsel and treat teenagers, advocates often cite the decline in birth rates among clinic patrons; detractors point out that birth rates are affected by abortion and that teenage pregnancy rates in the nation as a whole continue to climb. Neither statistic is a good measure of how well such clinics prevent teenage pregnancies. The relevant issue is whether pregnancy rates are lower among those who use the clinics than among comparable groups that do not.

The use of graphs may seem straightforward, but graphs, too, can be used to present information in a misleading way. Compare the two graphs in Figure 8-10, illustrating weight loss with a particular diet. The moral here is to read graphs carefully. Do not just glance at the overall picture.

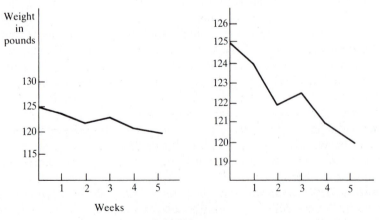

FIGURE 8-10

Bar graphs are a fine way of accurately presenting one-dimensional data—that is, information about the variation and changes in the magnitude of a *single* quantity. Many newspapers and television news programs try to make their graphics of one-dimensional data more dramatic by drawing pictures either of flat objects (e.g., dollar bills) that vary in area, or of three-dimensional objects (e.g., houses, barrels of oil, piles of money) that vary in apparent volume. Unfortunately, using pictures of objects of different sizes instead of bars of different lengths can be misleading if the diagrams are not drawn properly to scale. If one house, barrel of oil, or pile of coins, is supposed to represent a figure twice as large as another, then it should not be drawn twice as large in each of its three dimensions. If it is, it has eight times the apparent volume of the other, and will create the misleading impression that the larger figure is more than twice the size of the smaller one.

Even when the areas of two-dimensional figures are drawn so that they are directly proportional to the numerical quantity being represented, people differ in how they perceive their relative magnitudes. For example, when asked to compare the sizes of two circles, one of which has an area exactly twice that of the other, most people judge that the larger circle is less than twice the size of the smaller one. Thus, even though there may not be an intention to deceive, the use of an inappropriate graphic to represent numerical data can create a misleading impression.[8]

EXERCISES

Comment on the use of statistics in questions 1 through 8.

*1. The median price of a new house in 1969 averaged $25,600, but by 1979 it was up to $64,000 for a hike of 150 percent. Hamburger was in this bracket, too, selling for an average of 62 cents a pound in 1969, and $1.54 in 1979, up 148 percent. If inflation is not stopped promptly and effectively, tack another 10 years to these numbers and compare your likely buying power then.

2. "Dr. James Vaupel of the Institute of Policy Sciences and Public Affairs at Duke University, sought to dramatize the benefits of risk analysis by evaluating the often-heard admonition against eating too many eggs. Although eggs are high in cholesterol, and in some individuals may contribute to artherosclerotic disease, the risk entailed in eating them has, according to Dr. Vaupel, been greatly overstated. By cutting in half the average American's consumption of eggs (five per week) it is estimated that five thousand lives might be saved each year. Although this sounds like something worth doing, when stated in different terms it can be shown to be practically insignificant. For example, this proposed halving of egg consumption will extend the average American's life expectancy by only ten days; thus each egg consumed over an average lifespan of seventy-three years might reduce life expectancy by about a minute; further calculation shows that eating a half-dozen eggs involves one chance in a million of a death per year, thus qualifying as a 'micro-risk.'" [From Samuel C. Florman, *The Civilized Engineer* (New York: St. Martin's Press, 1987), p. 153.]

3. So far this year, Exxon has earned 726 million dollars from its oil and natural gas operations in the U.S. To do this, we sold the equivalent of 18 billion gallons of petroleum products. That works out to be a profit of 4 cents per gallon. In the same period, we invested 833 million dollars in the U.S. to find, produce, and deliver petroleum products to our customers in the future. (Exxon ad in *Time* magazine.)

4. (The following excerpt is from a piece that appeared in *Newsweek*, March 2, 1987, commenting on the record 54-point gain in the Dow Index on just one day during the previous week.) Save your enthusiasm. It was no big deal. The market had a good strong day: percentagewise, the Dow Jones industrial average was up 2.5 percent. But that was not enough to justify the hysteria. The simple truth is that the venerable Dow index distorts market movements. Twenty-five years ago a 50-point jump would have equaled about 10 percent. Today, a gain of that magnitude in an indicator whose total value now exceeds 2200 shouldn't startle anyone. What's needed is a little perspective; the Dow must be brought down to reality. Like any individual stock whose high price becomes an obstacle, it should be split, say, 10 for 1. . . . A 10 for 1 split would have reduced the record one-day gain to 5.41 points, a move more closely related to what actually happened to the prices of the 30 stocks making up the index. That day, for instance, Du Pont went up $5.88 a share, IBM $3.88 a share and Merck $4.50. Nice gains but nothing out of the ordinary.

5. In 1946, 8300 women drivers and 114,000 men drivers were involved in car accidents in Pennsylvania. Therefore, during this period men were about 14 times as likely to have accidents as women.

*6. (The following piece appeared in the "Letters" section of *Science*, September 5, 1986.) Eliot Marshall (News & Comment, June 27, p. 1596) should be chained to a roulette wheel in Atlantic City until he understands the nature of a probability estimate and the Monte Carlo fallacy.

Richard Feynman estimates the risk of a solid rocket booster failure on the shuttle at between 1 in 50 and 1 in 100. The fact that there was a failure on the 25th shuttle launch (50th booster launch) bears no relation to this estimate. If the first shuttle launch had failed—or if there had been no failure for 500 flights—Feynman's estimate could still be right. There is no relation between the probability of an event and the history of the event's occurrence.

Even worse is the imputation that NASA expects no failures in 280 years of daily launches. They are reported to expect a failure with a probability of 1 in 100,000 on every launch. The odds of one or more failures in 100,000 launches are thus over 63%. This is a far cry from expecting "not one equipment-based disaster."

7. In its annual review of cancer statistics released at the end of 1986, the National Cancer Institute (NCI) reported that the death rate for those under 55 years of age decreased nearly 7 percent between 1975 and 1984—from 38.2 per 100,000 to 35.7. NCI Director Dr. Vincent De-Vita, Jr., called the decline "one of the most encouraging cancer statistics we see this year." But in the same 10-year period, the rate at which cancers occurred in people younger than 55 rose about 2 percent, reaching 99.8 per 100,000 in 1984. This age group now accounts for 24 percent of all newly diagnosed cancers. Critics of NCI charge that, in fact, the nation is losing the war on cancer. Over the last decade, the incidence of diagnosed cases of cancer has been rising an average of 0.7 percent a year and the death rate has been increasing 0.5 percent annually. The NCI has countered that the total incidence and death rate obscure progress against a number of cancers because of the soaring numbers of deaths from lung cancer. If these are excluded, NCI officials hold, the overall cancer death rate has dropped significantly.

8. [The following passage is excerpted from an interview with Kenneth L. Fisher, author of *The Wall Street Waltz* (Chicago: Contemporary Books,

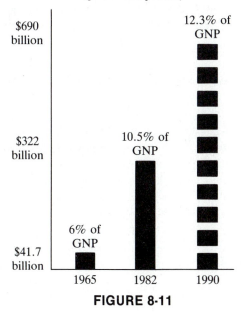

TOTAL HEALTH CARE COSTS

(public and private)

$690 billion

$322 billion

$41.7 billion

12.3% of GNP

10.5% of GNP

6% of GNP

1965   1982   1990

FIGURE 8-11

1987), published in *The Christian Science Monitor* on July 21, 1987.] . . . Fisher no longer worries that the United States government's deficit is the source of impending doom. Opening his book to the chart of net public debt as a percentage of gross national product, Fisher declares, "The deficit is a misnomer. The government is managing its finances well—within the realm of normalcy."

The chart shows federal debt as a percentage of GNP pushing the 40 percent mark now. But from 1940 to 1960 it was over 45 percent, and as high as 120 percent during World War II.

Fisher allows that the current trend is in the wrong direction but believes "we're probably 10 to 15 years away from a crisis environment."

9. Comment on the presentation of statistical information in Figure 8-11. (Taken from John K. Iglehart, "Fixed–Fee Medicine for Medicare: An Introduction," *Issues in Science and Technology*, Fall 1984, p. 97.)

Notes

[1]The drug testing example was adapted from a letter to the editor, published in *The New York Times*, September 16, 1986. The letter criticized a New York Times–CBS News poll, the results of which were published in *The New York Times*, September 2, 1986.

[2]When dealing with a finite population, the fraction x/y in decimal notation should not have more decimal places than $(N - 1)$, where N is the number of digits in the decimal representation of y. Thus, 50/100 should be written as 0.50, and 500/1000 should be written as 0.500.

[3]See the graphs in Edward R. Tufte, *The Visual Display of Quantitative Information* (Cheshire, CT: Graphics Press, 1983), p. 63.

[4]Described in Derek Rowntree, *Statistics Without Tears* (New York: Scribners, 1981), p. 188.

[5]For a more detailed discussion of this way of measuring strength of correlation, see Ronald Giere, *Understanding Scientific Reasoning*, 2nd ed. (New York: Holt Rinehart and Winston, 1984), pp. 179–201.

[6]See David M. Eddy, "Probabilistic Reasoning in Clinical Medicine: Problems and Opportunities," in Daniel Kahneman, Paul Slovic, and Amos Tversky, eds., *Judgement Under Uncertainty: Heuristics and Biases* (Cambridge: Cambridge University Press, 1982), pp. 249–267.

[7]Adapted from David M. Eddy, "Probabilistic Reasoning in Clinical Medicine: Problems and Opportunities," in Kahneman, Slovic, and Tversky, eds., *Judgement Under Uncertainty: Heuristics and Biases*, pp. 257–258.

[8]For more on the design and evaluation of statistical charts, see Chapter 2, "Graphical Integrity," in Edward R. Tufte, *The Visual Display of Quantitative Information*.

CHAPTER
9

Legal and
Practical Reasoning

Much of the reasoning we have been studying is concerned with determining what is true, or what we should believe. Critical thinking has another side: it is also essential in reaching rational decisions about what we should do. Should I file an income tax return? Should I sue my neighbor? Should the judge uphold my lawsuit and rule in my favor? We might reach decisions on the basis of hunches or intuitions but, as with deciding what to believe, that method is unreliable. Critical thinking and good reasoning are more likely to produce a decision that is consistent with our general goals, plans, and desires.

Arguments that deal with what we ought to do are examples of **practical reasoning.** In this chapter, we take up the problem noted at the end of Chapter 3: What is the best way of understanding the open-ended nature of practical arguments with *unconditional* conclusions? Having described some of the general features of such arguments, we then narrow our focus by examining one form of practical reasoning in more detail: legal reasoning. We examine the ways in which critical thinking is applied in courts of law, and how judges use the principles of practical reasoning to decide cases.

Special Problems with Practical Reasoning

Practical reasoning covers more than just deciding what is the practical or pragmatic thing to do. It also includes reasoning about legal and moral questions, and deciding what action is most consistent with my strong but *impractical* desires. Practical arguments may address the narrow question of what a specific person should do in a carefully defined circumstance, or they may be used in support of a conclusion as broad as "Nobody should ever cause unnecessary suffering." Practical reasoning poses its own unique set of problems which can make the evaluation of such arguments difficult.

The basic problem was mentioned in Chapter 3, in the section Argument Chains and Variations. Practical reasoning is essentially **open-ended** since there is always the possibility that new information can weaken or strengthen the relationship between the stated premises and the conclusion. Factors that had not been considered explicitly in the argument might still be relevant. For that reason, we noted in Chapter 3 that only practical arguments with a **conditional conclusion** (i.e., a conclusion qualified by a phrase such as "other things being equal") can be deductively valid.

But what about practical reasoning that is intended to lead to an *unconditional* conclusion? The ultimate goals of practical reasoning are action and choice, activities that, by their very nature, leave no room for conditions. In short, the basic problem of practical reasoning is this: How can we rationally support an unconditional conclusion given the open-ended nature of the argument?

Consider argument 9:1:

9:1. Humans can survive and be healthy without eating meat. Our current methods of raising food animals cause intense suffering that cannot be justified by appeal to some greater good. Therefore, those who eat meat ought to stop.

The conclusion of 9:1 is not qualified by a condition such as "other things being equal." The implication is that all the relevant considerations have already been taken into account, and that the conclusion now follows *unconditionally.*

It is important to be clear about the nature of practical arguments with unconditional conclusions—conclusions that reflect a firm choice or commitment to act. This does not mean that the correctness[1] of the conclusion is guaranteed by the premises, or that it is not subject to revision. Practical arguments share this quality with inductive arguments: their strength or weakness is a matter of degree, since even the strongest arguments we can think of *could* go wrong, in principle, and new evidence might lead us to revise our conclusions.

The problem of open-endedness can be seen as a problem about what is *not* in the argument—considerations that are not mentioned in the premises but might affect the relationship between premises and conclusion. This, again, is a property shared by practical reasoning and the inductive arguments studied in Chapter 4. In Chapter 4, we learned that inductive arguments are essentially *incomplete*; there is always the possibility of new evidence that could either weaken or strengthen them. The same is true of practical reasoning; there is always the possibility of new considerations that may affect the argument's strength. What sorts of considerations are these? To answer that question, we must first look more closely at what *is* in the argument.

No complete practical argument can consist solely of premises that describe a situation. In Chapter 3, we noted that the practical arguments we discussed there all included a premise with a prefix such as "We want it to be the case that. . . ." More generally, at least one premise must identify a goal toward which the action or decision is aimed.

The goal might be something we simply desire, or it might be something we desire because we think it is morally right, or essential to some other goal or good. Thus, not all arguments state the relevant goals in terms of what someone wants, but any example of practical reasoning must include the identification of a goal. We refer to the premise in which the goal is identified as the **guiding premise.**

In some cases, the guiding premise is only implicit. Such is the case with 9:1. Given the way the argument is stated, we can tell that the guiding premise must be something like "One should not cause [intense] suffering unless doing so can be justified by an appeal to some greater good."

Other premises in the argument, not surprisingly, will deal with facts about the situation that are relevant to the achievement of that goal. These premises are the **informing premises**; their function is to allow us to see how and why the guiding premise is relevant to the actual situation under consideration. In 9:1 the informing premise is the claim that meat eating is not necessary for survival or good health.

Together, the two sorts of premises should make it rational to believe that the action described in the conclusion will achieve (or contribute to) the goal described in the guiding premise, given the situation described in the informing premises. In 9:1 the informing premises are meant to establish that we can appeal to no greater good to justify the suffering caused by eating meat.

We can now summarize the two principal ways in which practical arguments with unconditional conclusions are open-ended. Each practical argument contains a guiding premise and an informing premise. The consideration of new informing premises can undermine the strength of the original argument and lead us to a different conclusion. In 9:1, for example, if we learn that pregnant or nursing women cannot obtain sufficient amounts of B vitamins from a meatless diet, our original conclusion would have to be changed.

Similarly, each practical argument assumes that its guiding premise is the most appropriate one to apply to the situation under consideration. This almost always involves a choice since, usually, there are conflicting principles that can be applied to the same situation. Since such competing principles usually exist, rival arguments can be constructed that lead to different conclusions. Choosing between guiding principles is discussed in the following section.

EXERCISES

In each of the following examples, identify the practical reasoning by (1) stating the decision that is being argued for, (2) identifying the guiding premise(s), and (3) identifying the informing premise(s). Keep in mind that some of the premises may be unstated.

*1. It is all too easy for the careful scientist to affect or misinterpret an experiment in light of her expectations. Scientists must remain objective, and for this reason are well-advised to make double-blind experiments the cornerstone of their research.

2. All children should be given basic instruction in computer science in their first few years at school, because within a decade the ability to use computers will be as necessary as literacy is today.

3. Loudspeakers should be located away from corners and at least three inches off the ground; otherwise, the bass will be amplified and drown out the treble.

4. The Reagan administration has not yet justified the moral values implicit in its decision to trade arms for hostages. Therefore, it is failing to do what it ought to do. A government that cannot justify its actions will lose the support of its people and the trust of its allies.

5. Our decision-making processes should be chosen with the aim of maximizing success. We should therefore ground such processes in logic.

Evaluating Practical Reasoning

Now that we have explored the general features of practical arguments, we turn to the problem of evaluating them. Part of the evaluation focuses on the argument itself, but we must remember this is only the first step. After evaluating the argument as stated, we must consider the factors that are not included in the argument, the factors responsible for its open-ended character.

Practical reasoning can take any of the general forms we have studied: categorical, propositional, or inductive. The arguments in 9:2 and 9:3 illustrate two of these possibilities.

9:2. A combination of increased exercise and reduced calorie intake is the only effective means of weight control. Since I want to lose ten pounds, I should definitely start to exercise and watch what I eat.

9:3. History is filled with examples of "more advanced" nations colonizing "more primitive" nations with the expressed intention of helping them. Instead, such colonization has inevitably led to gross injustice and ultimately to rebellion. The United States should therefore refuse to adopt a colonial attitude toward their Third World allies.

A necessary condition for acceptable practical reasoning is that the **underlying argument** satisfy the conditions covered in Chapters 2, 3, and 4. In 9:2 we can recognize that the underlying form is that of a categorical argument, and so we can put it into the following standard form (Remember that in Chapter 3 we decided to put the want/should prefixes in parentheses so that the underlying form can be seen more easily.):

> All effective methods of weight control are things which involve increased exercise and reduced caloric intake.
>
> (I want it to be the case that) some effective method of weight control is a form of behavior that I adopt.
>
> ---
>
> (I should bring it about that) some form of behavior I adopt involves increased exercise and reduced caloric intake.

By using either a Venn diagram or the five rules for categorical syllogisms, we can see that the underlying argument—that is, the argument without the phrases in parentheses—is valid. This is certainly a necessary condition for good practical reasoning with an underlying deductive form.

In 9:3 the use of past experience to predict what will happen suggests an underlying inductive argument, in this example, an induction to the future. To simplify the translation, we will abbreviate the prefixes as "(Want . . .)" and "(Should . . .)" whenever it will not cause any confusion or misunderstanding. Thus, when put into standard form, 9:3 looks like this:

> No colonized countries observed in the past have been helped by colonization.
>
> Colonized countries observed in the past are representative of Third World allies in the future.
>
> (Want . . .) Third World allies are helped by U.S. actions toward them.
>
> ---
>
> (Should . . .) The U.S. government does not engage in colonial activities.

One could object that the underlying inductive argument here is not reliable. The generalization in the first premise is probably false since, arguably, some countries have benefited from colonization, especially when self-government was quickly encouraged. Moreover, the R-premise would be more plausible if the sample of observed cases were restricted to colonies in the past that had more relevant similarities to Third World allies in the future. Nonetheless, the premises do lend some support to the conclusion when suitably restricted.

One pattern that is quite common in practical reasoning seems to involve an invalid argument form. Consider argument 9:4:

9:4. If we increase the memory of the computer, we will be able to make it run more efficiently. Of course, we want it to run more efficiently; so we should increase the computer's memory.

This argument has the form "If p, then q; we want q; therefore, we should bring it about that p." This is clearly based on the fallacy of affirming the consequent. Does that mean that it is bad reasoning? Often such arguments are bad, because other possibilities have been ignored; "p" is a hasty conclusion. However, some arguments of this form are actually disguised versions of a more complex argument.

A premise of the form "p → q" tells us that p is a sufficient condition for q; it is one way of bringing q about. That leaves open the possibility that there might be *other* ways of bringing q about. If p is the best way of achieving q, because all the other alternatives are unacceptable, then the resulting argument is strong. Such an argument can be represented schematically as follows:

q → (p V r V s)

(Want . . .) ~ r

(Want . . .) ~ s

(Want . . .) q

(Should . . .) p

The first premise tells us that for q to occur, either p or one of the other sufficient conditions for q must occur. If we can eliminate these other alternatives, then p is left as the only acceptable method for bringing q about. Thus, it is reasonable to infer that we should bring it about that p.

Obviously, interpreting an argument like 9:4 as if it really had this form involves some major revisions and additions. The principle of charity will support such an interpretation if and only if we have some reason to believe that the author of an argument intended or would accept these revisions and interpretations; only the context of the argument and our background knowledge can tell us whether this is so.

Once we have determined whether the underlying argument is deductively valid or inductively strong, we must also evaluate the premises themselves. This process is also guided by the considerations discussed in previous chapters. If the underlying argument is inductively reliable or deductively sound, we can go on to evaluate other factors that affect the practical reasoning obtained by adding the "(Want . . .)" and "(Should . . .)" prefixes. If the underlying argument is unsound or unreliable, the practical reasoning is unacceptable.

Since informing premises contain ordinary factual information, we can assess them as we would any other factual claim. Either directly (on the basis of our own experience and knowledge) or indirectly (by considering sources of testimony or reporting), we must determine whether the informing premises contain accurate information about the situation.

Evaluating the guiding premises is more difficult. Deciding whether the statement "I would rather be rich than famous" is reasonable is different from evaluating a statement like "It is never right to tell a lie," yet either might be a guiding premise. In the next section we discuss such evaluations in the context of legal reasoning, but a full treatment of the topic would raise questions in moral philosophy that cannot be covered adequately in this textbook. Nonetheless, we can identify a few standards, simply by paying attention to the demand that principles must be reasonable. At the very least, our principles should be **consistent** and must be **capable of justification.** Someone who defends capital punishment and at the same time employs a guiding premise such as "We must hold that all human life is sacred" is guilty of inconsistency. Someone whose practical reasoning involves the premise that "We should never negotiate with terrorists," but who is unable to give good reasons for that claim, is relying on an unjustified premise.

As noted earlier, our evaluation of practical reasoning cannot stop here; we must decide whether the guiding premise being used is the best one to apply in the given situation. To see how this is done, consider example 9:5, adapted from Extended Argument 5, 31–32:

9:5. Failure to limit freedom of speech in the case of pornography would allow innocent people to suffer violations of their rights, and the general welfare of the society would be damaged. It follows from this that society should ban certain sorts of pornography.

The mention of "freedom of speech" indicates that the author, Kathleen Okruhlik, is weighing at least one conflicting principle—the principle that one should not restrict the freedom of speech—against the guiding premises implicit in her argument. These premises might be stated as "A society should not allow the rights of innocent people to be violated" and "A society should protect the general welfare." Thus, the argument as stated in 9:5 assumes that these guiding premises should outweigh the general concern for freedom of speech.

An effective way of evaluating this assumption is to ask what the alternatives are. Thus, we should try to determine (a) whether any other principles apply to the same situation, and, if so, which one to follow, and (b) whether other facts about the situation make it less appropriate to apply the chosen principle.

In our example, we have already noted that a respect for the freedom of speech is also relevant to the debate over banning pornography. In Okruhlik's presentation of the argument (see especially paragraphs 30–32) she argues that there are good reasons for thinking the principle of free speech should be (and often is) overridden in cases in which the safety and rights of others are threatened. Having done so, her arguments are much more persuasive and less vulnerable to criticism, because she has given good reasons to think that the guiding premise she uses is more appropriate to the situation than its competitors. She has done this in part by adding informing premises which narrow the focus: premises which show that this is not an ordinary question of free speech, but an issue about an activity which causes harm. However, she also justifies the decision to use one guiding premise—that free speech should be restricted in cases where harm is done—as opposed to its competitor—that free speech should never be restricted—by pointing to other cases in which the former is given more weight. This is an implicit demand for **consistency** (treating like cases alike), one of the criteria for a reasonable premise noted earlier.

Because the use of a guiding premise almost always involves deciding to give it more weight than its competitors, we cannot fully evaluate the guiding premise without first identifying those competitors.

One effective method for trying to discover other facts or principles that might apply to a situation is to imagine the strongest possible arguments for the opposite conclusion. Playing devil's advocate in this way directs our attention to considerations that might weaken the original argument. Once we know what these potential objections are, we can then evaluate their strength in comparison to the original argument. In evaluating 9:5 we can see that freedom of speech does seem to be the basis for the strongest arguments against regulating pornography. It is, in fact, the argument most often used to support that position. Since Okruhlik has already considered this defense and criticized it effectively, this confirms our judgment that her argument is quite strong.

If the underlying argument of a practical argument (without the "want/should" prefixes) is deductively valid or inductively strong and the informing premises are true, we have a good foundation for practical reasoning. The special feature of practical reasoning—using guiding premises to reach an unconditional conclusion about what we should do—means that the soundness or reliability of the **underlying argument** is not sufficient to guarantee the truth of the conclusion. But if we have gathered a great deal of information about the situation, and have considered all the alternative guiding principles as well as we can, our conclusion is probably true, and our decision is probably correct.

Much more could be said about evaluating and justifying guiding premises but an adequate treatment would require theoretical work in ethics, social philosophy, and decision theory. Because these topics are too far-ranging to be taken up here, we turn instead to a more limited field of inquiry: legal reasoning.

EXERCISES

I. For each of the practice exercises for the section Special Problems with Practical Reasoning, decide whether the underlying argument is best reconstructed as a propositional, categorical, or inductive argument. Translate the underlying argument into standard form and evaluate it.

II. For each of the arguments you have just reconstructed, identify at least one other guiding principle that could be applied to the same case but lead to a different conclusion. Given that, and your evaluation of the underlying argument in Question I, how good is the practical reasoning in each case?

The Role of Arguments in Legal Reasoning

Practical reasoning plays an important role in the courtroom because judges are required to make decisions in a manner that is thoroughly reasonable. One of the basic principles of any rational society is that its rules should be *objective*. This means that laws and how they are applied cannot vary without reason. If we were to interpret laws and apply them *subjectively,* the rules could change from moment to moment, depending on who was doing the interpreting. One person might decide that burglary was not a particularly serious crime, and would favor a mild punishment for a convicted burglar. Someone else might think that burglary was heinous and, if she did not like the look of the accused, might impose a long jail sentence.

To avoid this kind of unfairness, a society needs a method of legal reasoning that is as objective as possible. A decision process is objective or impartial to the extent that it does not vary *merely* because two people wish to reach different conclusions. Objectivity, then, is a way of minimizing influences that should be irrelevant—influences that might result in a lack of uniformity in decisions about the same sorts of case. As we have emphasized all along, reasoning is objective in the desired way: arguments are valid or invalid, strong or weak, regardless of who produces them. Thus, demanding that judicial decisions should be supported by sound arguments is an effective method of reducing the subjectivity of these decisions.

When a judge reaches a decision, proper legal procedure requires that she produce a written report known as a **judicial opinion**. The opinion, which is published and becomes part of the public record, will not only describe the final decision; it will also include what the judge believes is a good argument in support of that decision. If the argument is sound or inductively reliable, any other judge confronted with the same sort of case must be bound by the same reasons. To justify a different decision, the second judge must either show that the new case is different from the first in some relevant way or identify a flaw in the argument that was given in support of the first decision.

Understanding that the primary goal of legal reasoning is to ensure continuity and objectivity helps put at least one debate about judicial decision in perspective. Many people, including some judges,[2] have claimed that judges decide, not on the basis of arguments, but according to their feelings or hunches, biases, background, and prejudices. This claim fails to recognize that legal reasoning is concerned with the *justification* of a decision, not necessarily with how the judge initially arrives at her conclusions. This is not to say that legal reasoning just provides a rationalization for any decision a judge happens to make. Rather, it provides a reliable method of selecting those beliefs that can be justified by good reasons; these are the beliefs that a judge is supposed to act on. In a sense it does not matter how a judge begins to formulate a decision, as long as that decision can eventually be justified in a rational and objective manner. In this way, the distinction between how a judge initially formulates a decision and how she justifies it is an example of the difference between the **context of discovery** and the **context of justification** discussed in Chapter 10.

Thus, when we evaluate an opinion, we do not have to speculate about a judge's decision-making procedure; we need only ask whether the reasoning gives adequate support to the decision that was eventually reached. In other contexts, we often construct arguments by first deciding what the conclusion should be and then trying to determine what premises would support that conclusion. That process may lead us to reject our initial conclusion if we cannot discover any good reasons in its favor, but it may also yield a sound argument that would make it rational to believe that the conclusion is true. The same is true of legal reasoning.

The rules of logic help ensure that different judges will agree on the correct decision in a particular case. Judges are also limited in what they can legitimately appeal to in their arguments: they must base their reasoning on the law. "The law" refers to the bills passed by Congress and various state and local legislatures, but it includes other things as well. The U.S. Constitution (and in some cases state constitutions) may be relevant. Various executive agencies, such as the Environmental Protection Agency, the Internal Revenue Service, local zoning boards, and many others, have the power to institute regulations that are binding in a court of law. Finally, a judge must also follow **common law** or **case law**. This means that decisions must be compatible with previous decisions about similar cases and with accepted legal practices and presuppositions. All of this means that two judges in the same jurisdiction will base their reasoning on a shared body of principles, not on their personal moral codes, likes and dislikes, prejudices, or other factors that would lead to inconsistent decisions.

Of course, conflicts between judges still happen; a higher court will sometimes overrule a lower court, and even Supreme Court Justices often enter dissenting opinions. The open-ended nature of practical reasoning in general carries over to legal reasoning, and this can lead to disputes. In most of the important legal issues, the dispute is not caused by new informing premises (although this might be important in a retrial which presents new evidence); rather, it has to do with the decision to use one guiding premise rather than another. In the next two sections, we explore some of the ways these decisions are justified.

EXERCISES

The questions below deal with the following excerpt from *Bowers* v. *Hardwick* 106 S.Ct. 2841 (1986), a Supreme Court decision in which a 5-4 majority upheld the constitutionality of Georgia's sodomy statute.[3] According to the Georgia statute: "A person commits the offense of sodomy when he performs or submits to any sexual act involving the sex organs of one person and the mouth or anus of another." Michael Hardwick was arrested for sodomy when the police visited his home and caught him performing consensual fellatio with another male in his bedroom. The charges against Hardwick were later dropped, but he sued Michael J. Bowers, the attorney general of Georgia, claiming the statute unconstitutional insofar as it criminalized sodomy between consenting adults.

Justice White delivered the opinion of the Court:
In August, 1982, respondent was charged with violating the Georgia statute criminalizing sodomy by committing that act with another adult male in the bedroom of the respondent's home. . . .

A divided panel of the Court of Appeals for the Eleventh Court reversed the finding of a lower court that the respondent had failed to state a claim . . . The Court [held] that the Georgia statute violated respondent's fundamental rights because his homosexual activity is a private and intimate association that is beyond the reach of state regulation by reason of the Ninth Amendment and the Due Process Clause of the Fourteenth Amendment. The case was remanded for trial, at which, to prevail, the State would have to prove that the statute is supported by a compelling interest and is the most narrowly defined means of achieving that end. . . .

The case does not require a judgment on whether laws against sodomy between consenting adults in general, or between homosexuals in particular, are wise or desirable. It raises no question about the right or propriety of state legislative decisions to repeal the laws that criminalize homosexual sodomy, or of state court decisions invalidating those laws on state constitutional grounds. The issue presented is whether the Federal Constitution confers a fundamental right of privacy upon homosexuals to engage in sodomy and hence invalidates the laws of the many states that still make such conduct illegal and have done so for a very long time. . . .

We first register our disagreement with the Court of Appeals and with respondent that the Court's prior cases have construed the Constitution to confer a right of privacy that extends to homosexual sodomy . . .

Three cases were interpreted as construing the Due Process Clause of the Fourteenth Amendment to confer a fundamental individual right to decide whether or not to beget or bear a child.

Accepting the decisions in these cases and the above description of them, we think it evident that none of the rights announced in those cases bears any resemblance to the claimed constitutional right of homosexuals to engage in the act of sodomy that is asserted in this case. No connection between family, marriage, or procreation on the one hand and homosexual activity on the other has been demonstrated, either by the Court of Appeals or by respondent. Moreover, any other claim that these cases nevertheless stand for the proposition that any kind of private sexual conduct between consenting adults is constitutionally insulated from state proscription is unsupportable. . . .

Even if the conduct at issue here is not a fundamental right, respondent asserts that there must be a rational basis for the law, and that there is none in this case other than the presumed belief of a majority of the electorate in Georgia that homosexual sodomy is immoral and unacceptable. This is said to be an inadequate rationale to support the law. The law, however, is constantly based on notions of morality . . .

Accordingly, the judgment of the Court of Appeals is reversed.

Justice Blackmun, dissenting [joined by Justices Brennan, Marshall, and Stevens]:

This case is no more about "a fundamental right to engage in homosexual sodomy" as the Court purports to declare . . . than *Stanley* v. *Georgia* (1969) was about a fundamental right to watch obscene movies, or *Katz* v. *United States* (1967) was about a fundamental right to place interstate bets from a telephone booth. Rather, this case is about "the most comprehensive of rights and the right most valued by civilized men," namely, "the right to be let alone." . . .

I believe we must analyze respondent's claim in the light of the values that underlie the constitutional right to privacy. If that right means anything, it means that, before Georgia can prosecute its citizens for making choices about the most intimate aspects of their lives, it must do more than assert that the choice they have made is an "abominable crime not fit to be named among Christians." . . .

The Court concludes today that none of our prior cases dealing with various decisions that individuals are entitled to make free of governmental interference "bears any resemblance to the claimed constitutional right of homosexuals to engage in acts of sodomy that is asserted in this case." . . . While it is true that these cases may be characterized by their connection to family . . . the Court's conclusion that they extend no further than this boundary ignores the warning . . . against "clos[ing] our eyes to the basic reasons why certain rights associated with the family have been accorded shelter under the Fourteenth Amendment's Due Process Clause." We protect those rights not because they contribute, in some direct and material way, to the general public welfare, but because they form so central a part of an individual's life. "[T]he concept of privacy embodies the 'moral fact that a person belongs to himself and not to others nor to society as a whole'". . .

*1. Identify the most important of Justice White's guiding premises.

2. Identify the guiding premises used by Justice Blackmun which conflict with those used by Justice White.

3. Does either Justice offer new informing premises which would justify the choice of guiding premises? If so, what are they?

4. Does either Justice compare the competing guiding premises in order to justify giving one more weight? If so, where?

The Structure of Legal Reasoning

Like any other form of practical reasoning, legal reasoning eventually leads to an argument that has a **decision statement** as its conclusion. We refer to this as the **decision argument**. A decision argument may have a conclusion such as "The court finds the defendant guilty of assault," "The plaintiff should not inherit the money left to him in his grandfather's will," or "The company's failure to perform adequate safety tests renders it liable for damages in this case."

Example 9:6 is a simple decision argument, adapted from *Cohen* v. *California*, 408 U.S. 15 (1971). In 1968, Paul Cohen was arrested for wearing a jacket that bore the words "Fuck the Draft" in the corridors of the Los Angeles County Courthouse. He was convicted of disturbing the peace. After several intermediate hearings, the U.S. Supreme Court agreed to review the conviction. Example 9:6 contains the final paragraph of the majority decision, written by Justice Harlan:

9:6. It is, in sum, our judgment that, absent a more particularized and compelling reason for its action, the State may not, consistently with the First and Fourteenth Amendments, make the simple public display here involved of this single four-letter expletive a criminal offense. Because that is the only arguably sustainable rationale for the conviction here at issue, the judgment below must be reversed.

This example illustrates the fact that decision arguments, like any other example of practical reasoning, have both guiding and informing premises. Thus, a decision argument justifies a decision by showing that a principle of action applies to a specific case. In this case, the guiding premise is contained in the first sentence, the informing premise in the first part of the second sentence, and the conclusion, or decision, in the last clause.

If the guiding premises and the informing premises are both straightforward, there is little work for the court to do. Indeed, most such cases would be decided out of court simply because the decision is obvious to all. The difficult cases, and the interesting ones, are those in which it is not clear which principles should appear in the decision argument, or which facts are relevant. In most cases, therefore, the decision argument must be preceded by arguments that justify the choice of principles and/or attempt to draw a conclusion about the relevant facts of the matter. In *Cohen* v. *California*, as in almost any Supreme Court case, the bulk of the arguments dealt with a justification of the guiding premise. 9:7 is an excerpt from Justice Harlan's opinion:

9:7. Against this background, the issue flushed out by this case stands out in bold relief. It is whether California can excise, as "offensive conduct" one particular scurrilous epithet from the public discourse, either upon the theory of the court below that its use is inherently likely to cause violent reaction or upon a more general assertion that the States, acting as guardians of public morality, may properly remove this word from the public vocabulary.

Arguments and evidence in support of the informing premise attempt to establish the relevant facts; these considerations are known as **questions of fact**. For the most part, arguments that lead to conclusions about facts are not in any way unique to practical or legal reasoning; they are exactly the sort of arguments covered in one or more of the other chapters of this book. Standards of testimony and reporting, reliable inductive reasoning, and supporting causal claims are but a few of the concerns that can be applied to arguments about the facts in a case.

One sort of premise that often appears in legal reasoning deserves special attention. Some premises make the claim that an action or event falls into a certain category or classification. A judge may have to decide whether an instance of leaving a gate unlatched is an instance of negligence, or whether a poorly made automobile wheel constitutes an imminent danger. As these examples suggest, the categories in these cases are technical legal ones.

Although these premises may look like ordinary factual claims, they often are not. If there is a clear, well-accepted, and precise definition of the category, the premise that claims an event belongs in this category is a factual claim. But the meanings of many legal terms evolve slowly and never have a precise and fixed definition. The following example illustrates how a term might be given a new interpretation. Example 9:8 is from *Thomas* v. *Winchester*, 6 N.Y. 397 (1852). Mr. Thomas purchased a drug labeled "extract of dandelion" for his sick wife. The jar had been mislabeled, and actually contained belladonna, a poison, and Mrs. Thomas became quite ill. The manufacturer, Winchester, and his agent, Gilbert, never had any direct dealings with Thomas or his druggist, and this posed a problem because common law suggested that liability due to negligence was limited to situations covered by a contract. The concept of an "imminent danger" was introduced here to expand the scope of liability in certain cases:

9:8. But the case in hand stands on a different ground. The defendant was a dealer in dangerous drugs. Gilbert was his agent in preparing them for market. The death or great bodily harm of some person was the natural and almost inevitable consequence of the sale of belladonna by means of the false label. . . . [The] distinction is recognized between an act of negligence imminently dangerous to the life of others, and one that is not so. In the former case, the party guilty of the negligence is liable to the party injured, whether there be a contract between them or not.

In this case, the premise in question is really a kind of guiding premise: it makes the claim, for example, that we *ought* to treat a mislabeled drug as an imminent danger. The justification is that the "natural and almost inevitable" nature of the consequence should render a negligent party liable for damages resulting from his negligence. When a judge uses such a premise, she must be prepared to justify it, and usually she cannot do so by referring to an explicit definition, since there usually is none. In *Thomas* v. *Winchester,* the justification is in the form of an argument that this case is different in important ways from ordinary cases of negligence that had been decided previously. Once a concept such as "imminent danger" has been introduced, a judge might then base her argument on the ways in which the concept has been applied in the past: in other words, she must appeal to **precedent.** Appeals to precedent are an important and interesting aspect of legal reasoning, and are explored in depth in the following section. For now, the point to remember is that premises that classify or categorize may not be ordinary factual claims.

The most interesting examples of legal reasoning deal with the justification of the guiding premise. These are known as **questions of law.** As we noted in the preceding section, "law" includes not only explicit legislation, but also executive regulations, constitutions, and common law.

Questions of law usually arise in one of three types of cases: if (a) law is unclear, or (b) a new sort of situation arises that had not been foreseen or mentioned in the law, or (c) two principles conflict.

In cases of the first type, the judge has to interpret the law. Her interpretation may be justified by an appeal to the intentions of the original lawmakers. Thus, even though no law explicitly mentioned the situation, it was decided that Elmer Riggs, who had murdered his grandfather, could not inherit the money left to him in his grandfather's will, even though the will had withstood all the tests of a legally valid document. Example 9:9 is an excerpt from Judge Earl's decision in *Riggs* v. *Palmer*, 115 N.Y. 506, 22 N.E. 188 (1889):

9:9. What could be more unreasonable than to suppose that it was the legislative intention in the general laws passed for the orderly, peaceable, and just devolution of property that they should have operation in favor of one who murdered his ancestor that he might speedily come into the possession of his estate? Such an intention is inconceivable. We need not, therefore, be troubled by the general language contained in the law. . . .

The second sort of case, in which a new situation is encountered, is handled in a similar way. In effect, the judge is asking "What would the law say if the legislators had considered this sort of case explicitly?" Such questions of law often arise when society or culture changes in ways that permit new kinds of activities. Thus, when the use of photographs first became widespread, there were no explicit guidelines for their use. Publishing an accurate photograph could not be considered libel, so it was suggested that people had a basic right to privacy which could be violated by the sorts of intrusions made possible by developing technology. That was the subject of *Roberson* v *Rochester Folding Box Company*, 171 N.Y. 538 (1902), in which the judge offered the argument reproduced in 9:10:

9:10. If such a principle be incorporated into the body of law through the instrumentality of a court of equity, the attempts to logically apply the principle will necessarily result, not only in a vast amount of litigation, but in litigation bordering on the absurd, for the right of privacy, once established as a legal doctrine, cannot be confined to the restraint of the publication of a likeness but must necessarily embrace as well the publication of a word-picture, a comment on one's looks, conduct, domestic relation or habits. . . . An examination of the authorities leads us to the conclusion that the so-called "right to privacy" has not as yet found an abiding place in our jurisprudence, and, as we view it, the doctrine cannot now be incorporated without doing violence to settled principles of law. . . .

Especially difficult questions of law arise when more than one principle might apply. In these cases, the judge must decide which of the principles should outweigh the other. Typical reasons given for choosing a principle may have to do with considerations of the goals of society, the rights of an individual, or the moral standards of the culture.

Although the proper evaluation of many questions of law requires a detailed knowledge of legal theory, the skills of critical thinking can help us identify when questions of law arise, and allow us to determine whether the judge's reasoning is valid.

Much of what goes on in legal reasoning is an attempt to take account of the open-ended nature of the arguments. When a judge argues that some facts about a case are irrelevant to the decision, or that certain principles do not apply or should be overridden, she is evaluating external factors that might apply, "other things being equal." The strength of the argument depends in large part on how successfully the judge identifies and evaluates these conflicting factors. We mentioned in the section "Evaluating Practical Reasoning" that playing devil's advocate is often a useful technique in this situation. The **adversary method** of having lawyers defend opposing sides is another version of the same technique. Ideally, the two sets of lawyers will, between them, bring out all the relevant facts and principles that the judge ought to consider. For this reason, the adversary method is an effective means of generating the background against which decisions can be reached in a reliable and rational manner.

EXERCISES

Review examples 9:6 through 9:10. Identify the guiding principle the judge invokes, and explain how it is justified. Construct a decision argument that uses this guiding principle to determine how the case should be decided. (The analysis of 9:6 is given in Appendix II.)

Analogy and Precedent

In the previous section we mentioned that legal reasoning often involves questions of classification, and that these questions are often decided on the basis of **precedent,** or previous judicial opinions. In this section, we explore the ways in which legal reasoning incorporates appeals to precedent. We will see that such appeals usually have the form of **arguments from analogy.**

When a judge reaches a decision and writes an opinion, that decision **sets a precedent** for all other judges who are later confronted with similar cases.[4] This means that, from then on, judges who must decide similar cases ought to reach the same conclusion unless they can supply good reasons for doing otherwise. The proper role of precedent in legal reasoning is the subject of much debate. It certainly seems odd that a principle should be accepted just because judges have used it before. However, if we recall the discussion in the section The Role of Arguments in Legal Reasoning, we can see that the special status of precedent is really a reflection of the demand for **consistency** in legal matters. Proper attention to precedent is meant to ensure that two judges will treat like cases in the same way.

Of course, it almost never happens that two cases are *exactly* alike. This means that an appeal to precedent would have to show that two cases are alike with respect to the facts that are relevant to the legal issue. In *Griswold* v. *Connecticut,* 381 U.S. 479 (1965), the Supreme Court had to decide whether it was constitutional for a state to pass a law forbidding the dissemination of information about birth control to married couples. Griswold was the executive director of the Planned Parenthood League in New Haven, Connecticut, and was arrested for violating such a law. The Supreme Court ruled that the law was unconstitutional, and Justice Douglas based his opinion on analogies with other cases involving education, as shown in 9:11:

9:11. The right to educate a child in a school of the parents' choice—whether public or private or parochial—is not mentioned [in the Constitution or Bill of Rights]. Nor is the right to study any particular subject or any foreign language. Yet the First Amendment has been construed to include certain of those rights.

By *Pierce* v. *Society of Sisters,* the right to educate one's children as one chooses is made applicable to the States by the force of the First and Fourteenth Amendments. By *Meyer* v. *Nebraska* the same dignity is given the right to study the German language in a private school. In other words, the State may not, consistently with the spirit of the First Amendment, contract the spectrum of available knowledge. . . .

The foregoing cases suggest that the specific guarantees in the Bill of Rights have penumbras, formed by emanations from those guarantees that help give them life and substance. Various guarantees create zones of privacy. . . .

The present case, then, concerns a relationship lying within a zone of privacy created by several fundamental constitutional guarantees. . . .

There are obviously many differences between teaching German and giving out information on birth control, differences that were used to support the law in question. Nonetheless, the Supreme Court opinion focuses on the qualities it considered relevant to the rights guaranteed by the First Amendment. The emphasis on similarities and the relevance of those similarities shows that the judge is using an argument from analogy. Much of the opinion is devoted to enumerating the ways in which *Griswold* was similar to the other cases cited: the dissemination of knowledge, the expression of one's belief as an extension of the right of assembly, the effect on privacy, and so on.

To evaluate appeals to precedent, we must consider two things. First, they are a form of argument from analogy. This means that the guidelines described in Chapter 4 will apply. Thus, we need to determine how inductively reliable the argument is. In particular, we need to decide whether the similarities that are mentioned are *relevant* to the conclusion.

Second, we must remember that most appeals to precedent, that is, claims that a situation should be classified in a certain way, are guiding principles, and hence themselves justifiable by open-ended practical reasoning. Such appeals are well-justified only if no alternative conclusions outweigh the factors cited in support of the decision. For that reason, we often find judges considering and then rejecting alternative precedents as being irrelevant (or at least less relevant).

Thus, we can evaluate appeals to precedent by the methods already discussed: a justifiable appeal to precedent will be a reliable argument from analogy in which no alternatives outweigh the decision that has been reached. Of course, many questions of legal theory come into play at this point, and a single chapter cannot hope to do justice to such a complex topic. Nonetheless, the insight we have gained into the structure of legal reasoning gives us not only a better understanding of how judicial opinions are justified, but also an example of practical reasoning at work.

EXERCISES

1. The following arguments, part of the opinion in *Riggs* v. *Palmer* (see example 9:9 for details) contain several analogies. Identify and write them in standard form for arguments from analogy.

"[These maxims] were applied in the decision of the case of *Insurance Co.* v. *Armstrong.* . . . There it was held that the person who procured a policy upon the life of another, payable at his death, and then murdered the assured to make the policy payable, could not recover thereon. Mr. Justice Field, writing the opinion, said . . . 'As well might he recover insurance money upon a building that he had willfully fired.' These maxims, without any statute giving them force or operation, frequently control the effect and nullify the language of wills. A will procured by fraud and deception, like any other instrument, may be declared void, and set aside, and so a particular portion of a will may be excluded from probate, or held inoperative, if induced by the fraud or undue influence of the person in whose favor it is."

2. Reconstruct the appeal to precedent in *Griswold* v. *Connecticut* (example 9:11) as an argument from analogy. How strong do you think it is?

*3. In *Village of Belle Terre* v. *Boras,* the Supreme Court held that zoning laws that prohibit more than two unrelated people from sharing a household were not unconstitutional. Justice Thurgood Marshall wrote a dissenting opinion. Identify, reconstruct, and evaluate the arguments from analogy in Marshall's opinion:

My disagreement with the Court today is based on my view that the ordinance in this case unnecessarily burdens appellees' First Amendment freedom of association and their constitutionally guaranteed right to privacy. . . . Constitutional protection is extended, not only to modes of association that are political in the usual sense, but also to those that pertain to the social and economic benefit of the members. The selection of one's living companions involves similar choices as to the emotional, social, or economic benefits to be derived from living arrangements.

The freedom of association is often inextricably entwined with the constitutional right to privacy. The right to "establish a home" is an essential part of the liberty guaranteed by the Fourteenth Amendment. And the Constitution secures to an individual the freedom to "satisfy his intellectual and emotional needs in the privacy of his own home" (*Stanley* v. *Georgia,* 1969). The choice of household companions . . . involves deeply personal considerations as to the kind and quality of intimate relations within the home. That decision surely falls within the ambit of the right to privacy protected by the Constitution . . . .

4. In *Adams* v. *New Jersey Steamboat Co.*, the court was asked to decide whether the operators of a steamboat were liable for the theft of property in the stateroom of one of the passengers on the boat. What is the argument from analogy in the opinion quoted here? What decision do you think follows from the argument?

. . . The principle upon which innkeepers are charged by the common law as insurer of the money or personal effects of their guests originated in public policy. It was deemed to be a sound and necessary rule that this class of persons should be subjected to a high degree of responsibility in cases where an extraordinary confidence is necessarily reposed in them, and where great temptation to fraud and danger of plunder exists by reason of the peculiar relation of the parties. . . . The relations that exist between a steamboat company and its passengers, who have procured staterooms for their comfort during the journey, differ in no essential respect from those that exist between the innkeeper and his guests. The passenger procures and pays for his room for the same reasons that a guest in an inn does. There are the same opportunities for fraud and plunder on the part of the carrier that was originally supposed to furnish a temptation to the landlord to violate his duty to the guest. A steamer carrying passengers upon the water, and furnishing them with rooms and entertainment is, for all practical purposes, a floating inn, and hence the duties which the proprietors owe to their charge ought to be the same. No good reason is apparent for relaxing the rigid rule of the common law which applies as between innkeeper and guest. . . .

Notes

[1]We refer here to the *correctness* of the conclusion rather than its truth, because the ultimate goal of practical reasoning is a decision or an action, and although these things can be called "correct" or "incorrect," it does not make sense to speak of a "true" or "false" action.

[2]See, for example, Jerome Frank, *Law and the Modern Mind* (Garden City, NY: Doubleday, 1963).

[3]We use the standard form of legal citation. The name of the case is given first, followed by the volume number and the name of the official state or federal recorder. The final number in parentheses is the year of the decision.

[4]This is oversimplified, since jurisdiction is also relevant. For a more detailed discussion of this point, and of legal reasoning in general, see Martin Golding, *Legal Reasoning* (New York: Knopf, 1984).

CHAPTER
10

Causal Reasoning

Talking and reasoning about causes is a pervasive feature of both everyday life and the sciences. Our language is peppered with causal verbs such as "produce," "result from," "prevent," and "leads to." (Even terms such as "kill" have causal implications, since a statement such as "John killed the porcupine" implies that John caused or in some way brought about the porcupine's death.) Many of our actions and decisions rely on practical reasoning whose premises contain statements about causal connections. In fact, making assumptions about cause-effect relations, often on flimsy evidence and sometimes even despite contrary evidence, is the principal way people try to achieve a coherent interpretation of events.[1] Because of this psychological tendency to draw hasty conclusions about causal relations, it is important to be aware of the basic features of good causal reasoning and to think critically about arguments that draw causal conclusions.

   The term "cause" is ambiguous. Some of its common meanings are discussed in the first section of this chapter. Despite this diversity of meanings, certain core elements in our notion of causality are worth pointing out. The first has to do with **temporal priority**. *Causes always precede their effects.*[2] If event A causes event B to happen, then A must occur *before* B does. We rule out the possibility that later events can have any causal influence on earlier ones; there is no such thing as "backwards" causation. Thus, in seeking the cause of an accident, such as the sinking of the Titanic, we confine our attention to the events that preceded it. This is not to deny that it is often useful to look at later events for evidence of what happened earlier, but nothing that happened after the accident can have had any causal influence on it.

The second core ingredient in our notion of causality is that of **physical connection**. It is difficult to be precise about this, but the basic idea is clear enough. If it is true that A caused B to happen, then B must have occurred *because of* A. It is not an accident or coincidence that B followed A; there must be some real, physical connection between the two events, some mechanism by which A *produced* B. Often this is the most difficult condition to satisfy, especially when A and B are widely separated in space and time. For example, take the case of diethylstilbestrol (DES), a nonsteroidal synthetic estrogen widely used in the 1940s and 1950s to prevent miscarriages. Though it is now well-established that there is a causal connection between women receiving DES during the first trimester of pregnancy and development of vaginal cancer in their daughters 10 to 20 years later, we still do not have a complete understanding of the mechanism involved.

It is sometimes claimed that there is a third basic element in our concept of causality, namely, **constant association** or **constant conjunction**. If events of type A cause events of type B, then whenever A occurs, B must follow; there must be a constant association between them. As we will see later, although constant association is characteristic of some types of causes (those that are sufficient for their effects), it does not hold for others (necessary causal conditions and probabilistic causes). To require that all causes must be constantly associated with their effects would drastically restrict the usual ways we use the term "cause." In the case of DES, for example, the incidence of vaginal cancer among daughters of women who took the drug during the relevant pregnancy is only about 14 in every 10,000. Thus, unlike temporal succession and physical connection, constant association is not an essential component of our concept of causation.

Different Types of Causes

We can use causal language either to talk about **the cause of a single event** (or of a particular thing or phenomenon) or to make **causal generalizations** about classes of events (or things or phenomena). Consider the four questions in 10:1:

10:1. What caused the fire in this house last night?

What caused the outbreak of Legionnaire's disease after a Philadelphia convention in 1976?

Does cigarette smoking cause lung cancer?

Do low-cholesterol diets prevent heart disease?

In the first two questions, we are asking about the causes of single events; in the last two, we are concerned with causal generalizations.

It is usually easy to tell whether a question or hypothesis concerns a single event or a causal generalization. But in either case the term "cause" and related concepts such as "produce," "prevent," "lead to," and "due to" are ambiguous. The word "cause" can mean different things depending on the context in which it is used.

In clarifying the meaning of a causal claim, it often helps to ask whether the cause in question is supposed to be a **necessary causal condition** or a **sufficient causal condition** for its effect. Consider the causal statement in 10:2:

10:2.   Feeding mice causes them to grow.

The statement clearly means that food is a *necessary* condition for growth, since without food mice would starve to death. But obviously food alone is not sufficient; mice also need water, oxygen, and a suitable environment to grow. Thus, in 10:2 "causes" means "is a necessary causal condition for."

In other contexts the term "cause" has a different meaning, as example 10:3 shows:

10:3.   Exposing mice to high levels of gamma-radiation causes them to die.

This statement asserts that gamma-irradiation is a *sufficient* condition for death. But mice can be killed in a variety of other ways, and so gamma-irradiation is not a necessary condition for death. Thus, in 10:3 "causes" means "is a sufficient causal condition for."

Some causes are both necessary *and* sufficient for their effects. In Newtonian mechanics, for example, a body will accelerate if and only if a net external force is acting on it.

Usually we are interested in sufficient conditions when we wish to *produce* a given result. For example, to make a mixture of hydrogen and oxygen gases combine to form water, it is sufficient to introduce a platinum catalyst. But this condition, though sufficient, is not necessary. We could equally well produce water from the gases by detonating the mixture with a spark. As long as at least one of the sufficient conditions for a phenomenon obtains, the result will follow.[3]

If we wish to *prevent* a certain event from occurring, we try to eliminate one of its necessary conditions. Outbreaks of typhoid fever, for example, can be prevented by immunization. They can also be prevented by avoiding all exposure to the typhoid bacillus. Whenever at least one of the necessary conditions for a phenomenon fails to obtain, the result will not occur.[4]

Our usual ways of thinking and talking about causes is somewhat loose and imprecise. When we describe N as "the" cause of E, and N is a necessary condition, we realize that, in most cases, N is not unique, since there are many necessary conditions for E apart from N. In singling out N as "the" cause we are drawing attention to the factor that is of most interest to us in that situation. For example, N might be a condition we can control to prevent future occurrences of E. Because the other necessary conditions lie outside our control, we ignore them.

When we describe S as "the" cause of E and S is a sufficient condition, we might mean one of two things. We might mean that S is the complete set of necessary conditions for E. In this case S would be unique. More often, when we regard S as a sufficient cause of E, we are assuming a certain context in which a number of other causally relevant factors are held fixed. In this case, there is no reason to expect S to be unique. We might focus on S as "the" cause because S is a factor we can employ to produce E. For example, we might say that negligence on the part of the operators was *the* cause of the explosion and fire that destroyed the unit IV reactor at the Chernobyl atomic power station in the Soviet Union on 26 April, 1986, even though we know there were other contributory factors such as weaknesses in the reactor design. We do so because, assuming all the other causal factors are held constant, it was the failure of the engineers to act as they should that was sufficient to produce the accident.

Thus far we have seen that causal statements can describe necessary causal conditions, sufficient causal conditions, or both. But some causes are neither necessary nor sufficient for their effects. Such causes are called **probabilistic causes**. Example 10:4 is a statement about a probabilistic cause.

10:4. Smoking causes lung cancer.

The causal connection between smoking and lung cancer is firmly established but, nonetheless, many smokers do not get lung cancer and some nonsmokers do. This is an example of a **probabilistic cause**. We can say that smoking is a **positive causal factor** for lung cancer. The distinctive feature of A's being a probabilistic cause of B is that, although A is physically connected with B when both occur, it is not the case that B always follows A. In this respect probabilistic causes are more like necessary causal conditions than sufficient ones. Thus, when A is a positive causal factor for B, we have $Pr(B/A) > Pr(B)$, or, equivalently, $Pr(B/A) > Pr(B/not\text{-}A)$. When A prevents B and thus is a *negative causal factor* for B, the inequality sign is reversed: A makes the occurrence of B less likely; $Pr(B/A) < Pr(B)$. (Probabilistic causes are discussed more fully in the sections Concomitant Variations, Correlations, and Causes and Randomized Controlled Experiments.)

Probabilistic causes are common in the biological, medical, and social sciences. Living organisms and social systems are extremely complex; we have only an incomplete grasp of the many factors that affect their behavior and properties. Because of their complexity, biological and social systems are, for all practical purposes, **stochastic**, not deterministic. A genuinely **stochastic system** has an element of chance or randomness that cannot be eliminated. Thus, in a stochastic system we *must* use a probabilistic conception of causality. In some cases, there may be an underlying deterministic set of causes, but they are complicated and largely unknown. This is the case with some well-established biological theories such as Mendelian genetics. Scientists have made considerable progress by treating genetic systems as stochastic, and the predictions of their theories have been amply confirmed by experiments.

The relationship between **laws of nature** and causality is a difficult topic that deserves more attention than we can give it here. Roughly speaking, laws of nature are **generalizations** such as Boyle's law, Dalton's law of constant composition, the principle of energy conservation, and Hubble's law, which express significant regularities in nature. Many of these laws are summarized in equations representing a functional dependence between the values of two or more physical quantities. Boyle's law, for example, is usually written as "PV = constant," where P and V are the pressure and volume of an ideal gas kept at constant temperature. Hubble's law, V = HD, relates the velocity of a galaxy, V, to its distance from the Earth, D; H is Hubble's constant.

Although all laws of nature are generalizations, not all of them are *causal generalizations*. Some, like Dalton's law of constant composition, have nothing to do with events or things happening. Whether or not a law of nature is regarded as a causal generalization depends on our understanding of the causal processes that underlie the regularity in question.

For example, Hubble's law of galactic recession is believed to result from the expansion of the universe following the Big Bang. Because of this initial explosion, faster-moving galaxies are now farther away from us (and from each other) than slower-moving ones; the relationship between velocity and distance is linear. Viewed in this way, the distance, D, of a galaxy is the causal result of its velocity, V. Thus, V is the cause of D, but D is not the cause of V. The lawlike statement summarized in the equation V = HD is simply a generalization. It says nothing about causality by itself; it merely expresses a functional dependence between two variables. We call it a "causal" generalization if we think there is a mechanism by which one of the quantities produces the other. The case of Boyle's law is similar. We normally think of causally producing changes in the pressure of a gas (at constant temperature) by changing its volume, but the equation PV = constant, by itself, is causally neutral.

It is important to resist the temptation to think of laws of nature as themselves being causes. The temptation arises because we say things like statement 10:5:

10:5. "Why is galaxy A moving twice as fast as galaxy B? Because of Hubble's law: A is twice as far away as B."

The "because" here is inferential, not causal. Given Hubble's law, if A is twice the distance of B from us, we can deduce the relation between their velocities. But, as we have seen, the greater distance of A does not cause its velocity to exceed that of B. Causality is a relationship between events. Laws of nature are not events. Some of them describe regularities between events and, in those instances in which the regularities are the result of a causal process, they can be called "causal" laws as a courtesy, so to speak. Which events are the effects and which the causes depends on the causal processes involved.

Finally, we need to discuss the notion of a **proximate cause**, which often plays a role in legal cases and historical narratives. The proximate cause of some event, F, is the event that lies closest to it in time and space. If we think of the events leading up to F as arranged in a causal chain (A, B, C, D, E, F) in which A causes B, B causes C, and so on, then the proximate cause of F is E. In this sense, the most common proximate cause of death in human beings is heart failure since, regardless of what produced it (asphyxiation, stroke, electrocution, or starvation), heart failure is usually the last link in the causal chain leading to death. Of course, some arbitrariness is involved in the identification of proximate causes because, in reality, causal chains are continuous. In practice, finding the proximate cause involves deciding which event is "close enough" to F to qualify as the closest. Thus, in ordinary contexts we regard flipping a switch as the proximate cause of a light bulb coming on even though there is a closer event: the beginning of the flow of electrons through the bulb's filament. Proximate causes, by their nature, usually concern single events.

EXERCISES

Explain the meaning of the terms "cause," "cures," "prevents," "because," and so on, used in the following statements. In each case decide whether (a) the statement is about a single event or a causal generalization, and (b) the cause is necessary, sufficient, probabilistic, or proximate.

*1. The cause of Legionnaire's disease is exposure to the bacterium *Legionella pneumophila*.

*2. Moderate exercise and a sensible diet can help prevent heart disease.

*3. The assassination of Archduke Ferdinand in Sarajevo caused the outbreak of World War I.

4. The drug Dapsone cured all the patients who were diagnosed as suffering from the early stages of Hansen's disease (leprosy).

5. Premature births are often caused by inadequate prenatal care.

6. Cystic fibrosis is caused by a recessive gene.

7. Pendulum clocks run slow in hot weather because the period of a pendulum is proportional to the square root of its length, and all materials expand as their temperature increases.

8. The red shift in the light emitted by distant galaxies is caused by their large velocities of recession.

9. The forest fire was caused by a period of exceptionally dry weather.

10. John Belushi died from a drug overdose.

11. Acne is not caused by eating greasy foods.

12. The Hindenberg disaster could have been prevented by using helium instead of hydrogen in the dirigible.

Mill's Methods

In the preceding section, we looked at different ways in which causal claims are understood. We now turn to consider how causal claims and hypotheses are discovered and justified.

John Stuart Mill, a nineteenth-century philosopher, codified the ways in which causal claims are justified. In *A System of Logic* (Book III, Chapter VIII, 1843), Mill proposed five "methods of experimental inquiry" for establishing causes. Mill named these "the method of agreement," "the method of difference," "the joint method of agreement and difference," "the method of residues," and "the method of concomitant variations." In this section we discuss the first four of these methods, reserving the method of concomitant variations for the following section. Taken together, these five methods are now known as **"Mill's methods."** Before we describe them, we need to clarify an important point about the general process of establishing a causal hypothesis.

Establishing a causal hypothesis involves two distinct stages which it is important to distinguish. First, one must *arrive at the hypothesis* that a causal connection exists. The second stage involves *testing the causal hypothesis* with appropriate experiments and observations. We mark the distinction between these two phases of causal investigation with the terms **the context of discovery** and **the context of justification.**

The same kinds of reasoning (both deductive and inductive) can occur in both contexts, since the reasons we have for thinking there might be a causal connection between A and B in the first place are also often reasons, however weak, for accepting the claim that A causes B (or that A caused B in a particular case.) But usually we require much more discriminating tests and evidence for accepting a causal claim than we do for advancing it in the first place. The two contexts differ in their level of rigor. A causal hypothesis might be advanced on the basis of hunches, intuition, casual observation, analogies, or superficial correlations. None of these suffices to prove that the causal claim is correct.

For example, we might guess that a tainted water supply is the cause of a particular epidemic of typhus, reasoning by analogy from similar outbreaks of typhoid and cholera in which polluted water was responsible. Proving that this hypothesis is true would require establishing that the water is, indeed, contaminated with the typhus bacterium, that drinking enough of it can produce the disease, and that all those who succumbed had drunk water from that source. (In this case the causal hypothesis would be refuted, because, unlike typhoid and cholera, typhus is transmitted by infected fleas and lice.)

Similarly, a physician who notices that several of her patients with the same disease were apparently cured after taking a certain drug might conjecture that the drug caused the recovery. The formation of this causal hypothesis belongs to the context of discovery. Proving that the drug is really a cure within the context of justification would (ideally) require a controlled experiment. After all, the symptoms of the disease might have disappeared regardless of whether the patients had received the drug (a case of spontaneous remission), or the apparent cure might result from other medications or changes in diet. Though they often lead us to initially entertain a causal hypothesis, casual observations, analogies, and mere correlations do not, by themselves, justify it.

The main reason our treatment of Mill's methods differs from his is that Mill did not distinguish between causes as necessary conditions and causes as sufficient conditions.[5] He also did not always carefully distinguish between the contexts of discovery and justification. In fact Mill thought that his rules could be used in both contexts—that is, as ways of discovering causal hypotheses in the first place and also as ways of testing causal claims once they have been arrived at. We will discuss Mill's methods from both points of view.

In the preamble to his description of the five methods (Book III, Chapter VII), Mill makes an important point about any causal investigation: at the outset we need to get a clear description of the phenomenon whose cause we seek. Although this requirement may seem obvious, the less we know about a field of inquiry, the harder it is to fulfill. In investigating the cause of an episode of food poisoning, for example, we need to ensure that the positive cases we examine are indeed all cases of food poisoning and not of some other complaint with similar symptoms, such as influenza. Similarly, in testing a causal generalization, we need some assurance that we really are examining repeated instances of the *same* phenomenon.

For this reason, it is standard practice in epidemiological investigations to construct a working definition of what constitutes a positive case. For example, when the form of bacterial pneumonia now known as Legionnaire's disease broke out among those who had attended a statewide convention in Philadelphia in 1976, the officers from the Centers for Disease Control defined a positive case of the illness as a person who had either attended the convention or been in the convention hotel, who had pneumonia or a fever of at least 102°F, and who had a cough. Thus, in the initial phases of the investigation apparently similar cases of so-called Broad Street pneumonia were excluded because its victims were not conventioneers, nor had they been inside the hotel.

In the search for the cause of the Philadelphia outbreak, one of the first steps taken was to find common factors among the infected persons. In seeking the cause of a phenomenon among the factors shared by all observed instances of it we employ **the method of agreement**. We can summarize this method as follows:

THE METHOD OF AGREEMENT

If several instances of P have only one antecedent condition, X, in common, then X is the cause of P.

To focus our discussion, let us consider example 10:6, which has been deliberately simplified to make the logic of our reasoning clear.

10:6. Four people all eat lunch at the same restaurant and then all four come down with food poisoning. Though none of the victims had chosen exactly the same items from the menu, there was one food item that all of them had consumed, namely, the egg salad. We conclude that the egg salad caused their illness.

In analyzing examples like this, it is convenient to represent the information in a table such as Table 10-1.[6]

TABLE 10-1

CASE	ANTECEDENT CONDITIONS						PHENOMENON (P)
	A	B	C	D	E	F	
1	*	*	*	—	—	—	*
2	*	—	—	*	*	*	*
3	*	*	—	*	—	*	*
4	*	—	*	*	*	—	*

The letters A, B, ..., F stand for the food items: A is egg salad, B is soup, C is pot roast, D is steak, E is apple pie, F is ice cream. The letter P stands for the phenomenon whose cause we seek, in this case, food poisoning. The asterisk means that a condition is present; a dash denotes its absence. Thus, individual 2 had egg salad, steak, apple pie, and ice cream, but she did not have either soup or pot roast. The asterisks in the column at the far right indicate that all four people contracted food poisoning.

In cases like this, when we inquire about "the" cause of P, we are looking for conditions that are either necessary for P, sufficient for P, or both. If X is a necessary condition for Y, then Y cannot occur when X is absent. This rules out B, C, D, E, and F, since each patron who became ill did not eat at least one of these items. This leaves A as a possible necessary condition for P. But can we conclude that A must be the culprit? This depends on a number of things. If more than one food is contaminated, then various combinations could be necessary or sufficient for P. For example, each of the four patrons had either soup or steak. So (B or D) might be a complex necessary condition for P whether or not the egg salad was also contaminated. If so, A need not be a necessary condition for P. Similarly, B and D could each be sufficient conditions for P and the egg salad might be entirely innocent. As we shall see later, the method of difference, and the joint method of agreement and difference, provide us with useful ways of ruling out candidates for sufficient conditions.

Before considering these further methods, we need to discuss a second point. Following Mill, we have summarized the method of agreement in the form of a conditional "if . . . then . . ." statement. If the cases share more than one antecedent condition, the method does not apply. If we take this literally, the method is useless since any given group of positive cases will always have a multitude of antecedent factors in common. In our example, all the persons who became ill ate lunch, they all patronized the same restaurant, they all drove automobiles to work, they all brushed their teeth in the morning, and so on. Usually we ignore these common factors because we are convinced they are causally irrelevant to cases of food poisoning. Thus, when we apply the method of agreement we are presupposing that we have already restricted the range of conditions to those that are potentially causally relevant. If, for example, we had overlooked the fact that all four of the customers had water with their meals, or ice in their drinks, then we would fail to uncover the cause if this had been the only source of contamination.

In real-life causal investigations in the sciences most of the hard creative work occurs at the outset in deciding which conditions to look at and knowing how to describe them. For this reason, we agree with Mill's critics that Mill's methods play only a minor role in the context of discovery and should more properly be regarded as falling within the context of justification. Thus, the "discovery" phase of the investigation consists of first coming up with the list of A, B, . . . , F as the possible causes of P. We then apply Mill's methods in the "justification" phase to infer inductively which, if any, of the hypotheses "A caused P," "B caused P," . . . "F caused P" is probably true.

As we have seen, one of the limitations of the method of agreement is that it tells us next to nothing about the sufficient conditions for P. We can remedy this defect by looking at negative cases, that is, cases in which P fails to occur. If X is a sufficient condition for P, then P must occur whenever X is present. Thus, if we find cases in which X is present but P is absent, we know that X cannot be a sufficient condition for P. As originally formulated by Mill, the method of difference applies to just a pair of contrasted cases—one in which P is present, the other in which P is absent.

THE METHOD OF DIFFERENCE

If two cases, one in which P occurs, and the other in which P does not occur, have exactly the same antecedent conditions with one exception, namely, that X is present in the first but absent in the second, then X is the cause (or a necessary part of the cause) of P.

In our food poisoning example, imagine that, among those who did not become ill, we find a patron (Case 5) who ate the same items as Case 3 with one exception: unlike Case 3, Case 5 did not have the steak. This is summarized in Table 10-2.

TABLE 10-2

CASE	ANTECEDENT CONDITIONS						PHENOMENON (P)
	A	B	C	D	E	F	
3	*	*	—	*	—	*	*
5	*	*	—	—	—	*	—

Applying the method of difference to this pair of cases, we would conclude that eating the steak was a sufficient condition for P, or perhaps more cautiously, as Mill suggests, that D is at least a "necessary part" of the sufficient condition for P. What Mill has in mind here is that D might not be sufficient by itself. Suppose that some people do not become sick even when they eat tainted food because they are immune to the toxins involved. (While this might seem far-fetched in this particular example, it is certainly a factor in many cases of infectious disease.) Thus, merely eating the tainted food is not sufficient to cause illness; one must also lack the appropriate immunity. If, in our example, both Case 3 and Case 5 lacked this form of immunity, then the antecedent clause of our statement of the method of difference would be satisfied even though D is not a sufficient condition for P. In this situation, if D were the only tainted food on the menu, the actual sufficient condition would be (D and non-N), where non-N denotes the absence of immunity N; D and non-N would each be "necessary parts" of this condition. Thus, D by itself would be a necessary but not a sufficient condition.

Just as with the method of agreement, the method of difference is reliable only when our choice of antecedent conditions includes the cause and when the cause is unique. The information in Table 10-2, for example, is consistent with the hypothesis that each of C, D, and E are sufficient conditions for P.

By combining conclusions from both methods, we can extract further information from Table 10-2. Case 5 rules out A, B, and F as sufficient conditions for P. As noted earlier, assuming there is only one cause and it is already on our list, Case 3 rules out C and E as sufficient conditions. That leaves us with D as the sufficient condition.

The biggest drawback with the method of difference is the difficulty of satisfying the antecedent, that is, of finding cases that are identical in all respects save one. Usually the closest we can come to realizing this condition is in **controlled experiments,** in which we can exercise a considerable degree of influence over the relevant variables. We discuss such experiments and their role in testing causal hypotheses in the section on Randomized Controlled Experiments. For the moment, it suffices to note that in nonexperimental situations, such as the food poisoning example, we are rarely if ever presented with pairs of instances in which there is only one relevant difference. It was this severe restriction of the range of cases to which the method of difference can be applied that led Mill to propose **the joint method of agreement and difference.** Unlike the method of difference, the joint method of agreement and difference does not require that any two instances must differ in only a single condition.

THE JOINT METHOD OF AGREEMENT AND DIFFERENCE

If several instances in which P occurs have only one antecedent condition, X, in common, while several instances in which P does not occur have nothing in common save the absence of X, then X is the cause (or a necessary part of the cause) of P.

We can illustrate the reasoning involved in the joint method in Table 10-3 by adding to Table 10-1 four more cases of people who did not get food poisoning, all of whom avoided the egg salad. (Note: Case 5 is now different from the one in Table 10-2.)

TABLE 10-3

CASE	ANTECEDENT CONDITIONS						PHENOMENON (P)
	A	B	C	D	E	F	
1	*	*	*	—	—	—	*
2	*	—	—	*	*	*	*
3	*	*	—	*	—	*	*
4	*	—	*	*	*	—	*
5	—	*	—	*	*	*	—
6	—	—	*	—	—	*	—
7	—	*	*	*	—	—	—
8	—	*	—	—	*	*	—

It should be noted that Table 10-3 does not contain any pair of cases that satisfies the method of difference. Each case in which P occurs differs from each case in which P does not occur in at least *two* respects. Thus, as Mill himself points out, the name "joint method of agreement and *difference*" is misleading because this method does not involve *any* application of the method of difference. It would be better to call it **"the double method of agreement,"** since the positive cases (1 through 4) use **the direct method of agreement** to identify A as a necessary condition; the negative cases (5 through 8) use **the inverse method of agreement** to identify A as a sufficient condition.

The entries in Table 10-3 make it highly probable (but not certain) that A is the cause of P in the sense that A is both a necessary and a sufficient causal condition for P. For the reasons mentioned earlier, the conclusion that A is the cause of P is only probable, not certain. Mill's methods involve inductive arguments, not deductively valid ones. The implicit premise of the underlying arguments is that the cause of P is unique and that it has been included in our list. In the usual run of cases in which we are not sure that this assumption is correct, Mill's methods provide us with a useful heuristic in the context of discovery for systematically narrowing the range of possible candidates for the necessary and sufficient causes of a phenomenon. But in the context of justification they cannot guarantee the truth of the conclusion.

The fourth of Mill's methods, and the last one we discuss in this section, is **the method of residues.** Mill regarded this method as "one of the most important among our instruments of discovery."

THE METHOD OF RESIDUES

If the known effects of antecedent conditions are subtracted from a complex phenomenon, P, then the residue of P is caused by the remaining antecedent conditions.

Consider the illustration of this method in 10:7:

10:7. A plant's growth pattern, P, can be analyzed in terms of three elements: (1) the development of large, healthy green leaves, (2) the development of strong stems and root structure, and (3) the production of fruit and flowers. Suppose we fertilize a test plot with a fertilizer labeled "10-10-10," indicating that it contains equal amounts of nitrogen, phosphorus, and potassium. We know that nitrogen promotes the healthy growth of leaves and that potassium encourages the development of stronger stems and roots. Our fertilized plants do well in these two categories; they also produce buds and flowers more prolifically than usual.

Since we know what caused the improved growth of leaves, stems, and roots, we can infer that the "residue," the increase in the number of buds and flowers, was caused by the phosphorus.

Mill relates the method of residues to the method of difference. Imagine that we had two cases: (ABC) followed by (QRS), and (BC) followed by (RS). If the *only* difference between the two cases is that, in the first, A and Q are both present whereas, in the second, they are both absent, then *the method of difference* would single out A as the sufficient cause of Q. In using the method of residues we do not have an actual case of (BC) followed by (RS); in our example, we did not fertilize some plants with a 10-0-10 fertilizer containing no phosphorus. Rather, we infer what that situation would be like from our previous knowledge that B causes R and C causes S.

It follows that the method of residues can be applied only in those situations in which we know how to "divide" P into parts. We must also know how to "add" the separate contributions of known causal factors like B and C. Even then, the method gives us no guidance on how to identify the condition or conditions responsible for the residue of P.

EXERCISES

1. Suppose your stereo system consists of just three components: a turntable, an integrated amplifier, and a pair of speakers. The left speaker sounds fine but the right one has developed an irritating buzz. Explain how, by rearranging the connections between the components, you could discover whether the fault lies in (a) the connecting leads, (b) the right speaker, (c) the amplifier, or (d) the turntable. Which of Mill's methods are you applying?

2. Alice, Beatrice, and Clarissa are all chain-smoking, coffee-guzzling friends who get little exercise and suffer from insomnia. They decide to make some changes in their life-styles. Alice and Beatrice quit smoking. Alice and Clarissa both stop drinking coffee; they also begin taking yoga classes together and swimming in the evenings. Beatrice is unwilling to give up coffee, and Clarissa is unable to stop smoking. Beatrice has no time for yoga classes and she detests chlorinated pools. Several weeks later, Alice and Beatrice are both sleeping much better, but Clarissa's insomnia persists. Using Mill's methods, what conclusions can you draw about the likely cause of Alice's cure?

*3. What causal conclusions can you draw from *each* of the following pieces of information? (a) Bob never gets an allergic reaction unless he eats shellfish. (b) On two occasions when Bob became ill the only shellfish he had eaten were shrimp, oysters, and crab, at one meal, and lobster, crab, clams, and oysters, at the other. (c) On two occasions when Bob did not become ill the only shellfish he had eaten were shrimp and clams, at one meal, and lobster, oysters, and clams, at the other. What can you infer from (a), (b), and (c) taken together?

4. Explain how you would set about investigating the cause of each of the following:

a. You come home from work to find that your dog is terribly ill. The next day you discover that two other dogs who live on your street are also very sick but the rest appear to be fine.

b. Every morning there is static interference on the bathroom radio.

c. Several friends tell you that they each tried to phone you over the weekend but were unable to reach you. You were at home that weekend, but made several trips out of the house for groceries. You did not hear the phone ring.

d. It comes to your attention that three letters you mailed on the same day never reached their destinations.

e. Though there has been a small increase in the price of electricity, your electricity bill for November is much higher than it was for the same 30-day period last year.

f. Each time you make a cup of instant coffee the hot water effervesces vigorously when added to the powered coffee in the cup.

*__g.__ About one-third of all the (female) victims of toxic shock syndrome are between the ages of 12 and 25.

Concomitant Variations, Correlations, and Causes

In many cases in which we suspect that a causal relation exists between two factors, changes in the magnitude of one of them are uniformly associated with changes in the magnitude of the other: the more current we pass through a resistor, the greater the amount of heat produced; the more a person is stressed, the higher his blood pressure; the more frequently the oil is changed in an engine, the less wear on its pistons; the higher the level of insulin, the lower the blood sugar level. In the first two of these examples, we have a uniformly positive association (increases in A are always matched by increases in B); in the last two, the association is uniformly negative (increases in A are always matched by decreases in B). Using this terminology, Mill's **method of concomitant variations** can be summarized as follows.

THE METHOD OF CONCOMITANT VARIATIONS

If changes in the magnitude of A and changes in the magnitude of B are always positively associated, or always negatively associated, then either A is the cause of B or B is the cause of A, or both A and B are the result of a common cause.

Mill's method of concomitant variations is especially useful when dealing with phenomena that vary in magnitude but for which we cannot easily produce or find a negative instance. For example, to establish that the acceleration of the planets in their orbits results from the sun's gravitational attraction, we cannot turn off the sun's gravitational field. But we can determine that the velocity of the planets in their elliptical orbits increases as they move closer to the sun and decreases as they move further away. Similarly, we might suspect a causal relationship between the average temperature of the Earth's atmosphere and the concentration of ozone in its upper layers, since increases in the former seem to be associated with decreases in the latter.

Inferences from concomitant variations to causes must be treated with caution. Part of this caution is built into the wording of the method. Notice, first, that the method requires that variations in A and variations in B are *always* associated in the *same* manner. Since our evidence usually consists of a relatively small number of observed cases, this means that we have to perform an *inductive generalization* from that evidence before we can apply the method. Second, no matter how numerous the instances in which changes in A are, say, positively associated with changes in B, if we find a single case in which the association is negative (i.e., an increase in A is followed by a decrease in B), then the antecedent clause in the statement of the method is not satisfied. Third, even if A and B always covary in the same manner, we should not infer from this alone that A is the cause of B. This is true for a number of reasons.

The first and most obvious reason is made clear in the statement of the method itself: instead of A being the cause of B, B might be the cause of A, or they might both be effects of a **common cause,** C.

One way of ruling out the first alternative is to see which comes first. If A always precedes B, then B cannot be the cause of A. But there might still be no direct causal connection between A and B at all if they are both effects of a common cause, C. For example, during a thunderstorm, the brighter the visible flash (A), the louder the clap of thunder (B). Variations in A are always uniformly associated with variations in B, but neither is the cause of the other. Both are effects of a common cause, the discharge of electricity in the air (C).

It should be borne in mind that even when A causes B, it does not follow that changes in A will always be matched by changes in B (nor does the method of concomitant variations imply this). Some causes manifest a **threshold effect.** For example, no relationship has ever been found between the development of cancer in daughters and the size of the dose of DES received by their mothers; in the photoelectric effect, the cutoff frequency is such that no electrons are released below it, regardless of the intensity of the incident light; beyond a certain, very small amount, all doses of cyanide are lethal to mammals.

Conversely, even an impeccable concomitant variation may be nothing more than a remarkable coincidence. The classic case of this is the variations in the average price of shares on the New York Stock Exchange matching variations in the intensity of solar radiation reaching the Earth. No plausible mechanism can connect the two phenomena, either directly (one being the cause of the other) or indirectly (both being joint effects of a common cause).

Though Mill himself paid little attention to probabilistic causes, the attempt is often made to extend the method of concomitant variations to include them by substituting "correlations" for "concomitant variations." Here is one version of such attempts:

THE METHOD OF CORRELATIONS

If A is always positively (negatively) correlated with B, then A is a positive (negative) causal factor for B, or B is a positive (negative) causal factor for A, or A and B are both the result of a common probabilistic cause.

Much of the previous discussion of Mill's method of concomitant variations applies to this new method. Our evidence is usually obtained from relatively small samples from the total population of As and Bs. We might, for example, examine several groups of people (say a thousand in each) and find that, in each group, rates of lung cancer (L) are higher among the smokers (S) than among the non-smokers. Just as before, we need to make an inductive inference to the generalization that smoking is *always* positively correlated with lung cancer. This is because the antecedent clause of our statement of the method of correlations says that L is positively correlated with S in every group. It is unlikely that this will be true even if, as we have good reason to suppose in this case, smoking is a genuine positive causal factor for lung cancer. Because smoking is a probabilistic cause, not a sufficient one, some groups (especially those containing relatively few people) are bound to show no correlation, or even show a negative one, purely by chance.

Cases of common causation are particularly interesting for probabilistic causes. Sir Ronald Fisher once speculated that the positive correlation between smoking (S) and lung cancer (L) might result from a genetic predisposition that causes both. Of course, there is no evidence for this hypothesis, but it is instructive to consider how we might rule it out. Let us suppose that the proponent of the Fisher's common cause hypothesis actually identified what this genetic factor is supposed to be. Let us call it "G" and pretend that we can tell, independently of their smoking habits, which people have it and which do not. We could now test the hypothesis by looking at the frequency of smoking and lung cancer in populations all of whose members have G. If the hypothesis were true, we would expect to observe that $Pr(L/S \& G) = Pr(L/non\text{-}S \& G)$. If G really is a common cause of L and S, then G should **screen off** L from S; people with G should be just as likely to develop lung cancer whether they smoke or not. In actual fact, though spokespersons for the tobacco industry sometimes vaguely allude to "something special" that distinguishes smokers who get lung cancer from those who do not, no one has ever said what, precisely, this "something" is. Thus, there is no reason to take the proposal seriously. But the important point is that hypotheses about common causation can be tested in the manner indicated.

A second problem that can arise in trying to infer causes from correlations is that other causal factors may be at work which interfere with the statistical relationship between A and B. These are sometimes referred to as **confounding causes**. Brian Skyrms gives the illustration reproduced in 10:8.[7]

10:8. Suppose that air pollution got so bad that most people in the cities refrained from smoking out of sheer terror of putting their lungs in double jeopardy, while many people in areas of the countryside with relatively little pollution felt that they could allow themselves the luxury of smoking.

As Skyrms explains, in this situation, we might well find that $Pr(L/S) < Pr(L/non\text{-}S)$. From this negative correlation alone, we might erroneously conclude that smoking *prevents* lung cancer. But if we include air pollution, P, as a further variable and use it to partition the class of smokers from the class of nonsmokers, then we would expect to observe that $Pr(L/S \& P) > Pr(L/non\text{-}S \& P)$, and $Pr(L/S \& non\text{-}P) > Pr(L/non\text{-}S \& non\text{-}P)$. The rates of lung cancer would be higher for urban smokers than for urban nonsmokers and higher for rural smokers than for rural nonsmokers. In Skyrms's illustration, smoking is negatively correlated with air pollution, which is a separate positive causal factor for lung cancer.

In extreme cases involving confounding causes, a positive correlation might exist between A and B even though A is, in fact, a *negative* causal factor for B. This can occur if A is positively correlated with a confounding cause, C, which is a positive causal factor for B and which overwhelms the effect of A. For example, a recent sex discrimination suit was brought against Stanford University on the grounds that rates of admission to its graduate school universitywide were lower for women than for men. But upon examination of the figures for each department, it was found that in most departments women were slightly more likely to be admitted than men. The reason this slight preference in favor of women was not reflected in the admissions figures for the university as a whole was a third relevant factor—a higher proportion of women than men were applying to the more popular departments, which, because of their greater number of applications, also had higher rejection rates.[8]

Some of the most persuasive statistical evidence that smoking is a probabilistic cause of cancer comes from studies of the relationship between the amount smoked and the frequency of disease. This evidence is described in 10:9:

10:9. Assume that we begin with a large population of smokers, which we then divide into subgroups ranging from light smokers (fewer than 5 cigarettes a day) to heavy smokers (at least 40 a day). In each subgroup smoking and lung cancer are positively correlated (and hence positively correlated for the population as a whole). But, in addition, there is a uniform association between the amount smoked and rates of lung cancer; the probability of developing cancer increases steadily as we proceed from the light to the heavy smokers.

The evidence described in 10:9 strongly supports the conclusion that smoking is a positive causal factor for lung cancer. This kind of reasoning, which we call **the method of concomitant correlations,** is common in epidemiological studies of disease.

THE METHOD OF CONCOMITANT CORRELATIONS

If increases in A are always positively (negatively) correlated with increases in B, then A is a positive (negative) causal factor for B, or B is a positive (negative) causal factor for A, or A and B are both the result of a common cause.

Like all the inductive methods discussed in this section, the method of concomitant correlations is fallible. The pattern in the observed correlations might be the result of common causes, confounding causes, or blind chance. As Mill himself emphasized in connection with the method of concomitant variations, these methods are reliable only to the extent that all other causally relevant factors are eliminated or neutralized through the use of appropriate controls. The best means of achieving this is through **randomized controlled experiments,** which are the topic of the next section.

For ethical reasons, we cannot perform controlled experiments that would involve giving potentially dangerous substances to healthy persons. We could not, for example, randomly assign some volunteers to smoke cigarettes while forbidding them to a control group. So, inevitably, many of the conclusions we wish to draw about the effects of substances on human beings have to rely on animal experiments and statistical studies using the kinds of methods discussed in this section. It is, however, important to distinguish **retrospective studies** from **prospective studies.**

Retrospective studies of smoking begin with lung cancer victims, comparing their smoking habits with those of an artificially constructed control group. In the medical literature, these investigations are called **case-control studies.** The control group consists of people who do not have lung cancer and who are matched with the cancer victims for age, sex, and other characteristics. Bias, whether conscious or unconscious, might enter into the selection of this group. There might, for example, be a tendency to omit or fail to recognize smokers. Since many case-control studies of disease are conducted in hospitals, the control groups are often selected from patients in the same institution who are suffering from other diseases. Also, in retrospective studies, the investigator has to rely on the testimony of the subjects (or their relatives) about such matters as diet and smoking habits in the years before the onset of illness. Apart from the obvious problem of faulty and incomplete memory, these reports might be influenced by the subjects' knowledge of their diagnoses.

Prospective studies start from the other end, first identifying smokers and nonsmokers and then recording their subsequent medical histories. Medical researchers and epidemiologists call these investigations **cohort studies.** Though neither type of study is truly randomized, prospective studies are generally more reliable and more informative than retrospective ones. In prospective studies there is usually less bias in the selection of the control group, and less uncertainty about people's habits, state of health, and cause of death; and, in the smoking example, they yield direct information about cancer rates among smokers, rather than the frequency of smokers among cancer victims. Moreover, prospective studies can open up new directions for research. For example, it was prospective studies of smokers that first revealed they experience higher rates of diseases other than lung cancer, such as heart disease.

EXERCISES

1. How would you investigate the claim that air pollution is a positive causal factor for lung cancer?

*2. In 1949, the U.S. Public Health Service launched a long-term prospective study in Framingham, Massachusetts, of the causal relationship between various diseases and life-styles. The major focus was on heart diesase. The initial group of 5209 men and women in the study were all judged to be healthy in 1949 and free of any heart disease. Discuss the causal significance, if any, of each of the following findings. (Reported in "A Guinea Pig Town," *Science 82,* December 1982.)

a. The more air people can suck into their lungs, the longer they live. Framingham residents with poor lung capacity tend to die young.

b. The thinnest Framingham subjects died youngest, even before those who were grossly overweight. (This led to the speculation, soon abandoned, that a few "excess" pounds could prolong life.)

c. Framingham studies of 55-year-old men show that those with high-density lipoprotein (HDL) levels as high as 65 have half as many heart attacks as those with the same blood pressure and life-styles who have HDL levels of only 45, which is the average for all Framingham men.

3. Discuss the causal significance, if any, of each of the following:

a. There is a constant association between the red shift of light emitted by a galaxy and its distance from the Earth. The more distant the galaxy, the larger the red shift.

b. The higher the altitude, the less energy it takes to bring a cup of water to the boil.

c. International studies reveal a strong positive association between a country's death rate from heart disease and its per capita consumption of refined sugar.

*d. Rates of different types of cancer for members of Mormon families who resided in southwestern Utah in the period 1951 through 1962 are significantly higher than those for all Utah Mormons. [See C. J. Johnson, "Cancer Incidence in an Area of Radioactive Fallout Downwind from the Nevada Test Site," *Journal of the American Medical Association* 251 (January 13, 1984): 230–236.]

*e. In September 1980, Proctor and Gamble voluntarily withdrew from the market their superabsorbent Rely tampon. Introduced at the beginning of the year, it was the only tampon to use polyester foam. Prior to 1980, cases of toxic shock syndrome (TSS) were very rare, but between January and September of 1980, 299 cases of TSS were reported to the Centers for Disease Control (CDC) in Atlanta. The CDC linked 71 percent of these cases to the use of Rely tampons by menstruating women. Since the recall, the number of reported cases satisfying the CDC's criteria for TSS has averaged about 30 to 35 new cases per month.

f. "A team of San Diego psychiatrists has compiled strong evidence closely linking drug and alcohol abuse to suicide among young people. . . . The researchers found that two-thirds of people under 30 years old who killed themselves in San Diego County between November 1981 and June 1983 were drug abusers. For 53% of them, substance abuse was the primary psychological problem. By contrast, an estimated 17% of the general population are drug abusers. . . . The principal investigator, Dr. Charles Rich said he believes that drug and alcohol use has ballooned because of social pressure and availability and is a direct cause—not a product— of the higher rates of depression. 'I would say they're depressed because of the drugs,' he said. 'It's entirely logical that drugs are the whole thing.'" (Reported in *The Purdue Exponent,* October 3, 1986)

g. In the 1970s, Danish researchers conducted a study of the "genetic influence in alcoholism" hypothesis on two groups of adopted Danish children. In group 1 were 55 children whose biological parents were alcoholics; in group 2 were 78 children whose natural parents were not alcoholics. In group 1, 10 of the children became alcoholics; in group 2, 4 became alcoholics. Only 7 percent of the foster homes of group 1 children had an alcoholic foster parent though 12 percent of group 2 children went to homes with an alcoholic foster parent. The researchers concluded that even after being separated from their natural parents as early as the first six weeks of life, the children of alcoholic parents were 3.5 times more likely to become alcoholic than the children of nonalcoholics. [From R. Fishman, *Alcohol and Alcoholism* (New York: Chelsea House Publishers, 1986)]

4. Using the materials cited, write a report on the following investigations of probabilistic causes. Focus on the following questions (where appropriate): Is the study retrospective or prospective? How were the control groups selected? What steps were taken to eliminate common causes and confounding causes?

a. Does the possession of an extra Y chromosome in XYY males cause a greater tendency toward aggression? [See H. A. Witkin et al., "Criminality in XYY and XXY Men," *Science* 193 (August 13, 1976):547–555.]

b. Is there a causal link between coffee drinking and pancreatic cancer? [See B. MacMahon et al., "Coffee and Cancer of the Pancreas," *New England Journal of Medicine* 304 (March 12, 1981):630–633; F. Clavel et al., "More on Coffee and Pancreatic Cancer," *New England Journal of Medicine* 316 (February 19, 1987):483–484.]

c. Does drinking alcohol increase a woman's risk of developing breast cancer? [See A. Schatzkin et al., "Alcohol Consumption and Breast Cancer in the Epidemiologic Follow-Up Study of the First National Health and Nutrition Examination Survey," *New England Journal of Medicine* 316 (May 7, 1987):1169–1173; W. C. Willett et al., "Moderate Alcohol Consumption and the Risk of Breast Cancer," *New England Journal of*

Medicine 316 (May 7, 1987):1174–1180; S. Graham, "Alcohol and Breast Cancer," *New England Journal of Medicine* 316 (May 7, 1987):1211–1213; "Drinking and Breast Cancer," *Newsweek,* May 18, 1987.]

Randomized Controlled Experiments[9]

The most rigorous way of testing an hypothesis about a probabilistic cause is to perform a **randomized controlled experiment.** For the sake of illustration, consider the problem posed in 10:10:

10:10.   We wish to test the hypothesis, H, that benzene causes leukemia in rats, or, in other words, that benzene (B) is a positive causal factor for leukemia (L). Because we are dealing with a probabilistic cause, we do not expect all rats that eat benzene to develop leukemia, nor do we expect all rats on a benzene-free diet to avoid getting the disease. But, if H is true, then we would expect the rates of leukemia to be higher among rats that consume benzene than among those that do not.

The simplest kind of controlled experiment to test hypotheses like H involves first dividing the test subjects (in this case, rats) into two groups of equal size—say a hundred animals in each. The **experimental group,** E, will receive benzene in regular, known amounts. The **control group,** K, will be maintained on a benzene-free diet. Ideally, the only difference between the two groups should be that E receives benzene and K does not. Thus, we select the animals from the same specially bred strain to minimize the genetic differences between them; we try to ensure that (with the exception of the benzene) they receive the same diet that is free from any other known carcinogens; we house and rear them under identical conditions.

A powerful technique for neutralizing the effects of variables that we cannot eliminate is **randomization.** We assign the rats to E and K at random from the original laboratory population. In tests of agricultural fertilizers we would go further: not only would we pick the seeds for the E and K groups at random from an initial population, we would also divide the field in which they are to be planted into adjacent plots and randomly assign batches from the E and K groups to those plots. In this way, we neutralize the disturbing effects of variations in soil quality on the results.

All these techniques—eliminating interfering variables, controlling relevant variables, and randomization—have a common aim, namely, to realize as closely as possible the conditions required by *the method of difference.* Ideally, the *only* difference between the two groups, E and K, should be the presence and absence, respectively, of the factor we are investigating.

In interpreting the results of a controlled experiment to test H, we need to consider the **null hypothesis,** H_0. In the benzene-rat example, the null hypothesis is that there is *no* causal relation between benzene and leukemia. In other words, H_0 asserts that benzene is neither a positive causal factor nor a negative causal factor for leukemia.[10]

If the null hypothesis were true, eating benzene should not make any difference to the cancer rates. If P_E is the proportion of the rats in the experimental group that get cancer, P_K the frequency of cancer in the control group, and d the difference between them, then we can summarize the prediction made by H_0 as follows:

H_0: $d = P_E - P_K = 0$, on average.

We say "on average" instead of "always" because the two groups, E and K, are samples of 100 animals randomly drawn from a much larger population. If H_0 is true, then E and K are samples from the same population, but even so, we do not expect to find exactly the same values of P_E and P_K each time the experiment is repeated. The situation is analogous to the model of simple random sampling described in Chapter 4. There, you will remember, we imagined a box containing 1000 balls: 600 white, 400 black. We do not expect to get exactly 60 white and 40 black each time we randomly select a sample of 100 balls. P_W, the proportion of white balls in the sample, will vary. But if we repeat the sampling process (with replacement) over and over again, we obtain a normally distributed sampling distribution curve (SDC) for P_W whose mean is 0.6; so, too, with the rats in our experiment. If H_0 is true and we were to repeat the same experiment many times, we would obtain a normally distributed SDC for d whose mean, representing the true value of d, is zero.

The standard deviation (SD) of the SDC for d can be calculated from the sample size, *n,* using Table 4-1 from Chapter 4. The calculation is straightforward when the E and K groups are *the same size:* simply multiply the SD value for a sample of size *n* given by Table 4-1 by the square root of 2. For *n* = 100, this gives a value of $(0.05)(1.414) = 0.0707$, or about 7 percentage points.

We will now suppose that the benzene-rat experiment has been performed. In group E, 15 of the rats developed leukemia, while in the control group, K, only 2 rats did. Since each group has 100 animals, we have found $d = P_E - P_K = 0.15 - 0.02 = 0.13$, or a net difference of 13 percentage points. Is this observed difference statistically significant? Does it show that the null hypothesis is false? To answer these questions we have to decide what level of significance to adopt. The usual choices, in increasing order of stringency, are 5, 1, and 0.1 percent.

Assume that we adopt the 5 percent significance level. This means that we shall reject H_0 as false whenever we obtain a result, R, such that $Pr(R/H_0) < 0.05$. In other words, we reject H_0 on the basis of R if the probability of getting R if H_0 is true is no greater than 5 percent.

By adopting a significance level of 5 percent, we indicate that we are willing to tolerate a 0.05 probability of committing a **Type I error.** A Type I error is made when we reject as false a null hypothesis that is true. By adopting a significance level of 5 percent we are specifying that such mistakes should not occur more frequently than once in every 20 trials. If we had adopted a 1 percent significance level, the probability of a Type I error would be reduced to no more than 1 in 100.

How do we decide whether the observed difference, d = 0.13, is significant at the 5 percent level? If H_0 were true, then since the SDC of d is normally distributed, 95 percent of all its values lie within 2 SDs either side of the mean, d = 0. In the benzene-rat experiment, 2 SDs = 0.14. So the observed difference lies just inside the crucial interval of −0.14 to +0.14. Thus, we would *not* reject the null hypothesis. The experiment is not significant at the 5 percent level, since the probability is slightly greater than 1/20 that we would have obtained the observed result even if the null hypothesis were true. The experiment has not established a causal link between benzene and leukemia.[11]

A second kind of error is associated with controlled experiments, namely, that of accepting the null hypothesis when it is actually false. This is known as a **Type II error.** In the benzene-rat example, it is easy to see how this might happen if the causal relation between benzene and leukemia, though positive, is very weak. Even when the benzene is given in large doses, the number of animals in E and K might simply be too small to reveal a significant difference. We could make our experiment more sensitive and hence decrease the probability of Type II error by increasing the number, *n,* of subjects in the two groups, E and K, from 100 to, say, 500.

For an experiment with any fixed number of subjects, *n,* the probabilities of the two types of error, Type I and Type II, are inversely related. One of them can be decreased only by increasing the other. Scientific researchers usually give priority to avoiding Type I errors, judging that it is more costly and misleading to falsely claim a causal relation when none exists than to miss detecting a small but genuine effect.

Randomized clinical trials (RCTs) on human subjects in medical research are based on the same general principles as randomized controlled experiments. RCTs are used to compare two (or more) therapies to see which, if any, is more effective. Typical examples include (a) comparing the effectiveness of a new drug for a disease with a drug already in use, (b) testing the effectiveness of a new drug (here the alternative "therapy" would be a pharmacologically inactive placebo), (c) comparing two alternative surgical procedures for a disease such as cancer.

Since human beings are involved in RCTs, there are important ethical constraints on the conduct of these experiments. The most important of these concern the **risk to the subjects** and the requirement of **informed consent.** The informed consent of the participants in a RCT is both morally and legally necessary. This means not only that the subjects should be made fully aware of any side effects or harm that may result from their participation, but also that they should realize the surgery, drug, or placebo they receive will be determined by a purely random mechanism. In particular, the subjects must know that the treatment they receive will *not* be based on any physician's judgment concerning what is best for each individual person.

The question of morally acceptable risk in RCTs can be controversial. Most people agree that no *healthy* human being, however willing, should knowingly be exposed to a significant risk of harm. Where people sometimes disagree is in deciding what risks are ethically permissible for patients suffering from serious or life-threatening diseases. As a general rule, the more serious the potential harm from an experimental treatment, the more comprehensive and informed should be the subject's consent.

EXERCISES

*1. George claims that he can tell whether a letter was written by a man or by a woman simply on the basis of the handwriting. You plan to test George's claim by collecting handwriting samples from 25 men and 25 women, and then presenting them to him in pairs. George is told that each pair consists of one piece written by man and one piece by a woman, and he is asked to identify which is which. What precautions would you take in performing this experiment? What is the null hypothesis? If the null hypothesis were true, how many correct identifications would you expect George to make (on average)? If George achieves 19 correct identifications, is the result significant at the 95 percent confidence level?

2. Explain how you would try to test the hypothesis that there is an audible difference between an expensive state-of-the-art amplifier and an inexpensive model. (For the details of one such test on a number of hi-fi enthusiasts, see the January 1987 issue of *Stereo Review.*)

3. Explain why the Salk polio vaccine was tested in 1954 in a randomized field trial rather than by distributing it widely and seeing whether the rates of reported polio cases decreased. Why did the study require the participation of more than 1,800,000 young children? Why were some children injected with a simple salt solution (a placebo) and why was the experiment performed double-blind (so that neither the children nor the physicians who evaluated their subsequent state of health knew who had received the vaccine and who had been given the placebo)? [See P. Meier, "The Biggest Public Health Experiment Ever: The 1954 Field Trial of the Salk Poliomyelitis Vaccine," in J. M. Tanur et al., *Statistics: A Guide to the Unknown;* and Allan M. Brandt, "Polio, Politics, Publicity, and Duplicity: Ethical Aspects in the Development of the Salk Vaccine," *International Journal of Health Services* 8 (1978):257–270.]

4. Explain the analogy between Type I and Type II errors and the specificity and sensitivity of diagnostic tests for disease in medicine. [The specificity of a test is the true negative rate, Pr(Neg/non-D); its sensitivity is the true

positive rate, Pr(Pos/D).] In a recent article the ELISA blood test for the HLTV-III AIDS associated antibody is described as having a specificity of 0.99 and a sensitivity of 0.82. If this is correct and the test is used *just once* to screen each unit of blood donated to a blood bank, what percentage of infected blood would go undetected? How would this figure be affected if the test was applied *twice* to each unit, and any unit that tested positive *at least once* was rejected? Usually in such tests, the specificity can be increased by adjusting the cutoff point between values judged "normal" and those judged "abnormal." As the specificity increases, the sensitivity decreases, and vice versa. If the ELISA test is adjusted so that its new specificity and sensitivity are both 0.9, what would be the effect on the inverse false-positive rate, Pr(not-D/Pos)? (See K. R. Howe, "How to Set a Cut Off Point for the ELISA Test," *Hastings Center Report,* April 1986, p. 43.)

5. The following description is adapted from "Is Vitamin C Really Good for Colds?" *Consumer Reports* (February 1976). Linus Pauling claims that large doses of vitamin C will prevent colds. This claim was tested in a randomized double-blind experiment performed at Toronto in the winter of 1971–1972. Volunteers were randomly assigned to two groups, E and K, each containing 500 subjects. Group E received 1 gram per day of vitamin C, and 4 grams per day at the first sign of a cold. Group K received a placebo. Throughout the winter, both groups were checked regularly for cold symptoms. At winter's end, 26 percent of the subjects in E had not had a cold compared with 18 percent in K. What is the causal hypothesis that was tested in the Toronto experiment? What is the null hypothesis? If the null hypothesis were true, what difference, $d = P_E - P_K$, would you expect to observe? What was the observed difference? Assume that for $n = 500$, the SD of the sampling distribution curve for d is 0.028. Is the result of the Toronto study significant at the 5 percent level? Is it significant at the 1 percent level? (This experiment is discussed in D. S. Moore, *Statistics: Concepts and Controversies,* pp. 72–73.)

6. Write a report on the design, conduct, and implications of the following RCTs.

a. The comparison of Halsted radical mastectomy with a less mutilating form of surgery for women with breast cancer. See U. Veronesi et al., "Comparing Radical Mastectomy with Quadrantectomy, Axillary Dissection, and Radiotherapy in Patients with Small Cancers of the Breast," *New England Journal of Medicine* 305 (1981): 6–11.

b. The test of the effectiveness of the anticholesterol drug, cholestyramine, in lowering blood cholesterol levels and preventing coronary heart disease. See "The Lipid Research Clinics Coronary Primary Prevention Trial Results," *Journal of the American Medical Association* 251 (January 20, 1984):351–364; "Hold the Eggs and Butter," *Time,* March 26, 1984.

   c. The test of the new drug adenine arabinoside (ara-A) as a treatment for herpes simplex encephalitis, a life-threatening brain disease. See J. Whitley et al., "Adenine Arabinoside Therapy of Biopsy-proved Herpes Simplex Encephalitis," *New England Journal of Medicine* 297 (August 11, 1977):289–294; J. J. McCartney, "Encephalitis and Ara-A: An Ethical Case Study," *Hastings Center Report* 8 (December 1978):5–7. These and other references, along with a summary of the experimental trial, can be found in T. L. Beauchamp and J. F. Childress, *Principles of Biomedical Ethics,* 2nd ed. (New York: Oxford University Press, 1983) pp. 318–319.

   7. Write a report on the merits and drawbacks of the alternative design for RCTs proposed in M. Zelen, "A New Design for Randomized Clinical Trials," *New England Journal of Medicine* 300 (May 31, 1979):1242–1245.

Notes

[1]A. Michotte, *The Perception of Causality* (New York: Basic Books, 1963), showed that people have an irresistible tendency to perceive sequences of events in causal terms, even when they are made aware that no such causal relations exist.

[2]Hence the adage "One cannot change the past." Whether this temporal asymmetry of the causal relation is logically necessary or contingent is discussed in Michael Dummett, "Bringing About the Past," and Samuel Gorovitz, "Leaving the Past Alone," *Philosophical Review* 73 (1964):338–371; both papers are reprinted in Peter A. French and Curtis Brown, eds., *Puzzles, Paradoxes, and Problems: A Reader for Introductory Philosophy* (New York: St. Martin's Press, 1987). Possible exceptions to the rule about temporal priority are cases of so-called simultaneous causation: the light bulb comes on "at the same moment" that the switch is thrown; the far end of a rigid rod moves "immediately" when its near end is pushed. A physical analysis of these examples reveals that, though it may be very short, there is always a temporal separation between the cause and the effect. Thus, these are not genuine exceptions to the rule.

[3]Does the converse also hold? That is, is it true that if an event occurs, at least one of its sufficient conditions must have obtained? The usual answer to this question is "Yes." The belief that every event has a sufficient cause underlies much of our reasoning in the sciences and in everyday life. We assume that for everything that happens, there is some prior state of the world that uniquely determines what happens later.

However reasonable or obvious this **principle of universal determinism** may seem to us, there is no guarantee that it is true. In fact, there is good reason to think it is false. In modern physics there is a highly successful theory, quantum mechanics, which implies that universal determinism is false. According to quantum mechanics, all systems are **stochastic,** not deterministic; they contain an irreducible element of chance. For example, if quantum mechanics is true, no sufficient cause determines that a radioactive nucleus will disintegrate when it does.

Even if we ignore quantum mechanics, there are contexts in which we find it convenient to treat systems as if they are stochastic. A good example of this is classical Mendelian genetics in which we assume that the genes transmitted to offspring are a random selection from each pair of genes possessed by the parents. Of course, if universal determinism holds, there must be some set of highly complicated factors that determine which particular genes get transmitted, but classical genetics says nothing about them. Similarly, in explaining the behavior of individual human beings, we can rarely find anything approaching sufficient causes for the things they do. I would be hard-pressed, for example, to specify the sufficient cause of my decision to have scrambled tofu for breakfast this morning. Much of the challenge in psychology and sociology stems from the difficulty of finding causal laws that determine the behavior of individuals or social groups.

[4]Again, it is pertinent to ask whether the converse holds. That is, is it true that if an event fails to occur at least one of its necessary conditions must have been absent? As before, the usual answer, "Yes," is based on our belief in universal determinism. We can reconstruct the reasoning involved as a reductio ad absurdum argument.

Let N be the complete set of necessary conditions for some later event E. Assume that N obtains but E does not occur. If universal determinism is true, there is some sufficient cause, S, for E. N must be part of S, since if N fails to obtain, E cannot occur. Let the remaining part of S be M. Thus, (N & M) is a sufficient cause of E. But since E cannot occur without M, M is a necessary condition for E. This contradicts our assumption that the set N is complete. Conclusion: If universal determinism is true, the complete set of necessary conditions for E is a sufficient condition for E. Thus, if E does not occur, at least one of its necessary conditions must have been absent. Moreover, if the principle of universal determinism is true, there can be only *one* sufficient condition for E, namely, the complete set of E's necessary conditions.

[5]Like most thinkers of his age, Mill believed in universal determinism. Thus, when Mill talks about "the" cause of a phenomenon, he means the strict concept of a sufficient condition, that is, the complete set of necessary conditions such that, given those conditions, the phenomenon must always follow. See Book III, Chapter V, Section 4, in which Mill defines the cause of a phenomenon as "the antecedent or the concurrence of antecedents, on which it is invariably and unconditionally consequent."

[6]For a more detailed account of Mill's methods and the use of tables of presence and absence, see Brian Skyrms, *Choice and Chance* (Belmont, CA: Dickenson, 1966), pp. 84–110.

[7]See Brian Skyrms, *Causal Necessity* (New Haven: Yale University Press, 1980), p. 160.

[8]See Peter J. Bickel, Eugene A. Hammel, and J. William O'Connell, "Sex Bias in Graduate Admissions: Data from Berkeley," in William B. Fairley and Frederick Mosteller, *Statistics and Public Policy* (Reading, MA: Addison-Wesley, 1977).

[9]The analysis of testing hypotheses about probabilistic causes in this section is adapted from Ronald W. Giere, *Understanding Scientific Reasoning*, 2nd ed. (New York: Holt, Rinehart and Winston, 1979), Chapter 12.

[10]Notice that while H_0 is a *contrary* of H, the two hypotheses are not contradictory: both cannot be true, but it is logically possible that benzene *prevents* leukemia, and hence is a negative causal factor. In that case, both H and H_0 would be false. The causal hypothesis and the null hypothesis will be contradictories only when the causal hypothesis asserts that a causal relation exists but does not specify whether it is positive or negative. Thus, consider the hypothesis H_1: Either benzene is a positive causal factor for leukemia or benzene is a negative causal factor for leukemia. H_1 is logically weaker than H since

H implies H_1, but H_1 does not imply H. The null hypothesis, H_0, for H_1 is the same as before, but now H_1 and H_0 *are* contradictories.

[11]This account implicitly adopts the **two-tailed test** of significance, since we have looked at both "tails" of the sampling distribution curve. The use of **one-tailed tests** is controversial since, at any chosen significance level, smaller differences will qualify as significant. At the very least, investigators should always say whether they are using a one-tailed or a two-tailed test when reporting that their results are significant at a given level. For further details see D. Rowntree, *Statistics Without Tears* (New York: Charles Scribner's Sons, 1981), Chapter 7, and R. Langley, *Practical Statistics* (New York: Dover Publications Inc., 1970), pp. 143–146.

APPENDIX I

Extended Arguments
1: Unfair Hurdles for Teachers
by
Albert Shanker

1. Every wave of education reform brings with it some good ideas and others that are attractive but not well thought out. The current reform wave is no exception.

2. One of the great virtues of the current wave is that it recognizes the classroom teacher as the key to a good education. (It's hard to believe that only a few years ago an earlier generation of reformers pinned their hopes on the creation of "teacher-proof" educational materials.) Many of the recent reports list recommendations designed to retain our teaching force and attract new talent, but it is inevitable that any discussion of teacher quality will also deal with the question of how to get rid of incompetents.

3. All of us were at one time students, and while we were lucky enough to have one, two or three great teachers who inspired us, the chances are good that we had just as many teachers at the other end of the quality spectrum. Of course, there are occasions when a given teacher rated as incompetent by one student or principal would be deemed satisfactory or even outstanding by others. Still, teaching has its share of incompetents, as does every other field, and the reform wave has resurrected some old "cures."

4. Most popular is the idea that tenure should be abolished so that teachers or faculty thought to be incompetent by their supervisors may be dismissed without the protection of tenure—the right to know why the discharge is being sought

and to challenge it before an impartial body that has the opportunity to hear both sides of the case. Somehow the public thinks that tenure gives teachers something that no one else enjoys—a special protection. It's just not so. What teachers have is no better than, and usually weaker and worse than, that enjoyed by other professionals—doctors, dentists, lawyers, pharmacists—and millions of workers in both the private and public sectors who can only be dismissed for "just cause."

5. But the real question is, would abolishing tenure lead to better teaching, better results in school? We don't have to abolish tenure in order to find out. Since at least two states do not have tenure—Mississippi and Texas—if tenure were the big stumbling block to improving education by easily removing incompetents, someone should be able to demonstrate the superiority of education in these two states. Anyone with the evidence ought to produce it. And if there is no evidence, it's time to put this idea back into mothballs.

6. A second idea is recertification. Even people who were really good five, ten, fifteen years ago get worn out—everyone knows that. Why require a "trial" to get someone out? Why not have all teaching certificates terminate after a specific period of time, such as five years? Most teachers' licenses would be renewed after five years, but some would not be, thus avoiding messy disputes and arguments.

7. The idea is appealing, but why apply it only to teachers? Why not to doctors, dentists, lawyers, pharmacists? Any of these whose performance deteriorates is likely to do at least as much damage as a teacher. If recertification were imposed on all of these and other job categories (and I don't mean a *pro forma* recertification but one that really reviews the desirability of granting another five years), it would be hard to ask that teachers be exempt, but it's just as unfair to subject teachers to this when no one else's certification is up for review. Also, we'd be sending a message to many who are now in college: In addition to having low pay and low prestige, the profession they're preparing to enter can easily be taken away from them every five years. We'd thus be adding exceptional insecurity to the other disadvantages of the job.

8. Third is the idea of retesting teachers. I've been a strong advocate of giving teachers tests before they're hired and requiring high passing marks in the subject matter to be taught. But why give a pencil-and-paper test to a teacher after five or ten years when you can spend a few hours in his or her classroom and find out by direct observation whether the teacher knows the subject and knows how to teach it? Of course, knowledge in a given field is always expanding. Shouldn't teachers be tested again to make sure they're keeping up with the latest advances?

9. Again, the answer is yes—but only if they're not singled out. The knowledge explosion in medicine, dentistry and pharmacy is much greater than new developments in the teaching of Shakespeare, Dickens, irregular French verbs, high school algebra or fourth-grade arithmetic. Here, too, if we're going to retest teachers to protect the public, it's going to be hard to convince teachers that they and only they should be retested.

10. You can't blame teachers for feeling that they're being made scapegoats when these proposals are floated by officials who are trying to hire teachers at $12,000, $13,000 and $14,000 a year, who don't bother giving teachers a test before they're hired, and who don't follow a policy of granting tenure only to those who meet very high standards during their probationary period.

2: Keeping Lawyers Out of the Hospital

"I will follow that system of regimen which, according to my ability and judgment, I consider for the benefit of my patients." (Hippocratic Oath)

1. The Bloomington attorney appointed as the legal guardian of Infant Doe last year is asking the State Supreme Court to consider reopening the case. He wants it on record that the parents of the child born with a deformed esophagus and Down's syndrome were wrong when they withheld food and medical treatment. The six-day-old child died, and the guardian now wants the court to set guidelines in case the same thing ever happens again.

2. Arguments over whether Infant Doe should or should not have been allowed to die can both be heard. The issue, however, is not what the decision is, but who will make it.

3. The question usually asked is: "Would you have let Infant Doe die?" The answer usually given is: "I don't know."

4. It's hard for any of us to know until we're in that situation, and until we've been advised by those who know best. Those of us isolated from the situation in the cold and separate chambers of judges and juries can't decide.

5. Rather, let it be decided by those closest to and most deeply involved in the pain of it, the parents—those who are in the midst of every hope, every disappointment. And, let the doctor help guide the decision. He is the expert few of us shall ever become. By granting him a license under the conditions of the oath above, we accept his decision.

6. Medicine has grown since the time those words were written, perhaps more so than its authors ever dreamed. It now has the flexibility to decide when the living can die and when the dying can live. Yet, as the legal community deals with medicine, it insists on using rigid standards carved in stone.

7. It simply can't. The situation is too complex and involved to fit a ready-

Courtesy of *Purdue Exponent*. Reprinted by permission.

made scheme. It's a highly individual matter, and can only be dealt with on that basis.

3: UN's Functions are Misunderstood
by
James Stegenga

1. The April 7 editorial belittling the United Nations for "its" inability to preserve peace between Britain and Argentina (and elsewhere) reveals a serious misunderstanding of the UN.

2. The UN is an intergovernmental organization. Governments are the members. It has only such authority and powers and resources as the member governments are willing to give it. It has no power of its own to prevent hostilities or force disputants to settle differences peaceably. It has no taxing power or military forces, no powerful central executive (president, prince, or dictator) accepted by all as licensed to enforce international order and law.

3. The world's governments (including the United States) have not been willing to grant the UN these abilities; for a variety of reasons, bad and good, these governments have so far deliberately kept the UN weak. It thus reflects the continuing divisions in the world. "It" should not be blamed for not doing what its members will not give it the ability to do.

4. (Would you blame a men's club for having crummy activities . . . if the members didn't show up for meetings, work on programs, pay their dues, work together harmoniously, encourage their friends to participate, and otherwise support the club? Or would you, instead, more sensibly blame the members for being quarrelsome, uncooperative, and stingy? Or if, say, the United Way fund didn't reach its goal, would you blame some abstraction called "the United Way" or would you, instead, more sensibly blame the volunteer staffers or the potential donors or the hard economic times?)

5. But perhaps you're planning a follow-up editorial urging the governments of the world to cede over to the UN real authority over the world's bickering peoples and real powers to regulate improper behavior by these same governments? Is your remedy for the flaws you see in the UN its speedy conversion into a tough, effective world government?

Letter to the Editor, *Lafayette Journal and Courier.*

6. Then when some thug threatened to upset the peace in some distant corner of the world, you could editorially applaud the UN Secretary General's stern announcement that he had dispatched his fleet to suppress the disturbance!

4: Some Animals Abused in Science Fairs

1. I recently served as a judge in the Regional Science Fair under your sponsorship, and have also had occasion to judge fairs at junior high level. I am an enthusiastic supporter of this means of communicating science to the community and regard it as an urgent task of the science profession.

2. One aspect of these fairs seriously mars my enthusiasm for them, and that concerns the use of live animals in Science Fair projects. In actual pharmaceutical and biological research, live animals suffer and die for substantial, measurable benefits. Laboratory animals suffer so that humans will not.

3. The purpose of a Science Fair project is different. The results will not be published or used by drug companies the way professional research will be. Science Fairs are to educate, to explain about science, not to develop new science.

4. These aims, to teach the methods of science, to train young people in the discipline of science, and to present the drama and excitement of science to us all, do not require live animals.

5. All of the science teachers in the area whom I have met have been more than sufficiently imaginative and creative to accomplish these educational aims in a variety of ways.

6. Nonetheless, every Science Fair contains boxes of mice, baby chicks, rabbits, goldfish subjected to extremes of heat, cold, noise, or dietary poisons for the "scientific" purpose of counting the survivors and assessing the level of physiological damage done.

7. No human pain will ever be alleviated by a high school student's observation in this last fair that mice subjected to 24-hour, day after day, unrelenting high noise levels become permanently deafened and fail to gain weight, or that, as in an earlier fair I have judged, goldfish will die if kept in acidic water, or that baby chicks kept at 120 degrees do not long survive.

8. For every project in which the animals have been handled with sympathy and intelligence—such as Miss Klinghammer's snakes of this recent fair—there are literally dozens throughout the country which amount to no more than calibrated torture.

Letter to the Editor, *Lafayette Journal and Courier.*

9. If a child drops a fish in acid to watch it die, that's sadism; if he first measures the pH, that's science. I object to this not only on human grounds, but also deeply resent the slur on science.

10. I have complained about this each time I have judged. It seems, however, that only you as the sponsoring agent are in a position to do something about it. If the *Journal and Courier* adopted the position—no Science Fair project using living animals (chordate) will be entered—that would put an end to it. Would you please give this policy serious consideration?

5: Pornography and Censorship
by
Kathleen Okruhlik

"Not a Love Story" is a film about pornography, produced by the National Film Board of Canada. In Ontario, censors approved the film only for educational viewing by specific groups. The following article consists of notes from a talk given by Kathleen Okruhlik after one such showing.

1. The film which we have just seen is itself a victim of censorship. In the province of Ontario it cannot be shown in public theatres, it cannot be publicly advertised, and no admission fee can be charged for viewing it. The people of this province are being *protected* from a film which seeks to establish that pornography is dangerous. The irony could hardly be more complete or more obvious.

2. One might argue that women have historically been among the chief victims of censorship. In the past, birth control information has been judged obscene and banned on that ground. Literature regarding abortion has been outlawed for the same reason. Sex education material has been, and still is, censored. *Our Bodies, Ourselves*, a feminist self-help book for women has been prosecuted in some jurisdictions. And today in Ontario . . . "Not a Love Story."

3. Some feminists have argued that *even in principle* censorship will always work against women in a sexist society—because the powers that enforce the censorship laws will be precisely the same powers that maintain the sexist societal

This article is reprinted by permission from the *Westminster Institute Review*, Vol. 2, No. 4, © 1983, published by the Westminster Institute for Ethics and Human Values, 361 Windermere Road, London, Ontario, Canada N6G 2K3. All rights are reserved.

structure. This is a very plausible argument that deserves to be taken seriously. I shall argue later that it is in fact decisive against our censorship laws as now written and interpreted. It is not so clear, however, that this argument precludes all legal controls against pornography.

4. In what follows, I should like to do three things: (1) discuss the conceptual and practical shortcomings of current obscenity legislation; (2) suggest (in passing) how we might have existing legislation re-interpreted on a case-by-case basis; and finally, (3) outline an alternative framework for understanding pornography within which a plausible case might be made for state intervention against some of its forms.

5. Before proceeding, however, it is essential that we establish a working definition of "pornography." It is especially crucial that we avoid the temptation to conflate it with "erotica." For purposes of this discussion, I shall adopt the sort of definition now common in the feminist literature; pornographic materials are *verbal or pictorial explicit representations of sexual behavior that have as a distinguishing characteristic the degrading and demeaning portrayal of the role and status of the human female.* The important thing to notice here is that not all sexually explicit materials are pornographic. Feminists are opposed not to sexual explicitness but to the degradation and abuse of women.

6. The legislation at issue here is chiefly s.159 (8) of the Criminal Code. (We should emphasize that this legislation deals with "obscenity" rather than pornography and that there is no guarantee that the two are co-extensive.) The objections to be considered here center chiefly around two aspects of the legislation and the manner in which it is interpreted: First: The final determination as to obscenity is made by the judge with reference to *community standards.* Second: The legislation as interpreted to date does not focus chiefly on degradation or violence but rather it concentrates on sexual explicitness. These two objections will be considered in turn.

7. When John Stuart Mill first articulated the now-standard objections to censorship, his motive was to oppose the "tyranny of the majority." His anti-censorship position was intended to place limits on a sort of democracy run wild by guaranteeing the free expression of minority viewpoints. He argued that society would be best served and the general societal welfare most enhanced if everyone had access to the marketplace of ideas. Without a free exchange of theories, society would stagnate; unpopular ideas would never get a chance to be developed to the point where they might be taken seriously; and everyone would suffer as a result. The loss to society would be obvious if the suppressed idea were true. But even if the unpopular view were false, consideration of it would serve to throw into greater relief the correct view.

8. This is a powerful argument, and I think it tells against any "community standards" test of obscenity. If community standards define obscenity, then the majority group receives additional power by virtue of the very fact that it is *already* powerful.

9. Such a definition of the censorable will inevitably reinforce rather than

challenge existing power structures. It can never provide a tool for attacking injustices which are approved of by the majority. So long as the majority is racist or sexist or religious, community standards legislation will be a tool against non-whites, women, and non-religious people. Films like "Not a Love Story" will continue to be banned while misogynistic magazines will flourish. Conservatism is built into and promoted by such legislation.

10. Two subsidiary points remain to be made about "community standards" legislation. First, what seems sometimes to underlie such a definition of obscenity is the view that what should be censored is that which causes a feeling of revulsion or repugnance in the average member of the community. But feelings of revulsion should be neither necessary nor sufficient in order to make material a candidate for censorship. Many things which disgust us are otherwise harmless; and much that is demonstrably harmful to some members of the community arouses no disgust in the majority. (We shall return later to the question of harm.) Emphasis on "community standards" and "disgust" has led not only to the banning of feminist materials, but to other abuses as well—for example, selective prosecution of homosexual materials.

11. Finally, there is a *practical* difficulty with the enforcement of "community standards" legislation. This involves the circularity of the community standards test: Something cannot be taken off the streets until deemed obscene; and nothing can be deemed obscene if it's on the streets. (The argument here seems to be that if it's on the streets, then it has been accepted; and if it's accepted, then it must be acceptable.)

12. For the reasons sketched above, both theoretical and practical, I would argue as strongly as anyone against any form of censorship based on a community standards criterion.

13. The second objection to current legislation concerns the fact that (as interpreted to date) it focuses on sexual explicitness rather than violence or degradation. The depiction of brutal behavior toward women is not generally judged to be obscene so long as they are at least half-dressed; but pictures of mutually consenting adults engaged in loving sexual intercourse may well be judged obscene if their genitals are exposed and particularly if "penile penetration of the vagina" is shown. The law prohibits the explicit portrayal of sexual intercourse, but does not generally prohibit the depiction of violence toward women. In seeking to change the focus of the law from "penile penetration" to violence feminists are undertaking much the same fight as the one they have waged in order to get the rape laws changed. In both cases, the real issue is the abuse and degradation of women: but that issue has been obscured by laws that focus exclusively on penis-in-vagina sex. Feminists are united in maintaining that explicit portrayals of sex need not be pornographic and that censorship of (nonpornographic) erotica cannot be justified. Feminists are also united in maintaining that pornography contributes to the oppression of women. The question which causes division within feminist ranks is a much harder one: What form should opposition to pornography take? In particular, should this opposition include calls for censor-

ship of some pornographic materials? That is the question to which we shall return shortly.

14. I have tried to argue so far that there are serious conceptual and practical flaws in the existing obscenity legislation and that we should hesitate before embracing it. If, however, one is reconciled to some form of censorship and despairs of getting new legislation enacted which focuses on abuse rather than explicit sex, one might choose to go the judicial rather than the legislative route. One might attempt to get the present law reinterpreted on a case-by-case basis by bringing charges under that clause which prohibits sex associated with violence. Perhaps in this way, new precedents could be established which reflect not a belief that sex is wrong, but a belief that violence and degradation are wrong.

15. This is largely a tactical suggestion. It still leaves open the prior question whether state controls on pornography can be justified on some *different* grounds than those embodied in current legislation.

16. Can a plausible case be made for *any* sort of state intervention against pornography? Traditionally, liberals have argued that the state has no business regulating any behavior which affects only oneself. However disgusting a certain behavior is, however deviant, however unpopular, the state cannot prohibit that behavior if it has no ramifications for others. Such a position has been defended above.

17. The state may consider intervention only if it can be shown that the given behavior has adverse effects on other people. It is not sufficient, moreover, that the effects be *adverse*; they must actually constitute a violation of the *rights* of others. (Standard example: If your superior performance at a job interview causes you to win the job over me, then your behavior has adversely affected me. It has not, however, led to any violation of my rights; so the state cannot outlaw your behavior.)

18. Very often, the consumption of pornography has been treated as a purely self-regarding act. One hears this argument very frequently these days regarding the cable TV controversy: "The government has no right telling me what I can watch in the privacy of my own living room."

19. This claim would be very plausible if the speaker promised never to leave his living room and if there were no other persons with him in that living room. If, however, he does other things besides watch pornography and, in particular, if he ever interacts with other people, then it's an open question whether the consumption of pornography is a purely self-regarding act. The fact that it is *viewed* privately is virtually irrelevant.

20. If the consumption of pornography leads him to treat women abusively and to violate their rights, then it is an other-regarding act, and the state has *prima facie* grounds for intervention. So the crucial question becomes: Do certain types of pornography actually increase aggression toward women? This is an empirical question which must be answered by employing empirical techniques.

21. Until recently, most researchers argued that pornography did *not* promote disrespect for and violence against women. The evidence cited originated

chiefly in the late 60's and early 70's, the most popular source of data being the report of the U.S. Presidential Commission on Obscenity and Pornography.

22. The studies on which this report was based have been subjected to extensive methodological criticism by feminists and non-feminists alike. A few of these criticisms are as follows: (1) In most of these studies, no distinction was made between pornography and erotica. Much of the material used was erotic rather than pornographic. Even if exposure to erotica did not increase aggression against women, this would have no bearing on the question that concerns us here. (2) In some of the experiments cited by the Presidential Commission, control groups were completely absent. (3) Much of the research was premised on acceptance of a "cathartic model" which was rejected *even at that time* by researchers working on the effects of violence in other (non-sexual) media. (4) Comments made by researchers betray strong sexist assumptions about the roles of women and men in sexual relations. These assumptions appear to color their interpretation of the data. (5) In longitudinal studies purporting to show that sexual crime decreases as pornography increases, authors failed to note that in Denmark (their favorite example), certain activities were decriminalized during the same period that pornography increased, thus artificially deflating sex crime figures. Furthermore, no distinction was made between crimes of violence such as rape and non-violent crimes such as "peeping Tom" offenses, and the authors failed to report that rape was *not* one of the crimes that decreased.

23. New tests have been designed more recently which seek to circumvent these criticisms. Notable among these are studies by Neil Malamuth and others by Edward Donnerstein. When care was taken to design the experiments in such a way as not to import some of the questionable assumptions characteristic of the old studies, the results were quite different from those cited by the Presidential Commission.

24. Both Malamuth[1] and Donnerstein[2] found (independently of one another) that exposure to violent pornography increased the levels of electric shock male subjects chose to deliver to a female confederate of the experimenter.

25. Malamuth and others report[3] that male subjects' self-reported likelihood of raping a woman was highly correlated with both their belief that women in the pornographic material presented to them had enjoyed being attacked and with their notion that women generally derive pleasure from being raped. Rape myths, of course, dominate the pornographic literature and reinforce these beliefs.

26. Malamuth found[4] that repeatedly exposing male subjects to violent pornography resulted in self-generated rape fantasies. It was also discovered[5] that male subjects who were first exposed to the type of rape portrayal typically found in pornography perceived less victim trauma upon hearing a more realistic rape depiction.

27. Some of this work is open to two sorts of objection. First, the data were obtained under conditions vulnerable to criticism in terms of "demand characteristics" and laboratory artificiality. Second, the undesirable effects were observed

only immediately after the exposure to violent pornography, leaving open the possibility that these effects might be limited in duration to a few minutes or hours.

28. To counter such criticisms, Malamuth and Check designed a field experiment in which subjects were assessed several days after viewing two movies without being made aware that there was any relationship between the survey of sexual attitudes and the viewing of the films. "The results indicated that exposure to films portraying violent sexuality increased male subjects' acceptance of interpersonal violence against women."[6]

29. My point in citing this literature is as follows: To indicate that it is intellectually dishonest for some proponents of pornography to continue citing the Presidential Commission report without acknowledging and coming to grips with the criticisms to which it has been subjected;

To suggest that there is a growing body of evidence pointing to the conclusion that consumption of pornography *does* increase aggression toward women;

To point out that *if* this is so, then we can no longer treat pornography as a purely self-regarding act.

If pornography does increase aggression toward women, then it is other-regarding, and the state has at least a *prima facie* right to intervene against it. This is a possibility which left-leaning intellectuals, particularly, must consider more seriously than they have in the past.

30. It might be objected here that because pornography is *literature*, of a sort, consumption of pornography differs from other behaviors because it receives special protection under the rubric "freedom of speech." But all the evidence suggests that we make exceptions to freedom of speech on exactly the same grounds that we allow the state to intervene in other behaviors. The state intervenes when failure to do so will cause the rights of innocent individuals to be violated. The standard litany is familiar to us all: We don't allow people to yell "Fire!" in a crowded theatre. We prohibit libel and slander. We forbid misleading advertising. We ban hate literature. We disallow publication of certain information if it will prejudice the outcome of a trial . . . And so on.

31. In all these cases the underlying principle seems to be the same: Failure to limit freedom of speech would allow innocent persons to suffer violations of their rights, and the general societal welfare would be damaged. Placing limits on the freedom of speech in these cases does not destroy the marketplace of ideas, but enhances and protects it.

32. The liberal tradition is for the most part a fine and honorable one. The best way to serve it in this case is to bear in mind the twin liberal ideals of equality and non-interference and to consider carefully which course of action will best serve those ideals. We have seen today that there is considerable evidence that blind loyalty to non-interference in the propagation of pornography may undermine the equality of women with men by exposing them to increased aggression. If this is so, we must give serious consideration to banning certain sorts of pornography. To concentrate exclusively on the rights of males to consume pornog-

raphy to the detriment of the right of women to walk with dignity and safety in their own communities is to betray and dishonor all that is good in the liberal tradition.

Notes

[1]N. M. Malamuth, "Erotica, Aggression, and Perceived Appropriateness." Paper presented at the Annual Convention of the American Psychological Association, 1978, Toronto.

[2]E. Donnerstein, "Aggressive-Erotica and Violence Against Women," *Journal of Personality and Social Psychology* 39 (1980): 269–277.

[3]See the following: N. Malamuth, S. Haber, and S. Feshbach, "Testing Hypotheses Regarding Rape: Exposure to Sexual Violence, Sex Differences, and the 'Normality' of Reports," *Journal of Research in Personality* 14 (1980): 121–137; N. M. Malamuth and J. V. P. Check, "Penile Tumescence and Perceptual Response to Rape as a Function of Victim's Perceived Reactions," *Journal of Applied Social Psychology* 10 (1980): 528–547; N. M. Malamuth, I. Reisin, and B. Spinner, "Exposure to Pornography and Reactions to Rape." Paper presented at the Annual Convention of the American Psychological Association, 1972, New York.

[4]N. M. Malamuth, "Rape Fantasies as a Function of Exposure to Violent Sexual Stimuli," *Archives of Sexual Behavior* 10 (1981): 33–47.

[5]Malamuth and Check, "Penile Tumescence."

[6]N. M. Malamuth and J. V. P. Check, "The Effects of Mass Media Exposure on Acceptance of Violence against Women. A Field Experiment," *Journal of Research in Personality* 15 (1981): 436–446.

6: Forbidden Knowledge
by
Stephen Stich

I

1. Much of the opposition to recombinant DNA research has focused on the potential hazards posed by the research process. Mayor Vellucci of Cambridge, Massachusetts, has conjured the image of "monsters" and "Frankensteins" that

Originally published in R. P. Bareikis, ed. *Science and the Public Interest: Recombinant DNA Research*, Indiana University Foundation, 1978. Reprinted by permission.

"may come crawling out of the laboratories into the sewers."[1] More responsible voices have raised troubling questions about the potential hazards posed by recombinant DNA research activities and the proper way to contain these hazards. But while safety has been the strident theme of the debate, there has been a persistent second theme, less sensational though ultimately perhaps more important. The issue raised by the second theme is not whether recombinant DNA research can be pursued safely, but whether it should be pursued at all. Those who raise the question are concerned that the knowledge to which recombinant DNA research could lead is knowledge that mankind simply should not acquire. The view that these critics would have us consider is that the knowledge of how to manipulate the genome of microorganisms and ultimately perhaps of people is knowledge that we ought not to uncover.

2. There is something radical, startling about this proposal. It conjures images of less enlightened times when ignorant, superstitious, fearful men held one or another domain of knowledge to be taboo. To embrace this doctrine of forbidden knowledge is to reject a fundamental part of our enlightened and hard-won moral views about knowledge and to return to the benighted moral standards of an earlier time. Or so it would appear. In any event, so it once appeared to me. But recently, and with considerable reluctance, I have come to believe that my former views were mistaken. I now think that there is knowledge which mankind ought not to acquire. What is more, I think that this conclusion, far from requiring the rejection of our enlightened moral views about knowledge, actually follows from those enlightened views. If we must now seriously consider imposing limits on what we allow ourselves to know, it is not because our moral principles have changed but rather because there has been a fundamental change in the sort of knowledge we have begun to uncover. In the pages that follow I will recount the reasoning that led me to these unwelcome conclusions. As a beginning I will sketch what I take to be enlightened moral views about knowledge.

II

3. The first of these is that knowledge is itself of intrinsic value. To know about the world and to understand its workings is one of the components of the good life. Other things being equal, the life of a knowledgeable person is better than the life of an ignorant person. This is not, of course, to say that knowledge is the only intrinsic good, but only that it is one of the things that makes a life worthwhile. Here a caveat may be needed. For it might be argued that not *all* knowledge is intrinsically valuable. Perhaps, for example, knowledge of the private peccadillos of my casual acquaintances is knowledge I am better off without. The point is well taken, but I will not pursue it here. Our present interest is scientific knowledge, knowledge about nature's laws and mechanisms. And on the enlightened view such knowledge is an intrinsic good.

4. In addition to being intrinsically valuable, scientific knowledge can also have considerable instrumental value, since the possession of knowledge may

allow us to achieve other ends which are also fundamental to a good life. Medical and agricultural knowledge are two obvious examples here. Each can, and does, lead to the alleviation of pain and an increase in physical well-being. In an entirely parallel way, some knowledge may be instrumentally harmful to its possessor. The knowledge of drugs and dosages which enables a temporarily despondent person to take his own life is perhaps an example.

5. Obviously knowledge can be used to help or harm not only its possessor but others as well. There are ways in which knowledge ought to be used and ways in which it ought not to be used. And as is the case with many other powerful tools, it is sometimes exceptionally difficult to decide whether a specific use ought or ought not to be undertaken.

6. So far I have been speaking of the value of knowledge for individuals and the obligations individuals have to use knowledge or refrain from using it. But each tenet of this "enlightened view" has a correlate for societies. The possession and dissemination of knowledge throughout a society is one of the features that makes it a good society. Knowledge may be instrumentally valuable or instrumentally harmful for a society. And there are some uses that a society ought to make of knowledge and other uses that it ought not to make.

7. Let us turn finally to the matter of forbidden knowledge. Of course, there may be certain *ways* of acquiring knowledge that we ought not employ because they are dangerous, or would infringe on the rights of others, or what have you. But this is quite a separate issue. The question we are asking is whether there is knowledge that we should not acquire by any means, no matter how safe and morally unproblematic the means may be. At first blush, it might seem that the enlightened view entails an unqualified negative answer. For, after all, possession of knowledge is an intrinsic good, and it may be an instrumental good as well. Surely there can be no reason why we ought not to acquire what is good. This conclusion can be strengthened by another strand often woven together with the enlightened view. This is the doctrine that freedom of inquiry is one of the marks of a good society, and that this freedom ought not to be restricted unless there are compelling reasons to do so.

8. Yet despite these considerations, I think it is clear that the enlightened view does allow that there is some knowledge we ought not to acquire. For the enlightened view recognizes that there is some knowledge which is instrumentally harmful for a person or a society to have. And so it is entirely possible that there may be some cases in which the instrumental harmfulness of the knowledge massively outweighs its intrinsic value. If there are such cases then the knowledge in question is knowledge we ought not to have. Moreover, in some of these cases the instrumental harmfulness of the knowledge may be so enormous as to count as a compelling reason for limiting the freedom of inquiry.

9. In an illuminating essay aimed at limiting the boundaries of the freedom of inquiry, Carl Cohen[2] considers one category of case in which the instrumental harmfulness of possessing knowledge would justify a restriction on research. These are the cases "where there is a *high* probability that the knowledge developed will be used with very injurious consequences." In Cohen's view, when the probability of very injurious consequences is moderate or low, there is no

justification for a restriction on research. But as I see the matter, Cohen has failed to focus on the fundamental point. It is not the probability of misuse alone which determines the magnitude of the instrumental harmfulness of knowledge. Rather, instrumental harmfulness is the *product* of the probability of misuse and the possible damage. Thus there may be some cases of knowledge which are overwhelmingly instrumentally harmful even though the probability of misuse is rather low.

10. While the possibility of such cases seems plainly compatible with the enlightened view, it is easy to see why it was often overlooked. Until Hiroshima and Nagasaki were reduced to rubble in a matter of seconds there was no serious candidate for membership in the category of knowledge which is so terribly instrumentally harmful that we should not have acquired it even if the probability of its misuse is relatively small. But the construction of the first atomic bombs marked a radical turning point in the history of science. For the first time science had given us knowledge which if misused might lead to the annihilation of civilization or even the extermination of all human life. With instrumental harmfulness of *that* magnitude, even a relatively small probability of misuse is enough to justify the conclusion that the knowledge which makes these terrors possible ought never to have been acquired.

11. The point was driven home to me recently when I asked a large undergraduate class at the University of Michigan what their subjective probability was that they themselves would die in an all-out nuclear war. My first proposal was 1 in 20 or higher; a scattering of students raised their hands. I lowered the proposal in steps to one in a thousand or higher, and by that point almost all the students had raised their hands. Is there anyone who would reckon the good, both intrinsic and instrumental, of the knowledge that makes nuclear weapons possible high enough to offset one chance in a thousand of all-out nuclear war?

12. I began with the claim that the enlightened view is compatible with there being knowledge we ought not to acquire. This is all I shall say by way of defending that claim. Our next job is to ask whether the knowledge likely to result from recombinant DNA research falls into the category of knowledge we ought not to have. But before turning to that question, let me comment briefly on the implications of our recent reflections. If there is knowledge which is so dangerous that it ought not to be uncovered, then we must think seriously about how we are to protect ourselves from it. It is a problem with no precedent. Our social institutions are not designed to limit inquiry; still less are they prepared to decide what inquiry to forbid and what to allow. It needs little imagination to see that in trying to institute social mechanisms for limiting inquiry, we run a genuine risk of crippling science. More ominous still are the potential dangers of the institutions that would be required to suppress or exterminate a body of knowledge once it has been discovered. There are no easy answers. But the problems must be faced while there is still time. If there is still time.

III

13. Now what shall we say of recombinant DNA research? Is it likely to lead to knowledge we ought not to acquire, and should it therefore be stopped?

The answers I would urge, though tentative, are both negative. There is no reason to think that recombinant DNA research will lead to knowledge we ought not to acquire; and if it is to be stopped, this should not be the reason. Recall that to show a body of knowledge ought not to be acquired requires showing that the instrumental harmfulness of the knowledge is so enormous that it outweighs both the intrinsic value and the instrumental value of the knowledge, and that the imbalance is so great that it outweighs the consideration due to the principle of free inquiry. I know of no convincing argument that the instrumental harmfulness of the knowledge resulting from recombinant DNA research is of this magnitude.

14. Here it might be protested that there *are* potentially disastrous uses of the knowledge that recombinant DNA research might produce. And indeed there are. Any science fiction buff can conjure a variety of grim scenarios each invoking the possible products of recombinant DNA research. Moreover, each of these scenarios is at least logically possible; we can have no *a priori* guarantee that one or another of them will not come to pass. But it is important to see that the mere logical possibility of such scenarios is not sufficient to establish that the knowledge at issue ought not to be acquired. In fact, if the mere logical possibility of disaster were sufficient to yield this conclusion, we would quickly reach the absurd conclusion that many types of research, including recombinant DNA research both *ought* and *ought not* to be pursued. For just as it is logically possible that pursuing recombinant DNA research will lead to an unthinkable catastrophe, so it is logically possible that failing to pursue recombinant DNA research will lead to an unthinkable catastrophe. It is, after all, at least logically possible that some natural event or some human activity unconnected with genetic research might bring about circumstances in which the capacity to alter plant or animal genomes quickly would be the only way to avoid disaster. One example of such a scenario might begin with a relatively swift change in world climate which drastically reduces the yield of most currently existing strains of agricultural plants.[3]

15. What is required in arguing that we ought not to acquire some knowledge is not merely a logical possibility of disastrous misuse, but a sufficiently high probability that the misuse will actually occur. And, of course, the lower the probability, the worse the consequences must be. This way of putting the matter is a bit misleading, for it suggests that it is possible to obtain objective estimates for the probabilities in question.[3] However, in many cases the best we can hope for is a reasonable subjective probability, and even that will often be hard to come by. Still, I am inclined to think that there is a clear distinction between the recombinant DNA case and the nuclear weapons case. Few of the imaginary scenarios involving recombinant DNA research are quite so terrible as the very real prospect of all-out nuclear war. And no thoughtful person would assess the probability of these DNA scenarios to be comparable with the likelihood of nuclear annihilation. So I am inclined to conclude that on the basis of currently available evidence the knowledge to be gained from recombinant DNA research is not knowledge we ought not to have.

16. Other observers have reached the opposite conclusion, and we would do well to ponder the reasons for the disagreement. As best I can tell, the reasons fall into two categories. First, there are those who disagree about the likelihood of the knowledge we might gain being disastrously misused. Here a distinction is needed. One way in which the knowledge might lead to catastrophe is through inadvertence. Some entirely laudatory plan for using the knowledge might misfire or have unanticipated terrible side effects. These are important concerns and they are not to be lightly dismissed. But the conclusion I would draw from them is that we should be very careful indeed in monitoring and regulating proposed applications of the knowledge we gain, rather than taking the draconian step of not permitting the knowledge to be discovered. Another way in which the knowledge might lead to disaster is by intentional misuse. Those who think this is likely often talk of a "technological imperative"—a force that compels us, sooner or later, to actualize any technological possibility simply because it can be done. I see no reason to take this talk of a technological imperative at all seriously. History does not support the contention that every morally repugnant use of technology will sooner or later be tried. Still less does it lead us to believe that every morally repugnant use of technology is bound to become widespread.

17. The second category of reasons for concluding that we ought not to have the knowledge recombinant DNA research may provide focuses on the question of the instrumental value of this knowledge. If knowledge is to be forbidden its potential harmfulness must outweigh its instrumental value, its intrinsic value and the value to be accorded the principle of free inquiry. When the instrumental value is potentially very great, the case for forbidding the knowledge is difficult to defend. Now this is just the way many people perceive the recombinant DNA issue. The potential medical, agricultural, and industrial value of the knowledge we may gain is enormous. Others, however, take a very different view of the value of these potential applications. On their view, we have reached a point of sharply declining marginal utility for industrial, agricultural and even medical advances. A new crop or a new cure, they argue, does little to enhance the overall quality of life. Our agricultural capacity is already sufficient, and would be vastly more than sufficient if we were to eliminate some of the more outrageous wastefulness in our diets. We have already controlled or eliminated many of the diseases that once scourged mankind. It is of little value to extend the average life span. Rather than adding to our years we should add to the quality of the years we have. Sufficient increases in human well-being will come through distributing the world's resources more fairly, and not through the application of yet another sophisticated technology. There is a great deal that needs to be said on this view. But to say it would require another paper, and a much longer one. For the present it will have to suffice simply to raise the issue.

Notes

[1]See, for example, the account in June Goodfield, *Playing God* (Random House, 1977), p. 186.

²"When May Research Be Stopped?," in D. A. Jackson and S. P. Stich, eds., *The Recombinant DNA Debate* (University of California Press).

³For more on this topic, cf. my "The Recombinant DNA Debate: Some Philosophical Considerations," in *The Recombinant DNA Debate*.

7: Handgun Bans: Facts to Fight With
by
Donald Kates, Jr.

1. The handgun debate has produced a plethora of emotional rhetoric on both sides of the issue, but very little hard research. On one side are the emotional bumper-sticker slogans full of patriotic posturing. On the other are equally emotional and sensationalized horror stories of innocent citizens killed by handguns, supplemented by supposedly neutral but, in fact, "result-oriented" social science research that is either misleading or downright inaccurate.

2. Gun owners nod enthusiastically at "Guns Don't Kill People, People Do" and "When Guns are Outlawed, Only Outlaws Will Have Guns," but such cliches are virtually useless in intelligent debate with someone who is not committedly pro-gun. Guns do kill people, just as knives and hand grenades do. If they didn't kill or injure or at least present that threat, they would be useless as instruments of self-defense. And even if "Only Outlaws Will Have Guns" if guns are outlawed, anti-gun forces have made it clear that they are willing to tolerate firearms possession by hardened criminals if a handgun ban would result in disarming the self-protection owner whom they believe responsible for murder.

3. If this characterization of murderers were accurate, banning handguns would seem an appealingly simple means of reducing domestic and acquaintance homicide. Most killings are not, however, perpetrated by the average noncriminal citizen whose law-obedient mentality (it is believed) would induce him to give up handguns in response to a ban. Refuting "the myth that the typical homicide offender is just an ordinary person" with "no previous criminal record," Professor Gary Kleck of Florida State University's School of Criminology notes FBI figures showing two-thirds of all murderers to have previous felony conviction records.

4. Moreover, a murderer's prior arrest record is likely to substantially underrepresent the real prior violence history. Unlike robbers, who generally strike at

---

Reprinted by permission from *1984 Guns and Ammo Annual*, 1984.

strangers, murderers' prior violence may have been directed against relatives or acquaintances, that is, the same kinds of people murderers end up killing. Such prior violent incidents may have never led to arrest or conviction, either because the victim did not press charges or because the police refuse to interfere in "a family affair." A study in Kansas City revealed that in 85 percent of domestic homicide cases, the police have had to be summoned to the home at least once before the killing occurred, and in 50 percent of the cases, the police had stopped beatings five or more times before the actual murder. In short, these people are criminals no less hardened than the professional robbers whom everyone agrees a handgun ban won't disarm. Unlike the average citizen, the typical murderer will not scruple to keep his gun in spite of a ban.

5. Unfortunately, the quality of most research associated with handgun control has been on a par with the sort found in UFO magazines. Another example is the tired old line about gun controls working in Europe and Japan. The gun bans of the European countries commonly compared to the U.S. were not enacted to reduce general violence (with which those countries have been little affected), but were enacted to prevent the assassinations and political terrorism from which England, Germany, and so forth, still suffer far more than we.

6. In fact, prohibitionists abruptly stopped referring to England in 1971 with the appearance from Cambridge University of the first in-depth study of that country's handgun permit law. This Cambridge study attributes England's comparatively low violence wholly to cultural factors, pointing out that until 1920 England had far fewer gun controls than most American states. Yet England had far less violence at that time than did those states or than England now has. Those who blame greater handgun availability for our greater rates of handgun homicide ignore the fact that rates of murder with knives or without any weapon (i.e., with hands and feet) are also far lower in England. The study's author rhetorically asks whether it is claimed that knives are less available in England than in the U.S. or that the English have fewer hands and feet than Americans. As a subsequent British government publication puts it, although "one reason often given for American homicide is the easy availability of firearms . . . the strong correlation with racial and linked socio-economic variables suggests that the underlying determinants of the homicide rate relate to particular cultural factors."

7. European comparisons would be incomplete without mention of Switzerland, where violence rates are very low though every man of military age is required to own a handgun or fully automatic rifle. Israeli violence is similarly low, though the populace is even more intensively armed. A comparison with handgun-banning Japan's low homicide rate is plainly inappropriate because of our vastly different culture and heritage and our substantial ethnic heterogeneity. (The only valid comparison reinforces the irrelevancy of gun bans: It is that Japanese–Americans, with full access to handguns, have a slightly lower homicide rate than their gunless counterparts in Japan.) An appropriate comparison to Japan would be Taiwan. Despite even more stringent anti-handgun laws, it has a homicide rate greater than ours and four times greater than Japan's. Similarly

the U.S. might well be compared to South Africa, a highly industrialized and ethnically heterogeneous country. Despite one of the world's most stringent "gun control" programs, South Africa's homicide rate, factoring out politically associated killings, is twice ours.

8. The moral of the story is that nothing about the correlation between levels of handgun ownership and violent crimes could lead one to conclude there is a cause and effect relationship. But it is simply taken for granted by many that there is a relationship, and they cite only those countries that have lower crime rates than America to "prove" it.

9. Writers on both sides of the barricade have too often started with conclusions and worked to justify them. For that reason, much of the best research has come not from conservative sources that have traditionally supported the right to own handguns, but from those who have converted to a position favorable to handgun ownership and feel a need to explain their aberrant positions.

10. In order to understand the preponderance of misinformation in the handgun ownership debate, it is necessary to trace some of the ideas that the anti-gun movement has used to justify its position. In my book *Firearms and Violence: Issues of Public Policy* (San Francisco: Pacific Institute for Public Policy Research, 1984), Gary Kleck of the Florida State University School of Criminology and David Bordua of the University of Illinois, Urbana, Department of Sociology have identified what they call "the key assumptions of gun control." The first we will consider for this article is:

People who buy guns for self-defense are the victims of self-deception and a mistaken belief in the protective efficacy of gun ownership. In fact, guns are useless for self-defense or protection of a home or business.

11. Fundamental to systematic discussion of these issues is the distinction between the self-defense value that gun ownership may have and its crime deterrence value. Anti-gun lobbyists are unassailably correct in asserting that a gun owner rarely has the opportunity to defend a home or business against burglars who generally take pains to strike only at unoccupied premises. But this fails to address two important issues of deterrence. Kleck and Bordua calculate that a burglar's small chance of being confronted by a gun-armed defender probably exceeds that of his being apprehended, tried, convicted and actually serving any time. Which, they ask, is a greater deterrent: a slim chance of being punished or a slim chance of being shot?

12. Even more important, fear of meeting a gun-armed defender may be one factor in the care most burglars take to strike at only unoccupied premises. In this connection, remember that it is precisely because burglary is generally a non-confrontation crime that victim injury or death is so very rarely associated with it—in contrast to robbery, where victim death is an all too frequent occurrence. If the deterrent effect of victim gun possession helps to make burglary an overwhelmingly nonconfrontational crime, thereby minimizing victim death or injury, that effect benefits burglary victims generally, even if the gun owners gain no particular self-defense value thereby.

13. The most recent evidence of the deterrent value of gun ownership appears in a survey taken in 10 major prisons across the United States by the Social

and Demographic Research Institute of the University of Massachusetts. It confirms earlier prison surveys in which inmates stated that (1) they and other criminals tried to avoid victims they believed may have been armed and that (2) they favor gun prohibition because, by disarming the victim, it will make their lives safer without affecting their access to illegal guns.

14. Increasingly, police are concluding and even publicly proclaiming that they cannot protect the law-abiding citizens and that it is not only rational to choose to protect oneself with firearms but societally beneficial because it deters violent crimes. Because of the lack of coherent evidence on the subject until the late 1970's, such views necessarily were only intuitively or anecdotally based. They were controverted by the citation of isolated, artificially truncated statistics supposedly showing that citizens rarely are able to kill criminals in self-defense. In fact, civilians justifiably kill about as many violent criminals across the nation as do the police. In California and Miami, private citizens kill twice as many criminals; in Chicago and Cleveland, three times as many.

15. Even when accurately reported, such statistics are unfair in that they underrepresent the full self-defense value of guns; as with the police, the measure of the success of armed citizens lies not in the number of criminals they kill, but in the total number whom they defeat by wounding, driving off, or arresting. In his paper for *Firearms and Violence,* Professor Wright concludes that incidents of people defending themselves with handguns are even more numerous than incidents of handgun misuse by criminals against citizens. In other words, while there are all too many crimes committed with handguns, there are even more crimes being foiled by law-abiding gun owners.

16. In his extensive study of Atlanta data, Philip Cook concluded that a robber's chance of dying in any one year in that city is doubled by committing only seven robberies because of the risk of counterattack by a potential victim. In addition to illustrating the self-defense value of handgun ownership, that is a pretty good indication of the kind of deterrent effect caused by gun ownership. Cook's work also shows that areas with the strongest anti-gun laws have the highest rates of crime. That in itself does not prove anything except the spurious nature of the data distributed by anti-gun forces that purports to prove the opposite. Since high crime rates often lead governments to seek solutions in gun bans, the correlation between gun control and high crime rates does not necessarily prove that bans cause violence. But more meaningful correlations can be found when examining the opposite case, where the public has actually increased the level of gun ownership.

17. The Orlando Police Department, when plagued with a sharply rising number of rapes in the city, undertook a firearms training program for women between October 1966 and March 1967. Kleck and Bordua studied the effects of the program and found that the rape rate in Orlando fell by almost 90 percent from a level of 35.91 per 100,000 inhabitants in 1966 to 4.18 in 1967. The surrounding areas and Florida in general experienced either constant or increasing rape rates during the same period, as did the United States in general. Another benefit from the program seems to have been the corresponding decrease in Orlando burglaries. Though the rape-protection program was well-publicized, the

anti-burglary aspect of gun ownership and training was not emphasized in the press. Burglars apparently made a connection between women's willingness and capability to defend their bodies and the increased risk of taking their property.

18. Similar programs have resulted in decreasing store robberies by as much as 90 percent in Highland Park and Detroit, Michigan, and New Orleans. Perhaps the most publicized is that of Kennesaw, Georgia, where the city council passed a kind of reverse gun control act requiring citizens to keep guns in their homes. In the ten months that followed, there was an 89 percent decrease in burglary.

19. These programs have been criticized on the theory that the crime rate has not been lowered but simply shifted to other areas. This does not appear to have been the case in Orlando. There rape fell by nine percent in the surrounding communities even as it fell by 90 percent in Orlando in the first year after the handgun training program was publicized. Also, criticisms that gun ownership is causing crime to shift to non-gun-owning areas are based on the perverse idea that defending oneself from rape or burglary is really an offense against others who do not.

20. It is not likely that women who are willing and able to protect themselves from rapists would have much sympathy with that view, even if it were true. To take the argument to its logical conclusion, one would have to admit that anybody who does anything to discourage crime (locking doors, calling for help, summoning the police, or staying indoors and out of alleys at night) is endangering the others who will not.

21. The evidence does show gun ownership acts as a deterrent to criminal activity for those who own them and those who do not. Opponents of handgun ownership get around that by saying:
Handguns are more dangerous to their owners and the family and friends of the owners than they are to criminals. Handguns kill more people through accident and criminal assault than they save.

22. Once again, there have been several widely quoted studies supporting this view that have become part of the conscious and subconscious rationale for banning handguns. One study, by Rushforth, purported to show that six times as many Cleveland householders died in gun accidents as killed burglars. It was discredited by Professor James Wright of the University of Massachusetts at Amherst in his paper for the 1981 annual meeting of the American Society of Criminology. Research done with San Francisco City Supervisor Carol Ruth Silver has indicated that between 1960 and 1975 the number of instances where handguns were used for defense exceeded the cases where they were misused to kill by a ratio of 15 to 1.

23. According to a monitoring of 42 of the nation's largest newspapers between June 1975 and July 1976, 68 percent of the time that police used firearms, they successfully prevented a crime or caught the criminal. On the other hand, the success rate for private citizens was 83 percent. This is not particularly surprising since the police must usually be summoned to the scene of criminal activity while the private gun owner is more likely to be there when it occurs. At the same time, Kleck and Bordua conclude that citizens who resist crimes with

weapons are much less likely to be injured than those who attempt to resist without weapons.

24. Anti-gun forces cover themselves in the question of self-defense by asserting that the absence of handguns will lead criminals to use other less dangerous weapons, lowering the death and injury rate in confrontations with criminals. The heart of the argument, as stated by Kleck and Bordua, is:
Guns are five times deadlier than the weapons most likely to be substituted for them in assaults where firearms are not available.

25. To begin with, the above statement does not differentiate between different types of guns. Most anti-gun measures are aimed at handguns because banning all guns is politically unlikely. Furthermore, the statement is based on the assumption that the second choice for a criminal who is denied a handgun would be a knife. In fact, a Massachusetts University survey of 10 major prisons indicates that in the majority of cases, a criminal denied access to a handgun will turn to a sawed-off shotgun or long rifle. Approximately 50 percent of all criminals and 75 percent of those with a history of handgun use said they would use a sawed-off shotgun or rifle. While handguns are slightly more deadly than knives, shotguns and rifles are three to eight times as deadly as handguns. If handguns disappeared but only 19 percent of criminals turned to long guns, the same amount of fatalities could be expected to occur. If 50 percent used shotguns or rifles, there would actually be an increase in assault-related deaths by as much as 300 percent.

26. Another danger associated with the upgrading of firearms due to a handgun ban is the increased risk of accidental wounds and fatalities due to the longer range of shotguns and rifles. This would be the likely consequence of a measure banning handguns but allowing the ownership of long guns for self-defense. A shot from a handgun that misses its target will usually come to rest in a wall much sooner than a shotgun or rifle blast, which is much more likely to continue on to impact whatever is on the other side of the wall. The danger of accidental death increases enormously when long guns replace handguns as the arm kept for home defense. Even now, long guns are involved in 90 percent of all accidental firearms deaths, though they probably represent less than 10 percent of the guns kept loaded at any one time.

27. So we see, handgun ownership is more than a civil liberty, it is valuable for society as a whole. Given the obvious nature of the analyses, it is surprising that the anti-gun forces in this country have succeeded to the degree they have.

28. Recent court decisions have made it clear that the government has no responsibility to protect the citizenry. In an important case, *Warren vs. District of Columbia*, three women brought suit against the local government because of lack of police action. Two men broke into their home and found one of the women. The other two were upstairs and called the police twice over a period of half an hour. After the woman downstairs had been beaten, raped and sodomized into silence, her roommates believed that the police had arrived. They went downstairs and "for the next 14 hours the women were held captive, raped, robbed, beaten, forced to commit sexual acts upon each other, and made to submit to the sexual demands of (their attackers)." The three women lost their suit

and an appeal because, as the courts universally hold, "a government and its agents are under no general duty to provide public services, such as police protection to any particular citizen."

29. This incident and many others like it took place in the city with the most stringent anti-gun law in the country. The D.C. law required handgun owners to register their guns and then disallowed the ownership of any new arms. Furthermore, the law made it illegal to keep a firearm assembled or loaded in the home for self-defense. There is a real ideological question as to whether a government can disclaim responsibility to protect its citizens and take away their means to protect themselves. Pragmatically though, one must admit that the government is basically unable to protect every citizen at all times, regardless of the legal position.

30. What good are handguns? The evidence has led many to believe that they are the largest single deterrent against crime. A recent study conducted by the Boston Police Department showed that the majority of high-ranking police administrators and police chiefs across the nation actually favor allowing law-abiding citizens to carry guns for self-protection. What can be done about the well-intentioned but misinformed foes of the handgun? Perhaps the most important thing would be the self-education of those who already defend that right. Only with intelligent, informed argument can the gun banners be convinced of the foolishness of their position. It is too easy to blame the media for bias or lack of information. Those who hold a position also have a responsibility to be informed and put those arguments forward. I hope that this article will help to do that.

8: Yellow Rain? An Expert Says the Charges Don't Hold Water
by
Saul Hormats

1. Considerable evidence has been put forward to support the Reagan administration's assertion that the Soviet Union violated arms control agreements in using chemical weapons such as "yellow rain" in Southeast Asia and Afghanistan. The evidence has been sufficient to persuade the U.S. Senate, which last

Reprinted by permission from *Washington Post National Weekly Edition*, March 12, 1984. (Until his retirement from Edgewood Arsenal in 1973, Saul Hormats directed development of chemical warfare munitions for the U.S. Army.)

month passed a resolution condemning the Soviets for their conduct, with not a single dissenting vote.

2. Thus far, the debate over yellow rain has focused less on whether the Soviets are using chemical weapons than on how they are doing it. Unfortunately, most of the testimony in the controversy has come from diplomats, politicians, analytical chemists and scientists with academic backgrounds. Almost completely lacking has been an assessment based on a military appreciation of chemical warfare agents, the munitions used to deliver such agents, and the logistics involved.

3. Such a military assessment raises grave questions about whether the Soviets have, in fact, engaged in the chemical warfare activities with which they have been charged.

4. In its report to Congress, the administration declared flatly that the Soviets had broken international agreements. It charged Moscow with "repeated violations" of the 1925 Geneva Protocol and of the 1972 Biological and Toxin Weapons Convention.

5. Chemical weapons were reported to have been used against the anti-Soviet guerillas in Afghanistan, but primarily against Hmong villages in Laos. The chemical warfare agent is said to be a mold fusarium (popularly called "yellow rain"), found naturally in infected crops and poorly stored grain.

6. The evidence supporting these allegations consists of a large number of interviews by State Department officials with Hmong refugees and "solid evidence" in the form of blood samples, twigs and leaves, rock scrapings and a contaminated Soviet gas mask purchased in Kabul, Afghanistan.

7. But the evidence seems less than solid to one who has worked in the chemical weapons field for 37 years.

8. To begin with, why would the Soviets or their allies have chosen chemical attack? Hmong villages are very small; 15 to 20 houses cover the equivalent of a city block. There are many conventional munitions (such as the antipersonnel shells used in Vietnam and Beirut) easily capable of destroying all the villagers. White phosphorus shells of the kind used in Beirut would destroy not only the villagers but the village itself. The Soviets must certainly have large quantities of these in their arsenal. Why, then, would they risk world condemnation by using chemical weapons?

9. Let us assume that the Soviets wanted to escape responsibility for attacking a village. They might then use a weapon that would not leave evidence of its use. This would rule out nerve agents and similar devices that have unmistakable effects. As a result, they might choose a device whose effect could be construed as resulting from naturally occurring food poisoning. Yellow rain would be one choice—but not a very probable one. Whether evading responsibility was the attacker's intent—or whether the intent was overt terror—there are cheaper and more effective techniques at hand.

10. There are many substances, well-known and available to weapons designers, that fill this bill. For example, an aerosol container the size of the smallest found on a supermarket shelf, slightly strengthened and modified and containing a solution of botulinal toxin type A, would kill everyone in a village if the poison

were released in or near it. Deaths would appear to have been caused by botulism food poisoning. The weight of such a munition might be less than half a pound.

11. Should the Soviets wish to incapacitate rather than kill Hmong villagers, an effective agent might well be staphylococcal entero-toxin. A munition quite similar in size and appearance to a paint spray can could cause a number of villagers to become extremely ill for a day or two, presumably from common "staph" food poisoning. Three or four of these devices would likely affect most of the villagers.

12. The above are chemical agents. Should the Soviets decide to engage in biological warfare, the agent might well be the micro-organism Coxiella burnetti, which causes Q-fever and is found in most parts of the world. The agent is easy to produce. Chills, fever, fatigue and weight loss can last for a month or longer and would be attributed to inadequate pasteurization of milk or milk products. Domesticated livestock and poultry would also be infected. The munition to do all this might weigh as little as two ounces.

13. Compared to these agents, yellow rain presents tremendous logistical problems.

14. Yellow rain itself has been reported by the State Department to contain only very small percentages of the supposed toxic ingredient, called T-2. Since one part yellow rain is reported to contain only one ten-thousandth part or less of T-2, and T-2 is only one fiftieth as toxic as our present lethal chemical agents, it would take some 500,000 times as much fusarium mold to attack a given target as would be required if a standard lethal chemical agent were used.

15. At a minimum, about 3,000 tons of yellow rain would be required to attack a village. To place this quantity on the target would require 20,000 to 30,000 shells—some two hours of fire from a full Soviet artillery division—or a minimum of 8,000 tons of bombs dropped from the air.

16. It is true the Soviets believe in massive air attack and artillery fire, but would they adopt this tactic in a remote mountain village of 15 to 20 families? A six-gun 122mm howitzer battery of the kind attached to a Soviet infantry regiment, firing one salvo of conventional shells weighing in all about 1,000 pounds, would leave little of the village.

17. Since none of the State Department reports of yellow rain incidents gives any indication of such physical destruction, one might assume that the agent was delivered as a cloud from large transport or cargo planes. However, fusarium is a solid and not a gas or volatile liquid. To be effective, it would have to be dropped from an aircraft as very finely divided particles and then inhaled by the people in the village. But if the necessary 3,000 tons were dropped in this way over a village, very little of the light, fluffy material would reach the target. Most of it would be carried away by the wind.

18. Evidence of chemical or biological attack is unmistakable to an experienced observer. The descriptions provided by State Department interrogators give no patterns whatsoever fitting any known type of chemical or biological attack.

19. Initially, the department's allegations dealt with clouds of a yellow gran-

ular substance delivered by shell or bombs. However, a careful examination of the incidents described in State Department publications indicates a wide variety of other agents and munitions.

20. For example, the Laotian village of Long Tienne was reported to have been attacked by aircraft dropping rectangular boxes releasing clouds of green and yellow gas. Victims were said to have suffered from dizziness, tension and dysentery.

21. A gas attack on Houi Xang was reported to have involved rockets emitting red and green clouds and tanks spraying large yellow drops, causing the people in the target area to suffer convulsions, vomiting and blisters on the upper torso.

22. Phu Nam was said to have been attacked with artillery and bombs emitting yellow smoke and dust. The victims suffered bleeding from their nostrils and mouths.

23. Pxu-Txoent was subjected to an attack in which small plastic bags broke in the air, releasing a wet yellow substance that caused coughing, vomiting and yellowing skin and eyes among those exposed to it.

24. These are but four of hundreds of reported incidents. Taking these all together, a very large number of different munitions would have to have been employed. Agents giving very different symptoms and effects are described. The colors of the toxins are not just yellow, but almost the entire spectrum. Delivery is by a variety of means, including plastic bags opened above the target, spray tanks, shells, bombs, grenades and rockets. The clouds of agents are composed of large granules, liquid drops, and very fine and, at times, invisible clouds.

25. Taking the State Department evidence at face value, several hundred combinations of agents and delivery systems seem to have been used. But it is unlikely that the Soviet Union has such a large number.

26. Judging by U.S. experience, it takes 10 years or longer to search for a new agent, research its toxicity and methods for dissemination and develop, test and produce it. Given the number of munitions and agents that the Soviets are said to have employed, they must have devoted several thousand years to the development and production of them! This seems more than a little improbable.

27. A very important part of a weapons development program is assuring reliability in combat. This involves extensive and prolonged tests to assure the ability of the munitions to withstand the rigors of storage, transport and delivery to the combat line.

28. These are long, time-consuming programs that cannot be significantly speeded up without seriously degrading the munitions' combat reliability. Even under the best conditions, there are always a certain number of malfunctions and duds. If the State Department allegations are accepted and the Soviet program had indeed been speeded up, it would be most surprising if their dud and malfunction rates were less than perhaps 5 to 10 percent.

29. Judging from the very large number of incidents that have been reported, there should be a very large number of duds and malfunctions that could serve

as indisputable proof of Soviet chemical weapon activities. Yet the best evidence put forward for the use of these weapons consists of moldy twigs, leaves and rock scrapings.

30. There are grave doubts, to say the least, about the validity of the allegations on which the administration's report and the Senate resolution rests. Certainly, individuals at the Defense Department and CIA also must have expressed their doubts. So it is difficult to understand why the secretary of defense and the director of the CIA persist in their positions, given the absence of acceptable evidence suggesting the Soviets have been or are engaged in chemical warfare.

31. The State Department's allegations appear to be based on imaginative responses to naive and gullible interrogators.

32. Our country would be better served if the Senate reconsidered its resolution condemning the Soviets and turned its attention to another question: Has Congress been misled, and if so, by whom?

APPENDIX II

Answers to Selected Exercises

Chapter 1: An Introduction to Arguments

Reasoning and Arguments

3. Not an argument: there is no conclusion. Without any information about the context in which these statements were made, we have no way of telling whether there is any implicit conclusion that the reader is supposed to draw from them.

6. An argument. The author is endorsing Russell's reasoning for the conclusion that even in a society which had eliminated destitution, laws would still be required. Russell's argument is being mentioned *and* used.

10. This is a borderline case. Strictly speaking it is not an argument but a statement, since the author is claiming that one of the causes of her opposition to the ERA is her awareness of the argument described. This claim is either true or false. It would be false, for example, if the author were lying or if she were deceived about her true motivations. But, presumably, the author also intends to endorse the argument mentioned in the passage. In that case, there is an argument here whose conclusion is "The ERA should not be adopted."

Getting to the Point: The Conclusion

4. The final conclusion is that congressmen are not interested in fighting the budget deficit. It is explicit and is indicated by the clue words "proved that." Underline "they are not interested in fighting the budget deficit."

9. The final conclusion, expressed by a rhetorical question in the last sentence, is that the responsible citizen should oppose school prayer. It is explicit and indicated by the clue word "therefore." Underline "the responsible citizen should oppose school prayer." The clue word "therefore" in the second sentence indicates the conclusion of an intermediate step in the argument, namely, that to permit school prayer is virtually the same as to endorse religion.

10. The final conclusion is that discrimination against gays is deplorable. It is implicit. One should *not* underline the phrase "discrimination against gays is deplorable" in the first sentence, since this is part of an "if . . . then . . . " statement. The clue phrase, "it becomes clear that" in the third sentence, indicates the conclusion of an intermediate step in the argument.

Giving Reasons: The Premises

I-4. This passage intends to give an argument. The conclusion: "Kennedy's arguments for gun control cannot be taken seriously" (indicated by the clue word "therefore") is inferred from the premise: "He has long been affiliated with anti-gun groups." Since the premise gives no plausible reason for thinking that the conclusion is true, the argument is a very poor one. But as long as the premise is *supposed to give* a reason for thinking that the conclusion is true, it satisfies our general conception of what arguments are.

I-8. There are no premises here and no conclusion. Stripped of its hyperbole and the specious analogy to the Stealth Bomber, the passage states, essentially, that the auto reverse cassette deck being offered for sale features the dbx noise-reduction system.

II-8. Most of this paragraph (6-1) is introductory, not argumentative. Mayor Vellucci's comments are a reason for thinking that the first sentence is true.

Outlining the Structure of Arguments

8. [¹The "total energy" of a physical system, a meaningful concept for flat space, is a meaningless concept if we allow for arbitrary space curvature.] {Since} [²the space of the entire universe can curve], [³the total energy of the universe is {thus} simply not a meaningful concept.] {This conclusion, that} [⁴the concepts of total energy and total energy conservation do not apply to the whole universe, is quite startling—but true.] {It implies that} [⁵*if we are to define nothing—the vacuum state—as it might apply to the whole universe, then we ought to look for features of the vacuum that do not use the concept of "total energy."*]

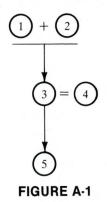

FIGURE A-1

13. [¹Animal liberationists insist that we have a moral obligation to efficiently relieve animal suffering.] [²The misery of wild animals is enormous.] [³In the natural environment nature ruthlessly limits animal population by doing violence to virtually every individual before it reaches maturity.] [⁴The path from birth to slaughter, however, is nearly always longer and less painful in the barnyard than in the woods.] {Thus,} [⁵the most efficient way to relieve the suffering of wild animals would be to convert our national parks and wilderness areas into humanely managed farms.] {It follows, therefore, that} [⁶*animal liberationists cannot be environmentalists*] {since} [⁷they must be willing to sacrifice the authenticity, integrity, and complexity of ecosystems for the welfare of animals.]

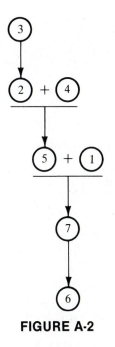

FIGURE A-2

17. *Forbidden Planet*, a 1956 MGM film, takes place on the distant planet Altair 4, in the year 2200. A rescue expedition from Earth finds only two survivors of an earlier landing party, Dr. Morbius and his daughter, along with the remnants of a long-extinct, highly advanced civilization, the Krell. An 8,000-cubic-mile power plant has continued to maintain itself for the 200,000 years since the Krell race vanished. It is powered by 9,200 nuclear reactors buried deep inside the planet. At the end of the film, the rescue party escapes in the nick of time as the planet is destroyed by an explosive chain reaction in the thermonuclear furnaces. [¹*This explosion of the entire planet is implausible.*] {Since} [²Altair 4's surface gravity nearly equals that of the Earth,] {we may infer that} [³the size of the planet is also similar.] [⁴Even exploded simultaneously, 9200 of our most powerful hydrogen bombs would not destroy a planet of Earth's size.] {One can only conclude that} [⁵the Krell nuclear power plants are each immensely greater, if they are to explode, than any hydrogen bomb built by man.] Besides, [⁶why would the Krell build in a simple mechanism to destroy their entire planet?]

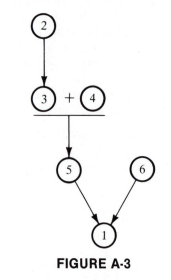

FIGURE A-3

Constructing Arguments

I. *List 2:*

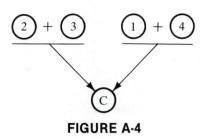

FIGURE A-4

Validity and Soundness

I-1.   All dogs are cats. All cats have eyes. Thus, all dogs have eyes.
II-1.   Yes. If the conclusion of a valid argument is false, then at least one of its premises must be false.
II-7.   Valid, since it is logically impossible for all its premises to be true and its conclusion false.

Chapter 2: Categorical Reasoning

Categorical Statements

4.   No *cowards* are *things that will die in a skydiving accident*. (E): Negative, universal. This example is an exception to the rule that sentences containing "never" are usually about times.
9.   Some vandals are things that left trash all over the campsite. (I): Affirmative, particular. OR: All *places in the campsite* are places where vandals left trash. (A): Affirmative, universal. This exercise illustrates that two nonequivalent translations may be possible. Which is best depends on the context—that is, whether the general topic is people or places.
15.   All *people who are not hypocrites* are people whom I can stand. (A): Universal, affirmative. The fact that this, not "All hypocrites are people I cannot stand," is the correct translation is best seen by noting that the original sentence can be restated as "I can stand anyone who is not a hypocrite."
20.   Some propositions are not *things that can be put into one of the four forms of categorical statement*. (O): Particular, negative.

Categorical Statements and Venn Diagrams

II-3.

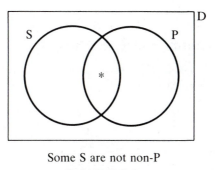

Some S are not non-P
FIGURE A-5

II-8.

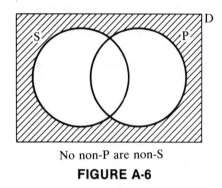

No non-P are non-S

FIGURE A-6

III-3. Since there is an asterisk in the area shared by S and P, "Some S are P."

Immediate Inferences

I-1. Some people are not things that can sing. (a) Some things that can sing are not people. Not equivalent. (b) Some things that cannot sing are not things that are not people. Equivalent. (c) All people are things that can sing. (d) Some people are things that cannot sing. (e) TRUE: Some things that cannot sing are people. Some things that can sing are things that are not people. FALSE: No people are things that cannot sing. No things that cannot sing are people.

I-3. No wild tigers are things that live in Africa. (a) No things that live in Africa are wild tigers. Equivalent. (b) No things that do not live in Africa are things that are not wild tigers. Not equivalent. (c) Some wild tigers are things that live in Africa. (d) All wild tigers are things that do not live in Africa. (e) TRUE: All things that live in Africa are things that are not wild tigers. No things that live in Africa are wild tigers. FALSE: Some things that live in Africa are wild tigers. Some wild tigers are not things that do not live in Africa.

II-3. Some S are not non-P = Some S are P (obverse).

II-4. No non-S are P = No P are non-S (converse) = All P are S (obverse). OR: No non-S are P = All non-S are non-P (obverse) = All P are S (contrapositive).

Categorical Syllogisms and Venn Diagrams

I-3. A categorical syllogism: (E = ecosystems; W = well-balanced systems; F = systems that are free from predators)

Some E are F

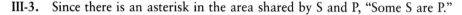

No W are F

Some E are not W

I-7.   Not a categorical syllogism. This type of argument with an "either . . . or
. . ." premise is best analyzed using propositional logic. See Chapter 3.
I.10.   Strictly speaking, this is not a categorical syllogism. Since "men" and "men
that I have met" are not equivalent, the argument has four terms. But since the
second premise, "Not everyone in the room is a man," is equivalent to "Some
people in the room are not men," this premise logically implies that some people
in the room are not men I have met. So, if we let M = men that I have met;
D = people I do not like; and R = people in this room; we get:

No M are D

Some R are not M

Some R are D

Notice that the class of people that I like is not the complement of the class of
people that I do not like, since there is a third category, namely, people that I
neither like nor dislike (i.e., people to whom I am indifferent).
II-3.

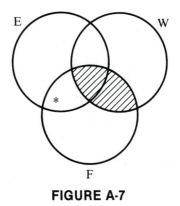

FIGURE A-7

Valid. To diagram the conclusion, we would need an asterisk in that portion of
the S-circle that is outside the P-circle, and there is already an asterisk there.
III-5.   (F = factual statements; G = things that provide a good reason for buying a product; A = advertisements; V = things that rest on a simple appeal to
vanity; D = things designed to sell a product.)

  (a) All G are F
  (b) Some A are V
  (c) All A are D
  (d) No V are F

(a) + (d)   (b) + (c)

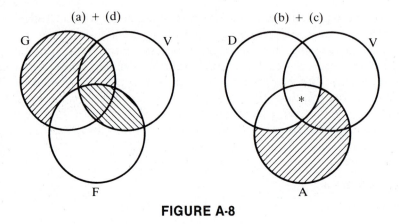

FIGURE A-8

From (a) + (d) we can infer (C1): No G are V. From (b) + (c) we can infer (C2): Some D are V. Combining these two, we get the following:

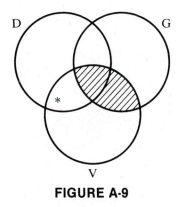

FIGURE A-9

From this diagram, we can infer: "Some D are not G."

Rules for Valid Categorical Syllogisms

I.

All S are M

All P are M

No S are P

This syllogism violates only Rule 1. All the other rules are satisfied. Note that Rule 4 is not violated because neither premise is negative.

II-4.   (N = *Napoleon*; F = French emperors; B = people born in France). We would normally translate both premises as universal, but since we know that

Napoleon actually existed, we have the option of using the particular form. If we do so, we get the following syllogism:

Some N are not B

All N are F
_____

Some F are not B

All five rules are satisfied: (1) The middle term, N, is distributed in the second premise; (2) B is distributed in the conclusion and in the first premise; (3) the second premise is affirmative; (4) we have a negative premise (the first) and a negative conclusion; (5) the conclusion is particular, and so is the first premise.

Note that if we translate both premises as universal statements, Rule 5 would be violated.

II-7. (T = trees on Main Street; E = elm trees; D = things with Dutch elm disease.)

All T are E

Some E are D
_____

Some T are D

(1) The middle term, E, is not distributed; the argument is invalid. (2) Nothing is distributed in the conclusion. (3) Both premises are affirmative. (4) There is no negative premise. (5) The conclusion is particular, and so is the second premise. The argument is invalid, since the first rule is violated.

Finding Missing Premises

7. (C = competent surgeons; E = experienced surgeons; N = men)

All E are C

??????????
_____

Some C are not N

The missing premise must contain N and E. Rule 1 does not restrict the missing premise, since the middle term, E, is already distributed in the first premise. To satisfy Rule 2, N must be distributed, and to satisfy Rule 5, the missing premise must be particular. Since (I) statements distribute neither term, the missing premise must be: "Some E are not N." Rules 3 and 4 are also satisfied by the complete syllogism; the first premise is affirmative, and we have a negative premise leading to a negative conclusion.

Argument Chains

I-3. (L = people who like Lucky's pizza; A = people who like anchovies; B = people who are boors; S = *Steven*)

(1) All L are A

(2) All A are B

(3) No S are L

(C) No S are B

(Notice that "No one except a boor likes anchovies" means "Only boors like anchovies"; hence the translation of premise 2.) The clue word "since" and the structure of the third sentence indicate that 3 is a premise in the final syllogism for C, and since neither of the other two stated premises contain L and B (the terms needed for the second premise of the argument), we can begin by looking for the missing premise. The missing premise must be affirmative (Rule 3), and B must be distributed in it (Rule 2). Thus, the only premise that will give us a valid syllogism is "All B are L":

(a) All B are L

(3) No S are L

(C) No S are B

We can now combine the two remaining premises to see what intermediate conclusion can be drawn from them:

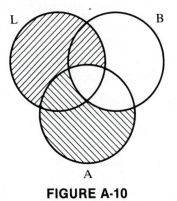

FIGURE A-10

The diagram indicates that the following is a valid argument:

(1) All L are A

(2) All A are B

(C1) All L are B

The entire chain, then, is as follows:

(1) All L are A   (a) All B are L

(2) All A are B   (3) No S are L

(C1) All L are B   (C) No S are B

Both syllogisms are valid, but the immediate inference from C1 to a is invalid, since an (A) proposition is not equivalent to its converse. Thus, the entire chain is invalid.

II-2. (A = sex acts between consenting adults; V = acts that are victimless crimes; H = acts of consensual homosexuality; L = acts that should be legalized.)

(1) <u>All A are V</u>

(C) All H are L

Since the stated premise and the conclusion have no terms in common, we know that there must be two syllogisms. If there is an argument chain, the conclusion of the first syllogism with 1 as one of its premises will be a premise in the second syllogism with C as its conclusion. Since the conclusion of the first syllogism will have either A or V as one of its terms, we know that the middle term of the second syllogism must be either A or V. We also know that both premises of the second syllogism must be affirmative (Rules 3 and 4) and H and the middle term must be distributed (Rules 2 and 1). Thus, there are two possibilities:

(a) All H are A	(a′) All H are V
(b) <u>All A are L</u>	(b′) <u>All V are L</u>
(C) All H are L	(C) All H are L

Either pair of premises seems acceptable, so we can now construct the first syllogism. On the first option, b would be the intermediate conclusion, and on the second option, it would be a′. If we tried to have a as the intermediate conclusion, the missing premise would have to distribute the middle term, V, and H; the only statement that distributes both terms is an E proposition, and such a premise violates Rule 4.

We can also eliminate b′ as an intermediate conclusion since V is distributed in it, and not in 1; any syllogism with 1 as a premise and b′ as the conclusion would violate Rule 2. Thus, there are two valid argument chains from 1 to C:

(1) All A are V	(1) All A are V
(d) <u>All V are L</u>	(d′) <u>All H are A</u>
(b) All A are L	(a′) All H are V
(b) All A are L	(a′) All H are V
(a) <u>All H are A</u>	(b′) <u>All V are L</u>
(C) All H are L	(C) All H are L

Either reconstruction is acceptable. Notice that both options use the same unstated premises: d = b′, and a = d′.

Chapter 3: Propositional Logic

Truth-Functional Operators

I-2. Logically complex. The atomic components are A = "Smith will win the race"; B = "Jones is entered." "Unless" is truth-functional. Clearly, "A unless B" is true if Jones does not enter and Smith wins or if Jones enters and Smith does not win. Similarly, "A unless B" is false if Smith fails to win even though Jones does not enter the race. What is debatable is whether "A unless B" is true if Jones enters and Smith still wins. If it is false in this case, then "unless" is equivalent to the exclusive disjunction; if it is true then "unless" is being used inclusively.

I-4. Logically atomic. "Believes that" is not a truth-functional connective.

I-9. Logically complex. Let R = "Taxes are raised"; D = "The budget deficit will decrease"; E = "Congress reduces the size of entitlement programs"; W = "Congress eliminates waste in the Department of Defense"; F = "Congress eliminates fraud in the Department of Defense." The whole statement can then be translated as the conjunction of "R → (~D V (W & F))" and "~R → (~D V (W & F))." This captures the truth-functional sense of "regardless of whether . . . or not" as well as the more familiar truth-functional operators "not," "unless," and "and."

II-3. (T V D). T = "Taxes are raised," and D = "The deficit will grow even larger."

II-4. (B → F). B = "A small business is successful," and F = "That small business is started on a solid financial base." Strictly speaking, neither B nor F is a proposition. The problem of representing generalizations correctly in propositional logic is addressed in the section of Chapter 3 on Argument Chains and Variations.

III-5. Let E = "Evelyn is in Paris," and F = "Fiona is in Rome." In standard form, the argument is as follows:

~(E & ~F)

E
_____

F

Using Truth Tables

I-5.

E	F	~F	E & ~F	(p-1) ~(E & ~F)	(p-2) E	(c) F
T	T	F	F	T	T	T
T	F	T	T	F	T	F
F	T	F	F	T	F	T
F	F	T	F	T	F	F

FIGURE A-11

The argument is valid.

II-4. Given the definitions of the two atomic propositions abbreviated by the letters P and Q, the argument in standard form is as follows:

$(\sim P \text{ V } \sim Q)$

$\underline{P \to Q}$

$\sim P$

P	Q	$\sim P$	$\sim Q$	(p-1) $\sim P \text{ v } \sim Q$	(p-2) $P \to Q$	(c) $\sim P$
T	T	F	F	F	T	F
T	F	F	T	T	F	F
F	T	T	F	T	T	T
F	F	T	T	T	T	T

FIGURE A-12

The argument is valid.

III-9.

M	P	$M \to P$	$\sim P$	$(M \to P) \& \sim P$	$\sim M$
T	T	T	F	F	F
T	F	F	T	F	F
F	T	T	F	F	T
F	F	T	T	T	T

FIGURE A-13

Since the entries in the two columns at the right differ in the third row, the propositions are not logically equivalent.

IV-1.

A	$\sim A$	$A \to \sim A$
T	F	F
F	T	T

FIGURE A-14

Since the column at the right contains both a "T" and an "F," $(A \to \sim A)$ is neither a contradiction nor a tautology. In fact, $(A \to \sim A)$ is logically equivalent to $\sim A$.

IV-4.

G	H	$\sim G$	$\sim H$	$\sim G \text{ v } \sim H$	$\sim(\sim G \text{ v } \sim H)$	$\sim(\sim G \text{ v } \sim H) \& \sim H$
T	T	F	F	F	T	F
T	F	F	T	T	F	F
F	T	T	F	T	F	F
F	F	T	T	T	F	F

FIGURE A-15

Since the column at the right contains only "F's," ($\sim(\sim G \ V \ \sim H) \ \& \ \sim H$) is a contradiction.

Some Common Forms of Argument

I-3.   Let C = "The jar will crack," B = "The water inside it boils," F = "The water inside it freezes." In standard form, the argument is as follows:

$$(F \ V \ B) \rightarrow C$$

$$\underline{\sim(F \ V \ B)}$$

$$\sim C$$

This is an instance of the fallacy of denying the antecedent, which is an invalid form of argument. The argument is invalid because it does not exemplify any other valid form.

I-8.   Let D = "Determinism is true," C = "All my actions are caused by events over which I have no control" = "I have no control over the events causing my actions," F = "Some of my actions are free." If we translate "Determinism is incompatible with free will" as "If determinism is true then none of my actions is free," we get

$$D \rightarrow C$$

$$\underline{C \rightarrow \sim F}$$

$$D \rightarrow \sim F$$

Since this is an instance of the valid form hypothetical syllogism (HS), the argument is valid.

II-6.   This is tricky since the statement given as a premise is a generalization about all persons. The best we can do is to translate it as "If a person can register to vote, then that person is a U.S. citizen," which we will abbreviate as "R → C." If we let S = "U.S. law allows noncitizens to vote," we get

$$R \rightarrow C$$

$$\underline{\sim S \ V \ \sim(R \rightarrow C)}$$

$$\sim S$$

This is an instance of the valid form DS.

III-6.   One possibility is to use DS. Let C = "I am an only child," S = "I have sisters," and B = "All my siblings are brothers."

$$(\sim C \ \& \ B)$$

$$\underline{\sim(\sim C \ \& \ B) \ V \ (\sim C \ \& \ \sim S)}$$

$$\sim C \ \& \ \sim S$$

Argument Chains and Variations

5. This is a good illustration of what can go wrong when more than one premise is hedged and when the hedged premises are not atomic propositions. Let S = "Jones is a neurosurgeon," M = "Jones is a man," N = "Jones has no formal medical training." The argument can be reconstructed as follows:

(Very likely)	$S \rightarrow M$
(Very likely)	$M \rightarrow N$
(Probably)	$S \rightarrow N$

The *underlying* form of argument here is valid (HS), and the conclusion is hedged more strongly than either premise, but because more than one premise is hedged, and the hedged premises are conditional propositions, not atomic ones, the argument is invalid. Notice that even if all neurosurgeons were men and thus only the second premise were hedged, the argument would still be invalid. In fact, since we know that all neurosurgeons have received formal medical training, we know that the conclusion is false. Since all the premises are true, in either version, both versions are invalid.

8. "There's no smoke without fire" is a generalization asserting that if there is smoke in a place, then there is fire in that place. Substitution gives us "If there is smoke in the foothills of southern France, then there is fire in the foothills of southern France," which we can abbreviate as "$S \rightarrow F$." Thus, we have

	$S \rightarrow F$
	S
(Probably)	F

Since the underlying form (MP) is valid, and the hedging has been carried through properly, the argument is valid.

Chapter 4: Inductive Arguments

Deductively Valid and Inductive Arguments Compared

2. Deductively valid. The premise "copper conducts electricity" means "*all* pieces of copper conduct electricity." It is not logically possible that every piece of copper conducts electricity and this piece of copper tubing will not.

3. This argument has several steps. The missing premises are (a) Siberia is in the Soviet Union and (b) oil is either heavy in sulfur or light in sulfur, but not both (i.e., the amount of sulfur cannot vary continuously). Assuming (a), the first step is an *inductive* argument from "20 percent of oil discovered previously in the Soviet Union is heavy in sulfur" to "There is a 20 percent chance that the new discovery in Siberia is heavy in sulfur." There is a valid deductive step from this intermediate conclusion to "There is an 80 percent chance that it is not the case that the new discovery is heavy in sulfur." Finally, using (b), it is deduced that there is an 80 percent chance that the new discovery is low in sulfur.

Inductive Strength and Inductive Reliability

5. False. An inductively weak argument can have a conclusion that is highly probable or even certain, just as a deductively invalid argument might have a true conclusion. Inductive strength concerns solely the relationship between the premises and the conclusion; it says nothing about the status of the conclusion considered by itself.

10. False. Any inductive argument, even a strong one with true premises, can have its inductive strength diminished by adding further premises, if these are appropriately chosen. Whether any such premises are *true* depends on the example. For example, assume that of the very large number of composers of whom we have knowledge none has lived to be older than 100 years and that we inductively infer from this that no composers (past, present, or future) live past their hundredth birthdays. This reliable inductive argument is weakened by adding to the premises the true statement that some human beings have survived past their hundredth birthdays.

Inductive Arguments from a Sample to a Population

3. Counting every one of such a large number of things is expensive and time-consuming. Also, people are likely to make errors because the task is so boring. Designing a better method depends on the contents and organization of the warehouse. It makes sense to count the largest parts (e.g., engines, transmissions), since they will be the most expensive, easily visible, and, one assumes, relatively few in number. Large boxes of the smallest parts (e.g., nuts, bolts, washers) can be weighed and their contents estimated by taking a random sample, weighing it, and determining its composition. If the parts of intermediate size are boxed and arranged by type (so that all the carburetors, say, are in one area of the warehouse and all the fuel pumps in another), their total number can be calculated by measuring the amount of space they take up and dividing by the mean volume of the boxes in which they are packed. If the boxes are of different sizes, and contain carburetors, fuel pumps, and other parts of different makes and sizes, then the mean volume of the boxes and the percentages of each subtype can be estimated from a random sample.

Statistical Generalizations Based on Simple Random Sampling

1. A score of 800 lies 3 SDs above the mean of 500; a score of 200 lies 3 SDs below the mean. Thus, 99.7 percent of all the scores lie between 200 and 800. Since the curve is symmetrical about the mean, $(0.3)/2 = 0.15$ percent of the scores lie above 800 (and, similarly, 0.15 percent lie below 200). Sixty-eight percent of the scores lie 1 SD either side of the mean. So the scores that are 1 SD below the mean and lower account for $(50 - 68/2) = 16$ percent of the scores. Thus, a score of 400 lies at the 16th percentile.

2. Imagine that the 100 coin tosses are a random sample from the infinite population of all possible tosses of the nickel. Let n be the true fraction of heads in the population. If the coin were fair, n would be exactly 0.5. For a sample of size 100, the SD of the sampling distribution curve is 0.05, or 5 percentage points. Hermione obtained a value of 0.58 (58 heads in 100 tosses). Thus, there is a 95 percent chance that n lies somewhere in the interval from 0.48 to 0.68, which includes the value 0.5. Thus, the fact that Hermione obtained 58 heads in 100 tosses does not show that the coin is biased.

Other Common Types of Inductive Argument

3. An SS to the conclusion that the Golden Dragon uses large amounts of MSG in its food followed by a practical inference.

5. IF.

Evaluating and Constructing Inductive Arguments

I-2. Inductively worthless. The premise concerns the percentage of male alcoholics who are married. The conclusion concerns the percentage of married men (and the percentage of bachelors) who are alcoholics. In terms of probabilities, this argument is trying to infer the values of $Pr(A/M)$ and $Pr(A/B)$ solely from the value of $Pr(M/A)$. For further details see the sections in Chapter 8 on Comparisons, Rates, and Correlations and Calculating the Odds.

II-4. IP. Observed primates (lemurs, monkeys, apes, and humans) all have good color vision [and observed nonprimates (cats, dogs, cattle, and horses) are all color blind]. The observed primates are representative of the loris, which is also a primate. Therefore, the loris also has good color vision.

III-3. The U.S. birth rate has declined each year for the last decade. The factors that influence the birth rate are not likely to change for the foreseeable future. Therefore, the U.S. birth rate will continue to decline.

Chapter 5: Arguments in Context

Mixed Argument Chains

3. As written, the argument in paragraph 11 is as follows:

(1) Something cannot be taken off the streets until deemed obscene.

(2) Nothing can be deemed obscene if it is on the streets.

(3) ????????

The implicit conclusion (3) is: "Nothing can be taken off the streets if it is on the streets." Thus, we get the following valid categorical syllogism:

(1) All T is D

(2) No D is S

(3) No T is S

6. In paragraph 9, Stich defines the instrumental harmfulness of K as the product of the probability that some harmful misuse of K will occur, times some measure of the amount of harm (or negative value) that such a misuse of K would produce. Stich's view is that only when the product Prob(K) × Harm(K) is unacceptably high should K not be acquired by us, *and* that K should not be acquired by us only if the product is too high. Thus, Stich assumes that the product Prob(K) × Harm(K) being unacceptably high is both a necessary and a sufficient condition for K to be a case of "forbidden knowledge." Stich's overall conclusion about the permissibility of continuing with recombinant DNA research involves a comparison with the knowledge that makes nuclear weapons possible. Let N stand for the scientific knowledge required for the manufacture and use of nuclear weapons; and let D stand for the knowledge involved in DNA research. Then Stich's argument in paragraph 15 for his conclusion that recombinant DNA research does not involve forbidden knowledge can be reconstructed as follows:

(1) Knowledge K should not be acquired by us if and only if the product Prob(K) × Harm(K) is unacceptably high.

(2) The product Prob(N) × Harm(N) is unacceptably high.

(3) Prob(D) < Prob(N).

(4) Harm(D) < Harm(N).

(5) It is not the case that D should not be acquired by us.

Apart from the difficulty, which Stich acknowledges, of measuring Prob(K) and Harm(K) in cases such as N and D (and hence the difficulty of justifying premises 2, 3, and 4), the preceding argument is not deductively valid. All that follows, logically, from the premises is that Prob(D) × Harm(D) < Prob(N) × Harm(N). It does not follow that the former product is not unacceptably high. Judging by his language (e.g., "I am inclined to conclude"), it is reasonable to assume that Stich did not intend his argument to be anything more than inductively reliable (i.e., inductively strong, and with true premises). Whether or not it is inductively strong depends on the magnitudes involved. (See Questions 2 and 3 in the section on Responding to Arguments.)

Reductio Ad Absurdum Arguments

2. Target Argument, T:

(1) If it is logically possible that [doing X] will lead to disaster, then we ought not to [do X].

(2) It is logically possible that [pursuing rDNA research] will lead to disaster.

(3) It is logically possible that [*not* pursuing rDNA research] will lead to disaster.

(4) We ought not to [pursue rDNA research] and we ought not to [*not* pursue rDNA research].

The first conjunct in the conclusion comes from premises 1 and 2, the second conjunct from 1 and 3. Stich gives the second conjunct of the conclusion in the simpler form, "We ought to pursue rDNA research." Presumably, this follows validly from "We ought not to not pursue rDNA research." Stich describes the conclusion as "absurd," but it does not have the explicit form of a contradiction, "P and not-P." The conclusion would be a contradiction if "We ought not to do X" implies "It is not the case that we ought to do X." Regardless of whether or not it is contradictory, one could claim that the conclusion is false on the basis of the general principle that "ought implies can." But, here again, a rather subtle principle has to be assumed, namely, that "We ought to do X" conjoined with "We ought not to do X" implies that "We ought to do X and not to do X." Since it is impossible for us both to do and not to do X, it follows that it is false that we have a moral obligation to do both of these things.

Thematic Outlines of Extended Arguments

Extended Argument 8:

Conclusion: The U.S. State Department's allegations that the Soviets have been using chemical weapons in Southeast Asia and in Afghanistan are false.
Alternatives: 8-12. (The Soviets could achieve their military goals more easily using other means.)
Yellow rain: 14-18. (The reports of the use of yellow rain are inconsistent with our current knowledge of the properties of the substance and how it could be delivered effectively.)
Variety: 19-26. (It is highly unlikely that the Soviets have had sufficient time to develop the wide variety of agents and delivery systems mentioned in the reports.)
Duds: 27-29. (It is highly suspicious that not a single dud weapon has been offered as physical evidence.)

Responding to Arguments

1. Since 5:21 is a valid argument chain (substitution followed by MT), any response must attack its premises. Since abortions are lethal for the fetus, the second premise of the second step is impregnable. Thus, in constructing a response, we must focus on the premise, "If eugenic abortions benefit the fetus, the fetus must exist to enjoy the outcome" and the generalization from which it is deduced, namely, "If an action benefits a being, then that being must exist to enjoy the outcome." We might question the generalization by considering how we think about the deaths of terminally ill adult human beings who are suffering great pain. In such cases we might well judge that a person is better off dying now rather than continuing to live in a pain-racked and hopeless condition. We might even contemplate acting to bring about or hasten such a death. Regardless of where one stands on the moral issue of euthanasia, it seems clear that there is a meaningful sense in which ceasing to exist can benefit someone, namely, that the person in question will have had a better life if it ends now than if it continues for a few more days or weeks. In cases in which an adult or a fetus benefits from death, one might say that the benefit is received at the same time as death occurs. The general point behind these remarks is that an individual can be benefitted in two different ways: by receiving something good and by being spared something bad. One way of sparing an individual something bad is by killing him or her. Thus, our response to 5:21 might consist of the following counterargument:

(1) A person or fetus can be benefitted by an action performed now, by being spared suffering in the future.

(2) If a person or fetus is killed now, he or she is spared suffering in the future.

(3) A person or fetus can be benefitted by being killed now.

If the conclusion of this argument is true, then the generalization that appears as the first premise of 5:21 is false.

Chapter 6: Words, Meanings, and Definitions

Analytic and Synthetic Statements

7. Analytic. The definition of the term "hominid" is such that the term applies to all forms of humanlike beings, extinct as well as living, and this includes Neanderthal man.

8. Synthetic. The truth of this claim depends on the historical pattern of human evolution, which can be determined only empirically. Many evolutionary biologists now regard Neanderthal man as an extinct subspecies of *Homo sapiens*, not as one of its ancestors.

What Is Said?

4. This statement is amphibolous. It can mean either "If you borrow money before December 31 to buy a truck, your monthly interest payments (for the duration of the loan) will be $98 a month" or "If you borrow money to buy a truck, the interest payments between now and December 31 will be $98 a month (with no indication of what the interest will be after that)." The two interpretations do not depend on the ambiguity of any one term.

7.   This statement relies on buzz-words. The terms "bandage," "special break," and "bias" are used to convey disapproval of tax relief for married couples, but no reasons are given to support this judgment. That is, the author fails to explain why such relief gives an unfair advantage to married couples.

What Is Suggested?

2.   The maxim of relation indicates that the first sentence, with its mention of "a woman's job," must be relevant to the topic. Thus, it suggests that a "woman's job" is *not* tough or exciting.

7.   The maxim of quantity requires that any relevant differences between the two cases should be mentioned. Since the speaker does not mention any, he suggests that all the differences between picking fruit from a tree and killing seals to obtain their pelts are irrelevant.

What Is the Issue?

I-5.   The key word is "tyranny"; its definition will determine whether or not majority rule constitutes tyranny. The speaker assumes a definition on which any curtailment of individual rights counts as tyranny.

What Should a Word Mean?

1.   The key terms are "cruel" and "unusual." The principle of charity dictates that we take both speakers to be using lexical definitions, since they are disputing what the 8th Amendment means, and hence what kinds of punishments it forbids. Person A takes "unusual" to refer to a comparison with other types of punishment, whereas B interprets it to mean "not in accord with accepted practice." B's definition is a more accurate reflection of standard usage. B's interpretation of "cruel" as meaning "painful" is also much closer to the lexical definition than A's. (Liberty is a basic human right, but the incarceration of criminals is not, for that reason, a "cruel" punishment.)

10.   The key terms here are "malpractice" and "negligence." A and B disagree about which stipulative definitions of these terms should be adopted in law. Both parties agree that if a patient suffers harm as a result of a physician's negligence, the physician is guilty of malpractice, but they disagree on what constitutes negligence: should it include not only surgical incompetence but also failure to obtain a patient's informed consent? They also disagree over whether the occurrence of harm should be a necessary condition for something to count as malpractice. B interprets "malpractice" in light of a broader conception of a doctor's duty toward patients, and would count something as falling within the definition if it violates that duty, regardless of whether harm ensues. (Aside from the harm issue, B's definition more closely reflects medical malpractice cases in U.S. law that

have been decided against physicians who failed to obtain the informed consent of their patients.) B's definition of malpractice might be judged preferable to A's from the point of view of protecting the rights of patients and giving them a greater chance to receive compensation for medical injuries; but without the harm requirement it would lead to a quagmire of litigation.

Chapter 7: Evaluating Sources of Information

Appropriate Subjects for Testimony

I-4.   Testimony is appropriate here because the answer depends on a medical evaluation of *your* state of health, not just on general knowledge about the preventive effects of exercise for the population at large.

I-6.   Testimony by itself, even from a qualified counselor, is inappropriate for answering this question since it depends on factors that only you can decide about.

Recognizing and Evaluating Testimony

I-2.   This passage can be considered from two points of view: as a newspaper giving a factual report of what the NRA said, and as the NRA making certain claims. Since there is no evidence that the newspaper is asking us to accept the claims made about the bill on the authority of the NRA, the newspaper is not making use of testimony. From the point of view of the NRA, it is making two sets of claims. The claim in the second sentence about the "anti-gun organization" is an example of factual reporting by the NRA. The first sentence contains three judgments: (a) that the bill is "repressive," (b) that it was "obviously" designed to discourage people from owning handguns, and (c) that the bill would make owning a handgun more difficult. The NRA is asking people to believe these claims, but no one is appealing to the NRA as an authority.

I-7.   Most of the first paragraph is factual reporting, although Khan is being appealed to as an expert on Pakistan's nuclear program. The second paragraph makes many appeals to authority: to the Reagan administration, "academic sources," Leonard Spector, and Robert Peck.

II-2.   Because of its strong interest in opposing any gun control measures, if anyone were to appeal to the NRA as an authority on statements a, b, and c, the testimony would be suspect on grounds of trustworthiness. Also, claim b is apparently an inference from the content of the bill, and the truth of claim c depends on what the bill says. Expertise is largely irrelevant; both are matters that any person could decide by reading the bill for herself.

II-7.   Although he is in an excellent position to know whether Pakistan has actually manufactured a nuclear bomb, Khan's testimony is not entirely trustworthy. Because of the tensions between Pakistan and India (which tested its own bomb in 1974), Khan may have had political reasons for claiming that Pakistan has already manufactured a nuclear weapon. As the other authorities cited in the second paragraph make clear, it is highly probable that Pakistan has enough weapons-grade plutonium to assemble an atomic bomb if it chooses to do so, but it may not have taken that final step. There is a consensus among the different authorities cited in the second paragraph, they are legitimate authorities on this matter, and there is no reason to suspect them of bias.

Factual Reporting

1.   Jefferson began writing his autobiography at age 77, in 1820, some 31 years after the Bastille was stormed. Presumably he was relying on his memory and his diary. As Jefferson himself points out, though he was in Paris at the time, he was not an eyewitness to the storming, but is reporting at second-hand the account given to him by M. de Corny, who did participate in the events described. Thus, we may have some mild doubts about the passage's authenticity. Though the account is written in a thoroughly objective manner, it is inadequate in some respects. Some of this incompleteness undoubtedly results from the confusion of the assault. As Jefferson admits, he has no idea how the revolutionaries gained access to this "fortification of infinite strength." We are not told whether M. de Launay ordered his men to fire on the crowd, how many people were killed in the assault, or whether the soldiers resisted.

4.   This account scores low marks as a piece of factual reporting. Couched in inflated language, the description of Ivan III's character and abilities in the first paragraph defies belief as a credible picture of any human being, however talented and ruthless; and it is largely undercut by the admissions made in the second paragraph.

Chapter 8: Statistics and Probability

Collecting Statistical Data

1-a.   The most direct test here would be to ask each public television station how many subscribers it has.

2-e.   This would not be an accurate indirect test of the number of tax cheaters, since the IRS does not take a simple random sample of all the returns. Apart from investigating any returns that look "suspicious," the IRS selects for audit a higher proportion of those in the higher income brackets.

Percentages and Averages

4.   Whether employed in industry or in teaching, economists with a Ph.D. earn more than those without it. Despite this, the mean salary of economists with Ph.D.s is $(150 \times \$20,000 + 50 \times \$40,000)/200 = \$25,000$, and the mean salary of those without the doctorate is $(50 \times \$15,000 + 750 \times \$31,000)/800$

= \$30,000. The apparent discrepancy results from the fact that 3 out of 4 of the economists with Ph.D.s work in the lower paid profession—namely, teaching—while 15 out of 16 of those without Ph.D.s work in industry, where the salaries are much higher.

Comparisons, Rates, and Correlations

4. The strength of the correlation between studying a foreign language (F) and being a woman (W) = $Pr(F/W) - Pr(F/not\text{-}W) = 60/100 - 15/100 = +0.45$. The strength of the correlation between W and F = $60/75 - 40/125 = +0.48$.

Understanding Probability Statements

I-1. Though expressed qualitatively, "more probable than not" corresponds to a quantitative probability greater than 0.5. Without further information, it is difficult to judge whether statement 1 is merely subjective or is objective. The phrase "at random" suggests that it is intended to be objective. If it is objective, then the empirical, relative-frequency approach gives the only plausible interpretation.

I-4. Quantitative, objective. The calculation presumably rests on the assumption that a person is just as likely to have been born on one particular day of the year as on any other. In other words, it assumes that all birth dates are equipossible. Thus, it uses the classical interpretation. The actual calculation would employ the At-least-one Rule. Thus, if we ignore leap years, the probability that at least 2 people out of 23 have the same birthday is 1 minus the probability that each of 23 people were born on different days.

II-4. Since Reagan *was* elected as president in 1984, the probability of that event is 1.0.

II-5. If the statement is made in 1990, say, then we want to know the chances that a 30-year-old male will live for at least another 10 years. Since we want this information *now* (in 1990) it can be based only on past evidence of the fraction of 30-year-old males who have survived to age 40.

Calculating the Odds

6. $Pr(F) = 0.8; Pr(M) = 0.2; Pr(Neg/M) = 0.95; Pr(Neg/F) = 0.2. Pr(Neg) = Pr(Neg/M) \times Pr(M) + Pr(Neg/F) \times Pr(F) = (0.95) \times (0.2) + (0.2) \times (0.8) = (0.2) \times (1.75). Pr(M/Neg) = Pr(Neg/M) \times Pr(M)/Pr(Neg) = (0.95)/(1.75) = 0.54$. Thus, it is now slightly more probable than not that the murderer is male.

Drawing the Correct Conclusion

1. Though the author has selected only two items, comparing the nominal costs of the same goods and services in 1969 and 1979 is a reliable way of measuring inflation during that decade since it reflects the decline in the purchasing power of the dollar. [The Consumer Price Index (CPI) published by the Bureau of Labor Statistics is based on more than 400 such items; it nearly doubled in the decade from 1969 to 1979.] What is entirely unwarranted is the author's projection of the same high rate of inflation into the next decade.

6. An instance of the Monte Carlo fallacy or "gambler's fallacy" is the error of thinking that the probability of getting heads on the next toss of a fair coin is greater if it is preceded by a run of tails. Since each toss is statistically independent, the chance of getting heads remains $1/2$ on each toss, regardless of the previous outcomes. Thus, the author is correct in stressing that "there is no relation between the probability of an event and the history of the event's occurrence." What is more debatable is the contention that Feynman could still be right even if there were no failures in 500 flights. If the chances of failure are $1/100$, the probability of 500 consecutive successes is 6.6×10^{-3}; if the chances of failure are $1/50$, the probability of 500 successes in a row drops even lower, to 4×10^{-5}. The calculation in the last paragraph is an application of the At-least-one Rule (280 years contain about 102,200 days). If the probability of failure is $1/100,000$, then the probability of at least one failure in 100,000 launches is $1 - (0.99999)^{100,000} = 0.63$.

Chapter 9: Legal and Practical Reasoning

Special Problems with Practical Reasoning

1. (1) Scientists should make double-blind experiments the cornerstone of their research. (2) Scientists should remain objective; and Scientists should avoid situations in which they affect or misinterpret experiments in light of expectations. (3) Objectivity is compromised if a scientist affects or misinterprets an experiment in light of expectations; and double-blind experiments reduce the possibility that expectations will lead scientists to affect or misinterpret an experiment.

Evaluating Practical Reasoning

I-1. There are two arguments here (see pages 254 and 258). The first can be reconstructed as a categorical argument:

(Want . . .) All scientists are people who are objective.

No people who affect or misinterpret experiments in light of their expectations are people who are objective.

(Should . . .) No scientists are people who affect or misinterpret experiments in light of their expectations.

The underlying argument is valid. The middle term (people who are objective) is distributed in the second premise. Both subject and predicate terms of the argument are distributed in the conclusion, and each is distributed in the appropriate premise. The first premise is affirmative, the argument contains a negative premise leading to a negative conclusion, and the conclusion is not particular.

The second argument is most easily reconstructed as a propositional argument:

If double-blind experiments are not used, then situations will obtain in which scientists may affect or misinterpret experiments in light of their expectations.

(Want . . .) It is not the case that situations will obtain in which . . .

(Should . . .) Double-blind experiments are used.

The underlying argument exhibits the form modus tollens, and is therefore valid.

II-1. An alternative guiding principle for the first case might be "Scientists should try to provide their subjects with the best possible treatment." This principle could be invoked in cases in which experimental drugs are tested on human volunteers, and it would lead to the conclusion that neither double-blind experiments nor any other sort of experimental design that uses a control group should be employed. This alternative is less plausible than the original guiding principle for two reasons: it applies to only a very limited number of cases, and it involves an assumption that is usually false—namely, that the scientist already knows which treatment is best. Thus, the original argument is quite good.

The Role of Arguments in Legal Reasoning

1. The basic issue in this case is whether Georgia must show a compelling state interest to justify its sodomy statute. A demonstration of compelling state interest is necessary if and only if the statute infringes on an area of privacy protected by the U.S. Constitution. The most important guiding premise in Justice White's opinion can be stated as follows: The constitutional right to privacy should not be interpreted to include protection of homosexual sodomy. His argument for this guiding premise is based on a comparison between this case and prior decisions which helped define the right to privacy.

The Structure of Legal Reasoning

9.f. The guiding principle in the decision argument in 9:6, *Cohen* v. *California*, is "If there are no other factors ["a more particularized and compelling reason"], the simple display of a single four-letter expletive should not be a criminal offense." This principle is justified by an appeal to the First and Fourteenth Amendments. The decision argument combines the guiding principle just stated with the informing premise "There are no other factors in this case" to justify the decision "The simple display . . . is not a criminal offense."

Analogy and Precedent

3. There are two arguments here, the first of which is an argument from analogy. This argument compares the choice of living arrangements to other modes of association that are protected by the Constitution:

> [Some] nonpolitical modes of association involve social or economic benefits to their members and are protected by the First Amendment.
>
> The selection of living arrangements and companions involves social, economic, and emotional benefits to those involved.
>
> Involving social and economic benefits to their members establishes that the selection of living arrangements and companions is similar to those nonpolitical modes of association already protected by the First Amendment.
>
> The selection of living arrangements and companions is protected by the First Amendment.

Since Marshall does not cite examples of other cases, the argument is difficult to evaluate. Certainly the properties shared by the cases are relevant: First Amendment protection presumably applies *because* social and economic benefits are involved. On the other hand, we cannot tell whether there are relevant dissimilarities between the cases or not. Thus, without the addition of more specific information, the argument is rather weak.

Chapter 10: Causal Reasoning

Different Types of Causes

1. A generalization about a necessary causal condition.
2. A generalization about a probabilistic cause.
3. A statement about the proximate cause of a single event.

Mill's Methods

3. From a we infer that eating shellfish is a necessary cause of Bob's illness. The positive cases in b have two items in common, oysters and crab, which, by the Direct Method of Agreement, suggests either oysters or crab as a necessary condition. The negative cases in c have the absence of crab in common, which, by the Inverse Method of Agreement, suggests crab as a sufficient condition. Putting all the cases together, we recognize that the second case in b and the second case in c satisfy the Method of Difference, strongly indicating the crab as a sufficient condition. The overall conclusion is that it is quite probable that eating crab is sufficient to cause Bob's illness. Eating crab might also be necessary, but it is quite possible that there are other kinds of shellfish, not mentioned in b and c, that could also provoke an allergic reaction in Bob.

4-g. There might be nothing to be explained here. Almost all cases of TSS occur in women who use tampons during menstruation. Since this group falls into the age range of 12 to 50, we would *expect* a third of the cases to be between 12 and 25. *If* older women are less susceptible to TSS, this might be because they have been exposed to the *S. aureus* bacterium (the organism responsible for TSS) more often, and thus have developed greater immunity to it. This hypothesis could be tested by measuring levels of antibody to TSS in both men and women of different ages to see whether they increase with age.

Concomitant Variations, Correlations, and Causes

2. (a) Poor lung capacity and premature death are probably the joint effects of a common cause, namely, suffering from various kinds of illness. (b) There is a confounding cause here, namely, life-threatening illness, which is positively correlated with significant weight loss shortly before death. Among healthy subjects, thinner people live longer. (c) This suggests that higher-than-average levels of HDL can prevent heart attacks.

3-d. Since about 70 percent of the population of Utah are Mormons, and Mormons experience significantly lower rates of cancer than the national average, it is important to avoid introducing religion as a confounding factor in this kind of study. Hence, the investigation was confined to Mormons. The study group or cohort consisted of 4125 Mormon families who lived in southwestern Utah during the period 1951–1962, downwind from the Nevada Test Site where atmospheric nuclear tests were conducted in the same period. The control group consisted of all Utah Mormons. Although the people in the study group were identified in the early 1980s, this is a prospective, not a retrospective study. The results provide convincing evidence that exposure to radioactive fallout is a positive causal factor for many types of cancer. Especially significant were the findings that (1) cancer rates were highest among those who lived in high-fallout areas; (2) the ratio of rates of cancer in radiosensitive organs to all other cancers was greater for those exposed to fallout.

3-e. The initial evidence implicating use of the Rely tampon as a causal factor for TSS was retrospective, since it was based on those women who already had the disease. The decrease in reported cases following the recall confirms this hypothesis. Since cases of TSS continued to be reported after the recall, clearly the Rely tampon is not the only causal factor involved. In 1985, researchers at Harvard reported that in the presence of either polyester foam or polyacrylate rayon *S. aureus*, a normally harmless bacterium, produces up to 20 times as much toxin as usual. This has led the makers of Playtex and Tampax tampons to withdraw all their superabsorbent brands that contain polyacrylate rayon fibers. (See "The Magnesium Connection," *Time* June 17, 1985.)

Randomized Controlled Experiments

1. Since the hypothesis is that George can tell the sex of authors *solely* from their handwriting, it is important to eliminate any other clues from the experiment. This suggests that the handwriting samples in each matched pair should be identical in their content and that those administering the test should not themselves know which is which. The null hypothesis, H_0, is that George cannot tell and is simply guessing. If H_0 were true we would expect George to make correct identifications roughly half the time; thus, about 12 or 13 out of 25. In a long series of repetitions of the same experiment, the mean frequency of correct guesses would be close to 0.5. Table 4-1 in Chapter 4 tells us that the SD of the SDC for a sample of size 25 is 0.11. So the 95 percent confidence interval for the null hypothesis is between 0.28 and 0.72, or in other words, between 7 and 18 correct guesses out of 25. Since George makes 19 correct identifications, the result is significant at the 95 percent confidence level.

Glossary

For more information about the terms defined, consult the index: a bold-faced page number in the index refers to the page on which the term is introduced and defined. Hyphenated numbers in parentheses after a definition refer to an example, figure, or table that illustrates the term's use.

(A) statement: a categorical statement of the form "All S is P."

accuracy (of a test): the degree to which the test actually measures the property it is designed to measure; also called the "validity" of a test. (8-2)

ambiguity: a word or phrase is ambiguous if it has more than one meaning. (6-7)

amphiboly: a special case of ambiguity, resulting from the grammatical structure of a phrase rather than the ambiguity of any individual word. (6-8)

analytic statement: a statement that is true or false solely by virtue of the meanings of the words used in the sentence that expresses it. Contrast with "synthetic statement." (6-1)

antecedent: the portion of a conditional statement in standard form that precedes the arrow; the portion introduced by "if."

argument from analogy (AA): an inductive argument in which the relevant properties of as few as two things are compared to draw a conclusion about a new property of one of the things. (4-8)

atomic statement: a statement that contains no truth-functional operators. (3-2)

attribute class (in a probability statement): that portion of the reference class containing the cases that have the property one is investigating. (Figure 8-6)

authenticity (of a report): the degree to which a report contains information that is based on observation rather than inference and has been transmitted reliably from its source.

begging the question: arguing in a manner that presupposes a statement one's audience believes to be false or is unwilling to accept as true. (5-28)

biconditional: a truth-functional statement of the form "p if and only if q," symbolized by a double-headed arrow: "p ↔ q."

buzz-word: a word or phrase calculated to elicit a positive or negative attitude without providing an objective reason for that attitude. (6-5)

categorical statement: a statement describing the relation between two categories or classes. In standard form, a categorical statement is one of the following types: (A) All S is P; (I) Some S is P; (E) No S is P; (O) Some S is not P. (Table 2-1)

categorical syllogism: an argument consisting of two premises and a conclusion, each of which is a categorical statement, and containing exactly three terms. One term appears in the conclusion and one premise, another appears in the conclusion and the other premise, and the third (the middle term) appears in both premises but not in the conclusion. (2-6)

circular argument: an argument containing premises that it is rational to believe only if one already believes the conclusion is true, for example, an argument whose conclusion merely repeats one of the premises. (5-22)

complement (of a class): a class that contains all and only those things not contained in the class of which it is the complement. Also, a term that names the complementary class: S and non-S are complementary terms.

conditional probability statement: a statement of the probability that one event (A) will occur given that another event (B) has already occurred: Pr(A/B).

confidence level: the probability that the true value in a population lies within the specified range. A confidence level of 95 percent is typical. (Figure 4-3; Table 4-1)

confounding cause: a causal factor that interferes with the statistical relationship between two other factors: a factor that diminishes the normal effect of a cause. (10-8)

consensus: the degree to which experts agree on a judgment; an important criterion of good testimony that reflects the probability that having the relevant expertise will lead someone to reach the correct conclusion.

consequent: the portion of a conditional statement in standard form that follows the arrow; the portion following "then."

context of discovery: the phase of an investigation during which one attempts to arrive at a hypothesis or explanation.

context of justification: the phase of an investigation during which one tests a hypothesis that has already been formulated.

contradictory statements: two statements that must have opposite truth values:

they cannot both be false and cannot both be true. If a statement is true, its contradictory is false, and vice versa. (Table 2-7)

contrapositive: a statement formed from a categorical statement by (a) exchanging the subject and predicate terms and (b) replacing each term with its complement. (Table 2-6)

contrary statements: statements that are inconsistent with one another: they cannot both be true, but, unlike contradictory statements, they might both be false.

conversational implicature: something that is suggested or implied by a remark, but is not stated explicitly.

converse: a statement formed by switching the subject and predicate terms of a categorical statement. (Table 2-4)

counterargument: an argument with a conclusion that is inconsistent with the conclusion of another argument. (5-18)

counterexample: an attempt to disprove a generalization by giving a specific case in which the generalization fails. (5-17)

crossover: a case in which an authority in one field is cited in another area in which the authority is not legitimate.

decision argument: an argument in legal or practical reasoning whose conclusion is a decision, a claim about what ought to be done, or a ruling in a legal case. (9-6)

deductively valid argument: an argument in which it is impossible for all the premises to be true and the conclusion false. (1-19)

dilemma: an argument with the form: p V q; p → r; q → s; therefore, r V s. The premises of a dilemma present two alternatives and specify the consequent of each; the conclusion claims that one of the two consequents will obtain.

direct test: a test based on observation of the actual property under investigation.

discovery: see "context of discovery."

disjunct: one of the components of a disjunction. Thus, in "A V (B & C)," "A" and "B & C" are both disjuncts.

disjunction: a truth-functional statement of the form "p or q," or "p V q." In propositional logic, "V" always stands for the inclusive "or." (3-4)

disjunctive syllogism (DS): an argument of the form: p V q; ~p; therefore, q. (3-11)

distributed term: if a categorical statement makes a claim about each member of a class, then the statement distributes the term naming that class. The subject term of any universal statement and the predicate term of any negative statement are distributed. (Table 2-3)

(E) statement: a categorical statement of the form "No S is P."

effective argument: an argument that is accepted by the intended audience as deductively sound or inductively reliable and that leads the audience to accept a conclusion it did not previously believe or increases the confidence with which the conclusion is accepted. More generally, an argument that is persuasive and useful.

enthymeme: a categorical syllogism with one premise left unstated. More generally, an argument with one or more missing premises. (2-13)

equivocation: moving back and forth between two different uses of an ambiguous word or phrase. (6-9)

exclusive "or": the connective in a statement that asserts that one or the other of two alternatives is true, but not both. (3-3)

guiding premise: the premise in a case of practical reasoning which identifies the goal being pursued or the rule or principle being followed.

hypothetical syllogism (HS): an argument of the form p → q; q → r; therefore p → r. (3-6)

(I) statement: a categorical statement of the form "Some S is P."

immediate inference: a form of reasoning that starts from a single categorical statement and concludes either that another categorical statement is true or that it is false. More generally, any argument with a single premise. Forms of immediate inference include conversion, contraposition, obversion, and contradiction.

inclusive "or": the connective in a statement which asserts that one or both of two alternatives is true; the standard interpretation of the disjunction in propositional logic. (3-4)

inconsistent statements: two statements that cannot both be true: contradictory or contrary statements.

indirect test: collecting data by measuring one thing in an attempt to investigate something else. (8-1)

induction to a particular (IP): an inductive argument in which the premise describes a property observed in a sample, and the conclusion ascribes that property to a new instance not included in the sample. (4-7)

induction to the future (IF): an inductive argument in which a premise describes a sample observed in the past, and the conclusion extends the observed pattern to all future cases of the same kind of thing.

inductively reliable argument: an inductively strong argument with true premises.

inductively strong argument: an argument in which the conclusion would be highly probable if the premises were true. (4-2)

inductively weak argument: an argument in which the conclusion would be more probable than not, but not highly probable, if the premises were true.

informing premise: a premise in practical reasoning that supplies factual information relevant to the application of a rule or the achievement of a goal.

inverse true negative rate: the probability that one does not have a disease, given negative test results: one element of the *predictive* accuracy of a test. Compare with "true negative rate."

inverse true positive rate: the probability that one has a disease, given positive test results: one element of the *predictive* accuracy of a test. Compare with "true positive rate."

justification: see "context of justification."

legitimacy (of an authority): the degree to which a source of information has the technical training, expertise, and background necessary to provide correct information and make reliable judgments in a specific area.

lexical definition: a standard, common, or accepted definition; the type of definition found in a dictionary.

logically equivalent statements: statements that always have the same truth value.

mean: the most common sort of "average," calculated by summing all the values in a set, and then dividing the total by the number of values.

median: a form of "average," calculated by arranging all the values in a set in ascending or descending order, and identifying the midpoint of that list.

mode: the value that occurs most frequently in a set.

modus ponens argument (MP): an argument of the form p → q; p; therefore, q. (3-8)

modus tollens argument (MT): an argument of the form p → q; ~q; therefore, ~p. (3-10)

necessary condition: a condition that must be met for something to obtain but does not automatically guarantee it will obtain. Thus, "Lee is a male" is a necessary condition for "Lee is a father."

nonsampling error: a weakness in inductive reasoning related to how the data about the sample was collected rather than how the sample was selected from the population.

null hypothesis: a hypothesis that there is no causal connection between two factors. Usually a null hypothesis is defined in relation to a specific causal hypothesis.

(O) statement: a categorical statement of the form "No S is P."

obverse: a statement formed from a categorical statement by (a) changing the quality of the statement, and (b) replacing the predicate term with its complement. The obverse is always logically equivalent to the statement from which it was formed.

practical argument: an argument concerned with what should be done, how one should act.

precedent: a legal ruling that is taken as a pattern to be followed in reaching a new decision. Appeals to precedent are a specific form of argument from analogy. (9-11)

presupposition: a statement that is entailed by another statement; if a statement is true, then all its presuppositions are also true. Thus, one of the presuppositions of "Sam is a father" is "Sam is male."

principle of charity: a guideline for reconstructing or analyzing arguments which requires that one reconstruct the argument in the strongest way consistent with the material given.

problem of induction: the question of how, or if, inductive arguments can be justified as reliable forms of reasoning.

R-premise: the premise in an inductive argument that describes the relationship between the sample and the population.

Reductio ad absurdum argument: an argument that proves a premise of another argument (see "target argument") is false by showing that the target argument is valid and its conclusion false.

reference class (in a probability statement): the larger class of which the attribute class is a subset. (Figure 8-6)

reference class (in a statistical statement): the class to which a specific case has been assigned. (4-9)

reliability (of a test): the degree to which repeating the test will yield the same results. Reliability is necessary but not sufficient for an accurate test.

sampling distribution curve: a graph that records the values obtained by repeated sampling from the same population; if the samples are randomly selected, the sampling distribution curve will approximate a standard bell curve. (Figure 4-1)

sampling error: a flaw in an inductive argument resulting from the way in which the sample was selected; a selection procedure that yields an unrepresentative sample.

slippery slope argument: an argument that reaches an illegitimate conclusion by using a vague term that blurs relevant distinctions. (6-6)

sorites: an argument chain composed entirely of categorical syllogisms. (Figure 2-21)

sound argument: a deductively valid argument with true premises.

standard deviation (SD): a number reflecting the way a curve spreads out from its mean. The smaller the standard deviation, the more sharply peaked the curve is. (Figure 4-2)

statistical generalization (SG): an inductive argument which concludes that a specified percentage of a population has a certain property, based on the premise that the same percentage of a sample has that property. (4-6)

statistical syllogism (SS): an inductive argument which uses a premise stating that a certain high percentage of a specified reference class has a property to support the conclusion that a specific member of that reference class has the property in question. (4-9)

stipulative definition: a definition that states how a word is to be used in a specified context, setting aside its normal or lexical meaning (if any).

strength of correlation: a measure of the extent to which one property is correlated with another. The strength of correlation between A and B is the fraction of Bs that are As minus the fraction of non Bs that are As. (Figures 8-2, 8-4)

sufficient condition: a condition which guarantees that something else is true, but may not be a necessary condition for its truth. "Smith has a daughter" is a sufficient condition for "Smith is a parent."

synthetic statement: empirical statement: a statement whose truth value is at least partially determined by empirical facts about the world. Compare with "analytic statement."

target argument: an argument that is the subject of a reductio argument. See "reductio ad absurdum argument."

tautology: a statement that is necessarily true.

testimony: appeal to an authority; the use of a specialized source of information to justify a claim in a technical area. (7-4)

true-negative rate: specificity: the probability of obtaining a negative result on a test, given that one does not have the disease being tested for; a measure of the retrospective accuracy of a test. Compare with "inverse true-negative rate."

true-positive rate: sensitivity: the probability of obtaining a positive result on a test, given that one has the disease being tested for; a measure of the retrospective accuracy of a test. Compare with "inverse true-positive rate."

truth-functional operator (or connective): a term that allows one to create a statement whose truth value depends solely on the truth value of its components and the definition of the truth-functional operator.

universal generalization (UG): an inductive argument that begins with a premise asserting that all members of an observed sample have a certain property and concludes that all members of the population from which the sample is drawn have that property. (4-5)

vague: a word or phrase is vague if there is considerable uncertainty which cases it applies to.

valid argument: see "deductively valid argument."

validity (of a test): see "accuracy."

Index

Numbers in **bold faced type** indicate a page on which the term is defined. The glossary also contains definitions of important terms.